W. KEBLE MARTIN, MA, DSc, FLS

THE CONCISE
BRITISH FLORA
IN COLOUR

with nomenclature edited and revised by Douglas H. Kent

and Foreword by
H.R.H. The Prince Philip, Duke of Edinburgh
KG, PC, KT, GMBE, FRS

SPHERE BOOKS LIMITED
30/32 Gray's Inn Road
London, w.c.1

First published in Great Britain in 1965 by
Ebury Press/Michael Joseph Ltd
Second Impression (with revisions) June 1965
Third Impression September 1965
Fourth Impression November 1965
Fifth Impression April 1967
Second (revised) edition 1969
Second Impression December 1969
Third Impression June 1971

© George Rainbird Ltd, 1965, 1969
First Sphere Books edition May 1972

Designed and produced by
GEORGE RAINBIRD LTD
Marble Arch House
44 Edgware Road, London W2

The text was set in
Monophoto Baskerville 8 on 9pt by
BAS Printers Limited, Wallop, Hampshire
The text and colour plates were printed and
bound by
C. J. Mason & Sons Ltd, Bristol
The colour plates and jacket were originated by
Charterhouse Litho Ltd, London

Foreword

I am delighted that Mr Keble Martin's beautiful paintings and drawings of British wild flowers have, at long last, been published.

It represents a life's work and has taken nearly sixty years to complete. Although there are many books of this kind, few of them cover virtually all the British Wild Flowers with such accuracy in the compass of one colourful volume.

The dedicated and painstaking skill which has gone into each plate in order to ensure complete accuracy in colour and detail will, I am sure, make this book invaluable to both amateur and professional botanists. I hope it will also stimulate new interests and bring delight to many thousands of readers.

Contents

Preface to the First Edition

In recent years many illustrated works on the British flora have issued from the press. It may appear at first sight to be superfluous to publish another. But there seem to be good reasons for this. The present work is on a somewhat different scale, comprising as it does some 1480 figures mostly in colour, drawn with all the care of which the draughtsman was capable, over a period of about sixty years. It is an attempt to attain scientific accuracy without losing the attractive appearance of the flowers. Although this work has been such a long while in preparation, an effort has always been made to keep it in touch with changing ideas through contact with leading botanists of each period. The drawings however are in a form in which their sequence could not be altered. With small exceptions this follows that of the National Herbarium at the British Museum, and *The London Catalogue of British Plants*, XIth Edition.

A further reason for desiring publication is that a number of experts have helped by selecting and identifying specimens for these drawings, thus ensuring suitable and accurate material for the purpose. In addition some three hundred of the specimens drawn were sent by a wide circle of botanists. Valuable help, as acknowledged below, has been given in the preparation of the short text, especially in bringing the nomenclature into accord with the Rules of the International Botanical Congress. The production of this work has therefore been very much a combined effort, and it is only fair to all these botanists that the result should be published.

Every figure of these plates was drawn direct from nature. The drawings were first made in the form of pen outlines on small separate sheets. On each sheet the name of the species was recorded, with the date, the place from which the specimen came, and the name of the sender, if any, or of the referee who named it. These sheets form four octavo loose-leaf volumes. We hope they may ultimately be made accessible for reference at the British Museum (Natural History Dept.) by the kindness of the Keeper of Botany.

In building up the plates the draughtsman's aim has been to show an average fragment, with its essential features, and to give each a place in the sun without crowding. He has tried where possible to show white or pale coloured flowers against green foliage, as in the hedgerow, though this was not always possible. These aims involved much patience in rearranging and redrawing. During the years there have always been gaps on the plates, because the necessary specimens could not be obtained. Some of these gaps have waited for twenty or even twenty-five years before being filled. The author's own visits to distant botanical spots have of necessity been rather few and brief. Owing to the pressure of the author's parochial work the specimens received by post sometimes perished. Some species difficult to obtain had to be sent in two or more seasons, but, owing to great kindness and much forbearance shown by correspondents, the gaps were all filled at last.

It was the desire to know the food plants of Lepidoptera that first promoted the effort to identify the plants required. Then the author was studying for his degree

5

in the Botany School at Oxford, under Professor S. H. Vines and Mr A. W. Church. It was Mr Church who specially urged his students to draw whatever they saw under the microscope and started them in the habit of drawing. The desire to help others in recognizing the plants around them led to the idea of this present work. In this the text is short, mentioning for the most part features that cannot be shown effectively in the figures.

It is an amateur work, which was from the beginning treated as a secondary interest and a recreation. For after further training at a Theological College the author was plunged at his own request in the Church work of large industrial parishes, which was happy work, but it left little time indeed for botany. Progress with these drawings was therefore slow and mostly confined to an annual holiday; and yet before 1918 work on the present lines was well under way.

For a few years, from 1921 to 1926, the author was in a small parish, and his work for a neighbouring housing estate had not yet begun. He had more time for this work, and several plates were redrawn. From 1949 he no longer held a benefice. And it happened that in five successive years as a Public Preacher he was in charge of some parish for more than six months in the winter, but had more interrupted engagements in the summer, and several other plates were redrawn.

We should like to make two suggestions about gathering flowers; first that it should be done sparingly, and secondly that collectors should be fully courteous to the owner of enclosed land.

We have tried to take care of the flowers, and only to gather rare species very sparingly or not at all. Often we have hidden them with foliage from less scrupulous fingers. And when leading walks or expeditions of field clubs, we have tried to persuade others to do the same. Unfortunately there was sometimes one in the party, who thought it his special privilege to pick the only specimen seen or even to come back afterwards and do so! It really is important that we should preserve rare and interesting flowers for future generations.

Real botanists understand this. Gathering the flower prevents the casting of seed. Even for drawing these figures we have sometimes been content with two florets from a good spike with an upper and a lower leaf. We have walked miles in mountain mist and rain to restore a small rare plant to its own niche.

We commend botanizing as a means of healthy recreation for young and old. It is an interest that takes us out to the beautiful places of the earth. And if we really know the wild flowers around us at home, the plants almost speak to us of their struggles to grow. This interest stays with us to the end of our pilgrimage. It is not exactly an armchair study. To fulfil it properly we need good boots, a compass and a companion, and must face the thorns and steep places, the dense clouds and sharp mountain thunderstorms or the tides and island crossings. But we take no undue risks. It is good fun and healthy.

We said that valuable help had been given in editing the short text. Mr Douglas Kent, formerly Editor of the *Proceedings of the Botanical Society of the British Isles*, has kindly helped much with it, making many adjustments, especially to the nomenclature, and adding a list of authorities for the names. The brief descriptions are indebted to the earlier Floras. The first pages were written before the publication of the Flora by Messrs Clapham, Tutin and Warburg; but the whole is now doubtless indebted in greater or less degree to this latter work. We gratefully acknowledge the debt, and commend that work to all who wish to make a more serious study of the British Flora. We have followed Mr H. W. Pugsley's *Prodromus of the British Hieracia* and his *Revision of Euphrasiae*, both of them published in the *Journal of the Linnean Society*, and also Dr C. E. Hubbard's *Grasses*.

We are much indebted to the Keeper of Botany and his staff at the British Museum (Natural History) and also to the Director and the Herbarium staff at the Royal Botanic Gardens at Kew. In both we have had valuable advice accompanied by the selection of suitable material from the National Herbaria for drawing. This has been especially the case in the choice of Sedges and Grasses, but in other groups also.

In drawing the figures we have had helpful advice or determination of specimens from those who have specialized in several groups. This was often coupled with the posting of fresh specimens as follows: *Fumaria*, H. W. Pugsley, who also personally conducted us around Cornwall in search of these; *Cruciferae* and many other groups, Dr G. C. Druce; *Rubus*, Wm. Watson, who himself wrote the notes for the text on those figured; the Rose plate was redrawn after kind criticism of N. Y. Sandwith; *Sorbus*, A. J. Wilmott; *Mentha*, R. Graham; *Salix*, R. D. Meikle; *Potamogeton*, Dr G. Taylor; *Cyperaceae*, E. Nelmes and A. W. Stelfox; *Gramineae*, Dr C. E. Hubbard. All these gave valuable help and we are much indebted to them. For other drawings we acknowledge with gratitude that many botanists past and present kindly helped by sending fresh specimens, carefully determined and posted for this work. They are too numerous to name here. Their names are on the separate drawings referred to above.

We wish further to acknowledge our debt to Dr W. S. Bristowe (of Spider fame, President of the Ray Society) for earlier research into the possibility of publication. We are extremely grateful to His Royal Highness the Duke of Edinburgh for his active interest and to Squadron-Leader David Checketts for introducing the project to Mr George Rainbird and his colleagues.

After these acknowledgements we hope that the plates may have a chance of speaking for themselves. The author is very conscious of their limitations.

Preface to the Second Edition

The past three years have been a period of considerable botanical study and experiment, and we are indebted to Mr Douglas H. Kent for adapting the text of this work to current botanical opinion, especially regarding closely related forms and subspecies, and in some cases, regarding nomenclature. In the text he has also described a number of additional established alien species. Mr Kent was formerly Editor of the *Proceedings of the Botanical Society of the British Isles*, and now, although busy in other ways, he has devoted much time and interest to making this *Concise British Flora* a standard work both for professionals and amateurs.

W. Keble Martin
Broadymead, Woodbury 1969

Glossary

achene A small dry indehiscent fruit, strictly of one free carpel.

acicle A very slender prickle or stoutish bristle.

acuminate Having a gradually diminishing point.

acute Sharply pointed but not drawn out.

alternate Arranged successively on opposite sides of a stem.

amplexicaul Clasping the stem with their base.

angle(d) (s) The meeting of two planes to form an edge.

annual A plant completing its life cycle from germination to death within one year.

anther The terminal portion of a stamen containing the pollen grains.

apex The growing point of a stem; the tip of an organ.

apiculate Furnished with a small broad point at the apex.

appressed Lying flat along the whole length of an organ.

arcuate Bent like a bow.

aril The exterior covering of the seed in certain plants, e.g. *Taxus baccata*, developed from the stalk or base of the ovule.

aristate Awned.

attenuate Gradually tapering to a point.

auricles Small ear-like appendages at the base of a leaf.

awn A bristle-like part.

axil The upper angle formed by the union of the stem and the leaf.

axillary Growing in an axil.

axis The central part of a plant, around which the organs are developed.

beak A pointed projection.

beard Awn.

biconvex Having a more or less rounded surface on both sides.

biennial A plant requiring two years to complete its life cycle, growing in the first year, and flowering and fruiting in the second.

bifid Divided halfway down into two parts.

bipinnate When the divisions of a pinnate leaf are themselves pinnate.

biserrate Doubly serrate.

blunt Ending in a rounded form, neither tapering to a point, nor truncate.

bract(s) Modified leaves intermediate between the calyx and the normal leaves.

bracteate Having bracts.

bracteoles Minute bracts.

bulb An underground organ which is really a modified plant bud with fleshy scales, yielding stem and roots.

bulbils Small bulbs or tubers usually arising in the axis of the leaves or amongst the florets of an inflorescence, but sometimes found on the root.

calyx The outermost of the floral envelopes.

campanulate Bell-shaped.

capillary Hair-like.

capitate Growing in heads; pin-headed.

capitulum A close cluster of sessile flowers.

capsule A dry, dehiscent fruit.

carpel A modified leaf of one, or several, of which the pistil is formed.

carpophore The continuation of the stalk between the carpels.

cauline Borne on the stem, not radical.

cernuous Nodding.

ciliate Fringed with hairs.

cladode A leaf-like branch, as in *Ruscus aculeatus*.

clasping Grasping.

claw The narrow base of a petal in certain genera, e.g. *Dianthus*.

cleft Deeply cut, but not to the midrib.

commissure The faces by which two carpels adhere, particularly in *Umbelliferae*.

confluent United at some part.

connate Similar organs distinct in origin but eventually becoming united.

connivent Making contact or converging.

contiguous Adjacent to each other; making contact at the edges.

cordate Heart-shaped.

corm Bulb-like fleshy underground stem, as in *Anemone*, etc.

corolla The petals as a whole.

corona The circumference or margin of a radiated compound flower, particularly in *Compositae*.

cotyledon(s) The first leaf or leaves of the embryo.

crenate With rounded marginal teeth.

crenulate Minutely crenate.

cruciform Cross-shaped.

cryptogam A flowerless plant.

cuneate Wedge-shaped.

cuspidate Spear-shaped at the tip.

cyme A flower-cluster of a broad and flattened type, as in *Sambucus nigra*.

deciduous Dropping off; shedding its leaves in the autumn.

decumbent Lying on the ground but tending to rise at the end.

decurrent Extending downwards, as when leaves are extended beyond their insertion and run down by a wing on the stem as in *Carduus* and *Cirsium*.

deflexed Bent sharply downwards.

dehiscent Opening to shed its seeds.

deltoid Shaped like an equilateral triangle.

dentate Toothed; notched.

denticulate Minutely toothed.

depressed When flattened vertically or at the top.

dichotomous Forked, parted by pairs from top to bottom.

diffuse Widely or loosely spreading.

digitate A compound leaf divided into five leaflets, as in *Aesculus hippocastanum*.

dioecious Having the sexes on different plants.

disk The central part of a capitulum in *Compositae* as opposed to the ray florets; the expanded base of a style in *Umbelliferae*.

elliptic(al) Oval but acute at each end.

elongate Much lengthened.

emarginate Slightly notched at the edges.

entire With an even margin; not toothed or cut at the edges.

epicalyx An involucre resembling an accessory calyx, as in *Malva*.

epichile The terminal part of the labellum of an orchid when it is distinct from the basal portion.

excurrent Where the stem remains central, the other parts being regularly placed around it.

exserted Protruding.

family A group of related genera.

fascicle(d) A close cluster or bundle.

fastigiate Tapering to a point like a pyramid.

filament The stalk of an anther.

filiform Thread-like.

fimbriate With fringed margin.

flexuose Zigzag.

floret A small flower, one of a cluster.

follicle A dry dehiscent fruit formed of one carpel opening by a ventral suture to which the seeds are attached.

fringe(d) With hair-like appendages on the margins.

frond The leaf-like part of a fern and other cryptogams.

fruit The ripe seeds and their surrounding structure.

gamopetalous Having the petals united at the edges in the form of a tube.

genus The smallest natural group containing related but distinct species.

gibbous Swollen on one side.

glabrous Smooth, devoid of hair or other clothing.

gland A wart-like structure on the surface, embedded or protruding, from any part of a plant.

glandular Having glands.

glaucous Covered with a bluish green bloom.

globose Round.

glume A small bract with a flower in the axil as in grasses.

hastate Spear-shaped.

herb Any non-woody vascular plant.

herbaceous Having the texture of leaves.

hirsute Hairy, with long, usually soft, hairs.

hispid Clothed with stiff hairs or bristles.

hooded Formed into a hood at the end.

hyaline Very thin and translucent.

hybrid A plant produced by the fertilization of one species by another.

hypochile The basal portion of the labellum in an orchid.

incumbent Resting or leaning upon.

inferior Below the ovary.

inflorescence The arrangement of the flowers on a stem or branch.

intercalary Inserted between or amongst others.

internode The space between two adjacent nodes.

involucre The whorl of bracts enclosing a number of flowers as in *Compositae* and *Umbelliferae*.

involute Having the margins rolled upwards.

keel(ed) The lower petal or petals when shaped like the keel of a boat as in *Vicia*, *Lathyrus*, etc.

labellum The lower petal of certain flowers, particularly orchids.

laciniate Jagged; deeply and irregularly divided into segments.

lanate Covered with soft, flexuous, matted hairs.

lanceolate Narrow, tapering at each end.

lateral Fixed on, or near, the side of an organ.

leaflet A subdivision of a compound leaf.

lemma The flowering glume of a grass.

lenticel Corky spots having the shape of a double-convex lens on young bark.

ligulate Strap-shaped.

ligule A small thin projection from the top of the leaf-sheath in grasses; a strap-shaped petal, e.g. in *Compositae*.

limb The border or exposed part of a calyx or corolla, as distinct from the tube or throat.

linear Slender.

linear-lanceolate Slender but tapering to a point at the tip.

lobed Said of leaves which are divided, but not into separate leaflets.

lunate Shaped like the new moon.

membranous Thin, dry and semi-transparent.

mucronate Abruptly tipped with a short, straight point.

muricate With sharp points or prickles.

nectary The honey gland of a flower.

nerve A vein or slender rib.

node A point in a stem where a leaf is borne.

notch An indentation.

ob- As a prefix means inversely or oppositely.

oblong Longer than broad.

obtuse Blunt.

ochrea Provided with a tubular membranous stipule.

opposite Growing in pairs at the same level on opposite sides of a stem.

orbicular Nearly round and flat.

oval Broadly elliptic.

ovary The vessel in which the seeds are formed.

ovate Egg-shaped.

ovate-oblong Egg-shaped, but much longer than broad.

ovoid Of a solid object which is egg-shaped in outline.

palea The inner bract or glume of a grass; the chaffy scales on the receptacle in many *Compositae*.

palmate Lobed or divided into more than three leaflets arising from a central point.

panicle A raceme with branching pedicels.

papillae Small elongated protuberances.

papillose Warty; having papillae.

pappus The tufts of hairs on achenes or fruits, particularly in *Compositae*.

pectinate Resembling the teeth of a comb.

pedicel The stalk of a single flower.

peduncle The stalk supporting either a flower or a flower-cluster.

pellucid Transparent.

peltate Shield-shaped with the stalk in the centre.

perennial A plant that lives for more than two years and usually flowers annually.

perfoliate With the leaf united round the stem, as in *Montia perfoliata*.

perianth The floral envelopes, calyx or corolla, or both.

pericarp A seed vessel, including the adhering calyx if present.

petal A flower leaf, often brightly coloured, forming part of a corolla.

petaloid Resembling a petal.

petiole A leaf-stalk.

petiolate Having a petiole.

pilose Hairy, usually with long soft hairs.

pinnate With leaflets arranged on opposite sides of a common stalk or rachis.

pinnatifid Deeply cut into segments nearly to the midrib.

pistil The female organ of a flower, consisting when complete of ovary, style and stigma.

pollinia A pollen mass composed of large numbers of cohering pollen grains.

polypetalous Having many separate petals.

pore A small aperture.

procumbent Trailing; lying loosely on the ground.

proliferous Bearing progeny as offshoots.

prostrate Lying closely on the surface of the ground.

pruinose Covered with a whitish bloom.
pubescent Covered with fine short hairs.
pyriform Pear-shaped.

raceme An unbranched inflorescence with flowers borne on equal pedicels.
rachis The axis of an inflorescence, compound leaf or branch.
radical Growing from the root.
ray The outer part of a compound radiate flower.
receptacle The uppermost part of the stem nearing the flowers.
recurved Bent moderately backwards in a curve.
reflexed Bent abruptly backwards.
reniform Kidney-shaped.
reticulate Marked with a network of veins.
retuse Terminating in a rounded end, the centre of which if slightly indented.
revolute Rolled or curved downwards.
rhizomatous Having the character of a rhizome.
rhizome An underground, creeping stem, producing roots and leafy shoots.
rhomboid(al) Similar in shape to a diamond in a pack of playing cards.
rib(bed) A primary vein; furnished with ribs.
rosette A cluster of leaves in circular form, as in *Plantago major*.
rotate (of a corolla) Wheel-shaped, circular and flat with a short tube.
rugose Wrinkled.

saccate Pouched.
sagittate Shaped like the barbed head of an arrow.
saprophyte A plant that lives on decaying vegetable matter.
scabrid Rough.
scale A thin scarious structure, often a degenerate leaf.
scape A leafless flower-stalk rising from the root.
scarious Very thin, dry and semi-transparent.
secund All turned to one side.
segment A division into which a plant organ, e.g. a leaf, may be cleft.
sepal A leaf of the calyx, the outer whorl of the perianth.
septate Divided into partitions.
serrate Toothed like a saw.
sessile Without a stalk.
setae Bristles.
sinuate Having a deep wavy outline.

sinuous Undulating.
sinus A depression between two teeth.
spadix A succulent spike with a fleshy axis, as in *Arum maculatum*.
spathe A large bract enclosing a flower cluster, usually a spadix.
spathulate Spatula-shaped.
spike An inflorescence in which the flowers are sessile round an axis.
spikelet A small spike; the inflorescence of grasses.
spine A thorn.
spur A slender projection from the base of a perianth segment, or of a corolla, as in *Aquilegia vulgaris*.
stamen One of the male reproductive organs of a plant.
staminodes Infertile, often reduced, stamens.
standard The large, often erect, posterior petal of a corolla in *Papilionaceae*.
stellate Star-shaped.
stigma The part of the pistil or style which receives the pollen.
stipule A leaf-like appendage usually at the base of the petiole.
stipulate Having stipules on it.
stolon A creeping stem which roots at intervals.
stoloniferous Having stolons.
striate(ions) Marked with slender streaks or furrows.
strict Narrow, upright and very straight.
style The space between the ovary and the stigma.
sub- Under or below.
subulate Awl-shaped.
succulent Juicy.

teeth Small marginal lobes.
terete Long and round, without ridges or grooves.
terminal Borne at the top of the stem.
testa The outer coat of the seed.
tomentose Densely pubescent, with woolly entangled hairs.
trifid Three-cleft but not to the base.
trifoliate Having three leaflets.
trigonous Of a solid body, three-angled, with plane faces.
triquetrous Triangular and acutely angled.
truncate As though abruptly cut off at the end.
tube The united parts of a corolla or calyx.
tuber A thickened part of an underground stem or root of one year's duration.
tubercle A small spherical or ovoid swelling.

umbel A type of inflorescence in which equal pedicels proceed from a common centre.
umbellate Having partial or secondary umbels.
unarmed Without spines or prickles.
undulate Wavy.
unisexual Of one sex only.

valvate When parts of a flower bud meet but do not overlap.
valve One of the pieces into which a capsule naturally separates at maturity.
vascular Furnished with vessels.
vernal Appearing in spring.
villous Covered with shaggy hairs.
viscid Clammy or sticky.
vitta(e) The aromatic oil tubes of the pericarp in many species of *Umbelliferae*.
viviparous Producing young plants instead of flowers.

whorl(ed) A ring of leaves or flowers around a stem at the same level as each other.
wing(ed) The lateral petals in the flowers of *Fumariaceae* and *Papilionaceae*; the flat membranous appendages of some seeds.

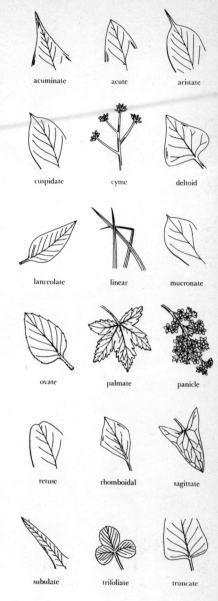

acuminate   acute   aristate

cuspidate   cyme   deltoid

lanceolate   linear   mucronate

ovate   palmate   panicle

retuse   rhomboidal   sagittate

subulate   trifoliate   truncate

attenuate

bipinnate

ciliate

cleft

crenate

cuneate

dentate

elliptic

emarginate

entire

filiform

hastate

oblanceolate

oblong

obovate

obtuse

orbicular

oval

pectinate

peltate

perfoliate

pinnate

raceme

reniform

serrate

spathulate

spike

tube

umbel

undulate

stigma

anther

style } pistil

stamen {

filament

corolla (petals)

ovary

perianth {

calyx (sepals)

FLORAL PARTS

The Plates

"O all ye green things upon the earth, bless ye the Lord.
Praise him and magnify him for ever."

Apart from certain details, the plants on the author's original plates were drawn life size. For this edition the plates have been reduced and therefore measurements given should be multiplied by $\frac{2}{3}$.

CLEMATIS
VITALBA

THALICTRUM
ALPINUM.

THALICTRUM
MAJUS.

GREATER
MEADOW
RUE.

THALICTRUM
MINUS.

VAR.
CAERULEA
VAR. PURPUREA.

THALICTRUM
ARENARIUM

ADONIS
ANNUA
PHEASANT
EYE

THALICTRUM
FLAVUM
COMMON
MEADOW RUE.

ANEMONE
NEMOROSA.
WOOD ANEMONE.

MYOSURUS
MINIMUS

PULSATILLA
VULGARIS.

PL 1

VAR. VERTUMNUS.

RANUNCULUS AQUATILIS.

×4

R. TRIPARTITUS.

RANUNCULUS TRICHOPHYLLUS.

×4

R. BAUDOTII.

RANUNCULUS CIRCINATUS.

R. TRIPARTITUS f. LUTARIUS.

VAR. CONFUSUS.

×5

R. FLUITANS.

R. HEDERACEUS.

×4

VAR. CALCAREUS.

RANUNCULUS OMIOPHYLLUS.

RANUNCULUS PELTATUS.

R. PELTATUS.

VAR. FLORIBUNDUS.

PL 2

RANUNCULUS
SCELERATUS.

RANUNCULUS
AURICOMUS

RANUNCULUS
ACRIS.

RANUNCULUS BULBOSUS.

VAR.
TENUIFOLIUS.

RANUNCULUS
LINGUA.

SUBSP.
SCOTICUS.

RANUNCULUS
REPTANS.

RANUNCULUS
FLAMMULA.

RANUNCULUS
REPENS.

RANUNCULUS
OPHIOGLOSSIFOLIUS.

RANUNCULUS
ARVENSIS.

RANUNCULUS
SARDOUS.

RANUNCULUS PARVIFLORUS.

RANUNCULUS
FICARIA

PL 3

CALTHA
PALUSTRIS

MARSH
MARIGOLD

TROLLIUS
EUROPAEUS
GLOBE FLOWER

HELLEBORUS
VIRIDIS
SUBSP.
OCCIDENTALIS.

HELLEBORUS
FOETIDUS.

ACONITUM
ANGLICUM.

AQUILEGIA
VULGARIS.
COLUMBINE

BERBERIS
VULGARIS.

WINTER
ACONITE
ERANTHIS
HYEMALIS.

CONSOLIDA
AMBIGUA.

BANE
BERRY
ACTAEA SPICATA

PAEONIA
MASCULA.

EPIMEDIUM
ALPINUM.

PL 4

PAPAVER HYBRIDUM

PAPAVER
ARGEMONE.

CHELIDONIUM
MAIUS

PAPAVER
SOMNIFERUM.

MECONOPSIS
CAMBRICA.

PAPAVER DUBIUM

PAPAVER
RHOEAS

ROEMERIA
HYBRIDA.

GLAUCIUM
FLAVUM.

NYMPHAEA
ALBA.

NUPHAR
LUTEA.

NUPHAR
PUMILA.

PL 5

CORYDALIS
LUTEA

CORYDALIS
CLAVICULATA

FUMARIA
CAPREOLATA

FUMARIA
OCCIDENTALIS

FUMARIA
PURPUREA

FUMARIA
BORAEI.

FUMARIA
MARTINII.

FUMARIA DENSIFLORA.

FUMARIA
BASTARDI.

FUMARIA
OFFICINALIS.

FUMARIA PARVIFLORA.

FUMARIA VAILLANTII.

MATTHIOLA
SINUATA

PL 6

WATER CRESS.

NASTURTIUM-OFFICINALE

RORIPPA AMPHIBIA.

RORIPPA SYLVESTRIS.

RORIPPA PALUSTRIS.

BARBAREA VERNA.

BARBAREA VULGARIS.

BARBAREA STRICTA.

ARABIS STRICTA.

CARDAMINE AMARA.

CARDAMINOPSIS PETRAEA.

CARDAMINE PRATENSIS.

CARDAMINE FLEXUOSA.

ARABIS ALPINA.

ARABIS GLABRA.

ARABIS HIRSUTA

CARDAMINE HIRSUTA.

PL 7

COCHLEARIA DANICA.

COCHLEARIA OFFICINALIS.

SUBSP. SPATHULATA

EROPHILA VERNA.

COCHLEARIA SCOTICA.

CARDAMINE IMPATIENS.

DRABA NORVEGICA.

CARDAMINE BULBIFERA.

DRABA AIZOIDES.

COCHLEARIA ANGLICA.

COCHLEARIA MICACIA

DRABA INCANA.

LOBULARIA MARITIMA.

ALLIARIA PETIOLATA.

ARABIDOPSIS THALIANA.

SISYMBRIUM IRIO. LONDON ROCKET.

SISYMBRIUM OFFICINALE.

DESCURAINIA SOPHIA.

DRABA MURALIS.

*HESPERIS MATRONALIS

PL 8

ERYSIMUM
CHEIRANTHOIDES.

BRASSICA OLERACEA.

BRASSICA RAPA
TURNIP.

RHYNCHOSINAPIS
CHEIRANTHOS

RHYNCHOSINAPIS
MONENSIS.

SINAPIS
ARVENSIS.
CHARLOCK.

SUBULARIA AQUATICA.

BRASSICA
NIGRA.
BLACK MUSTARD.

SINAPIS
ALBA.
WHITE MUSTARD.

DIPLOTAXIS TENUIFOLIA.

PL 9

CARDARIA
DRABA.

CORONOPUS
DIDYMUS.

CAPSELLA
BURSA-PASTORIS.

LEPIDIUM
RUDERALE.

DIPLOTAXIS
MURALIS.

CORONOPUS
SQUAMATUS.

LEPIDIUM
LATIFOLIUM.

THLASPI PERFOLIATUM.

X1

LEPIDIUM
HETEROPHYLLUM.

THLASPI
ALPESTRE.

THLASPI
ARVENSE.

LEPIDIUM
CAMPESTRE.

IBERIS
AMARA.

ISATIS TINCTORIA.

TEESDALIA
NUDICAULIS.

HORNUNGIA PETRAEA.

PL 10

RAPHANUS
RAPHANISTRUM

SUBSP.
MARITIMUS

SEA ROCKET
CAKILE
MARITIMA

X2

SEA KALE
CRAMBE
MARITIMA.

FRUIT OF
RAPHANUS
SATIVUS.

POLYGALA OXYPTERA.

TUBERARIA
GUTTATA.

RESEDA
LUTEOLA.

POLYGALA
SERPYLLIFOLIA

X 2

RESEDA
LUTEA.

POLYGALA
VULGARIS

POLYGALA
CALCAREA.

HELIANTHEMUM
APENNINUM

ROCKROSE
HELIANTHEMUM
NUMMULARIUM

POLYGALA
AMARA

HELIANTHEMUM
CANUM.

POLYGALA AUSTRIACA

PL 11

VIOLA ODORATA

V ODORATA

VIOLA PALUSTRIS.

VIOLA REICHENBACHIANA (=SYLVESTRIS)

V ODORATA × 3

VIOLA HIRTA

V. HIRTA VAR CALCAREA.

VAR. MINOR.

VIOLA LACTEA

VIOLA STAGNINA.

SUBSP. MONTANA.

VIOLA CANINA.

VIOLA CANINA.

VIOLA RIVINIANA.

VIOLA RUPESTRIS.

VIOLA ARVENSIS

SUBSP. CURTISII.

VIOLA TRICOLOR

VAR. LEPIDA.

VIOLA LUTEA.

VAR. OBTUSIFOLIA.

VIOLA NANA.

PL 12

FRANKENIA LAEVIS.

×2

SAPONARIA OFFICINALIS.

*DIANTHUS PLUMARIUS.

PETRORHAGIA NANTEUILII.

*DIANTHUS CARYOPHYLLUS.

DIANTHUS DELTOIDES

*VACCARIA PYRAMIDATA.

DIANTHUS CAESIUS. D.GRATIANOPOLITANUS.

DIANTHUS ARMERIA

VAR. QUINQUE- -VULNERA.

SILENE NUTANS

SILENE CONICA.

SILENE OTITES.

SILENE VULGARIS.

SILENE G.ALLICA.

SILENE ACAULIS.

SUBSP. MARITIMA.

PL 13

SILENE ALBA.

LYCHNIS FLOS-CUCULI. RAGGED ROBIN.

LYCHNIS VISCARIA.

EVENING CAMPION.

SILENE DIOICA. RED CAMPION.

LYCHNIS ALPINA.

SILENE NOCTIFLORA.

CERASTIUM FONTANUM. SUBSP. TRIVIALE. a b

AGROSTEMMA GITHAGO CORN COCKLE.

C. ALPINUM.

CERASTIUM CERASTOIDES.

CERASTIUM ARVENSE.

CERASTIUM GLOMERATUM.

C. PUMILUM.

CERASTIUM DIFFUSUM.

CERASTIUM SEMIDECANDRUM.

CERASTIUM ARCTICUM.

HOLOSTEUM UMBELLATUM.

MOENCHIA ERECTA.

PL 14

STELLARIA
NEGLECTA

MYOSOTON
AQUATICUM

STELLARIA MEDIA.

STELLARIA
NEGLECTA
VAR ELIZABETHAE.

STELLARIA
HOLOSTEA

STELLARIA
PALUSTRIS

STELLARIA
NEMORUM.

×6
STELLARIA
GRAMINEA

STELLARIA
ALSINE

MINUARTIA
RUBELLA

ARENARIA CILIATA

MOEHRINGIA
TRINERVIA

VAR GERARDI

ARENARIA
ANGLICA

MINUARTIA
HYBRIDA

MINUARTIA VERNA.

ARENARIA NORVEGICA

ARENARIA
SERPYLLIFOLIA.

ARENARIA
LEPTOCLADOS

PL 15

MINUARTIA SEDOIDES

SAGINA PROCUMBENS.

HONKENYA PEPLOIDES.

SAGINA INTERMEDIA

SAGINA APETALA SUBSP. APETALA

SAGINA APETALA SUBSP. ERECTA

SAGINA NORMANIANA.

MONTIA FONTANA

SAGINA SUBULATA.

x2½

SAGINA SAGINOIDES.

SAGINA MARITIMA

MONTIA PERFOLIATA.

x10

POLYCARPON TETRAPHYLLUM.

SAGINA NODOSA.

MONTIA SIBIRICA.

PERGULA ARVENSIS.

SPERGULARIA BOCCONII.

b   a
SPERGULARIA MARINA.

SPERGULARIA MEDIA.

SPERGULARIA RUBRA.

SPERGULARIA RUPICOLA.

PL 16

HYPERICUM
CALYCINUM.

H. ANDROSAEMUM.

HYPERICUM
MONTANUM.

TAMARIX
ANGLICA.

HYPERICUM
TETRAPTERUM.

H. MONTANUM

HYPERICUM
UNDULATUM.

HYPERICUM PULCHRUM.

ELATINE
HEXANDRA.

E. HYDROPIPER.

HYPERICUM
PERFORATUM.

HYPERICUM
LINARIFOLIUM.

HYPERICUM
HIRSUTUM.

HYPERICUM HUMIFUSUM.

HYPERICUM
MACULATUM.

HYPERICUM
ELODES.

PL 17

ALTHEA
OFFICINALIS.

MARSH
MALLOW.

ALTHEA
HIRSUTA.

LAVATERA
ARBOREA.

M.MOSCHATA
VAR.
HETERO-
PHYLLA.

MALVA
MOSCHATA

LAVATERA
CRETICA

MALVA NEGLECTA.

MALVA
SYLVESTRIS.

MALVA
PUSILLA.

TILIA
CORDATA.

TILIA PLATYPHYLLOS.

PL 18

LINUM

LINUM PERENNE SUBSP. ANGLICUM

LINUM BIENNE.

RADIOLA LINOIDES.

LINUM CATH -ARTICUM.

GERANIUM SANGUINEUM.

GERANIUM VERSICOLOR

GERANIUM PRATENSE.

× 2.

× 2.

GERANIUM SYLVATICUM

GERANIUM PHÆUM.

× 2.

GERANIUM MOLLE.

GERANIUM MOLLE
× 5.

GERANIUM PURPUREUM

GERANIUM ROTUNDIFOLIUM

GERANIUM PUSILLUM.

×5

GERANIUM LUCIDUM.

HERB ROBERT.

GERANIUM ROBERTIANUM.

GERANIUM COLUMBINUM.

GERANIUM DISSECTUM.

GERANIUM PYRENAICUM.

PL 19

ERODIUM
DUNENSE

ERODIUM
MARITIMUM

×2

ERODIUM
MOSCHATUM

ERODIUM
CICUTARIUM

×2

VAR.
PIMPINELLIFOLIUM

OXALIS
CORNICULATA.

WOOD
SORREL

OXALIS
ACETOSELLA.

ILEX AQUIFOLIUM

IMPATIENS
GLANDULIFERA.

IMPATIENS
NOLI-TANGERE.

IMPATIENS
CAPENSIS

RHAMNUS
CATHARTICUS.

EUONYMUS
EUROPAEUS.

ACER
PSEUDO-PLATANUS

ACER CAMPESTRE.

FRANGULA
ALNUS

PL 20

GENISTA
PILOSA.

GENISTA
ANGLICA.

ULEX
GALLII.

ULEX EUROPAEUS
X 4.

GENISTA
TINCTORIA

ONONIS RECLINATA

BAROTHAMNUS
SCOPARIUS.

ONONIS
SPINOSA.

VAR HORRIDA

ULEX
EUROPAEUS

ULEX
MINOR.

MEDICAGO SATIVA

ONONIS REPENS

TRIFOLIUM
ORNITHOPODIOIDES

MEDICAGO
FALCATA

MEDICAGO
VARIA

MEDICAGO LUPULINA

PL 21

MEDICAGO ARABICA.

MEDICAGO POLYMORPHA.

MEDICAGO MINIMA.

TRIFOLIUM SUBTERRANIUM.

TRIFOLIUM HYBRIDUM. ALSIKE.

MELILOTUS ALTISSIMA.

M. OFFICINALIS.

MELILOTUS ALBA.

TRIFOLIUM PRATENSE

TRIFOLIUM MEDIUM.

T. PRATENSE X 8

TRIFOLIUM REPENS.

TRIFOLIUM SQUAMOSUM

T. ARVENSE

TRIFOLIUM SUFFOCATUM.

TRIFOLIUM GLOMERATUM.

TRIFOLIUM OCHROLEUCON.

T. INCARNATUM →

TRIFOLIUM STRICTUM.

TRIFOLIUM BOCCONEI.

TRIFOLIUM STRIATUM.

TRIFOLIUM SCABRUM

TRIFOLIUM MOLINERII.

PL 22

TRIFOLIUM
DUBIUM

TRIFOLIUM
MICRANTHUM

TRIFOLIUM
CAMPESTRE.

TRIFOLIUM
AUREUM.

TRIFOLIUM
FRAGIFERUM

ANTHYLLIS
VULNERARIA

VAR. COCCINEA

LOTUS
ULIGINOSUS

LOTUS
CORNICULATUS

L. HISPIDUS × 10

LOTUS ANGUSTISSIMUS.

OXYTROPIS
CAMPESTRIS

LOTUS. TENUIS.

LOTUS
HISPIDUS.

OXYTROPIS HALLERI

PL 23

ASTRAGALUS DANICUS.

ASTRAGALUS GLYCYPHYLLOS.

VICIA HIRSUTA TARE.

VICIA TETRASPERMA

VICIA TENUISSIMA

ASTRAGALUS ALPINUS.

ORNITHOPUS PERPUSILLUS.

ORNITHOPUS PINNATUS.

VICIA OROBUS.

ONOBRYCHIS VICIIFOLIA.

VICIA CRACCA

WOOD VETCH

HIPPOCREPIS COMOSA.

VICIA SYLVATICA

VICIA SEPIUM

PL 24

VICIA LATHYROIDES.

VICIA SATIVA.

VICIA BITHYNICA.

VICIA ANGUSTIFOLIA

VICIA LUTEA

LATHYRUS APHACA

LATHYRUS SYLVESTRIS

LATHYRUS NISSOLIA

LATHYRUS PRATENSIS.

LATHYRUS TUBEROSUS.

LATHYRUS MONTANUS.

MARSH PEA.

LATHYRUS PALUSTRIS.

LATHYRUS MARITIMUS.

SEA PEA.

PL 25

BLACKTHORN.

PRUNUS SPINOSA.

PRUNUS CERASUS.

PRUNUS PADUS.

PRUNUS INSITITIA.

P. DOMESTICA.

PRUNUS AVIUM.

× 10
FILIPENDULA ULMARIA

FILIPENDULA ULMARIA

SANGUISORBA OFFICINALIS.

APHANES ARVENSIS.

SANGUISORBA MINOR.

ALCHEMILLA GLABRA.

ALCHEMILLA VESTITA.

ALCHEMILLA ALPINA.

AGRIMONIA EUPATORIA.

ALCHEMILLA CONJUNCTA.

FILIPENDULA VULGARIS.

PL 26

POTENTILLA STERILIS.
X 7.

P. STERILIS.

POTENTILLA
TABERNAEMONTANI.

POTENTILLA
CRANTZII.

P. NORVEGICA.

POTENTILLA
ARGENTEA.

POTENTILLA
ERECTA.

POTENTILLA
ANGLICA.

POTENTILLA REPTANS.

POTENTILLA
RUPESTRIS.

FRAGARIA
VESCA.

POTENTILLA
PALUSTRIS.

POTENTILLA
FRUTICOSA

SIBBALDIA
PROCUMBENS.

POTENTILLA
ANSERINA.

PL 27

RUBUS
IDAEUS.

RUBUS
CARPINIFOLIUS.
(SILVATICI)

RUBUS
SULCATUS.

RUBUS
SILVATICUS

(DISCOLORES)
RUBUS
ULMIFOLIUS.

(SUBERECTU

RUBUS
VESTITUS.
(VESTITI)

(PALLIDI)

RUBUS RADULA. (RADULAE)

RUBUS
EURYANTHEMUS.

PL 28

RUBUS CAESIUS.

RUBUS DASYPHYLLUS. (HYSTRICES)

RUBUS BELLARDII. (GLANDULOSI.)

RUBUS SAXATILIS.

G.RIVALE X URBANUM.

RUBUS CHAMAEMORUS.

GEUM RIVALE.

DRYAS OCTOPETALA.

GEUM URBANUM.

PL 29

ROSA
PIMPINELLIFOLIA
BURNET ROSE

ROSA TOMENTOSA

ROSA
VILLOSA.

ROSA
AGRESTIS.

ROSA
MICRANTHA.

ROSA
OBTUSIFOLIA

ROSA
SHERARDII.

SWEET BRIAR
ROSA RUBIGINOSA.

ROSA DUMALIS.

DOG
ROSE.
ROSA
CANINA.

ROSA
STYLOSA

ROSA
ARVENSIS.

PL 30

SORBUS
ARRANENSIS.

SORBUS
AUCUPARIA.

SORBUS
PORRIGENTI
-FORMIS

SORBUS
MINIMA

SORBUS
LATIFOLIA

SORBUS
ARIA.

SORBUS
TORMINALIS.

MALUS SYLVESTRIS

PYRUS
PYRASTER

PYRUS
CORDATA

CRATAEGUS
MONOGYNA

CRAETAGUS LAEVIGATA.

COTONEASTER
INTEGERRIMUS.

PL 31

SAXIFRAGA OPPOSITIFOLIA.

CHRYSOSPLENIUM OPPOSITIFOLIUM.

CHRYSOSPLENIUM ALTERNIFOLIUM.

SAXIFRAGA STELLARIS.

SAXIFRAGA URBIUM

SAXIFRAGA RIVULARIS.

SAXIFRAGA TRIDACTYLITES.

SAXIFRAGA NIVALIS.

SAXIFRAGA CERNUA.

SAXIFRAGA HIRSUTA.

SAXIFRAGA CESPITOSA.

SAXIFRAGA GRANULATA

SAXIFRAGA AIZOIDES.

SAXIFRAGA HIRCULUS.

SAXIFRAGA ROSACEA.

S. HYPNOIDES. VAR. PLATYPETALA

SAXIFRAGA HYPNOIDES.

PARNASSIA PALUSTRIS.

PL 32

RIBES UVA-CRISPA.

RIBES
RUBRUM.

♂ ♀ RIBES
ALPINUM.

RIBES
SPICATUM.

CRASSULA TILLAEA.

SEDUM
DASYPHYLLUM

RIBES NIGRUM

SEDUM
FABARIA.

ORPINE.

CRASSULA AQUATICA

SEDUM ANGLICUM.

SEDUM ALBUM

UMBILICUS
UPESTRIS.

SEDUM
VILLOSUM

SEDUM ACRE.

SEDUM FORSTERANUM.

SEDUM
REFLEXUM.

RHODIOLA
ROSEA.

PL 33

DROSERA
ROTUNDIFOLIA

DROSERA
INTERMEDIA

LYTHRUM
HYSSOPIFOLIA

DROSERA
ANGLICA

HIPPURIS
VULGARIS

LYTHRUM PORTULA

C. DEMERSUM.

C.
OBTUSANGULA

C. PEDUNCULATA

CALLITRICHE
HAMULATA.

LYTHRUM
SALICARIA.

MYRIOPHYLLUM
VERTICILLATUM.

MYRIOPHYLLUM
ALTERNIFLORUM.

CALLITRICHE
HERMAPHRODITICA.

×4

CALLITRICHE
STAGNALIS.

MYRIOPHYLLUM
SPICATUM

CALLITRICHE
PALUSTRIS.

CALLITRICHE
PLATYCARPA.

CALLITRICHE
TRUNCATA

CERATOPHYLLUM
SUBMERSUM.

PL 34

EPILOBIUM
ANGUSTIFOLIUM
ROSE BAY.

EPILOBIUM
HIRSUTUM

GREAT
WILLOW HERB.

EPILOBIUM
ALSINIFOLIUM

EPILOBIUM
ANAGALLIDIFOLIUM.

EPILOBIUM
PARVIFLORUM.

EPILOBIUM
MONTANUM

E. LAMYI.

EPILOBIUM
PALUSTRE.

EPILOBIUM
ROSEUM.

EPILOBIUM
TETRAGONUM.

EPILOBIUM OBSCURUM.

EPILOBIUM
LANCEOLATUM.

LUDWIGIA
PALUSTRIS.

CIRCAEA ALPINA.

CIRCAEA
LUTETIANA

PL 35

BRYONIA
DIOICA.

ASTRANTIA
MAJOR.

PHYSOSPERMUM
CORNUBIENSE.

ERYNGIUM
CAMPESTRE.

HYDROCOTYLE
VULGARIS

ERYNGIUM
MARITIMUM.

SANICULA
EUROPAEA.

BUPLEURUM
ROTUNDIFOLIUM.

BUPLEURUM
FALCATUM

HEMLOCK.
CONIUM
MACULATUM.

SMYRNIUM
OLUSATRUM.

BUPLEURUM BALDENSE.

BUPLEURUM
TENUISSIMUM.

x 4½

x 12

x 3

PL 36

TRINIA
GLAUCA.

CICUTA
VIROSA.

APIUM
GRAVEOLENS.

×3

CARUM
VERTICILLATUM.

CARUM
CARUI.

ETROSELINUM
EGETUM.

BUNIUM
BULBOCASTANUM.

SIUM
LATIFOLIUM.

REPENS.

×3

APIUM
INUNDATUM.

APIUM NODIFLORUM.

PL 37

BERULA
ERECTA.

AEGOPODIUM PODAGRARIA.

SISON
AMOMUM.

MYRRHIS
ODORATA.

PIMPINELLA
MAJOR.

CONOPODIUM
MAJUS

PIMPINELLA
SAXIFRAGA.

SCANDIX
PECTEN-
VENERIS.

CHAEROPHYLLUM
TEMULENTUM.

FLO. BUD × 18.

ANTHRISCUS CAUCALIS.

ANTHRISCUS SYLVESTRIS.

PL 38

OENANTHE
LACHENALII

OENANTHE CROCATA.
WATER DROPWORT.

OENANTHE
FISTULOSA

SESELI
LIBANOTIS

MEUM ATHAMANTICUM.

AETHUSA
CYNAPIUM.

OENANTHE
PIMPINELLOIDES.

OENANTHE
FLUVIATILIS

SILAUM
SILAUS

OENANTHE
AQUATICA

FOENICULUM
VULGARE

CRITHMUM
MARITIMUM.

PL 39

ANGELICA SYLVESTRIS.

LIGUSTICUM SCOTICUM.

×4

×6

PEUCEDANUM PALUSTRE.

PEUCEDANUM OFFICINALE.

PASTINACA SATIVA

HERACLEUM SPHONDYLIUM.

DAUCUS CAROTA.

CAUCALIS PLATYCARPOS.

TORILIS ARVENSIS.

TORILIS JAPONICA.

TORILIS NODOSA.

PL 40

HEDERA HELIX.

ADOXA
MOSCHATELLINA.
MOSCHATEL.

BUXUS
SEMPERVIRENS.

CHAMAEPERICLYMENUM
SUECICUM.

SWIDA
SANGUINEA.
DOGWOOD.

SAMBUCUS-
EBULUS.

VIBURNUM
OPULUS.

VIBURNUM LANTANA.

×2½

ELDER
SAMBUCUS NIGRA.

LONICERA
PERICLYMENUM.

LINNAEA BOREALIS.

LONICERA XYLOSTEUM.

PL 41

RUBIA
PEREGRINA.
MADDER

CRUCIATA
CILIATA.

GALIUM
VERUM.

GALIUM
PALUSTRE.

GALIUM
ALBUM

GALIUM
ULIGINOSUM.

GALIUM BOREALE.

×3
GALIUM
ALBUM
×6

GALIUM
SAXATILE.

×3

GALIUM
APARINE

GALIUM
PUMILUM.

SHERARDIA
ARVENSIS.

SWEET
WOODRUFF.

GALIUM
ODORATUM.

GALIUM TRICORNUTUM

GALIUM
PARISIENSE.
VAR. ANGLICUM.

GALIUM
DEBILE.

ASPERULA
CYNANCHICA.

PL 42

VALERIANELLA
DENTATA. ×7

VALERIANELLA
RIMOSA. ×5

×6

DIPSACUS
FULLONUM.

×8
V. ERIOCARPA.
Fruit

VALERIANA DIOICA.

♂

♀

×3

VALERIANELLA
LOCUSTA

VALERIANA
OFFICINALIS.

×6

VALERIANELLA
CARINATA.

×4

SCABIOSA
COLUMBARIA.

SUCCISA PRATENSIS.

DIPSACUS
PILOSUS.

KNAUTIA
ARVENSIS.

FIELD
SCABIOUS.

PL 43

EUPATORIUM CANNABINUM

x 3.

SOLIDAGO VIRGAUREA

CONYZA CANADENSIS.

ERIGERON ACER.

ERIGERON BOREALIS.

CRINITARIA LINOSYRIS

ASTER TRIPOLIUM.

x1½

FILAGO PYRAMIDATA.

ANTENNARIA DIOICA.

BELLIS PERENNIS.

FILAGO VULGARIS.

GNAPHALIUM NORVEGICUM

GNAPHALIUM SUPINUM.

GNAPHALIUM ULIGINOSUM.

FILAGO LUTESCENS.

FILAGO GALLICA

FILAGO MINIMA.

GNAPHALIUM SYLVATICUM.

PL 44

OTANTHUS
MARITIMUS

INULA
CONYZA.

INULA
CRITHMOIDES.

PULICARIA
VULGARIS.

PULICARIA
DYSENTERICA.

INULA
HELENIUM

ACHILLEA
MILLEFOLIUM

ACHILLEA
PTARMICA.

BIDENS
CERNUA.
VAR.
RADIATA.

BIDENS
TRIPARTITA.

ANTHEMIS
TINCTORIA

ANTHEMIS
ARVENSIS.

ANTHEMIS COTULA.

CHAMAEMELUM NOBILE.

PL 45

CHRYSANTHEMUM
LEUCANTHEMUM.

* CHRYSANTHEMUM
PARTHENIUM.

* PETASITES
FRAGRANS.

TUSSILAGO
FARFARA.

PETASITES HYBRIDUS.

C. SEGETUM.

CHRYSANTHEMUM
VULGARE.

MATRICARIA
RECUTITA.

ARTEMISIA
MARITIMA.

ARTEMISIA
VULGARIS

ARTEMISIA
CAMPESTRIS.

ARTEMISIA
ABSINTHIUM.

TRIPLEURO
-SPERMUM INODORUM.

* MATRICARIA MATRICARIOIDES.

PL 46

S VULGARIS AR RADIATUS

SENECIO SYLVATICUS

SENECIO SQUALIDUS

SENECIO JACOBAEA

x6

SENECIO ERUCIFOLIUS.

SENECIO VULGARIS

SENECIO AQUATICUS

MARSH RAGWORT

SENECIO CINERARIA.

SENECIO VISCOSUS.

ARCTIUM PUBENS.

SENECIO INTEGRIFOLIUS.

ARCTIUM LAPPA.

SENECIO SPATHULIFOLIUS

SENECIO PALUDOSUS.

CARLINA VULGARIS.

ARCTIUM MINUS

PL 47

CARDUUS
NUTANS.
NODDING
THISTLE.

CIRSIUM
PALUSTRE.

CARDUUS
TENUIFLORUS.

CARDUUS
ACANTHOIDES.

CIRSIUM
VULGARE.
(LANCEOLATUM)

SPEAR THISTLE.

CIRSIUM
HETEROPHYLLUM
MELANCHOLY
THISTLE.

CIRSIUM
ERIOPHORUM.

CIRSIUM
ARVENSE.
CREEPING
THISTLE.

CIRSIUM
DISSECTUM.

CIRSIUM
ACAULE.

PL 48

SERRATULA
TINCTORIA.

CENTAUREA NIGRA.

CENTAUREA
ASPERA.

ONOPORDON
ACANTHIUM.
SCOTTISH
THISTLE.

SAUSSUREA
ALPINA.

CENTAUREA
CALCITRAPA.

CENTAUREA
NEMORALIS.

CENTAUREA SCABIOSA.

CENTAUREA
JACEA.

CENTAUREA CYANUS.

PL 49

CICHORIUM
INTYBUS.

LAPSANA
COMMUNIS.

PICRIS
ECHIODES.

PICRIS
HIERACIOIDES.

ARNOSERIS
MINIMA.

CAT'S EAR
HYPOCHOERIS
RADICATA.

HYPOCHOERIS
MACULATA.

HYPOCHOERIS GLABRA.

CREPIS
TARAXACIFOLIA.

CREPIS
PALUDOSA.

CREPIS
FOETIDA.

CREPIS
MOLLIS.

CREPIS CAPILLARIS

CREPIS BIENNIS.

PL 50

HIERACIUM
HOLOSERICEUM.

HIERACIUM
EXOTERICUM
VAR
GRANDIDENS.

PILOSELLA
OFFICINARUM

HIERACIUM
BRITANNICUM.

HIERACIUM
LINGULATUM

HIERACIUM
VULGATUM.

HIERACIUM
ANGLICUM.

HIERACIUM
SCHMIDTTII

PL 51

HIERACIUM
LACHENALII.

HIERACIUM
UMBELLATUM.

HIERACIUM
LATOBRIGORUM

HIERACIUM
PERPROPINQUUM.

HIERACIUM
TRICHOCAULON.

HIERACIUM
MACULATUM.

PILOSELLA PELETERIANA.

PL 52

TARAXACUM
LAEVIGATUM.

LEONTODON
HISPIDUS.

LEONTODON
TARAXACOIDES.
COMMON HAWKBIT

TARAXACUM
OFFICINALE.
DANDELION.

LEONTODON
AUTUMNALIS.

MYCELIS
MURALIS.

ALPINE.
LETTUCE.

TARAXACUM
PALUSTRE.

CICERBITA
ALPINA.

WALL
LETTUCE.

LACTUCA
VIROSA.

LACTUCA
SERRIOLA.

SONCHUS
ASPER

SONCHUS OLERACEUS

SONCHUS PALUSTRIS.

CORN
SOW-THISTLE.

SONCHUS
ARVENSIS.

PL 53

TRAGOPOGON MINOR GOAT'S BEARD

CAMPANULA PATULA.

→ x3
JASIONE MONTANA

PHYTEUMA SPICATUM

WAHLENBERGIA HEDERACEA.

x 2

CAMPANULA GLOMERATA

x 2

CAMPANULA LATIFOLIA.

CAMPANULA RAPUNCULUS.

PHYTEUMA TENERUM

LEGOUSIA HYBRIDA.

CAMPANULA ROTUNDIFOLIA

LOBELIA URENS.

LOBELIA DORTMANNA.

CAMPANULA TRACHELIUM.

CAMPANULA RAPUNCULOIDES.

PL 54

VACCINIUM
MYRTILLUS.

VACCINIUM
VITIS-IDAEA.

VACCINIUM
ULIGINOSUM.

ARBUTUS
UNEDO.

E. MACKAIANA.

VACCINIUM
OXYCOCCUS

CRANBERRY.

×7

ERICA
TETRALIX

ERICA CILIARIS

ANDROMEDA
POLIFOLIA.

ARCTOSTAPHYLOS
UVA-URSI.

ERICA
VAGANS

LEDUM
PALUSTRE.

ERICA CINEREA.

DABOECIA
CANTABRICA.

PHYLLODOCE
CERULEA

×5

EMPETRUM NIGRUM.

ARCTOUS ALPINUS.

ERICA
HIBERNICA.

×4

CALLUNA VULGARIS.

PL 55

LOISELEURIA
PROCUMBENS.

PYROLA
MEDIA.

PYROLA
MINOR.

LIMONIUM
HUMILE.

×3

LIMONIUM
VULGARE.

×3

×3

×3

ORTHILIA
SECUNDA

LIMONIUM BINERVOSUM

LIMONIUM
TRANSWALLIANUM

MONOTROPA
HYPOPITYS.

ARMERIA
MARITIMA.

×1½

×3

PYROLA
ROTUNDIFOLIA.

MONESES UNIFLORA.

LIMONIUM
BELLIDIFOLIUM.

PL 56

PRIMROSE.
PRIMULA VULGARIS.

HOTTONIA PALUSTRIS.

OXLIP.
PRIMULA ELATIOR

PRIMULA VERIS.
COWSLIP.

PRIMULA SCOTICA

PRIMULA FARINOSA

P. VERIS x 4

DIAPENSIA LAPPONICA.

LYSIMACHIA THYRSIFLORA.

x 2

LYSIMACHIA VULGARIS

TRIENTALIS EUROPAEA.

*CYCLAMEN HEDERIFOLIUM.

LYSIMACHIA NEMORUM

LYSIMACHIA NUMMULARIA.

*LYSIMACHIA CILIATA.

PL 57

ANAGALLIS ARVENSIS.

ANAGALLIS MINIMA.

ANAGALLIS FOEMINA.

ANAGALLIS TENELLA.

GLAUX MARITIMA.

LIGUSTRUM VULGARE.

SAMOLUS VALERANDI.

CENTAURIUM PULCHELLUM.

EXACULUM PUSILLUM.

ASH

FRAXINUS EXCELSIOR.

VAR. SUBCAPITATUM.

CENTAURIUM ERYTHRAEA.

CICENDIA FILIFORMIS.

BLACKSTONIA PERFOLIATA.

CENTAURIUM CAPITATUM.

CENTAURIUM LITTORALE.

PERIWINKLE. VINCA MINOR.

CENTAURIUM SCILLOIDES.

PL 58

GENTIANA NIVALIS.

GENTIANELLA AMARELLA.

X4.

GENTIANELLA GERMANICA.

GENTIANELLA CAMPESTRIS.

GENTIANA VERNA.

X2

GENTIANA PNEUMONANTHE.

GENTIANELLA CAMPESTRIS VAR. BALTICA.

GENTIANELLA ANGLICA.

MENYANTHES TRIFOLIATA

BOG BEAN.

CYNOGLOSSUM OFFICINALE.

CYNOGLOSSUM GERMANICUM.

JACOB'S LADDER

POLEMONIUM COERULEUM.

NYMPHOIDES PELTATA.

PL 59

SYMPHYTUM
TUBEROSUM.

S. ASPERUM.

PULMONARIA
OFFICINALIS.

SYMPHYTUM
OFFICINALE.

PENTAGLOTTIS
SEMPERVIRENS.

×2

PULMONARIA
LONGIFOLIA.

MERTENSIA
MARITIMA

LYCOPSIS
ARVENSIS.

MYOSOTIS
ALPESTRIS.

MYOSOTIS
CAESPITOSA.

MYOSOTIS RAMOSISSIMA.

×3

MYOSOTIS
SCORPIOIDES

MYOSOTIS SECUNDA.

MYOSOTIS
STOLONIFERA.

MYOSOTIS
ARVENSIS.

MYOSOTIS
DISCOLOR.

MYOSOTIS
SYLVATICA.

PL 60

LITHOSPERMUM
PURPURO-
CAERULEUM.

LITHOSPERMUM
OFFICINALE.

LITHOSPERMUM
ARVENSE.

ECHIUM
VULGARE.

CALYSTEGIA
SEPIUM.

CUSCUTA
EPITHYMUM.

CUSCUTA
EUROPAEA.

CONVOLVULUS
ARVENSIS.

CALYSTEGIA SOLDANELLA.

SOLANUM
DULCAMARA.

SOLANUM
NIGRUM.

LYCIUM CHINENSE.

ATROPA BELLA-DONNA.

HYOSCYAMUS NIGER.

PL 61

VERBASCUM NIGRUM

V. PULVERULENTUM

*LINARIA
PURPUREA

LINARIA
VULGARIS.

KICKXIA
SPURIA × 4

VERBASCUM
THAPSUS

K. SPURIA

KICKXIA
ELATINE.

*CYMBALARIA
MURALIS.

VERBASCUM VIRGATUM

VERBASCUM
LYCHNITIS.

LINARIA
REPENS

CHAENORHINUM
MINUS.

*LINARIA
ARENARIA

MISOPATES
ORONTIUM.

PL 62

SCROPHULARIA
UMBROSA

SCROPHULARIA
NODOSA

SCROPHULARIA
SCORODONIA.

SCROPHULARIA
AURICULATA

MIMULUS GUTTATUS

X 10

SIBTHORPIA EUROPAEA

LIMOSELLA
AQUATICA.

VERONICA
HEDERIFOLIA.

VERONICA
TRIPHYLLOS.

V. PERSICA.

DIGITALIS
PURPUREA.

VERONICA
POLITA

V. FILIFORMIS.

VERONICA
AGRESTIS.

VERONICA VERNA.

PL 63

VERONICA FRUTICANS.

VERONICA ARVENSIS.

VERONICA SPICATA.

VERONICA SERPYLLIFOLIA.

VERONICA ALPINA.

VERONICA OFFICINALIS.

VERONICA MONTANA.

VERONICA CATENATA.

VERONICA SCUTELLATA.

VERONICA BECCABUNGA.

VERONICA CHAMAEDRYS.

VERONICA ANAGALLIS-AQUATICA.

EUPHRASIA MICRANTHA.

EUPHRASIA SCOTTICA.

EUPHRASIA NEMOROSA. ×2.

EUPHRASIA CONFUSA.

EUPHRASIA BREVIPILA.

EUPHRASIA ANGLICA. ×2

EUPHRASIA SALISBURGENSIS.

PL 64

PARENTUCELLIA
VISCOSA.

BARTSIA
ALPINA.

ODONTITES VERNA.

PEDICULARIS
SYLVATICA.

PEDICULARIS
PALUSTRIS.

MELAMPYRUM
PRATENSE.

RHINANTHUS
SEROTINUS

COW-WHEAT.

RHINANTHUS
STENOPHYLLUS.

RHINANTHUS
MONTICOLA

HAY
RATTLE.

RHINANTHUS
BOREALIS.

RHINANTHUS
MINOR.

R.LINTONI.

MELAMPYRUM
CRISTATUM.

MELAMPYRUM
SYLVATICUM.

MELAMPYRUM
ARVENSE.

PL 65

OROBANCHE
ALBA VAR. RUBRA.

OROBANCHE
RAPUM-GENISTAE.

OROBANCHE
ELATIOR.

O.RAMOSA.

O.PICRIDIS.

OROBANCHE
HEDERAE.

OROBANCHE
MINOR.

O.CARYOPHYLLACEA.

OROBANCHE
PURPUREA.

× 4.

Water

UTRICULARIA
VULGARIS.

UTRICULARIA
INTERMEDIA.

UTRICULARIA
MINOR.

PINGUICULA
LUSITANICA.

UTRICULARIA NEGLECTA.

PINGUICULA
GRANDIFLORA.

PINGUICULA VULGARIS.

LATHRAEA
SQUAMARIA.

PL 66

VERBENA
OFFICINALIS.

MENTHA
SUAVEOLENS.

MENTHA
LONGIFOLIA.

MENTHA
PIPERITA.

MENTHA
AQUATICA.

MENTHA
SPICATA.

MENTHA PULEGIUM.

MENTHA
GENTILIS.

MENTHA
SMITHIANA.

MENTHA
ARVENSIS.

LYCOPUS
EUROPAEUS.

ORIGANUM
VULGARE.

MARJORAM.

PL 67

THYMUS
SERPYLLUM

THYMUS
PULEGIOIDES.

CLINOPODIUM
VULGARE.

CALAMINTHA
NEPETA.

CALAMINTHA ASCENDENS

CALAMINTHA
SYLVATICA.

ACINOS ARVENSIS.

MELISSA
OFFICINALIS

SALVIA
PRATENSIS.

SALVIA
HORMINOIDES.

GLECHOMA
HEDERACEA

NEPETA CATARIA.

SCUTELLARIA
MINOR.

SCUTELLARIA
GALERICULATA.

PL 68

PRUNELLA
VULGARIS.

PRUNELLA
LACINIATA.

MELITTIS
MELISSOPHYLLUM.

MARRUBIUM
VULGARE.

STACHYS
ALPINA.

BETONICA
OFFICINALIS.

BETONY.

STACHYS
PALUSTRIS.

*STACHYS
ANNUA

GALEOPSIS
SPECIOSA.

GALEOPSIS
ANGUSTIFOLIA.

GALEOPSIS
TETRAHIT.
HEMP
NETTLE.

GALEOPSIS SEGETUM.

STACHYS
GERMANICA.

STACHYS
SYLVATICA.

STACHYS
ARVENSIS.

PL 69

LAMIUM
HYBRIDUM.

LAMIUM PURPUREUM.

LAMIUM
MOLUCCELLIFOLIUM.

LAMIUM
AMPLEXICAULE.

BALLOTA
NIGRA.

×2

LAMIASTRUM
GALEOBDOLON

LAMIUM
ALBUM.

TEUCRIUM
BOTRY

TEUCRIUM
SCORODONIA

*A GENEVENSIS.

TEUCRIUM
CHAMAEDRYS.

TEUCRIUM
SCORDIUM

AJUGA
PYRAMIDALIS

AJUGA CHAMAEPITYS

AJUGA REPTANS.

PL 70

PLANTAGO CORONOPUS

PLANTAGO MEDIA

×7

×6

PLANTAGO MAJOR.

PLANTAGO LANCEOLATA

CHENOPODIUM POLYSPERMUM

CHENOPODIUM VULVARIA

HERNIARIA GLABRA

CHENOPODIUM ALBUM

PLANTAGO MARITIMA.

×4

×10

SCLERANTHUS PERENNIS.

ILLECEBRUM VERTICILLATUM

SCLERANTHUS ANNUUS.

×10.

CORRIGIOLA LITORALIS.

LITTORELLA UNIFLORA.

PL 71

CHENOPODIUM
BOTRYODES.

CHENOPODIUM
RUBRUM.

CHENOPODIUM
GLAUCUM

CHENOPODIUM
MURALE.

CHENOPODIUM
FICIFOLIUM.

×10

×5

CHENOPODIUM
BONUS-HENRICUS.

ATRIPLEX
GLABRIUSCULA.

ATRIPLEX
LITTORALIS

ATRIPLEX
PATULA.

BETA
MARITIMA.

×2

HALIMIONE
PORTULACOIDES

ATRIPLEX
LACINIATA.

HALIMIONE PEDUNCULATA.

SALICORNIA
EUROPAEA.

SALICORNIA RAMOSISSIMA.

ATRIPLEX
HASTATA.

PL 72

POLYGONUM CONVOLVULUS

SUAEDA
MARITIMA

SALSOLA KALI

POLYGONUM
OXYSPERMUM
SUBSP. RAII

SUAEDA
FRUTICOSA

POLYGONUM
DUMETORUM

POLYGONUM
MINUS

POLYGONUM
MITE.

×2

POLYGONUM
LAPATHIFOLIUM

POLYGONUM
PERSICARIA

POLYGONUM
AVICULARE.

POLYGONUM
BISTORTA

POLYGONUM
ARENASTRUM.

POLYGONUM
HYDROPIPER

×4

POLYGONUM
VIVIPARUM

POLYGONUM
NODOSUM

POLYGONUM
AMPHIBIUM.

PL 73

RUMEX
SANGUINEUS.

RUMEX
CONGLOMERATUS.

RUMEX
LONGIFOLIUS.

R. PALUSTRIS
FRUIT ×2

RUMEX
RUPESTRIS.

RUMEX
MARITIMUS.

RUMEX
PULCHER.

OXYRIA
DIGYNA.

RUMEX
OBTUSIFOLIUS.

RUMEX
CRISPUS.

RUMEX
HYDROLAPATHUM.

RUMEX
ACETOSA. ×2

×4

RUMEX
ACETOSELLA.

PL 74

EUPHORBIA PEPLIS. ×5 ×1½

EUPHORBIA HYBERNA.

MERCURIALIS PERENNIS.

EUPHORBIA PLATYPHYLLOS.

EUPHORBIA AMYGDALOIDES. ×3½

EUPHORBIA HELIOSCOPIA.

EUPHORBIA LATHYRUS.

EUPHORBIA PEPLUS. ×3 ×4

EUPHORBIA CYPARISSIAS. ×3

EUPHORBIA PORTLANDICA. ×4

EUPHORBIA EXIGUA.

EUPHORBIA PARALIAS.

VISCUM ALBUM.

THESIUM HUMIFUSUM.

HIPPOPHAE RHAMNOIDES.

PL 75

ASARUM EUROPAEUM

DAPHNE LAUREOLA

D. LAURE-OLA. ×4

DAPHNE MEZEREUM.

ARISTOLOCHIA CLEMATITIS.

URTICA DIOICA.

×3

PARIETARIA JUDAICA.

ENGLISH ELM

ULMUS PROCERA.

ULMUS GLABRA WYCH ELM

BETULA NANA.

URTICA URENS.

MYRICA GALE SWEET GALE

HOP

HUMULUS LUPULUS

BETULA PENDULA.

BETULA PUBESCENS.

PL 76

ALNUS GLUTINOSA. ALDER.

×5

CARPINUS BETULUS. HORNBEAM

HAZEL

QUERCUS PETRAEA. SESSILE OAK

COMMON OAK QUERCUS ROBUR.

FAGUS SYLVATICA.

CORYLUS AVELLANA

SALIX TRIANDRA.

SALIX ALBA.

SALIX PENTANDRA.

SALIX FRAGILIS.

SALIX URPUREA.

×2

SALIX VIMINALIS.

SALIX LAPPONUM.

SALIX AURITA.

PL 77

SALIX
CAPREA.

SALIX
ATROCINEREA.

SALIX
PHYLICIFOLIA.

SALIX
ARBUSCULA.

SALIX
HERBACEA.

SALIX NIGRICANS.

SALIX
MYRSINITES.

SALIX
RETICULATA.

SALIX
REPENS

SALIX
LANATA

POPULUS NIGRA.

POPULUS TREMULA.

P ×CANESCENS.

POPULUS ALBA.

PL 78

LURONIUM NATANS.

BUTOMUS
UMBELLATUS.
FLOWERING
RUSH.

BALDELLIA
RANUNCULOIDES.

ALISMA
LANCEOLATUM.

SAGITTARIA
SAGITTIFOLIA
ARROW
HEAD.

ALISMA
PLANTAGO-
AQUATICA.

TRIGLOCHIN
MARITIMA.

DAMASONIUM
ALISMA.

TRIGLOCHIN
PALUSTRIS.

SCHEUCHZERIA
PALUSTRIS.

HYDROCHARIS
MORSUS-RANAE.

FROG-BIT.

WATER
SOLDIER

STRATIOTES ALOIDES.

ELODEA
CANADENSIS.

PL 79

HAMMARBYA
PALUDOSA.

LIPARIS
LOESELII.

NEOTTIA
NIDUS-AVIS

EPIPACTIS
ATRORUBENS.

CORALLORHIZA
TRIFIDA.

EPIPACTIS
HELLEBORINE.

EPIPACTIS
LEPTOCHILA

CEPHALANTHERA
RUBRA.

SPIRANTHES
SPIRALIS.

LISTERA
OVATA.

SPIRANTHES
AESTIVALIS.

LISTERA
CORDATA

CEPHALANTHERA
LONGIFOLIA.

GOODYERA REPENS.

CEPHALANTHERA
DAMASONIUM

PL 80

ORCHIS USTULATA

ORCHIS PURPUREA.

ORCHIS LAXIFLORA

ANACAMPTIS PYRAMIDALIS.

DACTYLORHIZA INCARNATA.

DACTYLORHIZA PRAETERMISSA

MONKEY ORCHID

ORCHIS SIMIA.

ORCHIS MASCULA.

MARSH HELLEBORINE EPIPACTIS PALUSTRIS.

ORCHIS MILITARIS.

ORCHIS MORIO.

DACTYLORHIZA ERICETORUM.

DACTYLORHIZA FUCHSII.

LIZARD ORCHID.

HIMANTO- -GLOSSUM HIRCINUM

DACTYLORHIZA PURPURELLA.

PL 81

O. FUCIFLORA.

OPHRYS
APIFERA.

OPHRYS
INSECTIFERA

HERMINIUM
MONORCHIS.

OPHRYS
SPHEGODES.

x3½

x4¼

VAR. TROLLII.

ACERAS
ANTHROPOPHORUM

PLATANTHERA
CHLORANTHA.

GYMNADENIA
CONOPSEA.

LEUCORCHIS
ALBIDA.

LADY'S SLIPPER
CYPRIPEDIUM CALCEOLUS.

COELOGLOSSUM
VIRIDE.

PLATANTHERA BIFOLIA

x4

PL 82

IRIS
PSEUDACORUS

ROMULEA
COLUMNÆ

CROCUS
PURPUREUS.

IRIS
FOETIDISSIMA.

SISYRINCHIUM
BERMUDIANA.

IRIS
SPURIA.

LEUCOJUM
AESTIVUM

LEUCOJUM
VERNUM.

NARCISSUS
PSEUDO-
NARCISSUS.

NARCISSUS
OBVALLARIS

TENBY
DAFFODIL.

GLADIOLUS
.LYRICUS.

×NARCISSUS
BIFLORUS.

LENT
LILY.

GALANTHUS
NIVALIS.
SNOWDROP.

PL 83

CONVALLARIA
MAJALIS.

POLYGONATUM
MULTIFLORUM.

TAMUS
COMMUNIS.

POLYGONATUM
ODORATUM.

ALLIUM
SCORODOPRASUM.

MAIANTHEMUM
BIFOLIUM.

POLYGONATUM
VERTICILLATUM.

SIMETHIS
PLANIFOLIA.

ALLIUM VINEALE.
CROW GARLIC.

ASPARAGUS
PROSTRATUS.

RUSCUS
ACULEATUS.

PL 84

LILIUM
PYRENAICUM

ALLIUM
SCHOENOPRASUM.

"ALLIUM
SIBIRICUM."

ALLIUM
OLERACEUM

ALLIUM
URSINUM.

ALLIUM
TRI-
QUETRUM

FRITILLARIA
MELEAGRIS.

TULIPA
SYLVESTRIS.

SCILLA
AUTUMNALIS.

MUSCARI
ATLANTICUM

SCILLA
VERNA.

ENDYMION
NON-SCRIPTUS.

ORNITHOGALUM
NUTANS.

ORNITHOGALUM
PYRENAICUM

ORNITHOGALUM
UMBELLATUM.

PL 85

GAGEA
LUTEA.

PARIS
QUADRIFOLIA.

TOFIELDIA
PUSILLA.

LLOYDIA
SEROTINA.

JUNCUS
SUBULIFLORUS

NARTHECIUM
OSSIFRAGUM.

COLCHICUM
AUTUMNALE.

JUNCUS
GERARDII.

JUNCUS
BALTICUS.

JUNCUS
TRIFIDUS.

JUNCUS
INFLEXUS

JUNCUS
COMPRESSUS.

x2

x2

JUNCUS
FILIFORMIS.

JUNCUS
TENUIS.

JUNCUS
SQUARROSUS.

JUNCUS
BUFONIUS.

x2

JUNCUS
EFFUSUS.

PL 86

JUNCUS
CAPITATUS.

JUNCUS
MUTABILIS

JUNCUS
ARTICULATUS.

JUNCUS
ACUTIFLORUS.

JUNCUS
MARITIMUS.

JUNCUS
ACUTUS.

JUNCUS
BIGLUMIS.

JUNCUS
TRIGLUMIS.

JUNCUS
SUBNODULOSUS.
BLUNT FLOWERED
RUSH.

LUZULA
PILOSA.

LUZULA
MULTIFLORA

JUNCUS
CASTANEUS.

LUZULA
FORSTERI.

LUZULA
ARCUATA.

LUZULA
SPICATA.

JUNCUS
OCHII

JUNCUS BULBOSUS.

LUZULA
SYLVATICA.

LUZULA
CAMPESTRIS.

PL 87

ACORUS
CALAMUS.

×2

SPARGANIUM
EMERSUM

SPARGANIUM
ERECTUM.

T. ANGUSTIFOLIA.

TYPHA
LATIFOLIA.

SPARGANIUM
ANGUSTIFOLIUM.

SPARGANIUM
MINIMUM.

ARUM
ITALICUM

ARUM
MACULATUM

SPIRODELA
POLYRHIZA.

LEMNA
MINOR.

LEMNA GIBBA.

LEMNA
TRISULCA.

PL 88

POTAMOGETON
POLYGONIFOLIUS

POTAMOGETON
GRAMINEUS.

POTAMOGETON
NATANS.

POTAMOGETON
COLORATUS

POTAMOGETON
LUCENS

POTAMOGETON
PERFOLIATUS

POTAMOGETON
PRAELONGUS.

POTAMOGETON
ALPINUS.

POTAMOGETON   NODOSUS

GROENLANDIA
DENSA.

PL 89.

POTAMOGETON
ACUTIFOLIUS.

POTAMOGETON
BERCHTOLDII.

POTAMOGETON
OBTUSIFOLIUS.

POTAMOGETON
FRIESII.

POTAMOGETON
CRISPUS

POTAMOGETON
PUSILLUS.

POTAMOGETON
TRICHOIDES

ERIOCAULON
AQUATICUM

POTAMOGETON
COMPRESSUS.

ZOSTERA
MARINA

RUPPIA
SPIRALIS

POTAMOGETON
FILIFORMIS.

POTAMOGETON
PECTINATUS.

NAJAS
MARINA.

ZANNICHELLIA
PALUSTRIS

PL 90

SCHOENUS
NIGRICANS.

SCIRPUS
SETACEUS.

B. RUFUS.

ERIOPHORUM
ANGUSTIFOLIUM.

SCIRPUS
LACUSTRIS.

SCIRPUS
MARITIMUS.

ERIOPHORUM
VAGINATUM

ERIOPHORUM
LATIFOLIUM

CYPERUS
LONGUS.

BLYSMUS
COMPRESSUS.

CLADIUM
MARISCUS.

S. TABERNAE-
-MONTANI.

KOBRESIA
CALICINA.

E. PALUSTRIS

SCIRPUS FLUITANS.

E. MULTI-
-CAULIS.

CYPERUS
FUSCUS.

SCIRPUS
CESPITOSUS.

RHYNCHOSPORA
ALBA.

ELEOCHARIS ELEOCHARIS
ACICULARIS. QUINQUEFLORA.

ELEOCHARIS
UNIGLUMIS.

SCIRPUS
SYLVATICUS.

RHYNCHOSPORA
FUSCA.

PL 91

CAREX MICROGLOCHIN.

CAREX DIOICA

CAREX PULICARIS.

CAREX PAUCIFLORA.

CAREX RUPESTRIS.

CAREX MARITIMA.

CAREX DISTICHA.

CAREX DIANDRA.

CAREX DIVISA.

CAREX PANICULATA.

CAREX ARENARIA.

CAREX APPROPINQUATA.

CAREX ECHINATA

CAREX DIVULSA.

CAREX REMOTA.

CAREX SPICATA.

CAREX OTRUBAE.

CAREX ELONGATA.

CAREX CURTA.

CAREX MURICATA

CAREX VULPINA.

CAREX OVALIS

PL 92

CAREX HUMILIS.

CAREX LIMOSA.

CAREX DIGITATA.

C. ORNITHO-PODA.

CAREX MONTANA.

CAREX PILULIFERA.

CAREX ERICETORUM.

CAREX BUXBAUMII.

CAREX ATRATA.

CAREX ELATA.

CAREX NIGRA.

CAREX ACUTA.

CAREX PAUPERCULA.

CAREX FILIFORMIS.

CAREX ATROFUSCA.

CAREX PALLESCENS.

CAREX NORVEGICA.

CAREX AQUATILIS.

CAREX CARYOPHYLLEA.

CAREX FLACCA.

CAREX CAPILLARIS.

CAREX BIGELOWII.

CAREX VAGINATA.

CAREX PANICEA.

PL 93

CAREX
PENDULA

CAREX
STRIGOSA.

CAREX
ROSTRATA.

CAREX
DISTANS.

CAREX
SYLVATICA.

C. EXTENSA

CAREX
LASIOCARPA

CAREX
HIRTA

CAREX
LEPIDOCARPA

CAREX
BINERVIS.

CAREX
DEMISSA.

CAREX
ACUTIFORMIS.

CAREX
RIPARIA.

CAREX
FLAVA.

CAREX
LAEVIGATA.

CAREX
PSEUDO-
-CYPERUS.

CAREX
STENOLEPIS.

CAREX SAXATILIS.

PL 94

A
ALPINUS

ALOPECURUS
AEQUALIS.

ALOPECURUS
PRATENSIS.

ANTHOXANTHUM
ODORATUM.

x2
ALOPECURUS
BULBOSUS.

GASTRIDIUM
VENTRICOSUM.

ARTINA
NNSENDII.

PHALARIS
ARUNDINACEA.

ALOPECURUS
GENICULATUS.

ALOPECURUS
MYOSUROIDES.

MILIUM
EFFUSUM.

AGROSTIS
STOLONIFERA.

x2

P. ALPINUM.

x4

x4

PHLEUM
PHLEOIDES.

PHLEUM
PRATENSE.

AGROSTIS
CANINA.

POLYPOGON
MONSPELIENSIS.

AGROSTIS
CANINA
VAR. MONTANA

HLEUM BERTOLONII.

PHLEUM
ARENARIUM.

AGROSTIS
SETACEA.

AGROSTIS
TENUIS.

PL 95

DESCHAMPSIA
CESPITOSA.

MIBORA
MINIMA.

CALAMAGROSTIS
CANESCENS.

x1

CALAMAGROSTIS
EPIGEJOS.

x1

SESLERIA
CAESULEA

DESCHAMPSIA
FLEXUOSA

CORYNEPHORUS
CANESCENS

AIRA
PRAECOX

AIRA
CARYOPHYLLEA

TRISETUM
FLAVESCENS.

H.PUBESCENS.

H.MOLLIS

x2

DESCHAMPSIA
SETACEA.

HOLCUS
LANATUS.

SIEGLINGIA
DECUMBENS.

CYNODON
DACTYLON

AMMOPHILA
ARENARIA.

AVENA FATUA

HELICTOTRICHON
PRATENSE.

ARRHENATHERUM
ELATIUS.

PL 96

YNOSURUS RISTATUS.

VAR. ALBESCENS.

KOELERIA CRISTATA.

MOLINIA CAERULEA.

MELICA NUTANS.

MELICA UNIFLORA.

CATABROSA AQUATICA.

GLYCERIA MAXIMA

x2 G. DECLINATA.

x2 BRIZA MEDIA.

DACTYLIS GLOMERATA.

x2 B.MINOR.

x2

GLYCERIA PLICATA.

POA ALPINA.

POA ULBOSA.

POA ANNUA.

POA COMPRESSA.

POA NEMORALIS.

P. SUBCAERULEA.

POA PRATENSIS.

x2

POA TRIVIALIS.

GLYCERIA FLUITANS

PL 97

PUCCINELLIA
RUPESTRIS.

CATAPODIUM
MARINUM.

× 2

VULPIA
BROMOIDES.

VULPIA
MEMBRANAC

PUCCINELLIA
DISTANS

P. FASCIC-
-ULATA.

CATAPODIUM
RIGIDUM.

VULPIA
AMBIGUA.

PUCCINELLIA
MARITIMA

VULPIA
MYUROS

×2

FESTUCA
OVINA.

×2
FESTUCA
TENUIFOLIA.

FESTUCA
RUBRA.

×2
FESTUCA
PRATENSIS.

FESTUCA
JUNCIFOLIA

FESTUCA
ARUNDINACEA

FESTUCA
ALTISSIMA.

FESTUCA
GIGANTEA.

PL 98

BROMUS
RAMOSUS.

BROMUS
COMMUTATUS.

BROMUS
ERECTUS.

AGROPYRON
PUNGENS.

AGROPYRON
JUNCEIFORME.

PARAPHOLIS
STRIGOSA.

AGROPYRON
REPENS.

AGROPYRON
CANINUM.

LOLIUM
PERENNE.

BROMUS
MOLLIS.

BROMUS
INTERRUPTUS.

NARDUS
STRICTA.

HORDEUM
MURINUM.

HORDEUM
MARINUM.

BROMUS
BRITENSIS.

BROMUS
STERILIS.

BRACHIPODIUM
SYLVATICUM.

BRACHIPODIUM
PINNATUM.

x2

HORDEUM
SECALINUM.

ELYMUS
ARENARIUS.

PL 99

PINUS SYLVESTRIS.

JUNIPERUS
COMMUNIS.

YEW   TAXUS
BACCATA.

JUNIPERUS COMMUNIS   VAR. NANA.

ABBREVIATIONS USED IN THE TEXT

agg.–aggregate   inflo.–inflorescence   var.–variety
flo.–flower(s)   o–absent   *–not native, alien
fr.–fruit(s)   subsp.–subspecies   ❈–indicates plant is illustrated

RANUNCULACEAE   **PLATE 1**

Clematis vitalba L. **Traveller's Joy, Old Man's Beard.** ¶Stems rope-like, climbing by twisted leaf stalks; flo. greenish; fr. feathery. Mostly on calcareous and alluvial soils in S. England, rarer and mainly introduced in N. Flo. July. ❈.

Thalictrum alpinum L. **Alpine Meadow Rue.** ¶Small, wiry, 3–8 in.; flo. purplish, drooping; stamens pendulous. On wet mountain turf and rocks, N. Wales and Yorkshire northward. Flo. July. ❈.

Thalictrum minus L. agg. ¶Closely related forms; leaflets variable, their length not much exceeding breadth; stamens drooping. Flo. June–Aug.
Subsp. *minus*. **Cliff Meadow Rue.** *T. montanum* Wallr. *T. collinum* auct. ¶Shortly creeping or not; branching above the middle; leaflets medium. On limestone sea cliffs, mountain rocks and chalk, local. ❈.
Subsp. *arenarium* (Butcher) Clapham. **Sand Meadow Rue.** *T. dunense* auct. ¶Stolons widely creeping; stem short, branched and leafy to base. On coastal sand dunes, from S. Wales and Norfolk northwards. ❈.
Subsp. *majus* (Crantz) Rouy & Fouc. **Greater Meadow Rue.** *T. kochii* Fr. ¶Stem 2–4 ft branching from about the middle; leaflets large. On shady rocks and river-sides, sometimes creeping on soft soils, Wales, N. England and Scotland. ❈.

Thalictrum flavum L. **Common Meadow Rue.** ¶Stems 2–4 ft stout, subsimple; leaflets oblong; flo. crowded; stamens erect. In damp meadows, ditches and stream sides. Flo. June–July. ❈.

Pulsatilla vulgaris Mill. **Pasque Flower.** *Anemone pulsatilla* L. ¶Stem 4–10 in.; leaves finely divided, hairy; flo. violet, silky outside; fr. feathery. On calcareous slopes, S. and E. England. Flo. April–May. ❈.

Anemone nemorosa L. **Wood Anemone.** ¶Rootstock horizontal; stem 6 in.; sepals petaloid, white, rarely lilac (var. *purpurea* DC. ❈) or pale blue (var. *caerulea* DC. ❈). Common in woods except on acid soils. Flo. March–April. ❈.

Anemone ranunculoides L. **Yellow Wood Anemone.** ¶Similar in habit to *A. nemorosa*; leaves deeply divided, very shortly stalked; sepals petaloid, golden yellow, solitary, or in pairs. Garden escape. Occasionally naturalized in woods and plantations. Flo. April–May.

Anemone apennina L. **Blue Anemone.** ¶Similar in habit to *A. nemorosa* but with a tuberous, blackish, elongated rhizome; stem leaves in whorls of 3, glabrous above pubescent below; flo. solitary, with 8–15 narrow, bright blue, rarely white, perianth segments. Garden escape. Occasionally naturalized in woods and plantations. Flo. April–May.

Adonis annua L. **Pheasant's Eye.** ¶Annual. Stem 8–15 in.; leaves finely divided; flo. scarlet; achenes with straight beak. In cornfields, S. and E. England, rarely naturalized. Flo. May–Sept. ❈.

Myosurus minimus L. **Mouse-Tail.** ¶Annual, 2–6 in.; leaves basal, linear; flo. greenish; sepals with spur; carpels many, spiked. Damp arable fields in England, rare. Flo. April–June. ❀.

PLATE 2

Ranunculus circinatus Sibth. **Circular-leaved Crowfoot.** ¶Leaves all submerged, segments short, in one plane, wheel like. In canals, ponds and slow streams, mainly lowland. Flo. June–Aug. ❀.

Ranunculus fluitans Lam. **River Crowfoot.** ¶Stems long and stout; submerged leaves 3–10 in.; flo. large, petals 5–8; stamens shorter than achenes. In rather rapid streams. Flo. June–Aug. ❀.

Ranunculus trichophyllus Chaix. **Dark Hair Crowfoot.** ¶Leaves all submerged, segments short, dark, rigid; petals narrow; achenes hairy, crowded. In ponds and slow streams, England and S. Scotland. Flo. June. ❀.

Ranunculus aquatilis L. **Water Crowfoot.** *R. heterophyllus* Weber. ¶Floating leaf segments wedge shaped or variously cut. Submerged leaves not rigid; peduncles short; stamens exceeding achenes. ❀.

Ranunculus peltatus Schrank. ¶Floating leaves with rounded segments; submerged leaves rather stiff; peduncles long and tapering; flo. large. Ponds and slow streams, common. ❀.
Var. *floribundus* (Bab.) Druce. ¶Petals not contiguous; peduncles short and slender. Now regarded as a mere habitat form and unworthy of varietal status. ❀.

Ranunculus penicillatus (Dumort.) Bab.
Var. *penicillatus*. *R. pseudofluitans* (Syme) Newbould ex J. G. Bak. & Foggitt. *R. peltatus* Schrank subsp. *pseudofluitans* (Syme) C. D. K. Cook. ¶Floating leaves alternate; submerged leaves long, tassel-like, much branched; flo. large. Fast-flowing streams in E. and S. England, the Midlands, Wales and Ireland. Flo. May–June.
Var. *calcareus* (Butcher) C. D. K. Cook. *R. calcareus* Butcher. ¶Similar to var. *penicillatus* but floating leaves absent; submerged leaves shorter and very much branched with up to 150 ultimate segments. Chiefly in calcareous streams in S.E. England and the Midlands. Flo. May–June. ❀.
Var. *vertumnus* C. D. K. Cook. *R. sphaerospermus* auct. angl., non Boiss. & Blanche. ¶Entire leaves absent; divided leaves globose to reniform in outline; shorter than mature internodes; segments rigid, much branched. Canals, ditches and slow streams in S. England and the Midlands. Flo. May–June. ❀.

Ranunculus baudotii Godr. **Seaside Crowfoot.** ¶Floating leaves cut into 3 subequal segments; submerged leaves rigid; stamens shorter than head of many achenes. Brackish water near sea. ❀.
Var. *confusus* (Godr.) Syme. ¶Is more slender with longer stamens. Now regarded as a mere habitat form and unworthy of varietal status. ❀.

Ranunculus tripartitus DC. **Little Three-lobed Crowfoot.** ¶Stems very slender; floating leaves small, with obovate or lobed segments; submerged leaves very fine or absent (f. *lutarius* ❀†); flo. minute, petals 3 mm.; achenes few, 3–5. In shallow pools, S. and W. England and Wales. Flo. May. ❀.

Ranunculus omiophyllus Ten. **Moorland Crowfoot.** *R. lenormandii* F. W. Schultz.

¶With floating leaves only, divided half-way into 3 rounded, crenate segments; petals 5–6 mm. In moorland pools, mostly in W. and N. Flo. May–Sept. ❀.

Ranunculus hederaceus L. **Ivy-leaved Crowfoot.** ¶Leaves notched, with shallow lobes broadest at their base; petals often hardly longer than the sepals. Creeping on mud and in shallow water throughout the British Isles, though rather local. ❀.

†*Ranunculus tripartitus* f. *lutarius* is possibly referable to the hybrid *R. omiophyllus* × *tripartitus*.

PLATE 3

Ranunculus sceleratus L. **Celery-leaved Crowfoot.** ¶Annual, 1–2 ft; petals small, yellow; receptacle elongated; achenes many. In muddy ditches and sides of ponds. Flo. May–Sept. ❀.

Ranunculus ophioglossifolius Vill. ¶Annual, $\frac{1}{2}$–1 ft; flo. small, $\frac{1}{4}$ in., pale yellow; achenes covered with tubercles. In marshes, Gloucestershire, formerly in Jersey and Dorset, very rare. Flo. June–July. ❀.

Ranunculus flammula L. **Lesser Spearwort.**
Subsp. *flammula*. ¶Suberect, 6–18 in.; basal leaves oval. Wet places. Flo. May–Sept. ❀.
Var. *tenuifolius* Wallr. ¶Fairly stout, arching, rooting at some nodes. ❀.
Subsp. *scoticus* (E. S. Marshall) Clapham. ¶Lower leaves without or almost without a blade. Gravelly lake margins, N. England, Scotland, Ireland. ❀.

Ranunculus reptans L. ¶Stem creeping, slender, rooting at every node; leaves linear-lanceolate; achenes with slender, curved beak. Sandy lake margins in N., very rare. Material previously referred to this species is now regarded as the hybrid *R. flammula* × *reptans*. Flo. July. ❀.

Ranunculus lingua L. **Great Spearwort.** ¶Stem 2–3 ft, hollow; leaves very large, ovate-oblong, clasping stem; flo. $1\frac{1}{2}$–2 in. wide. In marshes, fens and ditches, local. Flo. July–Sept. ❀.

Ranunculus auricomus L. **Goldilocks.** ¶Stem 1 ft; petals often imperfect; achenes on tubercles of receptacle, downy with hooked beak. In woods and thickets. Flo. April–July. ❀.

Ranunculus acris L. **Common Meadow Buttercup.** ¶Stem 1–3 ft without stolons; leaves with middle lobe subsessile; sepals not reflexed. Abundant in meadows. Flo. April–Sept. ❀.

Ranunculus repens L. **Creeping Buttercup.** ¶Stems 1–2 ft with leafy stolons rooting at nodes; mid lobe of leaves stalked; sepals not reflexed. Cultivated land and pastures. Flo. May–Aug. ❀.

Ranunculus bulbosus L. **Bulbous Buttercup.** ¶Stem 6–18 in., base bulbous; mid lobe of leaves stalked; sepals reflexed. Abundant in dry pastures. Flo. May–July. ❀.

Ranunculus sardous Crantz. **Pale Hairy Buttercup.** ¶Annual, 6–18 in.; sepals hairy, reflexed; achenes bordered and tuberculate. On damp arable, waste and grassland on heavy soils chiefly near the sea, local. Flo. June–Sept. ❀.

Ranunculus parviflorus L. **Small-flowered Buttercup.** ¶Stems prostrate, spreading; flo. very small; achenes few, bordered and with short, hooked tubercles. In arable land and short grass. Common in S.W. ❀.

Ranunculus arvensis L. **Corn Buttercup.** ¶Annual, 6–24 in.; fr. bordered and with long curved spines. Formerly common in cornfields, particularly on calcareous soils, mostly S. England. Flo. May–July. ✲.

Ranunculus paludosus Poir. **Jersey Buttercup.** ¶Plant with tubers and stolons; stem 6–12 in., silky; leaf segments narrow; flo. large, bright yellow. In Jersey only. Flo. May.

Ranunculus ficaria L. **Lesser Celandine.** ¶Tuberous; leaves cordate; flo. glossy yellow. Common. In shady places, axillary bulbils sometimes replace the often infertile frs. Flo. March–May. ✲.

PLATE 4

Caltha palustris L. **Marsh Marigold, Kingcup, Mollyblobs.**
Subsp. *palustris*. ¶Stems suberect, 1–2 ft; flo. 1¼ in. wide, bright yellow. In marshes, common. Flo. March–April. ✲.
Subsp. *minor* (Mill.) Clapham. ¶Stems decumbent or rooting; leaves often triangular; flo. few and smaller. On mountains in N. Flo. April–June.

Trollius europaeus L. **Globe Flower.** ¶Stems 1–2 ft; flo. 1 in., globular; perianth segments orbicular, pale yellow, inner (petals) with nectaries. Subalpine meadows. Flo. June–July. ✲.

Helleborus viridis L.
Subsp. *occidentalis* (Reut.) Schiffn. **Green Hellebore.** ¶Stems 1–2 ft; leaves glabrous beneath; flo. 1–1¾ in., green. In woods mostly on chalk in S. and E. England. Flo. March–April. ✲.

Helleborus foetidus L. **Stinking Hellebore.** ¶Stems 1–2 ft; flo. many, drooping, green with purple edges. In bushy places on calcareous soils in S. and W. England. Flo. Feb.–March. ✲.

Eranthis hyemalis (L.) Salisb. **Winter Aconite.** ¶Stems 4–6 in.; sessile leaflets forming an involucre; flo. bright yellow. Not native, naturalized in plantations. Flo. Jan.–March. ✲.

Aquilegia vulgaris L. **Columbine.** ¶Perennial, 1–2 ft; spur much curved inwards; fr. ¾–1 in. Native, on shady slopes and in woods, local, chiefly on the chalk. Flo. May–July. ✲.

Aquilegia pyrenaica DC. ¶Has spur less curved; fr. ½ in. Planted and naturalized in Caenlochan Glen, Clova Mountains, Angus.

Consolida ambigua (L.) P. W. Ball & Heywood. **Larkspur.** *Delphinium ambiguum* L. *D. ajacis* auct. ¶Annual, 12–18 in.; fr. of 1 pubescent follicle, tapering to beak. More or less naturalized in cultivated ground. Flo. June–July. ✲.

Aconitum anglicum Stapf. **Monk's Hood.** ¶Perennial, 2–4 ft; leaves light green, more narrowly divided than in Continental forms. Shady places by streams, S.W. England and Wales. Flo. May–June. ✲.

Aconitum napellus L. *sensu lato*. **Monk's Hood.** ¶Similar to *A. anglicum* but with darker green, less narrowly divided leaves. Garden escape. Naturalized on heaths and commons, in thickets, etc. Flo. May–June.

Actaea spicata L. **Baneberry, Herb Christopher.** ¶Rhizome stout; stem 1–2 ft, herbaceous; flo. white; berry black, poisonous. In woods on limestone, Yorkshire, Lancashire and Westmorland. Flo. May. ❀.

Paeonia mascula (L.) Mill. **Paeony.** ¶Stem 2 ft; flo. red; fr. large and downy. In rock clefts, Steepholme, Bristol Channel. Perhaps brought by monks in Middle Ages. Flo. May–June. ❀.

BERBERIDACEAE

Berberis vulgaris L. **Barberry.** ¶A spinous shrub, 4–6 ft; flo. yellow with irritable stamens. The host plant of the wheat rust. In hedges and copses. Flo. May–June. ❀.

Mahonia aquifolium (Pursh) Nutt. **Oregon Grape.** *Berberis aquifolium* Pursh. ¶Shrub with dark green, ovate, spinose, dentate, evergreen leaflets; flo. bright yellow in clustered, suberect, racemes; fr. globose, bluish black, pruinose. Commonly planted in woods and thickets, as pheasant cover, where it readily becomes naturalized. Flo. April–May.

Epimedium alpinum L. **Barrenwort.** ¶Rhizomatous; stem 12 in.; perianth segments red and pale yellow. In subalpine woods, not native. Flo. May. ❀.

NYMPHAEACEAE   PLATE 5

Nuphar lutea (L.) Sm. **Yellow Water Lily.** ¶Flo. 2–3 in. wide; stigma 10–20 rayed, margin entire. In canals, ponds and slow streams, floating from a creeping root. Flo. June–Sept. ❀.

Nuphar pumila (Timm.) DC. ¶Flo. 1–1½ in. wide; stigma with 8–10 rays projecting as teeth on the margin. Mostly in small lakes in Scotland, rare elsewhere. Flo. June–Aug. ❀.

Nuphar × spennerana Gaud. *N. intermedia* Ledeb. *N. lutea × pumila.* ¶Intermediate between *N. lutea* and *N. pumila.* Stigma with 9–14 rays. Northern Britain.

Nymphaea alba L. **White Water Lily.** ¶Flo. very large; stigma with 15–20 rays. In ponds, canals and slow streams. Frequently planted for ornamental purposes. Flo. July–Aug. ❀.

Subsp. *occidentalis* Ostenf. ¶Smaller in all parts. N. Scotland, etc.

PAPAVERACEAE

Papaver rhoeas L. **Common Red Poppy.** ¶Filaments of stamens not dilated; capsule round, glabrous; stigma rays 8–12. In cornfields, etc., abundant. Flo. all the summer. ❀.

Papaver dubium L. **Long Smooth-headed Poppy.** ¶Filaments not dilated above; capsule long, glabrous; stigma rays 6–12, lobes spreading. Cornfields and waste places. Flo. June–July. ❀.

Papaver lecoqii Lamotte. ¶Very near *P. dubium*, but sap always yellow; leaves more cut and acute; stigma lobes depressed. In calcareous fields, E. England, rare.

Papaver argemone L. **Long Rough-headed Poppy.** ¶Filaments dilated above; capsule long and bristly; stigma rays 4–6. In cornfields and dry places. Flo. June–July. ❀.

Papaver hybridum L. **Round Rough-headed Poppy.** ¶Filaments dilated above; capsule round and bristly; stigma rays 4–8. In sandy fields, mostly S. and E. England. Flo. June–July. ❀.

Papaver somniferum* L. **Opium Poppy. ¶Variable; leaves lobed, glaucous; flo. large, lilac, white or pink. A weed of cultivation, especially in fens, not native. ❀.

Meconopsis cambrica (L.) Vig. **Welsh Poppy.** ¶Perennial, 1–2 ft, with yellow sap. On damp shady rocks in S.W. England, Wales and Ireland, introduced elsewhere. Flo. June–July. ❀.

Glaucium flavum Crantz. **Yellow Horned-Poppy.** ¶Perennial, 1–3 ft; flo. yellow; pod up to 12 in. On shingly beaches. Flo. June–Oct. ❀.

*Roemeria hybrida (L.) DC. **Violet Horned-Poppy.** ¶Annual, 9–18 in.; flo. violet; pod 2–3 in. Casual, not native. ❀.

Chelidonium majus L. **Greater Celandine.** ¶Perennial, 1–3 ft; flo. ¾–1 in., yellow. In banks and hedgerows near houses. Probably introduced by herbalists. Flo. May–Sept. ❀.

FUMARIACEAE   **PLATE 6**

*Corydalis lutea (L.) DC. **Yellow Corydalis.** ¶Perennial, 6–12 in.; branched from root. On old walls. Flo. May–Sept. ❀.

Corydalis bulbosa* (L. emend. Mill.) DC. **Purple Corydalis. *C. solida* (L.) Sw. ¶Perennial, 6–10 in.; tuber solid; flo. purplish rose; bracts digitate. Naturalized on cultivated ground in few places. Flo. April–May.

*Corydalis cava (L.) Schweigg. & Koerte. *C. bulbosa* auct. *C. tuberosa* DC. ¶Resembling *C. bulbosa* but tuber hollow; small floral leaves entire; flo. white or purple, larger than those of *C. bulbosa*; bracts ovate, entire. Naturalized in a few places. Flo. April–May.

Corydalis claviculata (L.) DC. **Climbing Corydalis.** ¶Annual, stems 1–4 ft. In heathy woods and shady slopes, especially on peaty soil. Flo. June–Sept. ❀.

In the genus *Fumaria* Mr H. W. Pugsley gave liberal help both in finding and determining specimens for this work.

Fumaria occidentalis Pugsl. ¶Flo. very large, 12–15 mm.; lower petal with broad margin; fr. 3×3 mm., keeled and rugose. Field borders in Cornwall only, endemic. Flo. June. ❀.

Fumaria capreolata L.
Subsp. *babingtonii* (Pugsl.) P. D. Sell. **White Fumitory.** *F. pallidiflora* Jord. ¶Peduncle long; flo. large, 10–13 mm.; lower petal with narrow margin; upper petal narrow; wings not exceeding keel; fr. 2×2 mm., not keeled, pedicel recurved. In hedges and field borders. Flo. June. ❀.
Var. *devoniensis* Pugsl. ¶Flo. more suffused with pink; fr. 2½×2½ mm.

Fumaria purpurea Pugsl. ¶Peduncle long; flo. large, 10–13 mm., reddish purple; upper petal rather broad; wings exceeding keel; pedicel less recurved. In hedges and field borders mostly in W. and N., local, endemic Flo. June. ❀.

Fumaria martinii Clavaud. *F. paradoxa* Pugsl. ¶Peduncle much shorter than the long lax raceme; pedicel recurved in flo., straight in fr.; flo. 10–13 mm., light rose. In field borders mostly in Cornwall and Guernsey. Flo. June–Sept. �.

Fumaria bastardii Bor. ¶Peduncle shorter than lax raceme; flo. 9–12 mm.; upper petal narrow, without dark tip. Field borders in Ireland, Cornwall, Jersey, etc. Flo. June–Sept. ✻.

Fumaria muralis Sond. ex Koch.
Subsp. *muralis*. ¶Peduncle equalling lax few-flowered raceme; flo. 9–11 mm., upper petal apiculate, not broad. In field borders, rare.
Subsp. *boraei* (Jord.) Pugsl. **Few-flowered Fumitory.** *F. boraei* Jord. ¶Leaf segments broad and flat; raceme lax, few flowered; upper petal broad. On cultivated ground, common in West of England. Flo. May–Aug. ✻.
Subsp. *neglecta* Pugsl. ¶Raceme lax, many flowered; upper petal obtuse, not broad. Cultivated land in W. Cornwall, rare.

Fumaria densiflora DC. *F. micrantha* Lag. ¶Leaf segments linear, channelled; peduncle much shorter than the long raceme; sepals large and rounded; flo. small, 6–7 mm. In arable fields in E. England, rare or absent in W. Flo. June–Sept. ✻.

Fumaria officinalis L. **Fumitory.**
Subsp. *officinalis*. ¶Peduncle shorter than the many-flowered raceme; usually more than 20 flowered; sepals narrower than corolla; fr. truncate or retuse. In arable ground, chiefly on light soils. Flo. May–Sept. ✻.
Subsp. *wirtgenii* (Koch) Arcangeli. ¶Similar to subsp. *officinalis*, but raceme 10–20 flowered and sepals narrower. In arable ground, chiefly on chalky soils in E. and S.E. England.

Fumaria vaillantii Lois. ¶Leaves linear, flat, often glaucous; peduncle shorter than raceme; flo. small, 5–6 mm.; sepals minute. On chalky arable land, mostly in S.E. England, Flo. June–Sept. ✻.

Fumaria parviflora Lam. ¶Leaf segments small, linear channelled, very glaucous; raceme subsessile; flo. small white, 5–6 mm.; sepals minute. On chalky arable land. Flo. June–Sept. ✻.

CRUCIFERAE

Matthiola sinuata (L.) R. Br. **Sea Stock.** ¶Herbaceous, diffuse; lower leaves sinuate, dentate. On shores and cliffs of S.W. coasts, local. Flo. May–Aug. ✻.

Matthiola incana (L.) R. Br. **Hoary Stock.** ¶Shrubby and erect; lower leaves entire. On sea cliffs in I. of Wight, etc. Flo. May–July.

*Cheiranthus cheiri L. **Wallflower.** ¶Alien from Southern Europe naturalized on old walls, castles and rock cuttings.

PLATE 7

Nasturtium officinale R. Br. **Water Cress.** *Rorippa nasturtium-aquaticum* (L.) Hayek. ¶Perennial, stem 2–4 ft, rooting; seeds in two series; pods about 2 × 16 mm. Common in running water. Flo. May–Oct. ✻.

Nasturtium microphyllum (Boenn.) Reichb. *N. uniseriatum* Howard & Manton. *Rorippa microphylla* (Boenn.) Hyland. ¶Similar to above but seeds in one series, pods slender, 1 × 20 mm., leaves often smaller. Flo. May–Oct.

Nasturtium microphyllum × *officinale*. *Rorippa* × *sterilis* Airy Shaw. ¶Fr. dwarf and deformed with few good seeds. Common.

Rorippa sylvestris (L.) Bess. **Creeping Yellow Cress.** *Nasturtium sylvestre* (L.) R. Br. ¶Rootstock creeping; stem 9–18 in.; leaves pinnate; pods linear. On river banks and wet places. Flo. June–Sept. ⚥.

Rorippa islandica (Oeder ex Murray) Borbás, *Nasturtium palustre* (L.) DC. var. *pusillum* (Willd.) DC. ¶Plant prostrate; leaves with narrow and numerous lateral segments, together with a very small terminal lobe; petioles with inconspicuous wings and no auricles; pods 2–3 times as long as pedicels; sepals shorter than 1·6 mm.; flo. small, yellow. Sea coasts, very local and restricted, W. Ireland, I. of Man, Orkneys, W. mainland of Scotland. Flo. June–Sept.

Rorippa palustris (L.) Bess. **Marsh Yellow Cress.** *Nasturtium palustre* (L.) DC., non Crantz, *Rorippa islandica* auct., non (Oeder ex Murray) Borbás. ¶Root fibrous; stem 1–2 ft; leaves pinnatifid with irregularly toothed lateral segments, together with a very prominent ovate terminal lobe; petioles auricled; pods not more than *c.* 2 times as long as pedicels; sepals longer than 1·6 mm. Streamsides, marshes, damp waste ground, etc. S. Scotland southwards, common; local in Ireland. Flo. June–Sept. ⚥.

Rorippa amphibia (L.) Bess. **Amphibious Yellow Cress.** *Nasturtium amphibium* (L.) R. Br. ¶Rootstock stoloniferous; stem 2–3 ft; leaves serrate or pinnate; pods short. In watery places from York southward. Flo. June–Sept. ⚥.

Rorippa amphibia × *palustris* ¶Intermediate between the parents, with cauline leaves 2–3 times as long as broad and usually acutely serrate. A rare sterile hybrid, which occasionally occurs where the parents grow together, e.g. Thames between Hammersmith and Richmond.

Rorippa amphibia × *sylvestris* ¶Intermediate between the parents, with ripe pods up to 1–5 mm. broad and petals shorter than 3 mm. A fertile hybrid which often occurs where the parents grow together. Recorded from the Arun, Sussex; Thames, Oxford; frequent by the Severn in Shropshire, Worcestershire and Gloucestershire, etc.

Barbarea vulgaris R. Br. **Common Yellow Rocket, Winter Cress.** ¶Uppermost leaves undivided, toothed; flo. about 8 mm. wide; buds glabrous; pods ¾–1 in.; style 3 mm. Common in hedge banks. Flo. May–Aug. ⚥.

Barbarea stricta Andrz. **Lesser Yellow Rocket.** ¶Uppermost leaves undivided, toothed; flo. 5–6 mm. wide; buds downy at top; pods appressed, ¾–1 in.; style about 1 mm. Local, Yorkshire, Surrey, etc. Flo. May–Aug. ⚥.

*ptr*Barbarea intermedia* Bor. ¶Leaves all pinnatifid, terminal lobe oval; flo. 5–6 mm. wide; buds glabrous; pods ¾–1 in. Cultivated fields and waysides, local, not native. Flo. May–Aug.

*Barbarea verna (Mill.) Aschers. **American Cress.** *B. praecox* (Sm.) R. Br. ¶Upper leaves with linear-oblong lobes; flo. about 9 mm. wide; pods about 2 in. long, rather spreading. Naturalized in waste places. Flo. May–July. ⚥.

Cardaminopsis petraea (L.) Hiit. **Mountain Rock-Cress.** *Arabis petraea* (L.) Lam.

¶Stem 3–8 in.; leaves stalked spathulate, lower toothed; flo. white or tinted purple. On high mountains, N. Wales, Scotland, Tipperary, Leitrim. Flo. July. ❀.

Arabis alpina L. **Alpine Rock-Cress.** ¶Stem leaves clasping with rounded basal lobes, 3–6 teeth each side and clothed with stellate hairs; flo. white, 2 sepals saccate. In the mountains of Skye. Flo. July–Aug. ❀.

*Arabis caucasica Willd. **Garden Arabis.** *A. albida* Stev. ex Jacq. f. ¶Stem leaves with about 2 teeth each side, and basal lobes pointed; flo. rather larger than above. Garden walls. Flo. March–May.

Arabis stricta Huds. **Bristol Rock-Cress.** *A. scabra* All. ¶Perennial; stems erect, purple, 5–10 in.; leaves forming dense rosette, toothed, hispid; pod 2 in. long. On cliffs of R. Avon, Bristol. Flo. March–May. ❀.

Arabis hirsuta (L.) Scop. **Hairy Rock-Cress.** ¶Stem erect, leafy; rosette leaves stalked, hispid, subentire; pods 1–1½ in., stalked; stem leaves slightly clasping stem; seeds winged. Common on limestone rocks and walls. Flo. June–Aug. ❀.

Arabis brownii Jord. **Fringed Rock-Cress.** *A. ciliata* auct. ¶Like above but with stem leaves subglabrous or ciliate, with round base not clasping stem; seeds not winged. Sand dunes, W. Ireland. Flo. July–Aug.

*Arabis turrita L. **Tower Rock-Cress.** ¶Rosette leaves elliptical, stalked; stem leaves narrow, base cordate clasping stem, stellate hairy; flo. yellowish; pods 3–4½ in., recurved. On walls at Cambridge, formerly at Oxford and Kinross, now very rare.

Arabis glabra (L.) Bernh. **Glabrous Tower-Cress.** *A. perfoliata* Lam., *Turritis glabra* L. ¶Stem leaves glabrous, clasping stem; flo. yellowish; pods 1½–2½ in., erect; seeds not winged. On dry banks, local, rare in W. Flo. May–July. ❀.

Cardamine amara L. **Large Bitter Cress.** Stoloniferous, 1–2 ft; leaflets tapering below; flo. white; anthers purple. On moist meadows and riversides, local. Flo. April–June. ❀.

Cardamine pratensis L. **Cuckoo Flower, Lady's Smock.** ¶Perennial, 1–2 ft, sub-glabrous; flo. lilac, rarely white; anthers yellow. Common in moist meadows. Flo. April–June. ❀.

Cardamine hirsuta L. **Hairy Bitter Cress.** ¶Annual, 6–12 in.; basal leaves many, sparsely hairy; stamens 4; fr. pedicels erect. Abundant in open ground. Flo. March–Sept. ❀.

Cardamine flexuosa With. **Greater Bitter Cress.** *C. sylvatica* Link. ¶Biennial, 8–18 in.; basal leaves few; stamens 6; fr. pedicels spreading. Abundant in shade and moist ground. Flo. April–Sept. ❀.

**Cardamine trifolia* L. ¶Basal leaves with 3 roundish leaflets; flo. white or pale pink. Alien. Flo. April–June.

PLATE 8

Cardamine impatiens L. **Narrow-leaved Bitter Cress.** ¶Stem leaves with basal auricles like stipules; leaflets toothed; flo. small; pods spreading. On shady lime-stone rocks, local. Flo. May–Aug. ❀.

Cardamine bulbifera (L.) Crantz. **Coral Root.** *Dentaria bulbifera* L. ¶Root white and scaly; stem 1–2 ft with purple bulbils in axils; petals pink or lilac. In calcareous woods, very local. Flo. April–May. ❀.

Alyssum alyssoides (L.) L. **Hoary Alyssum.** *A. calycinum* L. ¶Plant 6 in., hoary with stellate hairs; flo. yellow; calyx persistent; pods rounded. Naturalized in arable land and sandy tracks. Flo. May–June.

Lobularia maritima (L.) Desv. **Sea Alyssum.** *Alyssum maritimum* (L.) Lam. ¶Plant 6–10 in., grey with forked hairs; calyx not persistent; petals white entire. On sandy ground near the sea, etc., not native. Flo. June–Sept. ❀.

Berteroa incana (L.) DC. *Alyssum incanum* L. ¶Plant 1–1½ ft, grey with stellate hairs; petals white, deeply bifid; stamen filaments toothed or winged at base. Casual in arable land.

Draba muralis L. **Wall Whitlow Grass.** ¶Stem 8–12 in.; stem leaves broadly ovate, sessile, dentate; flo. small; petals narrow, white. On limestone rocks and walls. Flo. April–May. ❀.

Draba incana L. **Hoary Whitlow Grass.** ¶Stem leafy, 2–10 in.; leaves lanceolate toothed, with stellate hairs; flo. white; pods twisted. On mountain rocks to 3000 ft. Flo. June–July. ❀.

Draba norvegica Gunn. **Rock Whitlow Grass.** *D. rupestris* R. Br. ¶Stem usually leafless, 1–3 in.; leaves mostly entire; flo. white; pods not twisted. Mountains in Scotland above 3000 ft, rare. Flo. July–Aug. ❀.

Draba aizoides L. **Yellow Whitlow Grass.** ¶Stem leafless, 2–5 in.; leaves acute, margins ciliate; flo. larger, 8 mm., bright yellow. On rocks and walls. Pennard near Swansea, doubtful native. Flo. March–May. ❀.

Erophila verna (L.) Chevall.
Subsp. *verna*. **Whitlow Grass.** ¶Stem 3–6 in.; leaves with forked hairs; pods boat shaped. On walls and dry places, mostly calcareous. Flo. March–May. ❀.
Subsp. *spathulata* (Láng) Walters. *Erophila spathulata* Láng. *E. boerhaavii* (Van Hall) Dumort. ¶With short forked hairs; pods obovoid, rounded at top; flo. smaller. Local. ❀a.
Var. *brachycarpa* (Jord.). ¶Pods orbicular; petals only 1·5 mm. ❀b.
Subsp. *praecox* (Stev.) Walters. *Erophila praecox* (Stev.) DC. ¶Leaves with long simple hairs; pod obovate. Local.

Cochlearia officinalis L. **Common Scurvy Grass.** ¶Lower leaves cordate, long stalked; pod subglobose; stems 4–10 in. On sea cliffs and shores. Flo. May–Aug. ❀.

Cochlearia pyrenaica DC. **Alpine Scurvy Grass.** *C. alpina* (Bab.) H. C. Wats. *C. officinalis* L. subsp. *alpina* (Bab.) Hook. ¶Lower leaves cordate; stem leaves triangular or ovate, lobed; pod obovate. On mountains. Flo. June–Sept.

Cochlearia micacea E. S. Marshall. ¶Pod 2–3 times as long as broad, tapering at apex; leaves small. ❀.

Cochlearia danica L. **Stalked Scurvy Grass.** ¶Lower leaves cordate; stem leaves stalked and lobed; flo. white or pinkish. On seaside cliffs and shores, also inland on railway ballast. Flo. Feb.–June. ❀.

Cochlearia scotica Druce. **Northern Scurvy Grass.** ¶Lower leaves suborbicular; stem leaves elliptical, sessile. On shores in N. Scotland. Flo. June–Sept. ❀.

Cochlearia anglica L. **English Scurvy Grass.** ¶Lower leaves ovate; upper leaves clasping stem; pods large obovoid. On muddy shores and estuaries. Flo. April–July. ❀.

Armoracia rusticana Gaertn., Mey. & Scherb. **Horse Radish.** *A lapathifolia* Gilib. ¶Leaves oblong, 1–2 ft long and 4 in. wide; root thick and used for flavouring. Alien from E. Europe. Flo. June–Sept.

Hesperis matronalis L. **Dame's Violet.** ¶Stems 2–3 ft; leaves 2–4 in., broadly lanceolate; flo. ¾ in., white or lilac. Alien, in plantations on waste ground, by waysides, river banks, etc. Flo. May–July. ❀.

Arabidopsis thaliana (L.) Heynh. **Thale Cress.** *Sisymbrium thalianum* (L.) Gay. ¶Annual; stem slender, 6–9 in.; flo. white. Common on dry banks and wall tops and in cultivated fields. Flo. April–May. ❀.

Sisybrium officinale (L.) Scop. **Hedge Mustard.** ¶Stem 1–2 ft, stiff and erect; pods hairy, appressed; flo. yellow. Common on hedge banks and waste land. Flo. June–Aug. ❀.
Var. *leiocarpum* DC. has glabrous pods.

Sisymbrium altissimum L. *S. pannonicum* Jacq. ¶Lower leaves with many triangular lobes, upper sessile with pairs of linear lobes; pods long, thin, spreading; peduncle 6–9 mm. Alien, naturalized in many waste places. Flo. May–Oct.

Sisymbrium orientale L. *S. columnae* Jacq. ¶Hispid; leaves petiolate, lobes few, 2–3 pairs; upper leaves hastate with oblong terminal lobe; pods long and thick; pedicel 3–4 mm. In waste places. Flo. May–Oct.

Sisymbrium irio L. **London Rocket.** ¶Glabrous, 1–2 ft; lower leaves many, with oblong lobes; upper leaves with hastate terminal lobe. In waste places, rare. Called London Rocket since it appeared in quantity after the fire of 1666. Flo. May–Oct. ❀.

Sisymbrium loeselii L. ¶Differs from *S. irio* in its bright yellow petals being about twice as long as sepals and in its young pods not over-topping the open flo. Waste places. Flo. June–Oct.

Descurainia sophia (L.) Webb ex Prantl. **Flixweed.** *Sisymbrium sophia* L. ¶Stem 1–3 ft, branched above, slightly downy; leaves finely divided; flo. small, pale yellow. In waste places. Flo. June–Aug. ❀.

Alliaria petiolata (Bieb.) Cavara & Grande. **Garlic Mustard.** *Sisymbrium alliaria* (L.) Scop. ¶Stem 2–3 ft; leaves broad, cordate or reniform, garlic scented; flo. white. Abundant in hedge banks. Flo. April–June. ❀.

PLATE 9

Erysimum cheiranthoides L. **Treacle Mustard.** ¶Stem 1–2 ft with a few forked hairs; leaves lanceolate; flo. yellow, often in a neat ring. In cultivated lowland fields, local. Flo. June–Sept. ❀.

Conringia orientalis (L.) Dumort. *Erysimum orientale* (L.) R. Br. ¶Stem 1–2 ft; leaves glaucous, oval, cordate, clasping the stem; flo. yellowish white. Introduced in cultivated land. Flo. May–July.

Camelina sativa (L.) Crantz. **Gold of Pleasure.** ¶Stem 2–3 ft; leaves oblong-lanceolate, with pointed auricles; flo. small, yellow; pods obovate, 6–9 mm. In arable fields, not native.

Subularia aquatica L. **Awlwort.** ¶Root of many white fibres; stem 1–3 in.; leaves all radical, subulate; pods ⅛ in. oblong. Margins of alpine lakes, N. Wales, N. England, Scotland. Flo. June–Aug. ✳.

Brassica oleracea L. **Wild Cabbage.** ¶Biennial, 1–2 ft; leaves very broad, glaucous; flo. in long spike and large. On sea cliffs in England and Wales. Flo. May–Aug. ✳.

*Brassica napus L. **Rape, Swede.** ¶Root spindle shaped; leaves glaucous; flo. yellow: Rape, grown for fodder. Root more tuberous; leaves glaucous; flo. pale orange: Swede. Flo. May–Aug.

*Brassica rapa L. **Turnip.** *B. campestris* L. ¶Root tuberous; leaves bright green; flo. overtopping the buds, bright yellow. Arable fields and river banks. Flo. May–Aug. ✳.

Brassica nigra (L.) Koch. **Black Mustard.** *Sinapis nigra* L. ¶Pods 4 angled, glabrous, appressed; beak short, narrow, seedless, valve 1 nerved. On riversides, cliffs and banks. Common near S.W. coasts. Flo. June–Aug. ✳.

Rhynchosinapis monensis (L.) Dandy. **Isle of Man Cabbage.** *Brassicella monensis* (L.) O. E. Schulz. ¶Mostly decumbent, glabrous; leaves radical, pinnatifid; pods spreading; beak 1–3 seeded; valves 3 nerved. On shores of N.W. coasts. Flo. May–June. ✳.

Rhynchosinapis cheiranthos (Vill.) Dandy. **Wallflower Cabbage.** *Brassicella erucastrum* auct. ¶Stem erect, branched, leafy, hispid below; leaves lobed, hispid beneath. On W. coasts and the Channel Islands. Flo. June–Aug. ✳.

Rhynchosinapis wrightii (O. E. Schulz) Dandy. **Lundy Cabbage.** *Brassicella wrightii* O. E. Schulz. ¶Like *R. cheiranthos* but more robust, erect 1½–3 ft, stem clothed with deflexed hairs; leaves very hairy; pods thicker, hairy with about 40 seeds; flo. larger, 2·5 cm. across. On Lundy Island, N. Devon only and endemic there. The sole host of 2 endemic beetles. Named after Dr Elliston Wright who observed the differences, and sent the plant to Prof. Schulz. (*Journal of Bot.*, Nov. 1936).

Sinapis arvensis L. **Charlock.** *Brassica arvensis* (L.) Rabenh., non L. *B. kaber* (DC.) L. C. Wheeler. ¶Hispid; pods spreading and longer than the conical beak; valves usually 3 nerved; seeds dark. Abundant in arable land. Flo. May–July. ✳.

*Sinapis alba L. **White Mustard.** *Brassica hirta* Moench, *B. alba* (L.) Rabenh. ¶Hispid with reflexed hairs; pods short, about 3 seeded, equalling the wide sword-like beak; seeds pale. On arable land, alien. Flo. June–Aug. ✳.

*Hirschfeldia incana (L.) Lagr.-Foss. **Hoary Mustard.** *Brassica adpressa* Boiss. ¶Hoary plant; pods very short, appressed with short 1-seeded beak; uppermost leaves narrow, entire, often subglabrous. Introduced in Sussex, Kent, Middlesex, Norfolk, Jersey and Alderney, etc. Flo. June–Sept.

Diplotaxis tenuifolia (L.) DC. **Wall Rocket.** ¶Stem leafy, branched, 1–2 ft; leaves glaucous, segments long and narrow; flo. long pedicelled. On walls, waste places, railway yards, etc. Flo. July–Sept. ✳.

PLATE 10

Diplotaxis muralis (L.) DC. **Annual Wall Rocket, Sand Rocket.** ¶Stem 6–15 in., simple or branched at base; leaves often mostly basal, lobed; flo. short stalked. Waste land and railway ballast. Flo. Aug.–Sept. ✳.

Diplotaxis erucoides (L.) DC. **White Rocket.** ¶Stem tall; leaf lobes toothed, terminal lobe large; flo. white or lilac. Introduced, weed of cultivated land, S. England. Flo. May–Sept.

Capsella bursa-pastoris (L.) Medic. **Shepherd's Purse.** ¶Basal leaves forming rosette; stem leaves amplexicaul; pods triangular or obcordate. A very common weed, but variable. Flo. all the year. ❀.

Capsella rubella Reut. ¶Similar to *C. bursa-pastoris* but with smaller flo., the petals scarcely exceeding the sepals; flo. buds red; apical notch of pod shallow. On waste ground in Sussex, Surrey, Bucks., etc., introduced. Flo. March–Sept.

Coronopus didymus (L.) Sm. **Swine Cress.** *Senebiera didyma* (L.) Pers. ¶Prostrate, foetid; petals minute or 0; pods stalked, small, of 2 rounded lobes. On bare waste ground mostly in S. and S.W. England, introduced. Flo. June–Sept. ❀.

Lepidium latifolium L. **Dittander.** ¶Stems 3 ft, branched; leaves large, basal lobed, upper oblong; flo. many; pods elliptical. In salt marshes, mostly in E. England, adventive on canal and river banks, in gravel pits, etc., in the London area. Flo. July–Aug. ❀.

Lepidium ruderale L. **Narrow-leaved Pepperwort.** ¶Stem $\frac{1}{2}$–1 ft; leaves mostly pinnate; petals usually 0; pods oval or nearly round, deeply notched. On waste land, especially near E. coast. Flo. May–July. ❀.

Lepidium sativum L. **Garden Cress.** ¶Stem 1 ft; lower leaves pinnatifid, upper entire, linear, not clasping the stem; pod deeply notched; narrowly winged above. A garden escape. Flo. June–Sept.

Lepidium campestre (L.) R. Br. **Field Pepperwort.** ¶Stem $\frac{1}{2}$–1 ft, branched at top; upper leaves clasping stem, soft and hairy; anthers yellow; pod papillose; style short. On dry banks. Flo. May–Aug. ❀.

Lepidium heterophyllum Benth. var. *canescens* Godr. **Downy Pepperwort.** *L. smithii* Hook. ¶Perennial; stems many, branched mostly from below or from base; stamens with violet anthers; pod nearly smooth; style longer than notch. On light soils and dry banks. Flo. May–Aug. ❀.
Var. *alatostylum* (Towns.) Thell. ¶Has the pod without a notch, wings continued to style.

Cardaria draba (L.) Desv. **Hoary Cress.** *Lepidium draba* L. ¶Stoloniferous; stem 1–2 ft, branched above; leaves oblong, sagittate, clasping the stem; pod cordate, tapering above. On arable land, not native. Flo. May–June. ❀.

Thlaspi arvense L. **Field Penny Cress.** ¶Glabrous annual, 1 ft or more; leaves clasping; pods very large, $\frac{1}{2}$–$\frac{3}{4}$ in., nearly round, broadly winged and notched. On cultivated land. Flo. May–Aug. ❀.

Thlaspi perfoliatum L. **Perfoliate Penny Cress.** ¶Annual, 3–8 in.; stem leaves deeply cordate; pods smaller; style short. On limestone fields, Worcestershire, Gloucestershire, Oxfordshire, Wiltshire, adventive on railway tracks elsewhere, rare. Flo. April–May. ❀.

Thlaspi alpestre L. **Alpine Penny Cress.** ¶Erect, 6–12 in.; stem leaves narrow, cordate; flo. white or pink; anthers often purple; style longer. On rocks and mountains, Somerset and N. Wales to Forfar. Flo. May–Aug. ❀.

Thlaspi alliaceum L. ¶Annual, 6–18 in. or more; stem hairy below; stem leaves with auricles; flo. white; fr. winged, with apical notch; whole plant smelling strongly of garlic. On cultivated land in S. England, introduced. Flo. April–June.

Iberis amara L. **Candytuft.** ¶Erect, 6–12 in.; leaves lanceolate, mostly lobed; flo. pink or white with outer petals larger; pods winged and notched. In chalky fields, mostly in S. England, local. Flo. July–Aug. ✿.

Teesdalia nudicaulis (L.) R. Br. **Shepherd's Cress.** ¶Stems 2–4 in.; leaves mainly radical with broad terminal lobe; flo. white, 2 outer petals longer; stamens 6 with minute white basal scale. On sand and gravel, often on acid soils. Flo. April–June. ✿.

Hornungia petraea (L.) Reichb. *Hutchinsia petraea* (L.) R. Br. ¶Stem 2–4 in., branched; leaves pinnate, lobes small; petals small, equal; pods elliptical. On limestone rocks and dunes in the W., local. Flo. March–May. ✿.

Isatis tinctoria L. **Woad.** ¶Stems 2–4 ft, branched; radical leaves oblong, crenate; stem leaves with basal lobes; flo. yellow; fr. pendulous. On chalk and clay especially near Tewkesbury, Gloucestershire. A prehistoric introduction. Flo. June–Sept. ✿.

PLATE 11

Crambe maritima L. **Sea Kale.** ¶Stem 1–3 ft; leaves broad and fleshy; flo. white; pods spherical or oval. On shingle and sea cliffs. This was first cultivated and introduced to Covent Garden by Mr Curtis in 1795 from the S. Devonshire coast, where it was plentiful, but it is now in consequence very rare. Flo. June–Aug. ✿.

Cakile maritima Scop. **Sea Rocket.** ¶Branches 1–2 ft; leaves mostly with oblong lobes; flo. lilac or white; pod of 1 or of 2 unequal cells. On sea sand and shingle. Flo. June–Aug. ✿.

Raphanus raphanistrum L.
Subsp. *raphanistrum*. **Wild Radish.** ¶Annual, 1–2 ft; leaf segments few; flo. pale yellow, golden, white, lilac or rarely, violet; pod slightly constricted; between 4 and 8 seeds. Arable land. Flo. May–Sept. ✿.
Subsp. *maritimus* (Sm.) Thell. **Sea Radish.** *Raphanistrum maritimus* Sm. ¶Biennial, very hispid; leaf segments many, often overlapping; pod deeply constricted; seeds 2–3. Sandy sea-shores and cliffs, local. Flo. June–Aug. ✿.

*Raphanus sativus L. **Radish.** ¶Root tuberous; stem often tall; pod inflated, scarcely constricted. An escape from cultivation, origin unknown. Flo. June–Sept. ✿.

RESEDACEAE

*Reseda alba L. ¶Stems erect, glabrous; leaves pinnate; petals 5–6, all trifid, white; stigmas usually 4. In waste places, introduced (but this is not the scented *R. odorata* of gardens). Flo. June–Aug.

Reseda lutea L. **Wild Mignonette.** ¶Leaves pinnate; petals 6, the lower entire, the lateral 2 cleft; stigmas 3. Mostly on chalky soil in England but frequently adventive by railways. Flo. June–Aug. ✿.

Reseda luteola L. **Dyer's Rocket, Weld.** ¶Stem erect, 2–3 ft; leaves oblong, entire; petals 5, 2 lower entire, lateral 3 cleft. On stony or calcareous soil, common. Flo. June–Aug. ✿.

CISTACEAE

Tuberaria guttata (L.) Fourr. **Spotted Rockrose.** *Helianthemum guttatum.* (L.) Mill.
Subsp. *guttata.* ¶Erect herbaceous annual, stellate hairy; upper leaves oblong with
stipules, much narrower than the lower; bracts absent; petals yellow with red spot.
On dry cliffs, rare, Channel Islands. Flo. June–Sept. ✳.
Subsp. *breweri* (Planch.) E. F. Warb. *Helianthemum breweri* Planch. ¶Similar to subsp.
guttata but branched from base; upper leaves with stipules, scarcely narrower than
the lower; bracts present. Rocky places nears the sea, rare, W. and N. Wales and
W. Ireland.

Helianthemum canum (L.) Baumg. **Hoary Rockrose.**
Subsp. *canum.* ¶Shrubby, dwarf; leaves hairy, green or greyish above and hoary beneath,
without stipules; flo. usually 2–5, yellow, $\frac{1}{2}$ in. wide. Limestone rocks, rare, S. Wales
to Westmorland, and isolated colonies in W. Ireland. Flo. May–July. ✳.
Subsp. *levigatum* M. C. F. Proctor. ¶Similar to subsp. *canum* but very prostrate; leaves
small, dark green, glabrous or subglabrous above; flo. usually 1–3, yellow, with
short inflo. Upper Teesdale.

Helianthemum nummularium (L.) Mill. **Common Rockrose.** *H. chamaecistus* Mill.
¶Shrubby, diffuse; leaves with stipules, white beneath; 2 outer sepals small; flo.
yellow, $\frac{3}{4}$ in. On dry and calcareous soils, common. Flo. June–Sept. ✳.

Helianthemum apenninum (L.) Mill. **White Rockrose.** *H. polifolium* Mill. ¶Shrubby,
hoary; leaves grey above and beneath, with stipules, margin revolute; flo. white.
On sea cliffs, Somerset and S. Devonshire, local. Flo. May–July. ✳.

Helianthemum apenninum × nummularium = H. × sulphureum Willd. ¶With sulphur-yellow
flo. sometimes occurs where the parents grow together.

POLYGALACEAE

Polygala vulgaris L. **Common Milkwort.** ¶Leaves lanceolate, lower small; flo. blue
(or white or pink); calyx wing as broad as fr., its lateral veins looping up with
central vein. Fairly common on rough pastures and banks, especially on chalky
soils. Flo. May–Sept. ✳.

Polygala oxyptera Reichb. ¶Stems prostrate; leaves narrow lanceolate; flo. pink or
white; calyx wing narrower than fr. On sandy shores and stony hills, local. This is
now regarded as a form of *P. vulgaris*. Flo. May–Aug. ✳.

Polygala serpyllifolia Hose. **Heath Milkwort.** *P. serpyllacea* Weihe. ¶Flower stem branched above; leaves all small elliptical; flo. deep blue-purple; calyx wing as wide as
fruit, its veins looping up. Common, especially on heaths and peaty moors. Flo.
May–Aug. ✳.

Polygala calcarea F. W. Schultz. **Chalk Milkwort.** ¶Lower leaves large, obovate; flo.
purer blue; calyx wing longer than fr., veins slightly rejoining or not. On chalk
downs in S. and E. England. Flo. May–July. ✳.

Polygala amara L. ¶Plant small, erect; lower leaves large, obovate; flo. blue; calyx
wings narrower than fr., its veins free. On calcareous rocks, W. Yorkshire and
Durham, rare. Flo. June–Aug. ✳.

Polygala austriaca Crantz. ¶Similar to above, plant more slender; lower leaves large, obovate; flo. small bluish lilac, white or pink; calyx wings $\frac{1}{2}$ width of fr., and scarcely branched. On calcareous downs in Kent and formerly in Surrey, very rare. Flo. June–Aug. ✿.

VIOLACEAE **PLATE 12**

(a) Leaves enlarging after flowering.

Viola palustris L. **Bog Violet.**

Subsp. *palustris*. ¶Stems white and creeping; leaves orbicular-reniform; flo. lilac, rarely white, with dark veins; spur short. In wet boggy places, especially on peat, widespread in Britain. Flo. April–July. ✿.

Subsp. *juressii* (Neves) Coutinho. *Viola epipsila* auct. angl. *V. juressii* Link ex Neves. ¶Leaves often with hairy petioles and more toothed than subsp. *palustris*; flo. larger; spur longer. In similar habitats to subsp. *palustris*. Mainly confined to S. England and Wales.

Viola odorata L. **Sweet Violet.** ¶Plant with stolons; leaves cordate; petioles and peduncles with deflexed hairs; stipules glandular; flo. fragrant, blue-purple, April. ✿. 'a'.

Var. *dumetorum* (Jord.) Rouy & Fouc. ¶Flo. white with violet spur; lateral petals bearded. Common in S.W. England. ✿. 'c'.

Var. *praecox* Gregory. ¶Summer leaves pointed; flo. small, blackish purple. Flo. early Jan.–March. ✿. 'b'.

Var. *subcarnea* (Jord.) Parl. ¶Flo. all pink. ✿. 'd'.

Var. *imberbis* (Leight.) Henslow. ¶Flo. white with violet spur; lateral petals beardless.

Viola × permixta Jord. (*V. hirta × odorata*). ¶Variable, flo. paler. ✿. 'x'.

Viola hirta L. **Hairy Violet.** ¶Plant without stolons; leaves triangular-cordate, hairy; flo. from rosette.

Subsp. *hirta*. ¶Leaves large, elongate; flo. large; spur hooked. On pastures and banks, mostly on calcareous soil. Flo. April. ✿.

Subsp. *calcarea* (Bab.) E. F. Warb. ¶Leaves shorter; flo. smaller, petals narrow; spur short and straight. Growing with subsp. *hirta* and intermediates. ✿.

(b) Leaves not enlarging after flowering.

Viola rupestris Schmidt. **Teesdale Violet.** ¶Small pubescent plants; leaves roundly cordate; flo. on short branches; spur short; capsule downy. On calcareous rocks and turf above Teesdale. Flo. May–June. ✿.

Viola reichenbachiana Jord. ex Bor. **Woodland Violet.** *V. sylvestris* auct. ¶Branched from the base; flo. lilac; spur long, red-purple; appendages of calyx small. In woodland glades and banks of lanes. Flo. April–May. ✿.

Viola reichenbachiana × riviniana. ¶Intermediate between the two parents, sometimes occurs where they grow together.

Viola riviniana Reichb. **Common Violet.**

Subsp. *riviniana*. ¶Branched freely from base; leaves cordate ovate; flo. blue-purple; spur broad, furrowed and pale. Common in woodland borders and hedge banks. Flo. April–June. ✿.

Var. *diversa* Gregory. ¶Plant dwarf and floriferous; petals and spurs variable in colouring. In upland pastures.

Subsp. *minor* (Gregory) Valentine. ¶Dwarf plant; leaves very small and often purple beneath; spurs yellow. In upland or moorland grass. ❀.

Viola canina L. **Dog Violet.**

Subsp. *canina*. ¶Branched from base; leaves cordate, prolonged; flo. almost pure blue; spur yellow. On heaths and sand dunes. Flo. April–June. ❀.

Subsp. *montana* (L.) Hartm. ¶Bushy plants with underground stems; leaves thin triangular; flo. pale blue; spur slender, green. In fens, Cambridgeshire and Huntingdonshire. Flo. April–June. ❀.

Viola × militaris Savouré (*V. canina × lactea*). ¶Intermediate between the two parents, sometimes occurs where they grow together.

Viola canina × riviniana. ¶Variable, but usually intermediate between the two parents, sometimes occurs where they grow together.

Viola × ritschliana W. Becker (*V. canina × stagnina*). ¶Occurs rarely where the two parents grow together.

Viola lactea Sm. **Pale Heath Violet.** ¶Upper leaves tapering at both ends; stipules larger with green teeth; petals pale, subacute. On heaths in S. and S.W. England. Flo. May–June. ❀.

Viola lactea × riviniana. ¶Intermediate between the two parents, sometimes occurs where they grow together.

Viola stagnina Kit. **Fen Violet.** ¶Plant with underground stems; leaves triangular; petals very pale, round; spur yellowish, bent downwards. Fens and limy marshes, E. England and Ireland. ❀.

Melanium Section. **Pansies.**

The British Pansies have sometimes been treated as belonging to several microspecies. Mr R. D. Meikle of the Kew Herbarium has kindly advised us to reduce them to the following arrangement.

Viola arvensis Murr. **Field Pansy** (including many named forms). ¶Annual plants with petals shorter than sepals. Very variable, with leaves lanceolate and hairy or finely pubescent or broadly oval and glabrous. The mid lobe of stipules may be rather broad and foliaceous or narrow and lanceolate. Widely spread in arable land especially cornfields. Flo. April–Oct. ❀.

The form with oval, glabrous leaves was figured as var. *obtusifolia*. ❀.

Viola tricolor L. **Tricolor Pansy** (including many named forms).

Subsp. *tricolor*. ¶Annual plants (except forma *lepida*); petals longer than sepals, often highly coloured; variable, with leaves ovate or oblong lanceolate; the mid lobe of stipules may be broad and crenate or narrow entire. In cornfields and other cultivated land. Flo. April–Sept. ❀.

Forma *lepida* Jord. ¶With shoots rising from twiggy underground stems. 'A form with perennial habit induced by environment.' R.D.M. ❀.

V. arvensis × tricolor (including *V. variata* Jord.). ¶'A very common, variable and widespread hybrid.' R.D.M.

Subsp. *curtisii* (E. Forst.) Syme. **Seaside Pansy.** *V. curtisii* E. Forst. ¶Perennial; underground stems rising 6 in. or more with slender branches at surface; flo. yellow; spur slender, exceeding small calyx appendages. Sand dunes on the W. coast and elsewhere. ❀.

'The hybrid *V. arvensis* subsp. *curtisii × tricolor* arises freely and has purple flowers.' R.D.M.

Viola lutea Huds. **Mountain Pansy.** ¶Perennial; stems slender, rising singly a few inches from underground rhizomes; leaf stipules with linear-lanceolate mid lobe; flo. large, 1–1¼ in., yellow or purple; spur long and slender. In mountain pastures, often on limestone. Flo. June–Aug. ❀.

Viola lutea × tricolor. ¶Intermediate between the two parents, sometimes occurs where they grow together.

Viola kitaibeliana Schult. **Dwarf Pansy.** *V. nana* (DC.) Godr. ¶Plant small in all its parts; flo. very small, pale, with short entire calyx appendages. On sand in Channel Islands, Scilly Isles and W. Cornwall. Flo. April–July. The small figure is labelled *V. nana.* ❀.

FRANKENIACEAE   **PLATE 13**

Frankenia laevis L. **Sea Heath.** ¶Stems prostrate, wiry; leaves small, oblong, heath-like, margins strongly revolute; flo. pink. On sand and gravel, S. and E. coasts. Flo. July–Aug. ❀.

CARYOPHYLLACEAE

Dianthus armeria L. **Deptford Pink.** ¶Stem 12–18 in., erect; leaves green, tapering; flo. clustered, crimson; calyx bracts acuminate, as long as calyx. On sandy soils, local and scarce. Flo. July–Aug. ❀.

Dianthus deltoides L. **Maiden Pink.** ¶Perennial, barren shoots green; flo. stems erect, slender; leaves lanceolate; calyx bracts ovate, near ½ length of calyx; petals pink with dark spot. On dry banks and hilly pastures, local. Flo. June–Sept. ❀.

Dianthus gratianopolitanus Vill. **Cheddar Pink.** *D. caesius* Sm. ¶Leaves on barren shoots linear-lanceolate, glaucous, rather blunt, edges rough; calyx bracts roundly ovate, ¼ length of calyx; flo. pink with shallow teeth. On limestone cliffs at Cheddar. Flo. June–July. ❀.

Dianthus plumarius L. **Wild Pink.** ¶Leaves on barren shoots linear, glaucous, very acute, with rough edges; calyx bracts ¼ length of calyx; petals cut nearly to the middle, fragrant. On old walls. The origin of the garden pink. Flo. June–Aug. ❀.

Dianthus caryophyllus L. **Wild Carnation.** ¶Leaves long, linear, glaucous with smooth edges; calyx bracts ¼ length of calyx; petal teeth shallow; very fragrant. The origin of the garden carnation, naturalized on old walls. Flo. July–Aug. ❀.

Dianthus barbatus L. **Sweet William.** Stem 1–2 ft, erect; basal leaves in a rosette; stem leaves broadly lanceolate; flo. short stalked in dense cymes; petals bearded, dark purple to pink, streaked with white. Garden escape, sometimes naturalized in chalky railway cuttings, etc. Flo. July–Aug.

Petrorhagia nanteuilii (Burnat) P. W. Ball & Heywood. *Kohlrauschia prolifera* auct. *Dianthus prolifer* auct. ¶Annual, erect, 6–18 in.; flo. clustered within inflated oval bracts; leaves linear; petals small, rose coloured, notched. On sand and gravel in S. England, rare. Flo. June–Oct. ❀.

Saponaria officinalis L. **Soapwort.** ¶Perennial, stoloniferous; stems 1–3 ft; leaves ovate; calyx cylindrical not angular. On banks of streams and rivers, S.W. England and Wales (elsewhere introduced). Flo. Aug.–Oct. ❀.

*Vaccaria pyramidata Medic. *Saponaria vaccaria* L. ¶Annual; stem 1–2 ft; leaves oblong; calyx inflated, 5 angled. Not native. Flo. June–July. ⁂.

Cucubalus baccifer L. ¶Plant long, climbing over bushes; leaves oval; calyx teeth broad and open; petals long, narrow, bifid, greenish white; fr. a black berry. In copses and bushy sea cliffs, very rare, perhaps introduced by migratory birds. Flo. July–Sept.

Silene vulgaris (Moench) Garcke. **Bladder Campion.** *S. cucubalus* Wibel.

Subsp. *vulgaris.* ¶Perennial, erect, 12–18 in.; branched above; bracts small, scarious; calyx inflated; petals white, rarely with a corona. On pastures and waste ground. Flo. May–Aug. ⁂.

Subsp. *maritima* (With.) A. & D. Löve. **Sea Campion.** *Silene maritima* With. ¶Plant decumbent; bracts leaf-like; flo. mostly solitary; petals broad, with a corona. On sea cliffs and shingle, common; rare by alpine streams. Flo. June–Aug. ⁂.

**Subsp. *macrocarpa* Turrill. ¶Plant slightly smaller than subsp. *vulgaris* with long stolons; leaves longer and narrower; petals pink or greenish. Introduced, but long naturalized on Plymouth Hoe, S. Devonshire. Flo. June–Aug.

Silene conica L. **Striated Catchfly.** ¶Annual, erect, 3–12 in.; calyx with many veins, conical in fr.; flo. pink. On sandy fields, mostly near E. and S. coasts, local. Flo. May–June. ⁂.

Silene gallica L. **Small Catchfly.** *S. anglica* L. ¶Annual, erect, 12–18 in.; leaves hairy; calyx viscid; petals slightly cloven, dull white or pink. On sandy and gravelly fields. Flo. June–Oct. ⁂.
Var. *quinquevulnera* (L.) Mert. and Koch. ¶Petals white with dark blotch. In Channel Islands and casual in S. England. ⁂.

Silene acaulis (L.) Jacq. **Moss Campion.** ¶Stems densely matted; leaves small, linear; flo. stalks short, solitary. On high mountain rocks from N. Wales northwards. Flo. July–Aug. ⁂.

Silene otites (L.) Wibel. **Spanish Catchfly.** ¶Stems erect, 1–2 ft, viscid below; leaves mostly radical; flo. small, yellowish, whorled. On sandy fields, Norfolk, Suffolk, Cambridgeshire. Flo. June–July. ⁂.

Silene nutans L. **Nodding** or **Nottingham Catchfly.** ¶Stem 1–2 ft, viscid above; flo. drooping. Flo. May–July. Cf. *Watsonia*, II, 80–90. ⁂.
Var. *salmoniana* Hepper. ¶Slender with narrow leaves; flo. yellowish; capsule 11–14 mm. on stalk (carpophore) 3–4·5 mm. On chalk in S.E. England, local.
Var. *smithiana* Moss. ¶Stronger plant; leaves broader; petals white; capsule 8–10 mm., carpophore 2–2·5 mm. On cliffs, local, E. Devonshire, E. Kent, Nottinghamshire, N. Wales, E. Scotland.

*Silene italica (L.) Pers. **Italian Catchfly.** ¶Stem 1–2 ft, hairy and viscid; flo. on opposite branches, suberect, yellowish white above; carpophore as long as capsule. Plant resembling *S. nutans*. In quarries, Kent, etc., rare, introduced from S. Europe. Flo. June–July.

PLATE 14

Silene noctiflora L. **Night-flowering Catchfly.** *Melandrium noctiflorum* (L.) Fr. ¶Stem 1 ft, hairy and viscid; calyx 10 veined; flo. fragrant at night, pale pink above; styles 3. Cultivated land, S. and E. England. Flo. July–Aug. ⁂.

Silene alba (Mill.) E. H. L. Krause. **White Campion.** *Lychnis alba* Mill. *Melandrium album* (Mill.) Garcke. ¶Flo. dioecious, white; fertile calyx ¾–1 in., teeth linear-lanceolate; styles 5; capsule teeth erect. Common. Flo. May–Sept. ❀.

Silene dioica (L.) Clairv. **Red Campion.** *Lychnis dioica* L., *Melandrium dioicum* (L.) Coss. & Germ.

Subsp. *dioica.* ¶Flo. dioecious, deep pink, rarely white; fertile calyx ½ in., teeth triangular; styles 5; capsule teeth revolute. Common in woods, etc. Flo. mostly May–June. ❀.

Subsp. *zetlandica.* (Compton) Clapham. ¶Similar to subsp. *dioica* but stem much stouter and densely hairy; basal leaves slender stalked; stem leaves narrower and pubescent on both surfaces; flo. larger. Orkney and Shetland.

Hybrids of *S. alba* and *S. dioica* are fairly common.

Lychnis flos-cuculi L. **Ragged Robin.** ¶Upper leaves narrow, glabrous; petals with 4 spreading segments, rose; coronal scales narrow. In marshes, wet meadows and fens, common. Flo. May–June. ❀.

Lychnis viscaria L. **Red Catchfly.** *Viscaria vulgaris* Bernh. ¶Stem 1 ft, very sticky at nodes; petals broad, slightly notched and with coronal scales. On rocks, N. Wales and Scotland, very local. Flo. June–July. ❀.

Lychnis alpina L. **Alpine Campion.** *Viscaria alpina* (L.) G. Don. ¶Rootstock branches ending in rosettes or flo. stems 3–8 in.; flo. clustered, dull rose, petals bifid. Alpine moors to 3000 ft, Cumberland and Clova Mountains. Flo. June–July. ❀.

Agrostemma githago L. **Corn Cockle.** *Lychnis githago* (L.) Scop. ¶Stem 1–2 ft; leaves linear; flo. large, solitary, purple, without corona; calyx leafy. In cornfields, becoming very rare. Flo. June–Aug. ❀.

Holosteum umbellatum L. **Umbellate Chickweed.** ¶Stem 2–6 in., viscid above; flo. umbellate, white or pale pink; sepals with broad scarious tips. On old walls, E. England, almost extinct. Flo. April–May. ❀.

Cerastium diffusum Pers. **Dark Green Chickweed.** *C. atrovirens* Bab., *C. tetrandrum* Curt. ¶Branched from base, 4–8 in. bracts leafy; sepals 4 (or 5) scarious, margin narrow; petals notched, veins branched. In sand, mostly near the sea. Flo. April–Oct. ❀.

Cerastium pumilum Curt. **Dwarf Chickweed.** ¶Stem 1–3 in.; lower leaves obovate stalked; sepals and small upper bracts with scarious margins; petals slightly notched, veins branched; fr. drooping, later erect. Calcareous banks mostly in S. England. Flo. April–May. ❀.

Cerastium semidecandrum L. **Scarious Chickweed.** ¶Upper half of bracts and tips of sepals broadly scarious; petals very slightly notched, veins simple. Common on dry soils. Flo. April–May. ❀.

Cerastium glomeratum Thuill. **Clustered Mouse-ear.** *C. viscosum* auct. ¶Stem glandular; bracts green, very hairy; flo. clusters dense; tips of sepals acute and hairy. Very common in fields. Flo. April–Sept. ❀.

Cerastium brachypetalum Pers. ¶Bracts herbaceous, petals and filaments ciliate, inflo. lax. Stems covered with spreading-ascending hairs. Railway cutting near Sharnbrook, Bedfordshire. First found 1947. Flo. May.

Cerastium fontanum Baumg.
Subsp. *triviale* (Murb.) Jalas. **Common Mouse-ear.** *C. holosteoides* Fr., *C. vulgatum*

auct. ¶Stems and lanceolate leaves hairy; flo. larger, not clustered; tips of sepals glabrous. Common in fields, larger flowered on mountains. Flo. April–Sept. ❀.

Subsp. *scoticum* Jalas & Sell. ¶Similar to subsp. *triviale*, but with longer petals, larger seeds bearing large tubercles and basal part of sepals prominently keeled. Scottish mountains, chiefly in Clova region.

Cerastium alpinum L. **Alpine Mouse-ear.**

Subsp. *alpinum*. ¶Plant greyish green, with soft long hairs and sometimes almost glandular hairs; leaves broadly ovate; bracts with scarious margins; seeds small with acute tubercles. On mountains, N. Wales, N. England and Scotland. Flo. June–Aug. ❀.

Subsp. *lanatum* (Lam.) Aschers. & Graebner. ¶Similar to subsp. *alpinum*, but whole plant lanate; glandular hairs absent. On mountains, Scotland.

Cerastium arcticum Lange. **Arctic Mouse-ear.**

Subsp. *arcitum*. *Cerastium edmondstonii* auct., non (H. C. Wats.) Murb. & Ostenf. ¶Leaves elliptic, yellowish green, margins sparsely ciliate, otherwise glabrous to slightly pubescent; bracts without scarious margins; seeds large, tubercles obtuse. On mountains, N. Wales and Scotland. Flo. June–Aug. ❀.

Subsp. *edmondstonii* (H. C. Wats.) A. & D. Löve., *C. nigrescens* Edmondst. ex H. C. Wats. ¶Plant dwarf, compact, densely tufted, purplish and glandular; leaves shorter, roundish and darker green. Serpentine rocks, Shetland.

Cerastium arvense L. **Field Mouse-ear.** ¶Stems prostrate; leaves narrow, downy; petals twice as long as sepals. On calcareous and sandy soils, local. Flo. April–Aug. ❀.

*Cerastium tomentosum L. **Snow-in-Summer.** ¶Perennial; similar to *C. arvense* but whole plant covered with dense silvery-white hairs; petals white, twice as long as sepals. Garden escape, naturalized in fields, on banks, etc. Flo. May–Sept.

Cerastium cerastoides (L.) Britton. *Stellaria cerastoides* L. ¶Stems prostrate, rooting, with alternate hairy line; pedicels slender, terminal. By high mountain rills, Cumberland and Scotland. Flo. July–Aug. ❀.

Moenchia erecta (L.) Gaertn., Mey. & Scherb. **Upright Moenchia.** *Cerastium quaternellum* Fenzl. ¶Glaucous 2–4 in.; sepals with broad white margins; petals 4 entire. On bare sandy and gravelly places in England. Flo. April–June. ❀.

PLATE 15

Myosoton aquaticum (L.) Moench. **Great Chickweed.** *Stellaria aquatica* (L.) Scop. ¶Stems long, soft and trailing; leaves subsessile; styles 5; capsule with 5 bifid valves. In wet places and streamsides. Flo. June–Aug. ❀.

Stellaria nemorum L. **Wood Stitchwort.**

Subsp. *nemorum*. ¶Leaves mostly long stalked; bracts decreasing gradually in size at each branching of inflo.; styles 3; capsule with 6 valves; margins of seeds with row of rounded tubercles. In wet shady places, N. Devonshire and Midlands to Scotland. Flo. May–Aug. ❀.

Subsp. *glochidisperma* Murb. ¶Similar to subsp. *nemorum* but bracts decreasing abruptly in size after first branching of inflo.; margins of seeds with long cylindrical papillae. In wet shady places, Wales and Monmouthshire. Flo. May–Aug.

Stellaria media (L.) Vill. **Chickweed.** ¶Stems annual with single line of hairs; sepals hairy; stamens 5; petals 5, rarely 0; anthers red. Abundant in cultivated land. Flo. all the year. ❀.

Stellaria pallida (Dumort.) Piré. *S. apetala* auct. ¶Stems procumbent, slender; leaves small, yellowish green; sepals small, 3 mm.; petals 0 or minute; stamens 3; anthers grey; seeds small and pale. In dunes, sandy places and pine woods. Flo. March–May.

Stellaria neglecta Weihe. **Greater Chickweed.** ¶Stems 1–3 ft with single hairy line; leaves broadly ovate, acuminate; pedicels and sepals usually hairy; stamens 10. In hedge banks. Flo. April–Aug. ❀.
Var. *elizabethae* (F. W. Schultz) Béguinot, *S. umbrosa* Opiz. ¶Pedicels and sepals glabrous; pedicels straight in fr., deflexed at base, later erect; fr. more sharply tubercled. Locally common in S.W. ❀.

Stellaria holostea L. **Greater Stitchwort.** ¶Perennial; angles of stems and leaf margins rough, scabrid; leaves widest below the middle; veins of sepals hardly visible, scarious margin narrow. Very common in hedges and sides of thickets. Flo. April–June. ❀.

Stellaria palustris Retz. **Marsh Stitchwort.** *S. glauca* With. ¶Angles of stem and leaf margins smooth; leaves glaucous, tapering from base; sepals 3 nerved, scarious margin wide; stamens red. In marshes and fens, local. Flo. May–July. ❀.

Stellaria graminea L. **Lesser Stitchwort.** ¶Stems 1–3 ft, diffuse; leaves bright green, margins smooth, ciliate below; bracts scarious, ciliate; sepals 3 nerved. Very common in grass. Flo. May–Oct. ❀.

Stellaria alsine Grimm. **Bog Stitchwort.** *S. uliginosa* Murr. ¶Stems 6–18 in., glaucous, diffuse; flo. branches short; lobes of adjacent petals near together. Common in boggy places. Flo. May–July. ❀.

Minuartia verna (L.) Hiern. **Vernal Sandwort.** *Arenaria verna* L. ¶Leafy shoots tufted; leaves linear, acute; sepals 3 veined; flo. stems few flowered; petals longer than sepals; seeds papillose. On calcareous rocks and moors in W. and N. Flo. June–Sept. ❀.
Var. *gerardii* (Willd.) Hiern. ¶Dwarf plant; leaves blunt, appressed. Kynance Cove, Cornwall. ❀.

Minuartia recurva (All.) Schinz & Thell. *Arenaria recurva* All. ¶Small perennial, densely caespitose; stems woody; leaves recurved, awl shaped; sepals 5–7, veined; flo. stems few flowered; petals white, twice as long as sepals; seeds smooth. Discovered on mountains in Cork and Kerry, Ireland in 1964. Flo. June–Sept.

Minuartia rubella (Wahlenb.) Hiern. **Mountain Sandwort.** *Arenaria rubella* (Wahlenb.) Sm. ¶Stems tufted, 2–4 in.; flo. branches mostly 1 flowered; leaves linear, blunt, 3 veined. On high Scottish mountains, very rare. Flo. July–Aug. ❀.

Minuartia stricta (Sw.) Hiern. *Arenaria uliginosa* Schleich. ex DC. ¶Small perennial tufts; leaves filiform, veinless; flo. stalks long, 1–2 in. erect, filiform. In Teesdale only, a plant of Arctic Circle. Flo. June–July.

Minuartia hybrida (Vill.) Schischk. **Fine-leaved Sandwort.** *Arenaria tenuifolia* L. ¶Stem annual, 4–6 in., much forked, glabrous, or glandular above; stamens 10. On sandy or chalky soils and walls, mostly in E. England. Flo. May–June. ❀.

Moehringia trinervia (L.) Clairv. **Three-veined Sandwort.** *Arenaria trinervia* L. ¶Stems diffuse, 8–12 in.; leaves broadly ovate, acute, 3–5 veined; seeds with an appendage. Common in shady places. Flo. May–July. ❀.

Arenaria serpyllifolia L. **Thyme-leaved Sandwort.** ¶Erect, rigid, pubescent; leaves and sepals ovate, acute; capsule 2·5 mm. wide. On dry places, cliffs and walls. Flo. June–Aug. ❀.

Arenaria leptoclados (Reichb.) Guss. **Slender Sandwort.** ¶Erect, very slender; leaves narrower; inflo. longer; sepals lanceolate; capsule only 1·5 mm. wide. Now regarded by some botanists as a subspecies of *A. serpyllifolia*, in which case the name used is *A. serpyllifolia* L. subsp. *leptoclados* (Reichb.) Nyman. Common on dry soil and walls. Flo. June–Aug. ❀.

Arenaria ciliata L.
Subsp. *hibernica* Ostenf. & Dahl. **Irish Sandwort.** ¶Small and prostrate; branches ascending 2–3 in.; leaves obovate, blunt, ciliate; petals exceeding 3 ribbed sepals. Ben Bulben, Co. Sligo. Flo. May–Aug. ❀.

Arenaria norvegica Gunn. **Arctic Sandwort.**
Subsp. *norvegica*. ¶Stems short; leaves obovate, blunt; sepals faintly 3 ribbed; capsule not constricted at top; teeth suberect. In stony places, Argyll, Sutherland, Hebrides and Shetlands. Flo. July–Aug. ❀.
Subsp. *anglica* Halliday. ¶Leaves lanceolate, acute; capsule constricted at the top, teeth revolute. On high calcareous rocks, W. Yorkshire. Flo. May–Sept. ❀.

PLATE 16

Honkenya peploides (L.) Ehrh. **Sea Purslane.** *Arenaria peploides* L. ¶Stolons creeping; leaves fleshy, margins membranous; flo. often dioecious; capsule globose. On sandy and pebbly seashores. Flo. May–Sept. ❀.

Minuartia sedoides (L.) Hiern. **Mossy Cyphel.** *Arenaria sedoides* (L.) F. J. Hanb., *Cherleria sedoides* L. ¶Stems in dense cushions; leaves linear; flo. solitary; petals usually 0, or minute. On Scottish mountains, local. Flo. June–Aug. ❀.

Sagina maritima Don. **Sea Pearlwort.** ¶Prostrate or erect; leaves blunt or apiculate; sepals suberect in fr.; petals 4 minute or 0. On seaside cliffs and rocks. Flo. May–Sept. ❀.

Sagina apetala Ard.
Subsp. *apetala*. **Ciliate Pearlwort.** *S. ciliata* Fr. ¶Very slender stems all flowering; outer sepals pointed, all appressed in fr., tips patent; petals minute or 0. Locally common in dry places, etc. Flo. May–Sept. ❀. The plants are apt to be glandular on dry heaths (*S. filicaulis* Jord.).
Subsp. *erecta* (Hornem.) F. Hermann. **Annual Pearlwort.** *S. apetala* auct. ¶Stems suberect, all flowering; leaves tapering, mucronate; sepals spreading in fr.; petals very minute. Locally common in bare places. Flo. May–Aug. ❀.

Sagina procumbens L. **Common Pearlwort.** ¶Branches spreading, prostrate from a central rosette; sepals blunt, spreading in fr.; pedicel top recurved in unripe fr. Common. Flo. May–Oct. ❀.

Sagina × *normaniana* Lagerh. **Scottish Pearlwort.** *S. procumbens* × *saginoides*, *S. scotica* (Druce) Druce. ¶Like the above but with fr. obviously smaller, 2·5 × 2 mm., about equal to sepals; stems more slender; rosette leaves longer. In wet turf on mountains in Scotland. Flo. July–Sept. ❀.

Sagina saginoides (L.) Karst. **Mountain Pearlwort.** *S. linnei* C. Presl. ¶Branches spreading from central rosette; petals 5, rounded, nearly equal to sepals; fr. large, 3·5–4 × 2·5 mm., exceeding appressed sepals. On mountains in Scotland. Flo. June–Aug. ❀.

Sagina intermedia Fenzl. **Alpine Pearlwort.** *S. nivalis* auct., *S. caespitosa* auct. ¶Small, densely tufted; petals 5; fruiting sepals suberect; pedicels short and straight. On mountain tops in Scotland, rare. Flo. June–Aug. ❀.

Sagina subulata (Sw.) C. Presl. **Heath Pearlwort.** ¶Stems tufted, glandular; leaves tapering, ciliate and hair pointed; petals 5; pedicels long and glandular. On dry heaths, local. Flo. June–Aug. ❀.

Sagina nodosa (L.) Fenzl. **Knotted Pearlwort.** ¶Leafy to top of stem, with many bundles of leaf buds in axils; petals large; fr. pedicels straight. In wet sandy places. Flo. July–Sept. ❀.

Spergula arvensis L. **Corn Spurrey.** *S. vulgaris* Boenn. ¶Plant scarcely viscid; seeds covered with club-shaped papillae. Common in sandy cornfields. Flo. June–Aug. ❀.
Var. *sativa* (Boenn.) Mert. & Koch. ¶Plant very viscid; seeds nearly smooth, with a narrow wing; leaves often grey-green.

Spergula morisonii Bor. *S. vernalis* auct. *S. pentandra* auct. non L. ¶Stems stiffly erect; leaves not furrowed beneath; seeds with a broad wing. On sandy cultivated ground, Sussex. First found in 1943.

Spergularia rubra (L.) J. & C. Presl. **Red Spurrey.** ¶Leaves flat; stipules silvery, torn; seeds tubercled, the margin thick, not winged. Common on gravelly and sandy soils. Flo. May–Oct. ❀.

Spergularia bocconii (Scheele) Aschers. & Graebn. *S. campestris* auct. non Aschers. ¶Plant covered with minute glands; branches dichotomous, bearing many small, short-stalked flo.; petals shorter than sepals; stipules broad. On dry sandy and rocky places on S.W. coasts and Essex, rare. Flo. May–Sept. ❀.

Spergularia marina (L.) Griseb. **Sea Spurrey.** *S. salina* J. & C. Presl. ¶Branches spreading or prostrate; leaves flat above, rounded beneath; bracts often leafy; calyx longer than petals, shorter than pedicels, a few of the seeds winged. Salt marshes by the sea. Flo. June–Aug. ❀.

Spergularia media (L.) C. Presl. **Perennial Sea Spurrey.** *S. marginata* Kittel. ¶Plant larger, subglabrous; upper bracts small; petals often exceeding calyx, pale pink; capsule almost twice length of calyx; seeds all winged. On muddy salt marshes. Flo. June–Sept. ❀.

Spergularia rupicola Lebel ex Le Jolis. **Rock Spurrey.** ¶Plant glandular; leaves short and fascicled; stipules acute, capsule not much exceeding calyx; seeds pear shaped, not winged. Sea cliffs and rocks. Flo. June–Sept. ❀.

Polycarpon tetraphyllum (L.) L. **Four-leaved Allseed.** ¶Leaves obovate, some opposite, some in whorls of 4; sepals hooded; petals minute, white. On sea cliffs in Scilly Isles, Cornwall, Devonshire, Dorset, and common in Channel Isles. Flo. June–July. ❀.

PORTULACACEAE

*_Montia sibirica_ (L.) Howell. _Claytonia sibirica_ L. _C. alsinoides_ Sims. ¶Succulent, 6–10 in.; stem leaves opposite but separate; flo. pink. Alien from N. America, spreading along streams, in damp woods, etc. Flo. May–July. ❀.

*_Montia perfoliata_ (Willd.) Howell. _Claytonia perfoliata_ Don ex Willd. ¶6–10 in.; stem leaves opposite and united; flo. smaller, white. Naturalized in cultivated ground. Flo. May–July. ❀.

Montia fontana L. **Water Blinks.** ¶All forms grow in trickles of water or in very wet places on acid soil, and of smaller size on pastures. Flo. May–Oct. ❀.

Subsp. _fontana._ ¶Seeds smooth and shining. In northern counties only.

Subsp. _chondrosperma_ (Fenzl) Walters. ¶Seeds dull, with rather coarse tubercles. Widely distributed.

Subsp. _amporitana_ Senn. Subsp. _intermedia_ (Beeby) Walters. ¶Seeds smaller, less than 1 mm., finely tuberculate with high tubercles. Widely distributed.

Subsp. _variabilis_ Walters. ¶Seeds more or less smooth, but not so shining as in subsp. _fontana._

TAMARICACEAE   PLATE 17

*_Tamarix gallica_ L. **Tamarisk.** ¶Shrub, 5–10 ft; branches slender; leaves minute, glaucous; flo. buds globose; stamens inserted in depressions of the disk. On sandy shores in S. England, planted. Flo. July–Sept.

*_Tamarix anglica_ Webb. ¶Very similar to above; leaves greener; flo. buds ovoid; stamens inserted on sharp elevations of the disk. Sandy shores, S. and E. England. Flo. July–Sept. ❀.

ELATINACEAE

Elatine hexandra (Lapierre) DC. **Waterwort.** ¶Plants matted, submerged; flo. stalked; petals 3; stamens 6; seeds nearly straight. In edges of lakes and reservoirs. Flo. July–Sept. ❀.

Elatine hydropiper L. ¶Similar to _E. hexandra_, but leaf stalked; flo. sessile; petals 4; stamens 8; seeds curved. In edges of lakes and pools, rare. Flo. July–Aug. ❀.

HYPERICACEAE

Hypericum androsaemum L. **Tutsan.** ¶Small shrub, 1–3 ft; slightly aromatic; flo. ¾ in.; leaves ovate, obtuse; stamens in 5 bundles; styles shorter than stamens; berry red, globose, becoming bluish black when ripe, indehiscent. In damp woods, hedgerows and shady ditches, mostly in W. Flo. June–Aug. ❀.

*_Hypericum inodorum_ Mill. _H. elatum_ Ait. ¶Similar to _H. androsaemum_, 1½–4 ft; leaves slightly smaller, strongly aromatic when bruised; flo. ½ in.; styles longer than stamens; berry dehiscent. Garden escape, naturalized in hedgerows and thickets particularly in S.W. England. Flo. June–Sept.

*_Hypericum hircinum_ L. ¶Similar to _H. androsaemum_ and _H. elatum_; stems quadrangular; leaves emitting a strong goat-like odour when bruised; flo. ½ in.; styles longer than stamens; berry dehiscent. Garden escape, naturalized in woods and thickets, rare. Flo. May–Sept.

*_Hypericum calycinum_ L. **Rose of Sharon.** ¶Stems many, creeping, ascending 18 in.; flo. 2–3 in. wide. From S.E. Europe, extensively naturalized in woods and wastes. Flo. July–Sept. ❊.

Hypericum perforatum L. **Perforate St John's Wort.** ¶Stem 2 ribbed; leaves elliptic, with many pellucid dots; sepals lanceolate, acute. Common, especially on calcareous soils. Flo. June–Sept. ❊.

Hypericum maculatum Crantz. _H. quadrangulum_ auct. _H. dubium_ Leers.

Subsp. _maculatum._ ¶Plant slender with few branches, usually at an angle of 30° from 4 ribbed stem; leaves oval; pellucid dots few or absent; densely reticulate; sepals ovate; obtuse; petals entire with glands on surface in forms of dots. In moist places chiefly in Scotland. Flo. July–Sept.

Subsp. _obtusiusculum_ (Tourlet) Hayek. ¶Plant stouter with many branches, usually at an angle of 50° from 4 ribbed stem; leaves oval, with pellucid dots; sparsely reticulate; petals sometimes crenate with glands on surface in form of streaks or lines. In damp woods, hedge banks, etc., widespread, but local. Flo. July–Sept. ❊.

Hypericum × desetangsii Lamotte (_H. maculatum_ subsp. _obtusiusculum × perforatum_). ¶Stem upright with 2 very prominent and 2 faint raised lines; leaves ovate-oblong, with or without large pellucid glandular dots. Sometimes occurs where the two parents grow together.

Hypericum tetrapterum Fr. **Square-stalked St John's Wort.** _H. quadrangulum_ L., _H. quadratum_ Stokes. ¶Stem 4 winged; leaves oval with pellucid veins and small dots; flo. ⅜ in.; sepals lanceolate, acute. In bogs and streamsides, common. Flo. July–Aug. ❊.

Hypericum undulatum Schousb. ex Willd. **Wavy St John's Wort.** ¶Stem 2 ribbed; leaves ovate with wavy edges and pellucid dots and veins; sepals ovate, acute; petals partly red outside. In bogs, Devonshire and Cornwall, and S. Wales. Flo. July–Aug. ❊.

Hypericum canadense L. ¶Stem erect, 3–6 in., 4 angled, reddish; leaves narrow, oblong; flo. ¼ in.; capsule dark red. In bogs and damp fields, W. Ireland, only.

Hypericum humifusum L. **Creeping St John's Wort.** ¶Stems slender, prostrate, 2 ribbed; flo. few, ⅜ in.; sepals unequal. On gravelly banks and heaths, common. Flo. June–Sept. ❊.

Hypericum linarifolium Vahl. **Narrow-leaved St John's Wort.** ¶Stems erect, nearly round; leaves narrow, obtuse, margin revolute; sepals acute with black glandular teeth. On rocks, S. Devon, Wales and Channel Islands, rare. ❊.

Hypericum pulchrum L. **Beautiful St John's Wort.** ¶Stems erect, round; leaves short, cordate, obtuse, with pellucid dots; buds red; blunt sepals and petals edged with black glands. On dry banks, fairly common. Flo. June–Aug. ❊. Forma _procumbens_ Rostrup. ¶Plant prostrate on sea cliffs and mountains.

Hypericum hirsutum L. **Hairy St John's Wort.** ¶Stem 2 ft, round, pubescent; leaves ovate, striate, with pellucid glands; flo. pale; sepals with black glands. In woodland borders. Flo. July–Aug. ❊.

Hypericum montanum L. **Mountain St John's Wort.** ¶Stem round; leaves, bracts and sepals with marginal black glands; inflo. dense; petals pale yellow. On calcareous soils, local. Flo. July–Aug. ❀.

Hypericum elodes L. **Bog St John's Wort.** ¶Plant softly tomentose; stems creeping or floating; leaves suborbicular; flo. few; petals erect. In spongy bogs, common. Flo. July–Aug. ❀.

MALVACEAE

PLATE 18

Althaea officinalis L. **Marsh Mallow.** ¶Stout, erect, 2–3 ft, velvety pubescent throughout; flo. clustered; epicalyx bracts 6–9, narrow; sepals ovate, acuminate. Marshes near sea. Flo. Aug.–Sept. ❀.

Althaea hirsuta L. **Hispid Marsh Mallow.** ¶Slender, hispid, spreading 6–18 in.; flo. solitary; epicalyx narrow; sepals long, setaceous. W. Kent and Somerset, rare, doubtful native. Flo. July–Aug. ❀.

Lavatera arborea L. **Tree Mallow.** ¶Stem 3–8 ft, stout, woody, pubescent; epicalyx bracts 3, connate, larger than calyx; fr. wrinkled. On sea cliffs and rocks. Flo. July–Sept. ❀.

Lavatera cretica L. **Lesser Tree Mallow.** *L. sylvestris* Brot. ¶Smaller plant, herbaceous, with stellate hairs; epicalyx shorter than calyx; fr. smooth. Plant like *Malva sylvestris*. W. Cornwall, Scilly Isles. Flo. June. ❀.

Malva moschata L. **Musk Mallow.** ¶Erect, 2 ft; stem leaves cut to narrow segments; flo. pink; fr. stalks erect; calyx enlarged; carpels hispid. On dry banks. Flo. July–Aug. ❀.
Var. *heterophylla* Lej. & Court. ¶Lower leaves entire, upper cut into about 3 broad segments. Flo. often more autumnal. ❀.

Malva sylvestris L. **Common Mallow.** ¶Leaves 2–3 in. wide, lobes folded, triangular; flo. rose-purple; fr. spreading; carpels reticulate, usually glabrous. Common. Flo. June–Sept. ❀.

Malva neglecta Wallr. **Dwarf Mallow.** *M. rotundifolia* auct. non L. ¶Prostrate, pubescent; leaves ½–1½ in. wide; flo. ¾ in., pale; epicalyx shorter than calyx; carpels pubescent, smooth. Common in S. England. Flo. June–Sept. ❀.

* *Malva pusilla* Sm. **Small Mallow.** ¶Epicalyx equalling deltoid calyx lobes; flo. ¼ in. wide; carpels netted, rugose, margined, meeting with a toothed edge. Introduced. Flo. June–Sept. ❀.

* *Malva parviflora* L. ¶Flo. ¼ in. wide; petal claws glabrous; calyx lobes broadly ovate, enlarged in fr.; carpels pubescent, edges winged and wavy. A rare alien. Flo. June–Sept.

* *Malva verticillata* L. ¶Plant erect, 2–2½ ft; flo. ¾ in. wide; carpels smooth, angles square; sepals enlarged in fr. Naturalized in a few places. Flo. July–Sept.

TILIACEAE

Tilia platyphyllos Scop. **Broad-leaved Lime.** ¶Twigs and under sides of leaves downy; flo. few, pendulous; fr. with prominent ribs. Woods by rivers Wye, Teme and Severn, elsewhere planted. Flo. June. ❀.

Tilia × vulgaris Hayne. **Common Lime.** *T. europaea* auct. *T. cordata × platyphyllos.* ¶Leaves green and glabrous beneath except hairs at axils of veins; flo. pendulous; fr. downy, slightly ribbed. In plantations, not native. Flo. July.

Tilia cordata Mill. **Small-leaved Lime.** ¶Twigs glabrous; leaves small, glaucous beneath with hairs at axils of veins; flo. erect; fr. thin walled, slightly angular. In woods and on cliffs, especially on limestone. Flo. July. ✿.

LINACEAE   PLATE 19

Radiola linoides Roth. **Allseed.** *R. millegrana* Sm. ¶Very small annual, 1–2 in.; repeatedly forked; flo. minute; sepals 3 cleft. In bare sandy places, sometimes with *Anagallis minima*. Flo. July–Aug. ✿.

Linum catharticum L. **White Flax.** ¶Annual, stem slender, 2–6 in.; leaves opposite, elliptic; petals white, suberect. On dry banks and basic soils, common. Flo. June–Aug. ✿.
    Var. *dunense* Druce. ¶Very small, about 1 in. long, quite prostrate. Dunes. ✿.

Linum perenne Mill. **Blue Flax.**
Subsp. *anglicum* Ockendon, *L. anglicum* Mill. ¶Perennial, 1–2 ft; leaves alternate, linear; flo. blue; sepals obovate, glabrous, less than ½ length of fr. On chalk and limestone. Flo. June. ✿.

Linum bienne Mill. **Pale Flax.** *L. angustifolium* Huds. ¶Perennial, 1–1½ ft; leaves linear; flo. very pale mauve; sepals ovate, ciliate, more than ½ length of fr. On dry banks, S. and S.W. England. ✿.

GERANIACEAE

Geranium sanguineum L. **Blood-red Geranium.** ¶Stems diffuse, 1–2 ft; flo. solitary, 1½ in. wide, crimson; peduncle long. On dry rocks and sea cliffs, local. Flo. July–Aug. ✿.
    Var. *lancastrense* (With.) Druce. ¶Stems procumbent; flo. pale pink. N. Lancashire coast.

Geranium macrorrhizum L. ¶Plant aromatic; stems erect, hairy, ½–1 ft; leaves smooth, 5 lobed; flo. in pairs on short peduncles; petals pink or red. Garden escape. Naturalized on walls and banks, chiefly in S.W. England. Flo. May–Aug.

Geranium versicolor L. **Streaked Cranesbill.** *G. striatum* L. ¶Stems erect, hairy, 1–2 ft; peduncle 2 flowered; petals emarginate, pale with purple veins. Shady places in S. and W., especially Cornwall. ✿.

Geranium endressii Gay. ¶Alien, similar to above, but petals more rounded, deep pink without darker veins. Garden escape. Naturalized on banks, in fields, etc. Flo. May–June.

Geranium endressii × versicolor. ¶Similar to above but petals pink with dark veins. Garden escape. Naturalized in fields, on banks, etc. Sometimes more frequent than either of the parents. Flo. May–June.

Geranium nodosum L. ¶Erect, glabrous, 1–2 ft; stem leaves with 3–5 large ovate, acute lobes; flo. pale rose-purple. Garden escape, sometimes confused with *G. endressii.* Flo. May–Sept.

Geranium phaeum L. **Dusky Cranesbill.** ¶Stems erect, 1–2 ft; flo. ¾ in., blackish purple, petals wavy; sepals awned. In plantations and waste places, not native. Flo. May–Aug. ✻.

Geranium sylvaticum L. **Wood Cranesbill.** ¶Erect, 1–3 ft; stem leaves sessile; flo. ¾ in., reddish purple; filaments filiform; fr. erect. In N. England and Scotland. Flo. June–July. ✻

Geranium pratense L. **Meadow Cranesbill.** ¶Erect, 2–4 ft; leaves nearly all petiolate; flo. 1¼ in., blue-purple; fr. reflexed; filaments wide at base. In meadows and banks. Flo. June–Sept. ✻.

Geranium platypetalum Fisch. & Mey. *G. ibericum* auct., non L. ¶Stems erect, 1–2 ft; leaves roundish, heart shaped, long stalked, deeply 5–7 lobed; woolly; flo. 1–1½ in. in pairs, or more, in open panicles; petals bluish violet to purple; calyx rough. Garden escape. Established on waste ground, in fields, etc. Flo. May–Aug.

Geranium pyrenaicum Burm. f. **Pyrenean Cranesbill.** *G. perenne* Huds. ¶Stems 2 ft, diffuse, downy; flo. ½ in., red-purple; petals deeply notched; carpels smooth. Roadsides and fields, S. and E. England. Flo. June–Aug. ✻.

Geranium molle L. **Soft Cranesbill.** ¶Prostrate, softly pubescent; flo. ⅓ in.; petals deeply notched; carpels wrinkled. Very common on cultivated and waste land. Flo. April–Sept. ✻.

Geranium pusillum L. **Small-flowered Cranesbill.** ¶Flo. ¼ in., lilac; petals notched; carpels smooth, keeled, hairs appressed. On cultivated fields and light soils. Flo. June–Sept. ✻.

Geranium rotundifolium L. **Round-leaved Cranesbill.** ¶Leaves round, lobes less deep; petals entire, flesh-pink; carpels keeled with spreading hairs. On cliffs, walls and banks, local. Flo. June–July. ✻.

Geranium dissectum L. **Cut-leaved Cranesbill.** ¶Leaves deeply cut; peduncles short; petals bifid, red-purple; carpels smooth, hairs erect. Common in hedge banks and arable land. Flo. May–Aug. ✻.

Geranium columbinum L. **Dove's-foot Cranesbill.** ¶Stems long, spreading; leaf segments narrow; sepals awned; petals rounded, pale rose. On dry, mainly calcareous soils. Flo. June–July. ✻.

Geranium lucidum L. **Shining Cranesbill.** ¶Stems red; leaves round and glossy, lobes shallow; petals rounded, pink. On shady banks, common on acid soils. Flo. May–Aug. ✻.

Geranium robertianum L. **Herb Robert.**
Subsp. *robertianum.* ¶Stems erect, rather hairy; petals spreading; anthers reddish; carpels wrinkled, downy. Common everywhere on banks. Flo. April–Oct. ✻.
Subsp. *maritimum* (Bab.) H. G. Bak. ¶Stem prostrate, succulent, red; leaves and flo. smaller; carpels glabrous. On shingle beaches.
Subsp. *celticum* Ostenf. ¶Stems reddish on nodes and petiole bases; flo. pale; fr. hairy, large. Limestone rocks, S. Wales and Galway.

Geranium purpureum Vill. **Lesser Herb Robert.**
Subsp. *purpureum.* ¶Plant upright; leaf segments narrow; stamens yellow; carpels much wrinkled, glabrous; fr. hairy or glabrous with closely set ridges. Sea cliffs, rocky places, etc., sometimes inland, Channel Islands, S. England, S. Wales and Ireland. Flo. May–Sept. ✻.

Subsp. *forsteri* (Wilmott) H. G. Bak. ¶Plant prostrate; petioles of rosette leaves very short; fr. hairy or glabrous, often occurring together; ridges less apparent. Stabilized shingle beaches, Guernsey, Hampshire and Sussex.

PLATE 20

Erodium cicutarium (L.) L'Hérit. **Common Storksbill.**
Subsp. *cicutarium*. ¶Leaves pinnate, leaflets cut to narrow segments; peduncles 6–9 flowered; petals rose, usually unspotted; filaments gradually enlarged at base. On light land and coast dunes. Flo. June–Sept. ⚹.
   Var. *pimpinellifolium* Cav. ¶Two upper petals with dark spot. ⚹.
Subsp. *dunense* Andreas. **Dune Storksbill.** *E. lebeli* Jord. ¶Stem short, stout, prostrate, very glandular, sticky; leaflet segments broader; peduncles 3–5 flowered; petals pale; filaments gradually enlarged at base; pit on carpel conspicuous. On coastal sand dunes. ⚹.
Subsp. *bipinnatum* (Willd.) Tourlet, *E. glutinosum* Dumort. ¶Plant very glandular, sticky; branches more slender, prostrate; peduncles 2–4 flowered; petals pale; filaments suddenly enlarged or dentate below; carpels with small pit at top. Sand dunes on coast, scarce.

Erodium moschatum (L.) L'Hérit. **Musky Storksbill.** ¶Leaves large, pinnate, leaflets ovate, coarsely toothed, smelling of musk; base of filament toothed.ʼ Seaside W. England, Ireland, introduced inland. Flo. June–Aug. ⚹.

Erodium maritimum (L.) L'Hérit. **Sea Storksbill.** ¶Branches prostrate; leaves small, oval, toothed or lobed, not pinnate; petals pale, often absent. On sea cliffs and exposed places inland. Flo. May–Sept. ⚹.

OXALIDACEAE

Oxalis acetosella L. **Wood Sorrel.** ¶Leaves radical from creeping rhizome; scape 1 flowered; petals white or rarely rose; capsule ovoid, 5 angled. In woods, common. Flo. April–May. ⚹.

*Oxalis corniculata L. **Yellow Sorrel.** ¶Stems prostrate, pubescent; trifoliate leaves with small stipules; flo. 1–7 together; pedicels reflexed in fr.; capsule oblong, hairy, erect. Chiefly in S. England, naturalized. Flo. June–Sept. ⚹.

*Oxalis europaea Jord. **Upright Yellow Sorrel.** *O. stricta* auct. ¶Stolons slender; stem erect, subglabrous; leaves purple tinted; stipules 0; flo. yellow, 2–6 together; fr. pedicel straight; capsule oblong. A garden weed, mostly in S.E. England.

*Oxalis articulata Savigny. *O. floribunda* Lehm. ¶Root tuberous; leaves radical; flo. many, ¾ in., rose-purple. Garden weed.

*Oxalis corymbosa DC. ¶Similar to *O. articulata* but with larger leaflets and flowers; leaflets with minute red dots on the margins; flo. purplish pink. Garden weed, common in London area.

*Oxalis latifolia Kunth. ¶Similar to *O. corymbosa* but leaves glabrous without red dots on margins. Introduced. Weed of cultivated ground in Devon and Cornwall. Flo. May–Sept.

*Oxalis tetraphylla Cav. ¶Leaflets 4; peduncles pubescent; flo. rose-red, similar in size to *O. corymbosa*. Naturalized in fields in Jersey. Flo. May–Sept.

*Oxalis pes-caprae L. **Bermuda Buttercup.** O. cernua Thunb. ¶Leaves many, springing from buried bulb; peduncles bearing flo. in umbels; flo. large, bright yellow. Frequent weed in bulb fields in the Scilly Isles, less frequent in Cornwall and Channel Islands. Flo. March–June.

*Oxalis incarnata L. ¶Similar to O. acetosella from which it differs in its slender, erect, bulbil-bearing stems. Garden escape, naturalized on walls and banks chiefly in S.W. England. Flo. May–July.

BALSAMINACEAE

Impatiens noli-tangere L. **Wild Balsam, Touch-me-not.** ¶Plant succulent, 1–2 ft; nodes swollen; flo. yellow, 1–3 together; spur tapering, point recurved. By streams, Lake District, N. Wales, introduced elsewhere. Flo. July–Sept. ✲.

*Impatiens capensis Meerb. **Orange Balsam.** I. fulva Nutt., I. biflora Walt. ¶Leaves ovate with shallow teeth; flo. orange; spur tapering, reflexed at tip. N. American plant, naturalized on river banks, mostly in S. and Midlands. Flo. June–Aug. ✲.

*Impatiens parviflora DC. **Small Yellow Balsam.** ¶Stem 6–18 in.; leaves ovate with many acute teeth; flo. 3–10 on peduncle, pale yellow; spur nearly straight. Naturalized in woods and wastes except in S.W. From Siberia. Flo. July–Sept.

*Impatiens glandulifera Royle. **Indian Balsam.** I. roylei Walp. ¶Stem stout, 4–6 ft; leaves opposite, teeth many, acute; flo. large, rose and pink; spur inflated, with short reflexed point. Spreading beside rivers, rarely on waste ground. Flo. July–Sept. ✲.

AQUIFOLIACEAE

Ilex aquifolium L. **Holly.** ¶Small tree 10–40 ft; flo. white, subdioecious; berries red, poisonous. Common in woods and hedges. Flo. April–May. ✲.

CELASTRACEAE

Euonymus europaeus L. **Spindle.** ¶Shrub 5–15 ft; flo. small, greenish; fr. beautiful, lobed and pink, with seeds enclosed in an orange aril (an aftergrowth from seed stalk). The plant harbours the 'Black Army' aphis. In copses and hedges, common in S. England, extending to S. Scotland and Ireland. Flo. June–July. ✲.

RHAMNACEAE

Rhamnus catharticus L. **Buckthorn.** ¶Shrub 5–10 ft; branches opposite, ending in thorns; flo. 4 partite, dioecious. On calcareous soil, chiefly in mid and S.E. England. Flo. May–July. ✲.

Frangula alnus Mill. **Berry-bearing Alder.** Rhamnus frangula L. ¶Branches alternate, without thorns; flo. white, 5 partite, perfect; fr. black when ripe. On peaty heaths and damp hedgerows. Flo. May–Sept. ✲.

ACERACEAE

*Acer pseudoplatanus L. **Sycamore.** ¶Tree 40–60 ft; flo. dense, pendulous; stamens twice as long as petals; juice not milky. Common everywhere, an ancient introduction. Flo. April–June, ❀ (fruit only).

*Acer platanoides L. **Norway Maple.** ¶Tree 40–60 ft; leaves shining on both surfaces; juice milky; flo. in erect corymbs. Introduced but readily regenerating. Flo. April–May.

Acer campestre L. **Common Maple.** ¶Small tree, 10–20 ft; flo. erect; stamens equalling petals; wings of fr. nearly in one line. Hedgerows from Yorkshire southward; introduced elsewhere. Flo. May–June. ❀.

PAPILIONACEAE PLATE 21

*Lupinus nootkatensis Donn ex Sims. **Lupin.** ¶Stems stout, herbaceous, subsimple, 1–2 ft; leaf petioles long; flo. blue. On river shingle, abundant in mid Scotland and Orkneys. Not native, from N.W. America. Flo. July–Aug.

*Lupinus arboreus Sims. **Tree Lupin.** ¶A woody shrub with many spreading branches; petioles short; flo. yellow. Locally naturalized and spreading, not native. Flo. June–Sept.

Genista anglica L. **Petty Whin.** ¶Stems 1–2 ft, woody, diffuse, spinous; leaves ovate, glabrous; flo. yellow. On damp heaths, up to 2000 ft, England and Scotland. Flo. May–June. ❀.

Genista pilosa L. **Hairy Greenweed.** ¶Stems ½–1 ft, woody, without spines; leaves ovate, silky beneath; flo. pubescent, yellow; pod downy. W. Cornwall, W. Wales, Sussex, rare. Flo. May–Sept. ❀.

Genista tinctoria L. **Dyer's Greenweed.** ¶Stems 1–2 ft suberect, striate; leaves oblong-lanceolate; flo. and pods glabrous. On rough grassy places, S. England to S. Scotland. Flo. July–Sept. ❀.
Var. *humifusa* L. (Dickson) Druce, non L. ¶Branches prostrate, hairy; pods hairy. W. Cornwall.

Ulex europaeus L. **Common Gorse, Furze.** ¶Stems 2–6 ft; spines furrowed and straight; flo. bracts ovate, about 4 × 2 mm.; calyx hairs spreading; flo. yellow. Abundant on heaths. Flo. March–May. ❀.

Ulex europaeus × gallii. ¶Very variable, but usually intermediate between the two parents, and probably common where they grow together.

Ulex gallii Planch. **Dwarf** or **Summer Gorse.** ¶Stems 1–3 ft; spines strong, slightly furrowed, often curved; bracts minute; calyx hairs appressed; flo. golden. On heaths and moors, common in W. England, Wales and S. Ireland. Flo. July–Oct. ❀.

Ulex minor Roth. **Small Furze.** *U. nanus* T. F. Forst. ¶Stems 1–3 ft; spines weak and slender; flo. bracts minute; flo. pale yellow and small. On heaths, Dorset to Sussex, Norfolk and Nottinghamshire. Flo. July–Oct. ❀.

Sarothamnus scoparius (L.) Wimm. ex Koch. **Broom.** *Cytisus scoparius* (L.) Link.
Subsp. *scoparius.* ¶Erect shrub, 1–6 ft; branches angular, green; leaflets 1–3, silky;

flo. large, bright yellow, sometimes blotched with red. On heaths. Widely distributed. Flo. May–June. ❀.

Subsp. *maritimus* (Rouy) Ulbr. Subsp. *prostratus* (C. Bailey) Tutin. ¶Stems prostrate; twigs and leaves densely silky. On sea cliffs, W. Cornwall, Pembroke, Lundy Island, Channel Islands and W. Cork.

Spartium junceum L. ¶A shrub similar to *Sarothamnus scoparius* but with terete stems and linear-lanceolate leaves. Naturalized on railway banks, etc., in S. England.

Ononis repens L. **Restharrow.** *O. arvensis* auct. ¶Stem rhizomatous, procumbent, hairy all round, usually without spines; pod shorter than calyx. Common on coasts and calcareous soils inland. Flo. June–Sept. ❀.
Var. *horrida* Lange. ¶Plant spinous. ❀.

Ononis repens × *spinosa*. ¶Very variable, but often intermediate between the two parents, and probably common where they grow together.

Ononis spinosa L. **Prickly Restharrow.** *O. campestris* Koch & Ziz. ¶Stem erect with two lines of hairs, usually spinous; pod decidedly longer than calyx. On rough pastures in England except S.W. Flo. June–Sept. ❀.

Ononis reclinata L. **Small Restharrow.** ¶Annual; stem 2–3 in.; viscid; fr. pedicels reflexed. In turf on sea cliffs, rare, S. Devon, S. Wales, Channel Islands. Flo. June–July. ❀. '

Medicago sativa L. **Lucerne.** ¶Erect 1–2 ft, bushy; leaflets 1 in.; flo. purple; pod $\frac{1}{4}$ in. wide, with 2–3 turns. From S.E. Europe, cultivated, locally naturalized. Flo. April–Aug. ❀.

Medicago × *varia* Martyn = *M. falcata* × *sativa*. *M. silvestris* Fr. ¶Variable; pod forming 1 ring; flo. yellow to green. ❀.

Medicago falcata L. **Yellow Medick, Sickle Medick.** ¶Usually procumbent; flo. $\frac{1}{2}$ in., yellow; pod sickle shaped, downy. On dry sand and gravel, Norfolk, Suffolk, Cambridgeshire, etc. Flo. June–July. ❀.

Medicago lupulina L. **Black Medick.** ¶Procumbent; flo. $\frac{1}{8}$ in., yellow, in small oval spikes; pods very small, netted circular, becoming black. In pastures, etc., very common. Flo. May–Aug. ❀.

PLATE 22

Medicago polymorpha L. **Fimbriate Medick.** *M. denticulata* Willd., *M. hispida* Gaertn. ¶Stem prostrate; stipules laciniate; flo. yellow, 1–5 on peduncle; pods netted, coiled, with spines usually long. On S. and E. coasts, introduced inland. Flo. May–Aug. ❀.

Medicago arabica (L.) Huds. **Spotted Medick.** *M. maculata* Sibth. ¶Leaflets usually with dark spot; stipules toothed; pods with 3–5 coils and curved spines. In pastures, mostly in E. and S. counties. Flo. May–Aug. ❀.

Medicago minima (L.) Bartal. **Small Medick.** ¶Prostrate, downy; leaves small; stipules subentire; peduncles very short; pods coiled and spinous. Sandy places in S.E. and E. England, introduced elsewhere, rare. Flo. May–July. ❀.

Melilotus altissima Thuill. **Yellow Melilot.** *M. officinalis* (Lam.) Hayne. ¶Stems erect, 2–3 ft; leaflets oblong, $\frac{3}{4}$ in.; petals all equal; pods acute, hairy. In fields and roadsides, S. England to S.E. Scotland. Flo. June–Aug. ❀.

Melilotus officinalis (L.) Pall. **Ribbed Melilot.** *M. arvensis* Wallr. ¶Similar to *M. altissima*, but wing petals and standard longer than keel, pale yellowish; pods mucronate, ribbed. Common on cultivated and waste land, not native. Flo. July–Sept. �.

Melilotus alba Medic. **White Melilot.** ¶More slender, 2–3 ft; flo. white; standard petal longer than keel or wing; pod netted. On cultivated waste land, not native. Flo. June–Aug. ✻.

Melilotus indica (L.) All. **Small Melilot.** *M. parviflora* Desf. ¶Plant small in all its parts; flo. small, pale yellow; standard longer than other petals; pods globular, netted. In waste places. Flo. July–Sept.

Trifolium ornithopodioides L. **Fenugreek.** *Trigonella ornithopodioides* (L.) DC. ¶Prostrate, glabrous; leaves trifoliate; flo. pink and white, 1–3 on peduncle; pod twice length of calyx. On sandy heaths mostly near the sea, local. Flo. June–Aug. ✻ on plate 21.

Trifolium subterraneum L. **Subterranean Clover.** ¶Stems prostrate, hairy; leaflets obcordate; flo. few, pale; sterile calyces adapted as anchors to bury pods. On dry pastures, mostly S. England. Flo. May–June. ✻.

Trifolium pratense L. **Red Clover.** ¶Leaves often white blotched; heads subsessile between leaves with broad stipules; flo. pale rose. In pastures, abundant. Flo. May–Sept. ✻.

Trifolium medium L. **Zigzag Clover.** ¶Leaflets longer; stipules linear, green, tapering; heads peduncled from opposite leaves; flo. deeper colour. In pastures, especially on clay soils. Flo. June–Sept. ✻.

Trifolium ochroleucon Huds. **Cream-coloured Clover.** ¶Pubescent; leaflets obovate; stipule tips subulate; flo. cream coloured; calyx tube ribbed, teeth subulate, lowest longest. On gravel and clay in E. counties, local. Flo. June–Aug. ✻.

Trifolium squamosum L. **Teasel-headed Clover.** *T. maritimum* Huds. ¶Leaf stipules long, tapering; heads shortly peduncled, pink; calyx teeth small in flo. becoming enlarged, foliaceous, spinescent, lowest longest, 3 veined. By the sea, S. and E. England, S. Wales. Flo. June–Aug. ✻.

Trifolium incarnatum L. **Crimson Clover.** ¶Stem with spreading hairs; leaflets obovate; calyx very hairy; flo. deep crimson. A fodder crop, persisting on roadsides, not native. Flo. June–Aug. ✻.

Trifolium molinerii Balb. ex Hornem. **Large Lizard Clover.** ¶Stem with appressed hairs; leaflets obcordate; flo. pinkish white; calyx spreading in fruit. In short grass on Lizard Head, Cornwall, and Jersey, native. Flo. June–July. ✻.

Trifolium stellatum L. **Starry-headed Clover.** ¶Stems short; leaves and ovate stipules softly hairy; heads globose, stalked; flo. small cream; calyx enlarged in fr., spreading, star-like. On shingle at Shoreham, Sussex, naturalized from S. Europe.

Trifolium arvense L. **Hare's-foot Clover.** ¶Stems ascending, hairy; leaflets narrow; heads oblong, stalked; flo. small, white, immersed in long, pink hairs of calyx. Sandy places. Flo. July–Sept. ✻.

Trifolium bocconei Savi. ¶Erect, 2–4 in.; heads ovate, terminal, often in pairs; stipules and calyx teeth subulate; flo. small, whitish. Lizard Head, Cornwall, and Jersey. Flo. July. ✻.

Trifolium striatum L. **Soft Clover.** ¶Leaflets silky with straight veins; stipules broad, striate; heads sessile; calyx ventricose, ribbed; flo. rose-pink. Sandy fields, often by sea. Flo. June. ⚥.

Trifolium scabrum L. **Rough Clover.** ¶Procumbent; leaflets pubescent, veins curved; heads sessile; flo. white; calyx tube cylindrical, teeth spreading in fr. On dry sandy places, mostly near the sea. Flo. May–July. ⚥.

Trifolium glomeratum L. **Flat-headed Clover.** ¶Leaves glabrous; heads axillary, semi-globose; flo. rose-pink; calyx teeth very acute, reflexed. On sand and gravel near S. and E. coasts. Flo. June. ⚥.

Trifolium suffocatum L. **Suffocated Clover.** ¶Stems short, nearly buried in sand; leaf petioles long; flo. heads sessile, often confluent; calyx teeth recurved. In sand on S. and E. coasts, local and rare. Flo. July–Aug. ⚥.

Trifolium strictum L. **Upright Clover.** ¶Erect, 2–6 in.; leaflets narrow, toothed; stipules broad; heads globose, peduncled; flo. pink; calyx ribbed. Lizard Head, Cornwall, and Jersey. Flo. June. ⚥.

Trifolium hybridum* L. **Alsike Clover. ¶Plant large, spreading, up to 3 ft; leaflets toothed; heads peduncled, ¾ in. wide; flo. pink and white, drooping over fr. A survival from cultivation, naturalized on roadsides. Flo. June–Aug. ⚥.

Trifolium repens L. **White** or **Dutch Clover.** ¶Closely creeping and rooting; leaf petioles long; heads long stalked; petals white or rosy, persistent, drooping over the fr. Flo. May–Oct. ⚥.

Trifolium occidentale D. E. Coombe. ¶Similar to *T. repens* from which it differs in its shorter stems, dark green, smaller leaflets without blotchy markings, fewer lateral veins, fewer-flowered heads and creamy white (never pinkish) flo. Dry warm rocks, pastures and sand dunes near the sea, Scilly Isles, W. Cornwall, and Channel Islands. Flo. March–June.

PLATE 23

Trifolium fragiferum L. **Strawberry-headed Clover.** ¶Creeping and rooting; leaves and heads long stalked; flo. pink; calyx of 2 lips, upper lip enlarging and covering fr. On stiff soils, mostly S. and E. England. Flo. July–Aug. ⚥.

Trifolium resupinatum* L. **Reversed Clover. ¶Slender, 4–9 in.; leaflets narrow, obovate; flo. small, pink, upside down; calyx inflated, woolly. Waste places and docksides, not native. Flo. July.

Trifolium aureum Poll. **Large Hop Trefoil.** *T. agrarium* auct. ¶Mid leaflet sessile; flo. up to 50 in head, bright yellow; style as long as pod. Naturalized in fields and roadsides, frequent in Scotland. ⚥.

Trifolium campestre Schreb. **Hop Trefoil.** *T. procumbens* auct. ¶Mid leaflet stalked; flo. yellow, up to 40 in head, standard deflexed; style shorter than pod. In pastures, common. Flo. June–Aug. ⚥.

Trifolium dubium Sibth. **Lesser Yellow Trefoil.** *T. minus* Sm. ¶Mid leaflet stalked; flo. yellow, up to 12 in head; standard folded over pod; style shorter than pod. Pastures and banks, common. Flo. June–Aug. ⚥.

Trifolium micranthum Viv. **Least Yellow Trefoil.** *T. filiforme* L. ¶Very slender; mid leaflet sessile; flo. 2–6, yellow; standard narrow and deeply notched; peduncle filiform. Sandy soil, chiefly S. England and Wales. Flo. June–July. ⚥.

Anthyllis vulneraria L. **Kidney Vetch.** ¶Stem and pinnate leaves silky; flo. usually yellow; heads in pairs; calyx woolly; pod small, 1 seeded. On calcareous and sandy soils and sea cliffs. Flo. June–Aug. ✿.
Var. *coccinea* L. ¶Small, with dark red flowers. Seaside. ✿.

Lotus corniculatus L. **Bird's-foot Trefoil.** ¶Decumbent; stipules ovate like leaflets; flo. bright yellow, 5–8 in head; calyx teeth erect, appressed in bud. Common everywhere. Flo. June–Aug. ✿.

Lotus tenuis Waldst. & Kit. ex Willd. **Narrow-leaved Bird's-foot Trefoil.** ¶Stems ascending, long and slender; leaflets and stipules linear; flo. 3–4 in head; calyx teeth erect. Stiff soils, absent or rare in N. Flo. June–Sept. ✿.

Lotus uliginosus Schkuhr. **Marsh Bird's-foot Trefoil.** *L. majus* auct. *L. pedunculatus* auct., non Cav. ¶Stoloniferous and tall; leaflets and stipules larger, ovate; flo. 6–10 in head; calyx teeth spreading in bud. Wet meadows and bogs, common. Flo. July–Sept. ✿. When branching in peat, less tall; leaflets smaller; standard petal very red backed and red veined. ✿.

Lotus hispidus Desf. ex DC. **Hairy Bird's-foot Trefoil.** ¶Plant small, hairy throughout; flo. 2–4 together; standard petal narrow; pod short and broad. On sea cliffs, Cornwall to Hampshire, Pembrokeshire and S. Ireland. Flo. July–Aug. ✿.

Lotus angustissimus L. **Long-fruited Bird's-foot.** ¶Prostrate; peduncles short; flo. 1–2, yellow (fading green); standard wide; pod narrow, 1 in. long. Near the sea, Cornwall to Kent and Channel Islands, introduced inland. Flo. July–Aug. ✿.

* *Tetragonolobus maritimus* (L.) Roth. *Lotus siliquosus* L. ¶Leaflets 3; peduncles exceeding leaves; flo. orange, 1 in. long; pod winged. Naturalized chiefly in Thames area (native as near as Pas de Calais).

Oxytropis halleri Bunge. *O. uralensis* auct. ¶Leaves 2–3 in., pinnate, leaflets acute; flo. pale mauve; pod abruptly pointed. Rocks up to 2000 ft in Scotland, local. Flo. June–July. ✿.

Oxytropis campestris (L.) DC. ¶Leaves 6 in., leaflets blunt; flo. yellow, touched with mauve; pod tapering. On rocks, 2000 ft in Perthshire and Angus, very rare. Flo. June–July. ✿.

PLATE 24

Astragalus danicus Retz. **Purple Milk-vetch.** ¶Erect, 2–6 in., pubescent; leaves pinnate; stipules connate; flo. erect; purple pods erect. Calcareous soils, Gloucestershire, Wiltshire and Chilterns to E. Scotland. Flo. June. ✿.

Astragalus alpinus L. **Alpine Milk-vetch.** ¶Prostrate, slender, elongate; leaf stipules free; flo. horizontal, whitish, purple tipped; pods pendulous. Rocks 2500 ft, Highlands of Scotland, rare. Flo. July. ✿.

Astragalus glycyphyllos L. **Wild Liquorice, Milk-vetch.** ¶Stems stout, spreading 2–3 ft; leaflets large; flo. greenish white; pods large and curved. On calcareous soils, local. Flo. June–Sept. ✿.

Ornithopus perpusillus L. **Least Bird's-foot.** ¶Stems slender; leaves pinnate; peduncle with leaf at top; flo. white, veined red, small; pod knotted. On sand and gravel, rare in N. Flo. May–July. ✿.

Ornithopus pinnatus (Mill.) Druce. *O. ebracteatus* Brot. ¶Stems slender; leaflets fewer, 3–4 pairs; peduncle without leaf at apex; flo. slightly larger, 6–8 mm., yellow. Scilly Isles and Channel Islands. Flo. July–Aug. ✄.

Coronilla varia L. **Crown Vetch.** ¶Spreading plant, 1–2 ft; leaves pinnate, leaflets oblong; peduncles long; flo. many, white and purplish; calyx teeth small; pod slender. Alien. Flo. June.

Hippocrepis comosa L. **Horseshoe Vetch.** ¶Slender, spreading, subglabrous plant; leaves pinnate; peduncles long; flo. yellow, deflexed; pod of crescent-shaped joints. Calcareous hills. Flo. May–Aug. ✄.

Onobrychis viciifolia Scop. **Sainfoin.** *O. sativa* Lam. ¶Erect, 1–2 ft; leaves long and pinnate; peduncle long; flo. in conical raceme, pink with darker veins; pod 1 seeded. Possibly native on the chalk, introduced on other soils. Flo. June–Aug. ✄.

Vicia hirsuta (L.) Gray. **Hairy Tare.** ¶Slender, 1–2 ft; leaflets narrow, 6–9 pairs; tendrils branched; peduncles $\frac{3}{4}$ in.; flo. small, pale mauve; pod hairy, 2 seeded. Common. Flo. May–Aug. ✄.

Vicia tetrasperma (L.) Schreb. **Smooth Tare.** ¶Leaflets 4–6 pairs, obtuse; peduncle 1–2 flowered; pod glabrous, 4 seeded. In grassy places and borders of thickets. Flo. May–Aug. ✄.

Vicia tenuissima (Bieb.) Schinz & Thell. **Slender Tare.** *V. gracilis* Lois., non Soland. ¶Leaflets 3–4 pairs, linear, acute; peduncle 1–4 flowered; flo. $\frac{1}{4}$ in.; pod 5–8 seeded. In grassy places and arable fields in S. England, local. Flo. June–Aug. ✄.

Vicia cracca L. **Tufted Vetch.** ¶Climbing, 2–6 ft; tendrils branched; stipules semi-sagittate; calyx gibbous; leaves sometimes silky. In hedges and thickets. Flo. June–Aug. ✄.

Vicia orobus DC. **Wood Bitter Vetch.** ¶Erect, stout, 1–2 ft; tendrils o; leaflets hairy; peduncle short; flo. white and purplish. In rocky woods, local. Flo. May–June. ✄.

Vicia sylvatica L. **Wood Vetch.** ¶Climbing, 2–6 ft; tendrils branched; lower stipules lunate, toothed. In rocky woods and sea cliffs, local. Flo. June–Sept. ✄.

Vicia sepium L. **Bush Vetch.** ¶Climbing, 1–3 ft; flo. head sessile; stipules semi-sagittate; pod glabrous. In hedges and grassy borders of thickets, very common. Flo. April–Oct. ✄.

PLATE 25

Vicia lutea L. **Yellow Vetch.** ¶Prostrate, tufted, 6–18 in.; flo. solitary; pod hairy; stipules triangular. On sea coasts, introduced inland, rare. Flo. June–Aug. ✄.

Vicia sativa L. **Common Vetch.** ¶Stout, 6–18 in.; flo. $\frac{3}{4}$ in., usually in pairs; pod erect 2–3 in. Naturalized in cultivated ground and roadsides. Flo. May–July. ✄.

Vicia angustifolia L. **Narrow-leaved Vetch.** ¶Fairly stout; leaflets narrowly oblong; flo. $\frac{1}{2}$–$\frac{3}{4}$ in., often 2 together; calyx gibbous; pods $1\frac{1}{2}$–2 in., spreading, bursting the calyx. On dry banks, meadows and grassy waste places. Flo. May–Sept. ✄.
Var. *bobartii* (E. Forst.) Koch. ¶Plant more slender; leaflets linear; flo. solitary; pod 1–$1\frac{1}{2}$ in., not bursting the calyx. A common form in S. and S.W. England, but many plants are intermediate.

Vicia lathyroides L. **Spring Vetch.** ¶Slender, pubescent, 3–8 in.; flo. solitary, $\frac{1}{4}$–$\frac{1}{3}$ in., calyx not gibbous at base, funnel shaped; leaflets obtuse, mucronate, $\frac{1}{4}$–$\frac{1}{3}$ in., pods $\frac{1}{2}$–1 in. In gravelly and sandy places, local. Flo. April–June. ❄.

Vicia bithynica L. **Bithynian Vetch.** ¶Perennial, 1–2 ft; leaflets ovate or linear; pod reticulate, hairy. In bushy places and sea cliffs, local. Flo. July–Aug. ❄.

Lathyrus aphaca (L.) L. **Yellow Vetchling.** ¶Stipules very large, leaf-like; leaflets 0; peduncle usually 1, sometimes 2 flowered. In dry calcareous sandy fields, mostly in S. England. Flo. May–Aug. ❄.

Lathyrus nissolia L. **Grass Vetchling.** ¶Stipules minute; petioles linear, leaf-like. In bushy and grassy places, local. Flo. May–June. ❄.

*Lathyrus hirsutus L. **Hairy Vetchling.** ¶1–2 ft; peduncle 2 flowered; leaflets 1 pair, linear-lanceolate; flower pale blue and crimson. In cultivated ground, Essex and Surrey, etc., not native. Flo. June–July.

Lathyrus pratensis L. **Yellow Meadow Vetchling.** ¶Stem angular 2–3 ft, not winged; leaflets 1 pair. Common in hedges and field borders. Flo. June–Sept. ❄.

*Lathyrus tuberosus L. **Tuberous Vetchling.** ¶Stem angled; leaflets obovate; peduncle 2–5 flowered; roots tuberous. In fields about Fyfield, Essex, and elsewhere, not native. Flo. June–Aug. ❄.

Lathyrus sylvestris L. **Wild Pea.** ¶Stem 3–6 ft, winged; leaflets large, sword-like; stipules large, semi-sagittate. In woods and especially on wet sea cliffs. Flo. June–Aug. ❄.

*Lathyrus latifolius L. **Everlasting Pea.** ¶Leaflets large, elliptic, glaucous; flo. 1 in.; stipules broad. On railways banks, etc., not native.

Lathyrus palustris L. **Marsh Pea.** ¶Stem winged, 2–3 ft; leaflets 2–3 pairs, lanceolate, with tendrils. In fens and boggy meadows, rare. Flo. June–Aug. ❄.

Lathyrus maritimus (L.) Fr. **Sea Pea.** *L. japonicus* Bigel.
Subsp. *maritimus.* ¶Stem angular; leaflets 2–3 pairs, oval; stipules large, ovate, hastate. On shingle sea beaches, local and rare, S. and E. England and S. Wales. Flo. June–Aug. ❄.
Subsp. *acutifolius* (Bab.) Pedersen. ¶Stem slender, straggling; leaflets elliptical-lanceolate. On shingle sea beaches, very rare, Shetland.

Lathyrus montanus Bernh. **Bitter Vetch.** *L. macrorrhizus* Wimm., *Orobus tuberosus* L. ¶Stem winged; leaflets 2–3 pairs; peduncle 2–4 flowered; stipules semi-sagittate. In woods and thickets, widespread but absent from much of E. England. Flo. May–Aug. ❄.

Lathyrus niger (L.) Bernh. **Black Bitter Vetch.** *Orobus niger* L. ¶Stem branched, not winged; leaflets 3–6 pairs; peduncle many flowered; stipules linear subulate. In rocky woods in Scotland, nearly extinct.

ROSACEAE   **PLATE 26**

*Prunus laurocerasus L. **Cherry Laurel.** ¶Small tree; leaves evergreen; obovate-acuminate, dark green, very glossy; flo. many in erect racemes; petals white; fr. ovoid, purple-black. Planted in woods and copses where it sometimes regenerates. Flo. April–June.

*_Prunus mahaleb_ L. ¶Small tree; leaves orbicular to broad-ovate, rounded or sub-cordate at base, pubescent on midrib beneath, otherwise glabrous; flo. fragrant, in 6–10-flowered racemes; petals white; fr. ovoid, black. Planted in woods and copses where it sometimes regenerates. Flo. April–May.

*_Prunus serotina_ Ehrh. **Rum Cherry.**¶Small tree, similar to _P. padus_, but with cylindrical slender racemes; flo. smaller on shorter peduncles; petals white; fr. ovoid, black; calyx persistent. Planted in woods and gardens where it sometimes regenerates; also bird-sown into other habitats. Flo. April–June.

Prunus spinosa L. **Blackthorn, Sloe.** ¶Shrub with many stout thorns; twigs black; leaves appearing after flo. Common in scrub, open woods and hedges. Flo. March–April. ❀.

*_Prunus domestica_ L. **Wild Plum.**

Subsp. _domestica_. ¶Large shrub or small tree without thorns; leaves large; petals greenish in bud; fr. oblong. Frequent in hedges, often near houses, not native. Flo. March–May. ❀.

Subsp. _insititia_ (L.) C. K. Schneid. **Bullace.** _P. insititia_ L. ¶Shrub with few or no thorns; twigs brown, pubescent; leaves appearing with the flowers; fr. globose. Frequent in hedges. Flo. March–May. ❀.

Prunus avium (L.) L. **Gean, Wild Cherry.**¶Small tree; leaves acuminate; flo. umbellate; calyx tube constricted; petals obovate; fr. red. Common in woods and hedges. Flo. April–May. ❀.

*_Prunus cerasus_ L. **Sour Cherry.** ¶Shrub with suckers; flo. umbellate; calyx crenate, tube not constricted; petals orbicular; fr. red, sour. In hedges in many places. Not native. Flo. April–May. ❀.

Prunus padus L. **Bird Cherry.** ¶Small tree; leaves acuminate; flo. smaller, in long often drooping raceme; fr. black, bitter. In woods, N. England and Scotland, introduced elsewhere. Flo. May. ❀.

*_Spiraea salicifolia_ L. ¶Shrub 4 ft; leaves simple, willow-like; flo. pink, in a dense panicle, planted and occasionally naturalized. Flo. July–Aug.

Filipendula ulmaria (L.) Maxim. **Meadow Sweet.** _Spiraea ulmaria_ L. ¶Herb 2–4 ft; leaves large, pinnate, usually white beneath; flo. cream. Common on wet meadows, ditches and riversides. Flo. June–Aug. ❀.

Filipendula vulgaris Moench. **Dropwort.** _F. hexapetala_ Gilib., _Spiraea filipendula_ L. ¶Herb 1 ft; leaves mostly radical; leaflets many, narrow, much cut; petals often 6 red outside. In chalk and limestone pastures. Flo. May–July. ❀.

Sanguisorba officinalis L. **Great Burnet.** ¶1½–3 ft, branched; flo. heads ovoid-oblong, crimson; stamens hardly exserted; fr. smooth, 4 winged. In damp meadows, local. Flo. June–Sept. ❀.

Sanguisorba minor Scop.

Subsp. _minor_. **Salad Burnet, Lesser Burnet.** _Poterium sanguisorba_ L. ¶1–1½ ft; stem leaves few; heads globose; lower flo. male; stamens long exserted; fr. finely reticulate, with 4 even ridges. On dry calcareous pastures, railway banks, etc. Flo. May–Aug. ❀.

Subsp. _muricata_ (Gremli) Brig. _Poterium polygamum_ Waldst. & Kit. _P. muricatum_ Spach. ¶Larger than subsp. _minor_, 1½–2½ ft; stem leaves several with narrow leaflets; heads often ovoid; fr. coarsely rugose with 4 irregular ridges. Naturalized in borders of fields, etc. Flo. May–Aug.

Acaena anserinifolia (J. R. & G. Forst.) Druce. ¶Fr. with 4 long barbed spines. Brought in sheep's wool from Australia and naturalized in some places. Flo. June–Aug.

Agrimonia eupatoria L. **Common Agrimony.** ¶Fr. deeply grooved throughout, lower spines spreading. Common on roadsides and waste ground. Flo. June–Aug. ⚥.

Agrimonia procera Wallr. **Scented Agrimony.** *A. odorata* auct. ¶Leaves stouter, glandular scented; fr. slightly grooved, lower spines deflexed. Waste places on heavy soils, less common. Flo. June–Aug.

Aremonia agrimonoides (L.) DC. *Agrimonia agrimonoides* L. ¶Differs from *Agrimonia eupatoria* in having flo. in few-flowered cymes, and receptacles without spines. Naturalized in woods in Scotland.

Aphanes arvensis L. **Parsley Piert.** *Alchemilla arvensis* (L.) Scop. ¶Lobes of stipules triangular, ovate, as long as broad; fr. sepals open. Common on bare soil in dry places. Flo. April–Oct. ⚥.

Aphanes microcarpa (Boiss. & Reut.) Rothm. ¶Lobes of stipules twice as long as broad; fr. sepals closed. Common, especially on acid soils. Flo. April–Oct.

Alchemilla alpina L. **Alpine Lady's Mantle.** ¶Leaflets all separate, white and silky beneath. Common on mountain pastures and rock crevices, N. England and Scotland. Flo. June–Aug. ⚥.

Alchemilla conjuncta Bab. ¶Leaflets connate at base, white and silky beneath. On rocks in Glen Clova and Arran, introduced elsewhere. Flo. June–July. ⚥.

Alchemilla glaucescens Wallr. *A. minor* auct. ¶Stems and petioles with dense silky hairs; leaves hairy, basal sinus closed. On limestone in Yorkshire, Ross, Sutherland and Leitrim. Flo. June–Sept.

Alchemilla filicaulis Buser.
Subsp. *filicaulis* ¶Similar to above, but upper stem and pedicels glabrous; leaves less hairy, stipules purplish. In mountain pastures. Flo. June–Sept.
Subsp. *vestita* (Buser) M. E. Bradshaw. *Alchemilla vestita* (Buser) Raunk. ¶Stems and petioles with spreading hairs; leaves hairy, basal sinus open; stipules purplish. Fairly common in natural pastures. Flo. June–Sept. ⚥.

Alchemilla subcrenata Buser. ¶Similar to *A. filicaulis* but stipules brownish not purplish; leaves undulate with broad lobes and coarse broad teeth. Grassland, Upper Teesdale and Weardale. Flo. June–Sept.

Alchemilla minima Walters. ¶Plant small; leaves very small, hairy on folds and on veins beneath, basal sinus open; stipules brown. On limestone, Ingleborough, Yorkshire. Flo. June–Sept.

Alchemilla monticola Opiz. *A. pastoralis* Buser. ¶Plant medium; stem and petioles with spreading hairs; pedicels glabrous; leaves orbicular, densely hairy on both surfaces, basal sinus closed. Pastures in Upper Teesdale and Weardale, introduced elsewhere. Flo. June–Sept.

Alchemilla acutiloba Opiz. ¶Lower stem with spreading hairs, glabrous above; leaf lobes with straight sides. In Upper Teesdale. Flo. June–Sept.

Alchemilla xanthochlora Rothm. ¶Plant large; stem and petioles with spreading hairs; pedicels and upper sides of leaves glabrous, lobes not overlapping. Fairly common. Flo. June–Sept.

Alchemilla glomerulans Buser. ¶Stem and petioles with appressed hairs; leaves hairy, lobes overlapping. On wet mountain rocks, Teesdale and mid Scotland northwards. Flo. June–Sept.

Alchemilla glabra Neygenf. *A. alpestris* auct. ¶Plant often large; lowest nodes of stem with appressed hairs, glabrous above; leaf lobes rather straight sided, with middle teeth on each side larger. Meadows, open woods, mountains, chiefly in the N. Flo. June–Sept. ❀.

Alchemilla wichurae (Buser) Stefánsson. *A. acutidens* auct. ¶Plant small; stems somewhat more hairy than in *A. glabra*; leaves orbicular in outline, basal sinus closed or nearly so. Grassland on basic soils, Yorkshire to Sutherland. Flo. June–Sept.

PLATE 27

**Alchemilla mollis* (Buser) Rothm. ¶Plant robust, very hairy; leaves shallowly lobed, epicalyx equalling the calyx. Garden escape. Naturalized in grassy places. Flo. June–Sept.

**Alchemilla tyttantha* Juz. *A. multiflora* Buser ex Rothm. ¶Plant robust; leaves hairy on both surfaces; stem with downward directed spreading hairs; flo. small, glabrous. Garden escape. Well naturalized in S. Scotland. Flo. June–Sept.

Sibbaldia procumbens L. *Potentilla sibbaldii* Haller f. ¶Stem woody, depressed; petals small, inconspicuous, yellow; leaves bluish green. On mountain-tops and rocks chiefly in N. Scotland. Flo. July. ❀.

Potentilla palustris (L.) Scop. **Marsh Cinquefoil.** *Comarum palustre* L. ¶Stem 18 in., from creeping base; leaflets oblong; flo. red-purple. In fens, marshy meadows and wet moorlands. Flo. June–July. ❀.

Potentilla fruticosa L. **Shrubby Cinquefoil.** ¶Shrub, 3 ft, silky; flo. yellow, partly one sexual. Very local, Teesdale, Lake District and W. Ireland. Flo. June–July. ❀.

Potentilla sterilis (L.) Garcke. **Barren Strawberry.** *P. fragariastrum* Pers. ¶Leaflets 3, silky beneath; flo. white; receptacle hairy. Common on heaths, banks and woodland borders. Flo. Feb.–May. ❀.

Potentilla rupestris L. **Rock Cinquefoil.** ¶Stems 1–2 ft, erect; leaves large and pinnate; flo. ¾–1 in., white. On rocks in Radnorshire and Montgomeryshire, rare. Flo. May–June. ❀.

Potentilla anserina L. **Silverweed.** ¶Stoloniferous; leaves pinnate, soft and very silky; flo. solitary. Common in waste ground, roadsides and damp pastures. Flo. July–Aug. ❀.

Potentilla argentea L. **Hoary Cinquefoil.** ¶Stems decumbent, woody; leaflets 5, slender, digitate, white beneath. On dry sandy grassland, local. Flo. June–July. ❀.

*Potentilla recta L. **Upright Cinquefoil.** ¶Stems erect, stout, 1–2 ft; leaves long petioled; leaflets 5, large, oblong; flo. 1 in. wide, yellow. A garden escape. Flo. June–July.

**Potentilla norvegica* L. ¶Stems 12–18 in., branched above; leaflets 3; sepals hairy; petals small. Introduced in many places. Flo. June–Oct. ❀.

**Potentilla intermedia* L. ¶Stem ascending; lower leaflets 5 obovate, upper 3 oblong; petals yellow; achenes rugose. Introduced from Europe. Flo. June–Sept.

Potentilla tabernaemontani Aschers. **Spring Cinquefoil.** *P. verna* auct. ¶Stem prostrate, rooting, branched below middle; leaflets $\frac{1}{2}$ in., flo. $\frac{1}{2}$ in., rather pale yellow; achenes smooth. On dry calcareous rocks and grass, local. Flo. April–June. ❊.

Potentilla crantzii (Crantz) G. Beck ex Fritsch. **Alpine Cinquefoil.** *P. alpestris* auct. ¶Stem ascending, branched above middle; leaflets 1 in.; flo. 1 in. achenes smooth; petals bright yellow, sometimes with an orange spot. On mountain rocks, local, from N. Wales northwards. Flo. June–July. ❊.

Potentilla erecta (L.) Räusch. **Common Tormentil.** *P. tormentilla* Stokes. ¶Rootstock sub-tuberous; stem slender, supported by other growth; cauline leaves sessile; radical leaves vernal only; petals 4. Abundant on heaths, moors and mountains, especially on acid soils. Flo. June–Sept. ❊.

Potentilla anglica Laichard. **Procumbent Cinquefoil.** *P. procumbens* Sibth. ¶Stems decumbent, rooting in autumn; radical leaves persistent; cauline leaves cuneate, with $\frac{1}{4}$ in. petiole; flo. $\frac{3}{4}$ in.; petals 5 or 4. On heaths, banks and wood borders, mostly on basic soil. Flo. June–Sept. ❊.

Potentilla reptans L. **Creeping Cinquefoil.** ¶Stem long, creeping, rooting, unbranched; leaflets mostly obovate, cauline similar; petals 5. On hedge banks, waste and cultivated land, on basic soil. Flo. June–Sept. ❊.

Fragaria vesca L. **Wild Strawberry.** ¶Runners long and slender; lateral leaflets sessile; receptacle covered by projecting achenes. Common on grassy banks and wood borders, especially on calcareous soil. Flo. April–July. ❊.

*Fragaria moschata Duchesne. **Hautbois Strawberry.** *F. elatior* Ehrh. ¶Runners few or none; lateral leaflets shortly stalked; flo. 1 in.; receptacle bare at base. Not native.

*Fragaria × ananassa Duchesne. **Garden Strawberry.** *F. chiloensis* auct. ¶Fruiting receptacle covered by achenes embedded in fr.; flo. $1\frac{1}{2}$ in. Not native.

PLATE 28

There are nearly 400 species of *Rubus* in this country, and the distribution of these both in this country and on the Continent is becoming better known. A valuable handbook on this genus by the late Mr Wm. Watson has been published. But in some cases accurate determination of specimens requires the experience of those who have made a special study of the genus. It is not our intention in this present work to figure or to describe more than about a dozen samples of leading groups, in order to illustrate the kind of gradation that is found throughout the genus.

Although the desired handbook has been published, this should not invalidate our small contribution to an understanding of the genus, because in drawing the figures here shown we had valuable help from the late Mr Wm. Watson himself. He selected and posted most of the samples illustrated, and he has very kindly written the following descriptions of the selected species. He is, however, not responsible for the specimen figured as *R. caesius*, and he points out that the specimen was a hybrid. The clothing of the stems is an essential feature in determining the species, and unfortunately the finer details of this clothing are on the borderline of visibility, and are not easily figured or reproduced.

Even in the few species chosen it will be observed that in the sub-genus *Eubatus* there is a gradation. We start with the *Suberecti*, which have no stalked glands or pricklets. Indeed, the first sample has the panicle almost unarmed. Then we come to a gradual increase of prickles, which are sometimes all equal or confined to the angles of the stem. And the series continues through an increase of stalked glands, acicles and pricklets to forms which have them all very numerous, unequal and distributed all over the stem. And the last sample of this sub-genus differs also in having only 3 leaflets to each leaf instead of 5–7.

The samples chosen for illustration are not always the same as those given in edition 1 of the British Flora by Messrs Clapham, Tutin and Warburg. Of those which are different *R. sulcatus* is near to *R. nessensis*, op. cit., p. 466. *R. silvaticus* is near to *R. pyramidalis*, p. 469. *R. euryanthemus* is near to *R. pallidus*, p. 477.

Sub-genus CYLACTIS

1. *Rubus saxatilis* L. ¶On wet limestone. Fr. red. ❀ on plate 29.

Sub-genus CHAMAEMORUS

2. *Rubus chamaemorus* L. **Cloud Berry.** ¶On elevated moors. Fr. ultimately amber. ❀ on plate 29.

Sub-genus IDAEOBATUS

3. *Rubus idaeus* L. **Raspberry.** ¶In woods and heaths. Fr. felted, red or amber. ❀.

Sub-genus EUBATUS. Fruit black.

    x Leaves 3–5 nate, or 3–7 nate. Groups 4–11.
    (*a*) Stem without stalked glands or pricklets. 4–7.

Section *Suberecti*

4. *Rubus sulcatus* Vest ex Tratt. ¶Stem tall, erect, furrowed; root creeping; panicle almost unarmed. ❀.

Section *Sylvatici*

5. *Rubus carpinifolius* Weihe & Nees. ¶Stem arching with strong yellow prickles; panicle racemose in the upper part; sepals patent under the fruit. ❀.

6. *Rubus silvaticus* Weihe & Nees. ¶Prickles small; leaflets narrow. ❀.

Section *Discolores*

7. *Rubus ulmifolius* Schott. *R. discolor* auct. ¶Leaves closely white felted beneath; leaflets convex, usually narrow. Stamens equalling the styles. ❀.

    (*b*) Stem with stalked glands, acicles and pricklets. 8–11.
    (1) Stem prickles subequal, seated on the angles. 8–9.

Section *Vestiti*

8. *Rubus vestitus* Weihe & Nees. ¶Densely hairy all over; prickles long, slender, straight, violet-purple; terminal leaflet round, short pointed and evenly toothed. ❀.

Section *Radulae*

9. *Rubus radula* Weihe ex Boenn. ¶Petals pink, rather small; prickles long and mostly straight; terminal leaflet ovate, gradually acuminate, white felted beneath. ❀.

    (2) Stem prickles unequal, not confined to the angles of the stem; stalked glands and acicles numerous, some rather long and gland tipped. 10–11.

Section *Apiculati*

10. *Rubus euryanthemus* W. C. R. Wats. ¶Petals white, narrow. ❀.

Section *Hystrices*

11. *Rubus dasyphyllus* Rogers. ¶Petals pink; leaves thick, soft beneath, principal teeth turned outwards; stalked glands very long. ❀.

xx Leaves all ternate. Groups 12–13.

Section *Glandulosi*

12. *Rubus bellardii* Weihe & Nees. ¶Petals white; leaflets subequal, regular, elliptical, evenly toothed. ❀.

Sub-genus GLAUCOBATUS

13. *Rubus caesius* L. ¶On wet or calcareous soils. Fr. black, pruinose. The figure represents a hybrid. ❀.

Numbers 7, 8, 11, 13 desiderate or tolerate a loamy, clayey or calcareous soil, the others are more narrowly restricted to soils that are siliceous or peaty or rich in humus.

Rubus saxatilis L. See text for plate 28.

Rubus chamaemorus L. See text for plate 28.

Dryas octopetala L. ¶Pedicel and calyx glandular; petals often 8; style feathery persistent. On basic rocks, local, N. Wales, Teesdale, N. Scotland and Ireland. Flo. June–July. ❀.

Geum urbanum L. **Herb Bennet, Wood Avens.** ¶Flo. erect, yellow; head of achenes sessile; style persistent as a hooked awn. Common in woods, hedges and shady lanes. Flo. June–Sept. ❀.

Geum rivale L. **Water Avens.** ¶Flo. nodding, red; head of achenes stalked; style persistent as a hooked awn. On wet rocks and shady banks, mainly in N. and N.W. Britain, local elsewhere. Flo. May–Sept. ❀.

Geum rivale × *urbanum* occurs occasionally. ❀.

PLATE 30

Rosa pimpinellifolia L. **Burnet Rose.** *R. spinosissima* auct. ¶Stem creeping, with many small straight prickles; leaflets 3–5 pairs; fr. purple. On sand dunes, cliffs and heaths, particularly near the sea. Flo. May–July. ❀.

Rosa rugosa Thunb. ¶Stem very prickly and rough; leaflets 2–4 pairs, elliptic; dark green and rugose above, felted below; flo. large, deep pink to white; fr. large, red; sepals erect, persistent. Commonly planted for hedging and occurring in woods, thickets on heaths and waste ground as a bird-sown introduction. Flo. June–Aug.

Rosa arvensis Huds. **Trailing Rose.** ¶Stem trailing, purplish; flo. white; fr. small; styles united in an exserted column. Common in S. and W., rare in the N. and introduced in Scotland. Flo. June–July. ❀.

Rosa stylosa Desv. **Long-styled Rose.** ¶Stem stout, erect; pedicels long, hispid; disk conical; styles united in an exserted column. On basic soils chiefly in S. England and S. Ireland, locally common. Flo. June–July. ❀.

Rosa canina L. **Dog Rose.** *R. systyla* Bast. ¶Pedicels 1–2 cm., subglabrous; sepals falling early; stigmas conical, narrower than disk. Common. Flo. June–July. ❀.

Rosa dumalis Bechst. **Short-pedicelled Rose.** *R. coriifolia* Fr. *R. afzeliana* auct. *R.*

glauca Vill. ex Lois., non Pourr. ¶Pedicels short, 1 cm., hidden in bracts; sepals persistent; stigmas flat, concealing disk. Common in N. England and Scotland, very rare in S. England. Flo. June–July. ✲.

Rosa obtusifolia Desv. ¶Leaves roundly ovate, pubescent or glandular beneath; pedicels short; sepals short, lobes broad. In England, except the N.W., local. Flo. June–July. ✲.

Rosa tomentosa Sm. **Downy Rose.** ¶Leaves pubescent, often densely so; pedicels up to 2 cm., glandular; sepals constricted at base; flo. 4 cm., pink; disk large, 4–6 times orifice. In hedges, etc., mainly on chalk. Flo. June–July. ✲.

Rosa sherardii Davies. **Northern Downy Rose.** *R. omissa* Déségl. ¶Leaves rather glaucous; pedicels $\frac{1}{2}$–$1\frac{1}{2}$ cm.; sepals short, slightly constricted, persistent; flo. often deep pink; styles villous; disk 3–$3\frac{1}{2}$ times orifice. Frequent in N. Britain, rare in S. Flo. June–July.

Rosa villosa L. **Soft-leaved Rose.** *R. mollis* Sm. ¶Prickles straight and slender; leaflets roundly oval, tomentose; sepals erect, persistent; pedicels short, hispid; fr. globose, hispid; flo. deep pink. Rather common in N. Britain, local in W. Midlands and Wales and introduced in S. England. Flo. June–July. ✲.

Rosa rubiginosa L. **Sweet Briar.** *R. eglanteria* auct. ¶Leaflets roundly oval, very glandular below and scented; pedicels short, glandular, hispid; fr. hispid; sepals persistent; flo. usually deep pink. Mostly on calcareous soils. Flo. June–July. ✲.

Rose micrantha Borrer ex Sm. **Lesser Sweet Briar.** ¶Stems arching; leaflets ovate, glandular beneath; pedicels long, hispid; sepals falling early; flo. pink; styles glabrous. Common in England and Wales, rare in Scotland and Ireland. Flo. June–July. ✲.

Rosa agrestis Savi. **Narrow-leaved Sweet Briar.** *R. sepium* Thuill., non Lam. ¶Stems arching; leaflets narrow, tapering to base; pedicels smooth; styles subglabrous; fr. smooth; sepals falling early. Mostly on calcareous soils, very local. Flo. June–July. ✲.

Rosa elliptica Tausch. *R. inodora* auct. ¶Similar to *R. agrestis*, but stems erect; leaflets obovate, tapering below only; styles hairy; sepals more persistent. Very rare, Somerset to Huntingdonshire.

PLATE 31

Sorbus aucuparia L. **Rowan, Mountain Ash.** *Pyrus aucuparia* (L.) Ehrh. ¶Leaves pinnate, all leaflets separate; flo. many, smaller than in other species. In woods and scrub, etc. on light soils, native in the W. and N., probably introduced, though readily regenerating elsewhere. Flo. May–June. ✲.

Sorbus pseudofennica E. F. Warb. ¶Small tree; leaves ovate-oblong, but some with free basal leaflets. Arran. Flo. May–June.

Sorbus intermedia agg. ¶Leaves elliptic with rounded ascending lobes, felted beneath; veins 7–11 pairs.
    S. arranensis Hedlund. ¶Leaves lobed at base about $\frac{1}{2}$ way to midrib; greyish felted beneath; veins 7–9 pairs; fr. ovoid. Arran. Flo. May–June. ✲.
    S. leyana Wilmott. ¶Leaves broader, cuneate at base; basal lobe nearly $\frac{1}{2}$ way to midrib; petals and fr. a little larger than in previous species. Breconshire. Flo. May–June.

S. minima (A. Ley) Hedlund. **Least White Beam.** *Pyrus minima* A. Ley. ¶Leaves elliptic, twice as long as broad, base lobed about ¼ way to midrib; petals 4 mm.; fr. small, 6–8 mm., subglobose. Limestone crags, Breconshire. Flo. May–June. ✿.

*S. intermedia (Ehrh.) Pers. *Pyrus intermedia* Ehrh. ¶Leaves elliptic, lobed at base ¼–½ way to midrib, yellowish felted beneath; fr. very oblong. Planted, but freely regenerating. Flo. May.

S. anglica Hedlund. **Cheddar White Beam.** *S. mougeotii* Soy.-Will. & Godr. var. *anglica* (Hedlund) C. E. Salmon. ¶Leaves broadly ovate, about 1½ times as long as broad; lobed ⅛–¼ way to midrib, greyish felted beneath; fr. subglobose, with few lenticels. On limestone rocks, Devon to Shropshire and Wales, also in Kerry. Flo. May.

Sorbus aria agg. ¶Leaves ovate or obovate, toothed or slightly lobed, white felted beneath; veins 7–14 pairs.

S. aria (L.) Crantz. *Pyrus aria* (L.) Ehrh. ¶Leaves oval, usually curved to base; veins 10–14 pairs; fr. longer than broad, scarlet; lenticels small. In calcareous woods, S. England, though frequently planted elsewhere. Flo. May–June. ✿.

S. × *thuringiaca* (Ilse) Fritsch. (*S. aria* × *aucuparia*). ¶Leaves oblong, sometimes with 1–3 pairs of free leaflets at base; serrate; green and glabrous above, greyish-green felted beneath; veins 10–12 pairs; fr. subglobose, scarlet; lenticels few, inconspicuous. Sometimes found where the parents grow together, also occurs as a planted tree. Flo. May–June.

S. × *vagensis* Wilmott. (*S. aria* × *torminalis*). ¶Tree, with wide crown and spreading branches; leaves ovate, deeply lobed, with acuminate lobes finely, and sometimes doubly, serrate, teeth small, yellowish green above, greenish-grey felted beneath; fr. brownish, longer than broad. In woods on limestone, Wye Valley. Flo. May–June.

S. leptophylla E. F. Warb. ¶Shrub, similar to *S. aria* but leaves yellow or dark green above; teeth curved on outer margins; veins *c.* 11 pairs. On limestone rocks, Breconshire. Flo. May.

S. wilmottiana E. F. Warb. ¶Shrub or small tree, similar to *S. aria* but leaves bright green above, teeth curved on outer margins; veins *c.* 8–9 pairs; fr. crimson. In woods on limestone, Cheddar Gorge. Flo. May–June.

S. eminens E. F. Warb. ¶Shrub or small tree similar to *S. aria* but leaves bright green above, teeth symmetrical; veins *c.* 10–11 pairs. In woods on limestone, Wye Valley and Avon Gorge. Flo. May–June.

S. hibernica E. F. Warb. **Irish White Beam.** ¶Leaves oval, shortly cuneate at the base; veins 9–11 pairs; teeth triangular, acute, turned outwards; fr. broader than long. In woods on limestone, Ireland. Flo. May.

S. porrigentiformis E. F. Warb. *S. porrigens* Hedlund, pro parte. ¶Leaves obovate, rounded above, tapering below, 1½ times as long as broad, greyish felted beneath; veins 8–10 pairs; fr. broader than long, crimson, with few large lenticels. In woods on limestone S. Devon to Mendips, Wye Valley and Wales. Flo. May–June. ✿.

S. lancastriensis E. F. Warb. ¶Shrub similar to *S. aria* but teeth of leaves symmetrical and pointing outwards; veins *c.* 8–10 pairs; fr. crimson with a number of large lenticels towards the base. On limestone rocks, Lancashire and Westmorland. Flo. May–June.

S. rupicola (Syme) Hedlund. **Rock White Beam.** ¶Leaves obovate, rounded above, length nearly double the breadth, white felted beneath; veins 7–9 pairs; fr. broader than long, with many rather smaller lenticels. On limestone rocks, S. Devon to Scotland and N. and W. Ireland. Flo. May–June.

S. vexans E. F. Warb. ¶Small tree, similar to *S. aria* but leaves obovate, with cuneate base; veins *c.* 8–10 pairs; fr. longer than broad, with few small lenticels. In rocky woods near coast, Somerset and S. Devon. Flo. May.

Sorbus latifolia agg. ¶**Broad-leaved White Beam.** ¶Leaves with triangular lobes; veins 7–9 pairs; fr. orange, subglobose or longer than broad. ✂.

S. bristoliensis Wilmott. ¶Leaves obovate; anthers pink; fr. longer than broad, bright orange, with small lenticels. In rocky woods on limestone, Avon Gorge. Flo. May–June.

S. subcuneata Wilmott. ¶Leaves elliptic, tapered at the base; white felted beneath; anthers cream; fr. subglobose, brownish orange. In open oakwoods, Somerset and Devon. Flo. May–June.

S. devoniensis E. F. Warb. ¶Leaves ovate, round at base, with shallow triangular lobes; greyish-green felted beneath; fr. subglobose. In woods, Devon, E. Cornwall and Ireland. Flo. May–June.

Sorbus torminalis (L.) Crantz. **Wild Service Tree.** *Pyrus torminalis* (L.) Ehrh. ¶Leaves oval, deeply lobed, green beneath; fr. elongated, brown. In woods on clay and limestone in England. Flo. May–June. ✂.

Pyrus pyraster Burgsd. **Pear.** *P. communis* auct. ¶Flo. on very short rachis; petals broad, very concave, white; fr. 2–4 cm., sometimes tapered into stalk. Throughout England, not common. Flo. April–May. ✂.

Pyrus cordata Desv. **Lesser Pear.** ¶Leaves rather small, round, subglabrous; flo. on longer rachis, smaller; petals narrow, obovate, pink; fr. very small, 1–2 cm., obovoid or round. In hedges near Plymouth, very rare. Flo. April–May. ✂.

Malus sylvestris Mill. **Crab Apple.** *Pyrus malus* L. ¶Small tree; flo. in an umbel; styles united below. In woods. Flo. May. ✂.

*Malus domestica Borkh. **Cultivated Apple.** *Malus sylvestris* Mill. subsp. *mitis* (Wallr.) Mansf. *Pyrus malus* L. var. *mitis* Wallr. ¶Similar to *M. sylvestris* but young twigs tomentose, glabrous later; buds hairy; leaves obtuse, pubescent beneath; pedicels, calyx, etc., woolly; fr. largish, sometimes sweet. Naturalized in hedges, woods, etc. Flo. May.

*Mespilus germanica L. **Medlar.** ¶Small thorny tree; stalks pubescent; leaves large; sepals persistent, linear. Naturalized in hedges, mostly in England. Flo. May–June.

Crataegus laevigata (Poir.) DC. **Two-styled Hawthorn.** *C. oxyacanthoides* Thuill. ¶Leaf lobes broader than long, without axillary hairs beneath; styles 2. In woods on heavy soils, S. and E. England, the Midlands, Wales and Ireland; rare in N. and introduced in Scotland. Flo. May–June. ✂.

Crataegus × media Bechst. (*C. laevigata × monogyna*). ¶Hybrids, intermediate between the two species are common where the parent plants grow together.

Crataegus monogyna Jacq. **Common Hawthorn.** ¶Leaf lobes longer than broad, very variable, with hairs in axils beneath, style 1. Common in hedges, etc., though often planted. Flo. May–June. ✂.

Cotoneaster integerrimus Medic. ¶Leaves 1 in. or more, rounded at base; petals erect, pink. On rocks, Great Orme's Head, Caernarvon. Flo. April–June. ✂.

Cotoneaster microphyllus Wall. ex Lindl. ¶Leaves ½ in. or less, obovate; petals white and spreading. Introduced from India. Bird-sown from gardens and naturalized on banks, in chalk pits, etc. Flo. May–June.

Cotoneaster simonsii Bak. ¶Leaves ½ in. or more, green and glabrous above, sparsely pubescent beneath, cuneate at base; petals erect, pink. Bird-sown from gardens and naturalized on cliffs, heaths, etc. Flo. May–July.

Cotoneaster horizontalis Decne. ¶Similar to *C. simonsii*, but procumbent with horizontal spreading stems; leaves small, dark green, glabrous above. Bird-sown from gardens and naturalized on cliffs, old walls, in chalk pits, etc. Flo. May–July.

SAXIFRAGACEAE   **PLATE 32**

Saxifraga oppositifolia L. **Purple Saxifrage.** ¶Stems many, prostrate; leaves many, opposite; flo. rose-purple, solitary. On mountain rocks, mostly in N. Britain. Flo. April–June. ❀.

Saxifraga nivalis L. **Clustered Alpine Saxifrage.** ¶Leaves in basal rosette, broadly obovate; stem naked; flo. in a close head. On higher mountain rocks, mostly in Scotland, rare. Flo. July–Aug. ❀.

Saxifraga stellaris L. **Starry Saxifrage.** ¶Stems with small rosettes of subsessile leaves; sepals reflexed. Common on wet mountain rocks and streamsides. Flo. June–July. ❀.

Saxifraga hirculus L. **Yellow Bog Saxifrage.** ¶Erect, leafy, with prostrate basal branches; lower leaves petiolate; flo. yellow, ovary free. On wet moorland grass, N. England, Scotland and Ireland, rare. ❀.

Saxifraga aizoides L. **Yellow Mountain Saxifrage.** ¶Prostrate with ascending branches; leaves sessile; flo. several, yellow, ovary partly inferior. Common on wet mountain rocks, Wales to N. Scotland and in Ireland. Flo. June–Aug. ❀.

Saxifraga umbrosa L. ¶Leaves oval with obtuse teeth, terminal tooth shorter and broader; petiole shorter than blade, very ciliate. Yorkshire, introduced before 1800.

Saxifraga spathularis Brot. **St Patrick's Cabbage.** *S. umbrosa* auct., non. L. ¶Leaves, oval, with triangular equal teeth; petiole longer than blade, sparsely ciliate. On mountain rocks in Ireland. Flo. June–Aug.

Saxifraga spathularis × *umbrosa* = *S.* × *urbium* D. A. Webb, *S. umbrosa* L. var. *crenatoserrata* Bab. **London Pride.** ¶Leaves subacute, with equal angular teeth; flo. stem less glandular, sterile. ❀.

Saxifraga hirsuta L. *S. geum* L. *S. lactiflora* Pugsl. ¶Leaves orbicular or reniform, cordate, crenate; petiole slender, much longer than blade. On rocks in S.W. Ireland. Flo. May–July. Figure is probably that of *S.* × *polita* auct. = *S. hirsuta* × *spathularis*. ❀.

Saxifraga tridactylites L. **Rue-leaved Saxifrage.** ¶Plant small, annual, glandular; leaves 3–5 lobed, upper entire. On light dry soils and wall tops. Flo. April–June. ❀.

Saxifraga granulata L. **Meadow Saxifrage, Bulbous Saxifrage.** ¶Stem with large bulbils at base; leaves cordate, with round lobes. In meadow grass, in England, except the S.W., where it is an introduction, rare in Wales. Flo. April–June. ❀.

Saxifraga cernua L. **Lesser Bulbous Saxifrage.** ¶Stem erect, with small red bulbils in axils; flo. terminal or none. On rock ledges on mountain tops, Perthshire and Argyll, very rare. Flo. July. ❀.

Saxifraga rivularis L. **Alpine Rivulet Saxifrage.** ¶Stems weak, trailing, ascending in flo.; leaves reniform, 3–7 lobed. On wet rocks on high mountains in Scotland, very rare. Flo. July–Aug. ❀.

Saxifraga cespitosa L. **Tufted Saxifrage.** ¶Plant small, compact; leaf lobes oblong, obtuse; glandular hairs short, dense. On mountain rocks, Wales and Scotland, very rare. Flo. May–July. ❀.

Saxifraga hartii D. A. Webb. ¶Similar to *S. cespitosa*, but plant looser, leaves larger and densely covered with short glandular hairs, lobes subacute; petals larger, pure white. Sea cliffs, Arranmore Island, Donegal. Flo. May–June.

Saxifraga rosacea Moench. **Irish Saxifrage.** ¶Plant rather compact, with erect barren branches, and few longer glandular hairs. On wet mountain rocks, W. Ireland, local. Flo. June–Aug. ❀.

Saxifraga hypnoides L. **Mossy Saxifrage.** ¶Barren branches long and prostrate, often with axillary tufts; leaf lobes acute, aristate. On mountain rocks, Somerset and Wales to N. Scotland, and Ireland. Flo. May–July. ❀.
Var. *platypetala* Sm. ¶Axillary leaf buds few or o; petals broad, contiguous, flat. ❀.

Chrysosplenium oppositifolium L. **Golden Saxifrage.** ¶Upper leaves opposite; basal leaf petiole equalling blade. Common, especially on acid soils, but rare in parts of E. England and the Midlands. Flo. March–May. ❀.

Chrysosplenium alternifolium L. **Alternate-leaved Golden Saxifrage.** ¶Upper leaves alternate or only 1; basal petioles longer than blade. Often on basic soil, local, absent from extreme W. Britain. Flo. March–June. ❀.

PARNASSIACEAE

Parnassia palustris L. **Grass of Parnassus.** ¶Flo. solitary; stamens 5, and 5 staminodes, fringed with stalked glands. On wet moorlands, and fixed sand dunes, absent from the S.W., and now very rare in S. England and the Midlands. Flo. July–Sept. ❀.

GROSSULARIACEAE

PLATE 33

Ribes rubrum L. **Red Currant.** *R. sylvestre* (Lam.) Mert. & Koch. ¶Inflo. drooping; receptacle with a raised rim; sepals broader than long. In woods and beside streams, frequent. Flo. April–May. ❀.

Ribes spicatum Robson. **Upright Red Currant.** *R. petraeum* auct. ¶Inflo. erect; receptacle deeper, without raised rim; sepals circular. In woods on limestone, N. England to N. Scotland. ❀.

Ribes nigrum L. **Black Currant.** ¶Leaves strong smelling; flo. drooping, campanulate; fr. black. In woods and by streams, locally native. Flo. April–May. ❀.

*Ribes sanguineum Pursh. **Flowering Currant.** ¶Leaves bluntly lobed, pubescent

beneath; flo. pink; fr. dark bluish black, pruinose. Garden outcast or bird-sown from gardens, naturalized by streams, etc. Flo. April–May.

Ribes alpinum L. **Alpine Currant.** ¶Flo. dioecious in erect spikes; male numerous, small; female few; fr. red. On limestone rock, mainly N. England and Wales. Flo. April–May. ✻.

Ribes uva-crispa L. **Gooseberry.** *R. grossularia* L. ¶Stems spinous at the nodes; flo. 1 or 2; fr. usually bristly. In woods and hedges, native, or bird-sown from gardens. Flo. March–April. ✻.

CRASSULACEAE

Crassula tillaea L.-Garland. **Mossy Tillaea.** *Tillaea muscosa* L. ¶Plant small and reddish with minute, crowded, oval leaves; flo. very small, axillary. On sandy soil, local, S. Devon to Norfolk. Flo. June–July. ✻.

Crassula aquatica (L.) Schönl. *Tillaea aquatica* L. ¶Leaves linear, not crowded; flo. minute, axillary. On wet mud, perhaps only casual. Flo. June–July. ✻.

Umbilicus rupestris (Salisb.) Dandy. **Pennywort.** *Cotyledon umbilicus-veneris* auct. ¶Leaves peltate; petals united in a tube; stamens 10. On rock crevices and walls, common on acid soils. Flo. June–Aug. ✻.

Rhodiola rosea L. **Roseroot.** *Sedum rosea* (L.) Scop., *S. rhodiola* DC. ¶Rootstock thick and fleshy; flo. dioecious with 4 linear petals. In rock crevices, Wales to Scotland, and Ireland. Flo. May–Aug. ✻.

Sedum telephium L. **Orpine, Livelong.** *S. purpureum* auct.
Subsp. *telephium*. ¶Leaves flat, rounded at base; flo. reddish purple, rarely white. In woods. Flo. July–Sept.
Subsp. *fabaria* (Koch) Kirschleger. *Sedum fabaria* Koch. ¶Leaves all tapering at base, sometimes shortly stalked. Flo. July–Sept. ✻.

*Sedum spurium Bieb. *S. stoloniferum* auct. ¶Stems procumbent, creeping, forming dense mats with numerous ascending branches; leaves opposite, flat, obtuse; flo. pink in flat terminal cymes. Garden escape. Naturalized on hedge banks, waste ground, etc. Flo. July–Sept.

*Sedum dasyphyllum L. **Thick-leaved Stonecrop.** ¶Stems procumbent or ascending; leaves roundly obovoid, glandular. On walls and limestone rocks. Not native. Flo. June–July. ✻.

Sedum anglicum Huds. **English Stonecrop.** ¶Prostrate with short, erect, forked flo. stems; leaves spurred. On rocks especially granite, and sandy soil, abundant. Flo. June–Aug. ✻.

Sedum album L. **White Stonecrop.** ¶Prostrate, with erect much-branched flo. stems; leaves not spurred. On limestone rocks, Mendips and S. Devon, on walls elsewhere. Flo. June–Aug. ✻.

Sedum acre L. **Wall Pepper.** ¶Creeping, with ascending flo. stems with few short branches; leaves hot tasting. On limestone rocks and walls, railway tracks and on basic soils. Flo. June–July. ✻.

*Sedum sexangulare is similar to *S. acre*, without hot taste and with smaller flo. Not native.

Sedum forsteranum Sm. **Rock Stonecrop.** *S. rupestre* L. pro parte.

Subsp. *forsteranum.* ¶leaves linear, erect, tufted at ends of branches; flo. stems slender, tall, usually green, sometimes glaucous, branched; inflo. convex in flo. Local on damp rocks and cliffs, Devon to Wales. Flo. June–July. ✳.

Subsp. *elegans* (Lej.) E. F. Warb. *Sedum elegans* Lej. *S. rupestre* L. subsp. *elegans* (Lej.) Syme. ¶Similar to subsp. *forsteranum* but glaucous and usually more robust; inflo. flat-topped in flo. Local on dry rocks and cliffs, Devon to Wales. Flo. June–July.

*Sedum reflexum L. **Reflexed Stonecrop.** ¶Leaves stout, recurved, equally distributed, not tufted; flo. larger. On old walls and rockeries, common, not native. Flo. June–Aug. ✳.

Sedum villosum L. **Hairy Stonecrop.** ¶Annual, erect, glandular, shortly branched; petals ovate pink. On wet mountain rocks, Yorkshire to N. Scotland. Flo. June–July. ✳.

*Sempervivum tectorum L. **Houseleek.** ¶Leaves in a close persistent rosette, thick, obovate, mucronate; petals red. An ancient introduction, planted on walls and roofs.

DROSERACEAE   PLATE 34

Drosera rotundifolia L. **Sundew.** ¶Leaves orbicular, spreading, long petioled; flo. stem from centre. Common on wet moors and peat bogs. Flo. June–Aug. ✳.

Drosera anglica Huds. **Great Sundew.** ¶Leaves 4 in., tapering into petiole; flo. stem from centre. In wet peat bogs, local. Flo. July–Aug. ✳.

Drosera × obovata Mert. & Koch. (*D. anglica × rotundifolia*). ¶Similar to *D. intermedia* but with a straight scape up to 3 times as long as the leaves. This sterile hybrid sometimes occurs where the two parents grow together.

Drosera intermedia Hayne. **Long-leaved Sundew.** *D. longifolia* auct. ¶Leaves 1½ in., obovate, tapering into petiole; flo. stem from base of rosette. On damp peaty moors, fairly common in the W. Flo. June–Aug. ✳.

SARRACENIACEAE

*Sarracenia purpurea L. **Pitcher Plant.** ¶Plant stout, up to 1 ft tall, with large erect clusters of root-leaves, splashed with green and purple; leaves tubular with a flap at the apex, the whole forming a 'pitcher', often containing water in which small insects drown; flo. purple, 1 in. wide, solitary or in few-flowered racemes, nodding on leafless stems; top of style umbrella shaped. Introduced from N. America and naturalized in bogs in Roscommon and Westmeath, Ireland. Flo. June–July.

HALORAGACEAE

Hippuris vulgaris L. **Mare's Tail.** ¶Leaves narrow, linear, whorled; submerged leaves longer, more flaccid; flo. sessile; perianth almost 0; stamen 1. Pools and slow streams. Flo. June–July. ✳.

Myriophyllum verticillatum L. **Whorled Water Milfoil.** ¶Leaves mostly 5 in a whorl, pectinate; floral bracts leaf-like, variable; lower flo. female. In ponds and slow streams, scarce. Flo. July–Aug. ❧.

Myriophyllum spicatum L. **Spiked Water Milfoil.** ¶Leaves usually 4 in a whorl; flo. spike long, erect; bracts very short; upper flo. male with red petals. Ponds and slow streams. Flo. June–July. ❧.

Myriophyllum alterniflorum DC. **Alternate-flowered Water Milfoil.** ¶Leaves 3 or 4 in a whorl; flo. spike short, drooping in bud; petals yellowish. In lakes and slow streams and peaty water. Flo. May–Aug. ❧.

CALLITRICHACEAE

Callitriche stagnalis Scop. **Mud Water Starwort.** ¶Leaves usually roundly obovate, about twice as long as broad, at least 3 veined; submerged leaves never linear; bracts usually deciduous; fr. nearly round, freely produced. In ponds, ditches, canals, on wet mud, etc., very common, and widespread, up to 3000 ft. Flo. May–Sept. ❧.

Callitriche platycarpa Kütz. *C. polymorpha* auct. ¶Leaves usually obovate or rhomboid, about 3 times as long as broad, 1 veined in submerged plants; bracts usually persistent; fr. small, nearly round, sparsely produced; styles long, deflexed, persistent. In similar habitats to *C. stagnalis*. Very common and widespread, but rarely occurring above 500 ft. Flo. May–Sept. ❧.

Callitriche obtusangula Le Gall. ¶Leaves rhomboid-spathulate, forming rosettes; bracts persistent; fr. rather square, longer than broad, the edges rounded with shallow groove; styles long, persistent. In ponds, ditches, streams, etc., locally common in S. England, rarer in the N. Flo. May–Sept. ❧.

Callitriche palustris L. *C. verna* auct. ¶Similar to *C. platycarpa*, but fruit small, 1 mm., turgid, narrowed below in side view, edges keeled, converging above in end view; styles short, 2 mm., erect, soon falling off. The figure was drawn from a Devon specimen, but it is now said that all the available British material formerly referred to this species belongs to *C. platycarpa*. ❧.

Callitriche hamulata Kütz. *C. intermedia* Hoffm. ¶Leaves linear, widened and emarginate at apex; bracts deciduous; fr. small, sessile, black, about as long as broad; styles reflexed. In lakes, ditches, slow streams, etc., probably widespread. Flo. April–Sept. ❧.

'*Callitriche pedunculata*' DC. ¶A complex plant which may be conspecific with *C. hamulata* or a subspecies or variety of that plant. It is said to differ in being smaller, with shorter leaves, and brown (not black) fr. borne on slender peduncles. ❧.

Callitriche hermaphroditica L. *C. autumnalis* L. ¶Leaves linear $\frac{1}{2}$–$\frac{5}{8}$ in. long, widest at base; fr. large, 2 mm., of 4 separate winged lobes. In lakes and streams, chiefly in N. Britain. Flo. May–Sept. ❧.

Callitriche truncata Guss. ¶Leaves linear, $\frac{1}{4}$ in., only slightly wider at base; fr. small, 1 mm., edges not winged. In ponds and ditches in S. half of England, rare. Flo. May–Sept. ❧.

CERATOPHYLLACEAE

Ceratophyllum demersum L. **Hornwort.** ¶Leaves once or twice forked; fr. with 2 spines at the base. In ponds and dikes. Flo. July–Sept. ❁.

Ceratophyllum submersum L. ¶Leaves 3 times forked; fr. without spines. In ponds and dikes. Flo. July–Sept. ❁.

LYTHRACEAE

Lythrum portula (L.) D. A. Webb. **Water Purslane.** *Peplis portula* L. ¶Stems prostrate, rooting; petals often 6, small, soon falling. Common on mud, especially on acid soils. Flo. June–Sept. ❁.

Lythrum salicaria L. **Purple Loosestrife.** ¶Perennial, 2–4 ft; flo. ½ in., clustered; styles and stamens of variable length. On river banks, ditches and marshes, common. Flo. June–Aug. ❁.

Lythrum hyssopifolia L. **Hyssop-leaved Loosestrife.** ¶Annual, ½–1 ft; flo. ⅓ in., singly in axils. In pools that dry up, local and uncertain in appearance. Flo. June–July. ❁.

ONAGRACEAE   **PLATE 35**

Epilobium angustifolium L. **Rose Bay.** *Chamaenerion angustifolium* (L.) Scop. ¶Flo. horizontal; stamens long and drooping; petals a little unequal. In woodland clearings, waste and burnt ground. Flo. July–Sept. ❁.

Epilobium hirsutum L. **Great Willow Herb.** ¶Stems 4 ft, terete, hairy; leaves sessile, hairy; stigma 4 lobed. In ditches and streamsides, common. Flo. July–Aug. ❁.

Epilobium parviflorum Schreb. **Hairy Willow Herb.** ¶Stems 1–3 ft, terete, hairy; leaves oblong, sessile, softly hairy; stigma 4 lobed. In ditches and damp ground, common. Flo. June–Aug. ❁.

Epilobium montanum L. **Broad-leaved Willow Herb.** ¶Stem slender, terete; leaves stalked, ovate, acute; stigma 4 lobed. Common in woods, hedges and cultivated ground. Flo. June–Aug. ❁.

Epilobium lanceolatum Seb. & Mauri. **Spear-leaved Willow Herb.** ¶Stem with 4 slight ridges; leaves stalked, lanceolate; stigma 4 lobed. On dry banks, in woods and rock cuttings in S. England. Flo. July–Sept. ❁.

Epitobium roseum Schreb. **Pedicelled Willow Herb.** ¶Stem with 2 raised lines; leaves stalked, tapering below; stigma entire, equalling style. On damp waste and cultivated ground. Flo. July–Aug. ❁.

Epilobium adenocaulon Hausskn. ¶Stem 2–3 ft with 4 raised lines and glandular hairs; leaves rounded below; flo. small, pale; stigma entire, shorter than style. Introduced from N. America and spreading rapidly in woods, marshes, by streamsides, on waste grounds, walls, etc. Flo. June–Sept.

Epilobium tetragonum L. **Square-stalked Willow Herb.** *E. adnatum* Griseb.
Subsp. *tetragonum*. ¶Leaves oblong, shining, sessile; stigma entire; fr. 2½–4 in., plant with small autumn rosettes. In ditches and damp lanes. Flo. July–Aug. ❁.

Subsp. *lamyi* (F. W. Schultz), Léveillé. **Scarce Willow Herb.** *Epitobium lamyi* F. W. Schultz. ¶Leaves short stalked, lanceolate, glaucous; stigma entire; capsule 2½–4 in., downy. In damp places in S. England. Flo. July–Aug. ✤.

Epilobium obscurum Schreb. **Thin-runner Willow Herb.** ¶Stem with stolons and 4 raised lines; leaves short, sessile; stigma entire; capsule 1½–2½ in. Common in ditches and wet shady places. Flo. July–Aug. ✤.

Epilobium palustre L. **Bog Willow Herb.** ¶Stem terete, with slender stolons; leaves linear-lanceolate; buds drooping; stigma entire. On peaty moorland bogs, marshes, etc., common. Flo. July–Aug. ✤.

Epilobium anagallidifolium Lam. **Alpine Willow Herb.** *E. alpinum* auct. ¶Stem 4 in., stoloniferous; leaves small, elliptical; flo. drooping. By mountain springs, N. Yorkshire northwards. Flo. July–Aug. ✤.

Epilobium alsinifolium Vill. **Chickweed Willow Herb.** ¶Stem 2–8 in., with white stolons; leaves ovate, dentate; flo. drooping. By mountain streams, Wales and N. Yorkshire northwards. Flo. July–Aug. ✤.

*Epilobium nerterioides Cunn. *E. pedunculare* auct., non Cunn. ¶Stems slender, creeping; leaves suborbicular; capsule 1½–2 in., glabrous. Introduced from New Zealand. Garden escape. Spreading by streamsides, on wet rocky places, moors, etc., chiefly in S.W. and N. England, N. Wales, Scotland and Ireland. Flo. June–July.

Ludwigia palustris (L.) Ell. ¶Stem prostrate below; flo. axillary, subsessile; stamens 4, no petals. In shallow pools, New Forest and Jersey. Flo. June. ✤.

*Oenothera biennis L. **Evening Primrose.** ¶Stem without bulbous hairs; leaves lanceolate; flo. erect, petals 1 in. Garden escape. On sand dunes and waste places. Flo. June–Sept.

*Oenothera erythrosepala Borbás. *O. lamarkiana* auct. ¶Stem with bulbous hairs; leaves broadly lanceolate; petals 2 in., buds angular. Garden escape. On roadsides and waste places. Flo. June–Sept.

*Oenothera stricta Ledeb. ex Link. *O. odorata* auct. ¶Stem subsimple, erect, glandular; leaves linear-lanceolate; petals 1½ in., becoming red. Garden escape. Mostly on sand dunes. Flo. June–Sept.

*Oenothera parviflora L. ¶Has inflo. drooping; flo. smaller (⅔ in.). Garden escape. On waste ground, etc. Flo. June–Sept.

*Fuchsia magallenica Lam. *F. gracilis* Lindl. *F. riccartonii* auct. ¶Shrub, up to 6 ft; leaves toothed, oval-acuminate; flo. small, solitary, pendulous; sepals bright red; petals plum-purple; stigma and stamens exserted; berry black. Cultivated for hedging purposes and naturalized in S.W. England and W. Ireland. Flo. June–Sept.

Circaea lutetiana L. **Enchanter's Nightshade.** ¶Rhizomes overwintering; plant hairy; leaf base truncate, margin slightly denticulate; bracteoles o; flo. widely spaced. Common in shade. Flo. July. ✤.

Circaea alpina L. **Alpine Enchanter's Nightshade.** ¶Tubers overwintering; plant subglabrous; leaf base cordate, margin strongly dentate; flo. bracteolate, clustered when open. Very local, in shady places, Wales, N.W. England, Arran. ✤.

Circaea × intermedia Ehrh. *C. alpina × lutetiana.* ¶Intermediate in most characters and always sterile. More widely dispersed in Wales, N.W. England, Scotland and N. Ireland, in areas where *C. alpina* has long been extinct.

CUCURBITACEAE

PLATE 36

Bryonia dioica Jacq. **White Bryony.** *B. cretica* L. subsp. *anglica* Tutin. ¶Climbing by tendrils; leaves 5 lobed; flo. greenish white, male with 5 stamens, female with 3 bifid stigmas; berry red. Common in S.E. and mid England. Flo. May–Aug. ⚥.

UMBELLIFERAE

Hydrocotyle vulgaris L. **Marsh Pennywort.** ¶Stem creeping, rooting; leaves orbicular; flo. in small sessile whorls; fr. laterally compressed. Common in peaty bogs. Flo. July–Sept. ⚥.

Eryngium maritimum L. **Sea Holly.** ¶Very glaucous; radical leaves suborbicular; bracts very broad, lobes spine pointed; flo. blue. On sandy sea-shores. Flo. July–Aug. ⚥.

Eryngium campestre L. ¶Pale green; radical leaves pinnate; bracts with narrow lobes; flo. white. In grass mostly near S.W. coasts, very local and rare. Flo. July–Aug. ⚥.

*Astrantia major L. **Melancholy Gentleman.** ¶Radical leaves broadly lobed; bracts lanceolate; umbels simple; outer flo. male. Naturalized in a few grassy places, especially in Shropshire. ⚥.

Sanicula europaea L. **Sanicle.** ¶Radical leaves roundly lobed; flo. in 2–3 partial umbels; outer male; calyx long and sharp; fr. with hooks. Woods on basic soils. Flo. May–Aug. ⚥.

Physospermum cornubiense (L.) DC. *Danaa cornubiensis* (L.) Burnat. ¶Leaf segments stalked, laciniate; umbel rays and pedicels long; fr. broad. Local, in woods, Cornwall, rare in S.W. Devon and Buckinghamshire. Flo. July–Aug. ⚥.

Conium maculatum L. **Hemlock.** ¶Stem 6 ft, spotted; foliage poisonous; fr. suborbicular; vittae 0. In damp roadsides, hedges and river banks, common. Flo. June–Sept. ⚥.

*Smyrnium olusatrum L. **Alexanders.** ¶Leaves broad and celery-like; fr. becoming black; commissure narrow. On cliffs and hedge banks, particularly near the sea in S. and mid England, Wales and Ireland, introduced. Flo. April–May. ⚥.

*Smyrnium perfoliatum L. ¶Similar to *S. olusatrum*, but with roundish upper leaves clasping the stem. Naturalized in grassy places, rare. Flo. May–June.

*Bupleurum fruticosum L. ¶Evergreen shrub up to 8 ft; stems slender, sometimes purplish; leaves bluish green, alternate oblong-lanceolate, entire, mucronate; flo. small, greenish yellow in terminal umbels; bracts and bracteoles reflexed. Garden escape. Naturalized in a few localities, particularly in S. Midlands. Flo. July–Aug.

Bupleurum rotundifolium L. **Thorow-wax.** ¶Stem 6–12 in.; leaves elliptic, upper perfoliate; bracteoles broadly ovate. In cornfields on basic soils, very rare. Flo. June–July. ⚥.

Bupleurum baldense Turra. *B. opacum* (Ces.) Lange. *B. aristatum* auct. ¶Plant 1–4 in.; bracteoles ovate, concealing the sessile flowers. On dry banks near the sea, Devon, Sussex and Channel Isles. Flo. June–July. ⚥.

Bupleurum tenuissimum L. ¶Annual; slender, wiry, erect, 6–12 in.; bracts and bracteoles subulate. On salt marshes. Flo. July–Sept. ⚥.

Bupleurum falcatum L. ¶Perennial; stem hollow; upper leaves and bracteoles linear-lanceolate. In hedges and waste places, in Essex. Flo. July–Oct. ⚥.

Trinia glauca (L.) Dumort. **Honewort.** ¶Stem 3–6 in.; leaf segments linear; male umbels $\frac{1}{2}$ in., female $1\frac{1}{2}$. On dry limestone hills, S. Devon and N. Somerset. Flo. May–July. ❀.

Apium graveolens L. **Wild Celery.** ¶Leaves with broad segments, lower segments stalked; umbels subsessile. In wet places and ditches, mostly near the sea. Flo. June–Aug. ❀.

Apium nodiflorum (L.) Lag. **Procumbent Marsh-wort.** *Helosciadum nodiflorum* (L.) Koch. ¶Ascending from a creeping base; leaves pinnate; umbels often nearly sessile. In muddy ditches and edges of ponds, common in S. England, the Midlands and Ireland, local in Wales and N. England, rare in Scotland. Flo. July–Aug. ❀.

Apium nodiflorum × repens. ¶Intermediate between the two parents, often with a coarse stem and peduncled umbels, though the peduncles vary greatly in length. This very rare hybrid sometimes occurs in the absence of the parents.

Apium repens (Jacq.) Lag. ¶Stem entirely creeping; leaf segments broadly oval; umbels peduncled. In wet places, local, Oxfordshire, E. Yorkshire and Scotland. Flo. July–Aug. ❀.

Apium inundatum (L.) Reichb. f. **Floating Marsh-wort.** *Helosciadum inundatum* (L.) Koch. ¶Floating; segments of submerged leaves capillary, of upper 3 lobed; umbel rays $\frac{1}{4}$ in. In ponds and dikes, rather local. Flo. June–July. ❀.

Apium × moorei (Syme) Druce. (*A. inundatum × nodiflorum*). ¶Similar to, but larger than, *A. inundatum*, but with linear segments to lower leaves. This sterile hybrid sometimes occurs where the parents grow together.

Cicuta virosa L. **Cowbane.** ¶Stem 5 ft, hollow; leaf segments linear-lanceolate; bracteoles many. In ditches and marshes, rare, except in Ireland where it is local. Flo. July–Aug. ❀.

*Ammi majus L. ¶1–2 ft, glaucous; leaves pinnate or bipinnate, serrate; bracts several, pinnate; bracteoles linear; fr. oblong-ovoid. On waste ground, etc., introduced, scarce. Flo. July–Sept.

Petroselinum crispum* (Mill.) Nyman. **Parsley. *Carum petroselinum* (L.) Benth. ¶Leaves deltoid, tripinnate; bracts with hyaline margins; flo. yellowish. Naturalized on walls and rocks, especially limestone. Flo. June–Aug.

Petroselinum segetum (L.) Koch. **Corn Parsley.** *Carum segetum* Benth. ¶Leaves linear, simply pinnate, segments ovate; bracts subulate; flo. white, anthers purple. On grass, particularly near the sea, chiefly in S. England. Flo. Aug.–Sept. ❀.

Carum verticillatum (L.) Koch. **Whorled Caraway.** ¶Perennial; stem solid; leaf segments capillary and whorled; bracts lanceolate, anthers pink. In damp acid meadows, mostly W. England to W. Scotland. Flo. July–Aug. ❀.

*Carum carvi L. **Common Caraway.** ¶Biennial; stem striate, hollow; leaf segments linear; fruit used for flavouring. Naturalized, rather rare. Flo. June–July. ❀.

Bunium bulbocastanum L. **Tuberous Caraway.** *Carum bulbocastanum* (L.) Koch. ¶Perennial; root a black 1 in. tuber; leaf segments narrow; fr. oblong. On chalky banks and grass in Hertfordshire, Buckinghamshire, Bedfordshire and Cambridgeshire, local. Flo. June–July. ❀.

Sium latifolium L. **Water Parsnip.** ¶Stem 6 ft, hollow, grooved; petioles sheathing; leaf segments regularly serrate. In fens and marshes, mostly in E. England, local. Flo. July–Aug. ✲.

PLATE 38

Berula erecta (Huds.) Coville. **Narrow-leaved Water Parsnip.** *Sium erectum* Huds., *S. angustifolium* L. ¶Stem 1–2 ft; leaf segments 1–2 in., irregularly serrate; flo. 2 mm. In marshes and ditches. Flo. July–Sept. ✲.

Sison amomum L. **Stone Parsley.** ¶Umbels small, with few rays and few minute flo.; plant aromatic. Hedge banks in S. England and Midlands, common on basic soils, local in Wales. Flo. July–Sept. ✲.

*Falcaria vulgaris Bernh. ¶Leaves with long linear or strap-shaped segments, regularly serrate; flo. small, yellow. Naturalized in a few places in S. and E. England. Flo. July.

Aegopodium podagraria L. **Goutweed, Ground Elder.** ¶Stem 2 ft, hollow, with white rhizomes; leaflets broad; fr. without vittae. In waste places and as a garden weed. Flo. May–July. ✲.

Pimpinella saxifraga L. **Burnet Saxifrage.** ¶Stem subterete, rough; leaflets ovate or in linear segments; styles much shorter than petals. In grass except on acid soils. Flo. July–Aug. ✲.

Pimpinella major (L.) Huds. **Greater Burnet Saxifrage.** *P. magna.* L. ¶Stem ridged, glabrous, purple below; leaves broad, simply pinnate; styles equalling petals. In grass and road borders, mostly in E. England. Flo. June–July. ✲.

Conopodium majus (Gouan) Loret. **Pignut.** *C. denudatum* Koch., *Bunium flexuosum* Stokes. ¶Root tuberous; petioles sheathing; leaf segments and fr. narrow; styles short. In woods and shaded sides of fields. Flo. May–June. ✲.

Myrrhis odorata (L.) Scop. **Sweet Cicely.** ¶Plant 2 ft, aromatic; male flo. on shorter rays; fr. 1 in., oblong with ridges. In grass and hedge banks, N. England and S. Scotland, introduced elsewhere. Flo. May–June. ✲.

Chaerophyllum temulentum L. **Chervil.** ¶Stem hairy, purple spotted, swollen below nodes; leaves dark green, hairy. Common in hedge banks, except in mid Wales, Scotland and Ireland where it is local. Flo. June–July. ✲.

*Chaerophyllum aureum L. ¶Stem glabrous, swollen; leaves yellow-green, glabrous above; fr. ½ in. Naturalized locally in Perthshire and elsewhere. Flo. July.

Scandix pecten-veneris L. **Shepherd's Needle.** ¶Umbels of 1–2 rays only; bracteoles ciliate; fr. with long beak, 1–2 in. In cultivated land, mostly in S. and E. England. Flo. April–July. ✲.

Anthriscus caucalis Bieb. **Bur Chervil.** *A. vulgaris* Pers., non Bernh., *A. neglecta* Boiss. & Reut. ¶Stem glabrous; peduncle short; rays few; flo. minute; fr. oval, muricate. Hedges and waste places, often near the sea, mostly in S. and E. England. Flo. June–July. ✲.

Anthriscus sylvestris (L.) Hoffm. **Cow Parsley.** ¶Stem pubescent; peduncle long; rays many; flo. 3–4 mm.; fr. oblong, smooth. Common except in N. Scotland and S. Ireland. Flo. April–June. ✲.

*_Anthriscus cerefolium_ (L.) Hoffm. **Garden Chervil.** ¶Stem pubescent above nodes; peduncles very short, pubescent; flo. 2 mm.; fr. 10 mm., smooth. Introduced from E. Europe, naturalized in some waste places. Flo. May–June.

PLATE 39

Seseli libanotis (L.) Koch. ¶Leaf lobes oblong; peduncle long; rays, bracts and fr. pubescent; fr. ovoid. On chalk hills, local, Sussex to Cambridgeshire. Flo. July–Aug. ✼.

Foeniculum vulgare Mill. **Fennel.** ¶Stem 3–4 ft, striate, glaucous; leaf segments long, capillary, scented. On sea cliffs from Wales and Norfolk southwards, on waste ground inland. Flo. July–Oct. ✼.

Crithmum maritimum L. **Samphire.** ¶Stem 1 ft; leaves fleshy; rays stout; fr. corky. On sea cliffs of W., S. and S.E. Flo. June–Sept. ✼.

Oenanthe fistulosa L. **Common Water Dropwort.** ¶Stem a hollow tube; leaf segments linear; blade shorter than hollow petiole. In shallow pools, dikes and marshes, mostly S. England, Midlands, S. Wales and Ireland. Flo. July–Sept. ✼.

Oenanthe pimpinelloides L. **Corky-fruited Water Dropwort.** ¶Tubers distant, obovate; stem solid; leaf blade longer than petiole; fr. cylindrical. In meadows, S. England. Flo. June–Aug. ✼.

Oenanthe silaifolia Bieb. ¶Roots thickened from base; stem hollow ribbed; rays thick in fr.; fr. constricted below. In damp meadows, S. England and Midlands, rare. Flo. June.

Oenanthe lachenalii C. C. Gmel. **Parsley Water Dropwort.** ¶Roots cylindrical; stem solid; rays slender; fr. ovoid, reddish. In salt marshes and fens. Flo. June–Sept. ✼.

Oenanthe crocata L. **Hemlock Water Dropwort.** ¶Stem 4–5 ft, hollow, grooved; leaves with broad segments; umbels 6–8 in. wide. In boggy places and beds of streams, mostly in S. and W. Britain. Flo. June–July. ✼.

Oenanthe aquatica (L.) Poir. **Fine-leaved Water Dropwort.** _O. phellandrium_ Lam. ¶Segments of submerged leaves capillary; peduncles short; fr. 3–4 mm. In ponds, dikes and fen ditches. Flo. June–Sept. ✼.

Oenanthe fluviatilis (Bab.) Colem. **River Water Dropwort.** ¶Segments of submerged leaves cut into narrow lobes; peduncles short; fr. 5–6 mm. In ponds and streams, N. to Lincolnshire, local in Ireland. Flo. July–Sept. ✼.

Aethusa cynapium L. **Fool's Parsley.** ¶Stem 1–2 ft, hollow, striate; outer bracteoles long, deflexed; poisonous. Common in cultivated land, except in N. England and Scotland where it is local. Flo. July–Aug. ✼.

Silaum silaus (L.) Schinz & Thell. **Pepper Saxifrage.** _Silaus flavescens_ Bernh. ¶Stem 1–2 ft, solid, striate; bracteoles linear with scarious edges; flo. yellowish. In meadows and grassy places, mostly in S. and E. England, local. Flo. June–Aug. ✼.

Meum athamanticum Jacq. **Spignel, Bald-Money.** ¶Stem hollow, 1–2 ft; leaves finely divided, aromatic; fr. ovoid; ridges acute. In grass on mountain meadows, local. Flo. June–July. ✼.

Ligusticum scoticum L. **Lovage.** ¶Stem red below; leaf segments 1–2 in. broad; fr. ridges prominent, acute. On rocky coasts, Northumberland northwards. Flo. July. ❊.

Selinum carvifolia (L.) ¶Stem ridges prominent, acute; leaf segments lanceolate, mucronate, minutely serrate; fr. ovoid; ridges winged. In damp meadows, Cambridgeshire, formerly in Nottinghamshire and Lincolnshire. Flo. July–Oct.

Angelica sylvestris L. **Wild Angelica.** ¶Stem hollow, purple; petioles inflated, sheathing; leaf segments ovate, serrate; flo. pink and white. Common by streamsides, in damp meadows, etc. Flo. July–Sept. ❊.

*Angelica archangelica L. *Archangelica officinalis* Hoffm. ¶Stem hollow, green; leaf segments decurrent; flo. greenish white. Naturalized on some river banks. Flo. July–Sept.

*Levisticum officinale Koch. ¶Stout, strongly aromatic, perennial up to 6 ft; stems glabrous; leaves pinnate; leaflets obovate-cuneate, deeply toothed; flo. small, yellow, in terminal umbels; fr. with 10 narrowly winged ribs. Garden escape. Naturalized in wet places, thickets, etc., in Scotland. Flo. July–Aug.

Peucedanum officinale L. **Sea Hog's Fennel.** ¶Stem solid; leaf segments long, 1–3 in., narrow, linear, entire. On banks by the Thames estuary, local. Flo. July–Sept. ❊.

Peucedanum palustre (L.) Moench. **Marsh Hog's Fennel.** ¶Stem hollow; leaf segments with lanceolate lobes, finely serrate. In fens and marshes, Somerset and Sussex to S. Yorkshire. Flo. July–Sept. ❊.

*Peucedanum ostruthium (L.) Koch. ¶Stem hollow; leaf segments few, broad, serrate; fr. suborbicular. Naturalized in moist meadows, Wales and Yorkshire to N. Scotland, and N.E. Ireland. Flo. July–Aug.

Pastinaca sativa L. **Wild Parsnip.** ¶Stem hollow, furrowed; leaf lobes broad, ovate, lobed; flo. yellow. In grassy places mainly on calcareous soil in S. and E. England, S. Wales, Midlands and Ireland. Flo. July–Aug. ❊.

Heracleum sphondylium L. **Hogweed, Cow Parsnip.** ¶Leaf segments broadly ovate, irregularly cut, petals of outer flo. enlarged. Common everywhere. Flo. June–Sept. ❊.
Var. *angustifolium* Huds. ¶Has leaves with linear-lanceolate segments.

*Heracleum mantegazzianum Somm. & Lev. **Giant Hogweed.** ¶Differs from *H. sphondylium* in its enormous size (stems up to 10 ft tall, red spotted); leaves and panicles very large. Naturalized by rivers, etc. Flo. June–Sept.

* Tordylium maximum L. ¶Stem 3–4 ft; leaves simply pinnate; lobes ovate to lanceolate; fr. with thick whitish ridges. In hedges, marshes and bushy slopes, Essex, formerly in Oxford, Buckinghamshire, Middlesex, etc., rare, introduced. Flo. June–July.

*Coriandrum sativum L. **Coriander.** ¶Stem solid, 1–2 ft; lower leaves pinnate; lobes ovate; upper leaves bipinnate; umbels small; fr. orbicular. In waste places, introduced. Flo. June.

Daucus carota L. **Wild Carrot.**
Subsp. *carota*. ¶Leaf lobes lanceolate, acute; umbels concave in fr.; spines hooked at tip, separate below. Common near the sea and on calcareous soil. Flo. June–Aug. ❊.

Subsp. *gummifer* Hook. f. *D. gummifer* Lam., non All., *D. gingidium* auct. ¶Leaf lobes more ovate, obtuse; umbels flatter; spines straight at tip, confluent at base. Cliffs by the sea in S. and W. England. Not very distinct.

*Caucalis latifolia L. **Great Bur-Parsley.** ¶Leaves simply pinnate; flo. 5 mm.; bracts 3–5; inner flo. long pedicelled, male. Casual in cultivated fields, not native. Flo. July.

*Caucalis platycarpos L. **Small Bur-Parsley.** *C. lappula* Grande., *C. daucoides* L. 1767, non L. 1753. ¶Leaves 2–3, pinnate; flo. 2 mm.; bracts 0; outer flo. long pedicelled, male. Not native. Flo. June–July. ❀.

Torilis arvensis (Huds.) Link. **Spreading Hedge Parsley.** *T. infesta* (L.) Spreng. ¶Umbels long pedicelled; rays 3–5; bracts 0–1; fr. spines curved, not hooked; style glabrous. Probably introduced, in cultivated fields, scarce. Flo. July–Sept. ❀.

Torilis japonica (Houtt.) DC. **Hedge Parsley.** *Caucalis anthriscus* (L.) Huds. ¶Umbels long pedicelled; rays 5–12; bracts 4–10; fr. spines hooked; style hairy. Common in hedgerows. Flo. July–Aug. ❀.

Torilis nodosa (L.) Gaertn. **Knotted Hedge Parsley.** ¶Stem prostrate; umbels nearly sessile, short rayed; bracts 0; carpels with straight or hooked spines. In dry places, mostly on calcareous and alluvial soils, chiefly in S. and E. England. Flo. May–July. ❀.

BUXACEAE

PLATE 41

Buxus sempervirens L. **Box.** ¶Leaves coriaceous; flo. clusters 1 female and several male with 4 stamens. On calcareous soil, Gloucestershire to Kent, introduced elsewhere. Flo. April–May. ❀.

ARALIACEAE

Hedera helix L. **Ivy.** ¶Flowers tomentose, 5-merous; styles united; fr. black, globose. Climbing everywhere. Flo. Oct.–Nov. ❀.

CORNACEAE

Chamaepericlymenum suecicum (L.) Aschers. & Graebn. **Dwarf Cornel.** *Cornus suecica* L. ¶Stem creeping with erect shoots; flo. surrounded by 4 white bracts. Among heather on mountains in Scotland, local and rare in N. England. Flo. July–Aug. ❀.

Swida sanguinea (L.) Opiz. **Dogwood Cornel.** *Cornus sanguinea* L., *Thelycrania sanguinea* (L.) Fourr. ¶Shrub 6–10 ft; twigs red; petals 4, valvate; calyx teeth very small. Common on calcareous and other soils in S. England, local in Wales and Ireland, probably introduced in N. England and Scotland. Flo. June–July. ❀.

ADOXACEAE

Adoxa moschatellina L. **Moschatel.** ¶Rhizome creeping, white; lateral flo., with 5 petals, facing N.S.E. and W. as clock tower; upper flo., with 4 petals facing sky; fr. green. In shady lanes and banks. Flo. April. ❀.
A symbol of Christian watchfulness.

CAPRIFOLIACEAE

Sambucus nigra L. **Elder.** ¶Shrub or small tree; stipules o or small; flo. 5 together, cream-white. Common in hedges and waste places, except in N. Scotland. Flo. June–July. ❊.

Sambucus ebulus L. **Danewort.** ¶Stem about 4 ft, herbaceous; stipules prominent, ovate; flo. 3 together, pinkish white. In waste places, local. Flo. July–Aug. ❊.

*Sambucus racemosa L. **Red-berried Elder.** ¶Shrub; leaves ovate-lanceolate; stipules replaced by large glands; flo. creamy white in dense panicle-like cymes; berry globose, scarlet. Bird-sown from gardens and naturalized in woods and hedges, particularly in N.E. England and E. Scotland. Flo. April–May.

Viburnum lantana L. **Wayfaring Tree.** ¶Leaves oval, wrinkled, pubescent; fr. oval, becoming black; flo. all equal. In hedges, common in the S., especially on calcareous soils, introduced elsewhere. Flo. June–July. ❊.

Viburnum opulus L. **Guelder Rose.** ¶Leaves lobed, glabrous above; outer flo. enlarged and sterile; fr. globose, scarlet. In woods and very damp hedgerows. Flo. June– July. ❊.

*Symphoricarpos rivularis Suksd. **Snowberry.** *S. albus* auct., *S. racemosus* auct. ¶Small shrub; twigs slender; leaves orbicular, entire; flo. small, pink, campanulate, 3–6 in terminal spikes; berry ½ in., white. Garden escape. Widely naturalized in hedges and thickets. Flo. June–Aug.

Linnaea borealis L. ¶Stems slender, pubescent, creeping, forming a mat; flo. pendulous, pink; fr. an achene. In shade, E. Scotland, rare. Flo. June–Aug. ❊.

Lonicera periclymenum L. **Honeysuckle.** ¶Climbing to 30 ft; upper leaves free, often downy beneath; flo. yellow, numerous. Common in woods and hedgerows. Flo. June–Sept. ❊.

Lonicera xylosteum L. **Fly Honeysuckle.** ¶Stem slender, climbing; leaves broadly ovate, pubescent; flo. ½ in. long, in pairs on peduncles ½ in.; berry red. Possibly native in a few woods on calcareous soils in Sussex, elsewhere bird-sown or escaped from gardens, rare. Flo. May. ❊.

*Lonicera caprifolium L. **Perfoliate Honeysuckle.** ¶Stems glabrous, climbing; leaves ovate, green above, glaucous below; upper leaves united at their bases; flo. pale yellow, in terminal whorls, sometimes with additional axillary whorls; bracts large; berry orange-red. Bird-sown or escaped from gardens and naturalized in hedges and thickets, rare. Flo. May–June.

*Leycesteria formosa Wall. **Flowering Nutmeg.** ¶Shrub, leaves opposite, ovate-acuminate; flo. ¾ in., purplish, funnel-shaped, sessile, in whorls enclosed by large claret-coloured leaf-like bracts; berry ¾ in., dark purplish brown. Bird-sown from gardens and naturalized in woods and hedges. Flo. June–Sept.

RUBIACEAE   **PLATE 42**

Rubia peregrina L. **Madder.** ¶Stems climbing by downward prickles; leaves shining; flo. yellowish, 5 cleft; fr. black. In hedgerows near the sea and on sea cliffs, chiefly in S. and S.W. England, Wales and W. Ireland. Flo. June–Aug. ❊.

Cruciata ciliata Opiz. **Crosswort.** *C. laevipes* Opiz., *C. chersonensis* (Willd.) Ehrend., *Galium cruciata* (L.) Scop. ¶Stem 1½ ft; leaves 4 in whorl, 3 veined, hairy; flo. yellow; fr. small, smooth. Common, especially on calcareous soils but rare in W. Wales, and N. Scotland, and introduced in Ireland. Flo. May–June. ❀.

Galium boreale L. **Northern Bedstraw.** ¶Stems 1 ft; leaves 4 in whorl, 3 veined; flo. white; fr. bristles hooked. In moist rocky places in N. England, Scotland and Ireland. Flo. July–Aug. ❀.

Galium verum L. **Lady's Bedstraw.** ¶Stems 1½ ft; leaves many, narrow, 1 veined, downy beneath; flo. yellow; fr. smooth. Common in dry places. Flo. July–Sept. ❀.

Galium album Mill. subsp. *album*. **Hedge Bedstraw.** *Galium mollugo* auct., non. L., *G. erectum* Huds. pro parte. ¶Stems 1–3 ft, trailing on hedges or upright; leaf margins rough with forward prickles; flo. branches spreading; fr. 1–2 mm. Common on banks, in pastures, etc., especially on calcareous soils, in S. England, local in the Midlands, N. England and Wales, rare in Scotland and Ireland. Flo. June–Sept. ❀.

Galium × pomeranicum Retz. (*G. album* subsp. *album × verum*). *G. × ochroleucum* Wolf ex Schweigg. & Koerte. ¶Intermediate between the two parents, with pale yellow flo., sometimes occurs where the parents grow together.

Galtium saxatile L. **Heath Bedstraw.** *G. harcynicum* Weig. ¶Stems procumbent, matted, 4 angled, glabrous; flo. branches shorter than internodes; fr. with tubercles. Common on peaty heaths. Flo. July–Aug. ❀.

Galium pumilum Murr. **Slender Bedstraw.** ¶Stems often hairy below; leaves lanceolate, margin revolute, ciliate; flowering branches usually longer than internodes; fr. faintly granular. On limestone and chalk from S. England northwards to Lincoln, local. Flo. June–Aug. ❀.

Galium sterneri Ehrend. *G. pumilum* Murr. subsp. *septentrionale* Sterner ex Hyland. ¶Similar to *G. pumilum* but more prostrate; leaves oblanceolate to linear; flo. cymes more compact, forming a pyramidal panicle (panicle open in *G. pumilum*); fr. covered with tubercles. On calcareous and limestone slopes and rocks from mid Wales to N. Scotland, also in W. and N.E. Ireland, local. Flo. June–Aug.

Galium palustre L. **Marsh Bedstraw.** ¶Stem 3 ft, nearly smooth, supported by other plants, black when dry; flo. 3–4 mm. wide, fruit rugose. Common in wet meadows. Flo. June–Aug. ❀.
Var. *elongatum* C. Presl. ¶More robust, less branched, flo. 4·5 mm.

Galium debile Desv. **Pond Bedstraw.** ¶Stem nearly smooth; leaves narrow, linear, subglabrous, margin slightly rough; flo. pinkish white; fr. granular. In ponds, rare, Devon, Hampshire and Channel Islands. Flo. May–July. ❀.

Galium uliginosum L. **Fen Bedstraw.** ¶Slender stems and leaf margins rough with backward prickles; leaves 6–8 in whorl, mucronate, green when dry; fr. granular. In fens and boggy meadows, local. Flo. July–Aug. ❀.

Galium parisiense L. **Wall Bedstraw.** *G. anglicum* Huds. ¶Small, slender stems with backward prickles; leaves with forward prickles, flo. very small, greenish white; fr. small, granular. On walls and dry places, mostly S.E. England, rare. Flo. June–July. ❀.

Galium aparine L. **Goose Grass, Cleavers.** ¶Climbing, 3–4 ft, stems and leaves with deflexed prickles; fr. large, 4–6 mm., with hooked prickles. Common in hedge banks. Flo. June–Aug. ❀.

Galium tricornutum Dandy. **Corn Bedstraw.** *G. tricorne* Stokes pro parte. ¶1 ft stems and leaf margins very rough with backward prickles; fr. large, 3–4 mm., granular, recurved. Calcareous fields, mostly S. England and S. Midlands, local. Flo. June–Sept. ⚘.

Galium spurium L. **False Cleavers.** *G. vaillantii* DC. ¶Similar to *G. aparine* but branches with more numerous 3–9 flo., greenish, with only 2 floral bracts instead of a whorl; fr. glabrous or with hooked hairs. In arable fields, in S. and E. England, local. Flo. July.

Galium odoratum (L.) Scop. **Sweet Woodruff.** *Asperula odorata* L. ¶Rhizomatous; stem 1 ft; flo. funnel shaped, tube equalling limb, white, fragrant; fr. with hooked hairs. Woods chiefly on calcareous soil. Flo. May–June. ⚘.

Asperula cynanchica L. **Squinancy Wort.** ¶Stock woody; branches prostrate; flo. few, funnel shaped, pale pink; fr. tubercled. On dry calcareous soils, chiefly in S. and E. England, S. Wales and W. Ireland, local. Flo. July–Aug. ⚘.

Sherardia arvensis L. **Field Madder.** ¶Stems prostrate; flo. in involucre, pink, tube much exceeding limb; sepals 4, 2 bifid, crowning the fr. Arable land, common in S. Britain, local in Ireland and in N. Scotland where it is mainly confined to the E. coast sand dunes. Flo. June–July. ⚘.

VALERIANACEAE

PLATE 43

Valeriana dioica L. **Lesser Valerian.** ¶Plant stoloniferous; stem 1 ft; lower leaves entire; flo. dioecious, pale pink. Local in marshes, throughout England and Wales. Flo. May–June. ⚘.

Valeriana officinalis L. **Valerian.** *V. sambucifolia* Mikan f. ¶Stolons short or 0; stem 3 ft; leaves all pinnate, very variable. Common in ditches, damp woods and on chalk downs. Flo. June–Sept. ⚘.

*Valeriana pyrenaica L. **Pyrenean Valerian.** ¶Stolons absent; stem 2 ft, downy, erect; basal leaves large, petiolate, cordate, toothed; upper leaves pinnate; lower pairs of leaflets oblong-acuminate; terminal leaflet broadly ovate-cordate; leaflets deeply and irregularly serrate; flo. pale pink, rarely white, in terminal corymbs; fr. glabrous. Naturalized in woods chiefly in S.W. and N. England and Scotland. Flo. June–July.

*Centranthus ruber (L.) DC. **Red Valerian.** ¶Stem 2 ft; leaves ovate; flo. rose-red, sometimes white, with slender tube and long spur. Garden escape. Naturalized on walls, rocks and banks, chiefly in S. England, the Midlands, Wales and E. Ireland. Flo. June–Aug.

Valerianella locusta (L.) Betcke. **Lamb's Lettuce.** *V. olitoria* (L.) Poll. ¶Fr. suborbicular, corky; calyx 0 or 1 minute point. Common in cultivated soil and hedge banks, chiefly in S. England. Flo. April–June. ⚘.

Valerianella carinata Lois. ¶Fr. oblong, nearly square in section, not corky; calyx faintly 1 toothed, sterile cells nearly confluent, as figure. Chiefly in S. and S.W. England, local. Flo. April–June. ⚘.

Valerianella rimosa Bast. ¶Inflo. lax; calyx teeth minute; sterile cells together larger than fertile one, and confluent. Cultivated ground, chiefly in S. England, local. Flo. July–Aug. ⚘.

Valerianella dentata (L.) Poll. ¶Inflo. lax; calyx 4 lobed, 3 lobes very small; fr. not corky. In fields, chiefly in S. and E. England, local. Flo. June–July. ✵.

*Valerianella eriocarpa Desv. ¶Fruit pilose; calyx deeply 5 lobed and strongly net veined. Naturalized in a few places. Flo. May–June. ✵ (fruit only).

DIPSACEAE

Dipsacus fullonum L. **Common Teasel.** *D. sylvestris* Huds. ¶Stem 4–5 ft; involucre long erect; bracteoles exceeding purple flo. and ending in flexible or stiff spine. In fields and hedge banks, on stream banks, waste ground, etc., chiefly in S. and E. England. Flo. July–Aug. ✵.

Dipsacus pilosus L. **Small Teasel.** ¶Stems 3–4 ft; bracteoles shorter than white flo., heads subglobose. In ditches and by calcareous streams, in England, local. Flo. Aug. ✵.

Knautia arvensis (L.) Coult. **Field Scabious.** *Scabiosa arvensis* L. ¶Stem 2 ft; bracts ovate; bracteoles 0; calyx teeth 8; petals 5. On dry banks and pastures. Flo. May–June. ✵.

Scabiosa columbaria L. ¶Stem 2 ft; bracts and bracteoles linear; calyx teeth 5; petals 5. On calcareous banks and pastures, but very rare in Scotland and absent from Ireland. Flo. July–Aug. ✵.

Succisa pratensis Moench. **Devil's Bit Scabious.** *Scabiosa succisa* L. ¶Stem 18 in.; bracteoles elliptic; calyx teeth 4; petals 4, blue-purple. In fens and damp meadows, common. Flo. June–Sept. ✵.

COMPOSITAE   **PLATE 44**

Eupatorium cannabinum L. **Hemp Agrimony.** ¶Stem 3 ft; inflo. of many small heads; each with oblong bracts and 5–6 reddish florets. Common in ditches and sides of streams, but local in N. England and Scotland. Flo. July–Sept. ✵.

Solidago virgaurea L. **Golden Rod.** ¶Stem 1–2 ft; flo. bracts in many rows; flo. golden; achenes ribbed. Common on heaths, dry banks and cliffs chiefly in the S. and W. Flo. July–Sept. ✵.

*Solidago altissima L. **Tall Golden Rod.** *S. canadensis* auct., non L. ¶Stem pubescent, 3–5 ft; leaves lanceolate, 3 veined, unequally toothed, roughish above, pubescent below; flo. small, golden yellow in numerous recurved racemes, forming a large pyramidal panicle. Garden escape. Naturalized by rivers, streams and lakes, and established on waste ground, etc., very common. Flo. Aug.–Nov.

*Solidago gigantea Ait. *S. serotina* Ait. ¶Similar to *S. altissima*, but stem glabrous below, up to 3 ft; leaves 3 veined, glabrous below except on midrib; flo. larger, ray florets exceeding disk florets, golden yellow, in compact erect corymbose panicles. Garden escape. Naturalized by rivers, streams and lakes, and established on waste ground, etc., common. Flo. Aug.–Nov.

*Solidago graminifolia (L.) Salisb. *S. lanceolata* L. ¶Stems glabrous, up to 3 ft; leaves linear-lanceolate, 3–5 veined entire, glabrous except on veins beneath; flo. small, ray florets not exceeding disk florets, golden yellow, in erect corymbose panicles. Garden escape. Naturalized on hedge banks, etc., rare. Flo. July–Sept.

Bellis perennis L. **Daisy.** ¶Plants forming a close mat; achenes without pappus. Abundant in short grass. Flo. all the year. ✤.

Aster tripolium L. **Sea Aster.** ¶Stem 18 in.; leaves fleshy; ray florets mauve or absent. Common in salt marshes. Flo. July–Sept. ✤.
Several alien species of *Aster* are spreading from gardens.

Crinitaria linosyris (L.) Less. **Goldilocks.** *Aster linosyris* (L.) Bernh. ¶Stem 1 ft; leaves linear; flo. all tubular, golden and fertile. On limestone cliffs, rare, S. Devon, Somerset, Wales, Lancashire. Flo. Aug.–Sept. ✤.

Conyza canadensis (L.) Cronq. *Erigeron canadensis* L. ¶Stem 18 in.; leaves linear; heads many, small, $\frac{1}{8}$ in. across, white. Alien in cultivated and waste ground, chiefly in S. and E. Britain. Flo. Aug.–Sept. ✤.

Erigeron acer L. **Blue Fleabane.** ¶Stem 10–12 in.; heads many, small; ray florets small, mauve; pappus red. On dry sandy and calcareous banks, chiefly in S. and E. Britain. Flo. July–Aug. ✤.

Erigeron borealis (Vierh.) Simmons. **Alpine Fleabane.** *E. alpinus* auct., non L. ¶Stem 6 in.; leaves mostly basal; heads solitary, $\frac{3}{4}$ in.; rays mauve. Rock ledges at about 3000 ft, mid Scotland. Flo. July–Aug. ✤.

Erigeron mucronatus DC. ¶Stem slender, μp to 6 in.; basal leaves obovate-cuneate, 3 lobed or coarsely toothed at apex; upper leaves linear-lanceolate; rays in 2 rows, white above, purple below. Naturalized in S. and S.W. England and the Channel Islands. Flo. July–Aug.

Filago vulgaris Lam. **Cudweed.** *F. germanica* auct. ¶Flo. in spherical clusters of about 30 heads, not overtopped by leaves. Common on sandy and acid heaths. Flo. July–Aug. ✤.

Filago lutescens Jord. *F. apiculata* G. E. Sm. ¶Flo. in clusters of about 15 heads, overtopped by leaves; flo. bracts red tipped. Sandy fields in S. and Central England, rare. Flo. July–Aug. ✤.

Filago pyramidata L. *F. spathulata* C. Presl. ¶Branches horizontal; clusters of about 12 5-angled heads, overtopped by leaves; flo. bracts yellow tipped. S. England, rare. Flo. July–Aug. ✤.

Filago minima (Sm.) Pers. ¶Flo. in small clusters of 3–6 heads, not overtopped by leaves; tips of flo. bracts blunt, yellowish. Common on sandy and gravelly soils. Flo. June–Sept. ✤.

Filago gallica L. ¶Flo. in small clusters of 2–6 heads, overtopped by leaves; tips of flo. bracts yellowish. In S. and E. England on gravel, rare. Flo. July–Aug. ✤.

Antennaria dioica (L.) Gaertn. ¶Dioecious and stoloniferous; stem 3–6 in.; leaves woolly, white beneath; flo. bracts often pink. On heaths and mountains, chiefly in N. Britain and W. Ireland. Flo. June–July. ✤.

Anaphalis margaritacea (L.) Benth. **Everlasting.** ¶Dioecious; stem 1–2 ft and leaves very woolly; flo. yellowish with woolly bracts. Garden escape. Naturalized in meadows, by streams and on wall tops, chiefly in Wales and Scotland. Flo. Aug.

Gnaphalium uliginosum L. **Marsh Cudweed.** ¶Stem 4–5 in. with woolly branches; flo. bracts pale brown, overtopped by leaves. Common in damp places and waysides. Flo. July–Aug. ✤.

Gnaphalium luteoalbum L. **Jersey Cudweed.** ¶Stem 12 in., branched; leaves oblong;

flo. bracts yellowish, not overtopped by leaves. Native in Channel Islands, introduced in E. England. Flo. June–Aug.

Gnaphalium sylvaticum L. **Wood Cudweed.** ¶Stem 6–9 in.; leaves linear-lanceolate; heads in a long leafy spike; bracts brown and green. Woods and heaths on acid soil, local. Flo. July–Sept. ❀.

Gnaphalium norvegicum Gunn. ¶Leaves lanceolate; heads in a short spike, ¼ length of stem; bracts dark brown. On mountains in Central Scotland. Flo. Aug. ❀.

Gnaphalium supinum L. **Creeping Cudweed.** ¶Stems creeping, ascending 2–3 in.; heads very few; bracts dark brown. Mountains in Scotland. Flo. July–Aug. ❀.

PLATE 45

Inula helenium L. **Elecampane.** ¶Stem 3–4 ft; flo. heads 2–3 in. across, golden; bracts broad. Fields and waste places. Flo. July–Aug. ❀.

Inula conyza DC. **Ploughman's Spikenard.** *I. squarrosa* (L.) Bernh. ¶Stem tough, 2 ft; inner flo. bracts purplish; outer florets tubular or very shortly ligulate. On dry calcareous soil, mostly in S. and mid Britain. Flo. July–Sept. ❀.

Inula salicina L. ¶Stem 18 in.; leaves elliptical, cordate at base; flo. few, 1 in.; ligules narrow, golden. Beside Lough Derg, Ireland. Flo. July–Aug.

Inula crithmoides L. **Golden Samphire.** ¶Stems and narrow leaves bright green, thick and fleshy; flo. golden. Salt marshes and wet rocks by the sea, S. and W. coasts. Flo. July–Aug. ❀.

*Telekia speciosa (Schreb.) Baumg. *Buphthalmum speciosum* Schreb. ¶Plant robust, hairy, strongly aromatic, superficially resembling *Inula helenium*; stem 3–4 ft; leaves alternate, glabrous above, hairy below; lower leaves triangular-cordate, double toothed, stalked; upper leaves ovate, sessile, with simple teeth; florets subtended by linear filiform scales (absent in *Inula*); flo. heads large with orange-yellow ray florets and very large prominent disk; bracts ovate, mucronate. Garden escape. Naturalized in wet places, chiefly in Scotland, though long known at Woodwalton Fen, Huntingdon. Flo. July–Sept.

Pulicaria dysenterica (L.) Bernh. **Fleabane.** ¶Stem 2 ft, woolly; leaf base cordate; flo. heads 1 in.; outer florets spreading, golden. Common in wet meadows and ditches, but local in mid Wales and Ireland and very rare in Scotland. Flo. Aug.–Sept. ❀.

Pulicaria vulgaris Gaertn. **Lesser Fleabane.** ¶Stem 1 ft; leaf base rounded; flo. heads ⅔ in., pale yellow; outer florets erect. Wet, muddy places in S. England, very rare. Flo. Aug.–Sept. ❀.

Bidens cernua L. **Nodding Bur-Marigold.** ¶Leaves simple, lanceolate, serrate; flo. heads nodding; sometimes (var. *radiata* DC.) with broad, yellow rays. In ponds and ditches, mostly S. and mid Britain and Ireland. Flo. July–Sept. ❀.

Bidens tripartita L. **Bur-Marigold.** ¶Leaves usually tripartite, stalked; terminal leaflet broad; flo. heads erect, yellow. In ponds and ditches. Flo. July–Sept. ❀.

*Bidens frondosa L. ¶Leaves usually pinnate with 3–6 separate leaflets; flo. heads erect on long stalks; disk florets yellow; achenes blackish, densely tubercled. By canals and rivers, chiefly in W. Midlands and S. Wales, introduced from N. America. Flo. July–Oct.

Galinsoga parviflora Cav. ¶1–2 ft, much branched; leaves ovate; flo. heads small; rays short, white; disk yellow; pappus of silvery scales, not awned. Alien, common in London area. Flo. May–Sept.

Galinsoga ciliata (Raf.) Blake. *G. quadriradiata* auct. ¶Closely resembles *G. parviflora* but stem is thickly clothed with spreading hairs; pappus scales awned. Alien, common in London area.

Ambrosia artemisiifolia L. **Ragweed.** *A. elatior* L. ¶Annual; stem erect, shortly hairy, up to 2 ft; leaves short stalked, in pairs, pinnatifid, dark green above, grey felted beneath; flo. small, greenish yellow; male flo. short stalked in clusters on drooping terminal spikes; female flo. solitary, or in small clusters in axils of upper leaves. Established on waste ground, though often only casual. Flo. July–Oct.

Ambrosia psilostachya DC. ¶Similar to *A. artemisiifolia*, but stem up to 18 in.; leaves smaller, thicker, less pinnatifid and more heavily grey felted beneath. Naturalized on dunes in Lancashire and Ayrshire. Flo. July–Oct.

Achillea millefolium L. **Yarrow, Milfoil.** ¶Stoloniferous; stem 1 ft; leaves finely divided; flo. heads ¼ in., white or pink. Common in grass. Flo. June–Aug. ✳.

Achillea ptarmica L. **Sneezewort.** ¶Stoloniferous; stem 2 ft; leaves linear-lanceolate; flo. heads few, ½ in., white. Common in wet meadows and on moors. Flo. July–Aug. ✳.

Otanthus maritimus (L.) Hoffmanns. & Link. *Diotis maritima* (L.) Desf. ex Cass. ¶Stem woolly, 6–10 in.; leaves woolly, white; flo. heads yellow, bracts woolly. Sandy sea-shores in S. England and S.E. Ireland, almost extinct. Flo. Aug. ✳.

Anthemis tinctoria L. **Yellow Chamomile.** ¶Perennial; stem 2 ft; ray florets golden; disk scales lanceolate, subulate. Garden escape. Naturalized in fields, etc. Flo. July–Aug. ✳.

Anthemis cotula L. **Stinking Chamomile.** ¶Annual; stem 18 in., foetid; flo. heads ¾ in.; ray florets white; disk scales linear; achenes tubercled. On basic soils, common in England, but local in Wales and very rare in Scotland and Ireland. Flo. July–Sept. ✳.

Anthemis arvensis L. **Corn Chamomile.** ¶Annual; slightly scented; flo. heads 1 in.; ray florets white; disk scales lanceolate, cuspidate; achenes rugose at top. On basic soil, local, and very rare in Ireland. Flo. June–July. ✳.

Chamaemelum nobile (L.) All. **Sweet Chamomile.** *Anthemis nobilis* L. ¶Perennial; sweetly aromatic; flo. heads 1 in.; rays white; disk scales oblong; achenes 3 ribbed. Sandy soil and moorland borders, mostly S. Britain and S. Ireland, introduced elsewhere. Flo. June–July. ✳.

PLATE 46

Chrysanthemum segetum L. **Corn Marigold.** ¶Annual; stem 1 ft, thickened below the flo.; rays yellow; bracts with broad scarious margins. In cultivated fields. Flo. June–Aug. ✳.

Chrysanthemum leucanthemum L. **Ox-eye Daisy.** ¶Perennial; stem 18 in.; leaves simple; flo. heads solitary; rays white. Common on basic soil and in pasture. Flo. June–Aug. ✳.

*_Chrysanthemum parthenium_ (L.) Bernh. **Feverfew, Bachelor's Buttons.** ¶Perennial; stem 18 in.; leaves pinnate; flo. heads many; rays white. In cultivated soil and waste places. Flo. July–Aug. ✵.

Chrysanthemum vulgare (L.) Bernh. **Tansy.** _Tanacetum vulgare_ L. ¶Perennial; stem 2 ft, tough; leaves fragrant, lower bipinnate; heads golden; rays 0. On hedge banks, common. Flo. July–Sept. ✵.

Tripleurospermum maritimum (L.) Koch. **Scentless Chamomile.**
Subsp. _maritimum._ ¶Leaf segments short, fleshy; disk nearly flat, without scales; achenes with elongate oil glands at top. At the seaside. Flo. July–Sept.
Subsp. _inodorum_ (L.) Hyland. ex Vaarama. _Matricaria inodora_ L. ¶Leaf segments long and mucronate; oil glands on achenes nearly circular. Common in cultivated land. ✵.

Matricaria recutita L. **Wild Chamomile.** _M. chamomilla_ L. ¶Annual; fragrant; flo. heads ¾ in.; disk conical, without scales; rays white, soon reflexed. On cultivated land, mostly S. and mid England, casual in Scotland and Ireland, local. Flo. June–July. ✵.

*_Matricaria matricarioides_ (Less.) Porter. _M. suaveolens_ (Pursh.) Buchen. ¶Annual; aromatic; flo. heads greenish; disk conical, hollow; rays none. Alien, common on farm tracks and waste places. Flo. June–July. ✵.

*_Cotula coronopifolia_ L. ¶Aromatic, stem ascending; leaves toothed or pinnatifid, with sheathing base; heads ¼ in., yellow; rays 0; marginal achenes winged. Established on waste ground, etc., rare. Flo. July–Aug.

Artemisia vulgaris L. **Mugwort.** ¶Aromatic; stem 3 ft, tough, grooved, reddish; leaves dark green above, white beneath. Waysides and waste places. Flo. July–Sept. ✵.

*_Artemisia verlotorum_ Lamotte. **Chinese Mugwort.** ¶Similar to _A. vulgaris_, but with long rhizomes and lower part of scape semi-woody and naked; leaflets longer and narrower, darker green, less white beneath and very aromatic; inflo. much more leafy. Naturalized by rivers, streams and roadsides and established on waste ground, common in the London area especially near the Thames. Flo. Oct.–Dec.

Artemisia norvegica Fr. **Norwegian Mugwort.** ¶Plant tufted, greyish, hairy, up to 4 in.; basal leaves stalked with toothed cuneate lobes; upper leaves sessile, pinnate; flo. heads yellow, up to ½ in. across, usually solitary, but sometimes 2–4 together, nodding; bracts with greenish midrib and wide dark brown margins. In mountains in W. Ross, very rare. Flo. July–Sept.

*_Artemisia stellerana_ Bess. **Dusty Miller.** ¶Stem creeping, ascending 1 ft; leaves white felted, with rounded lobes; heads ⅜ in.; bracts white; flo. yellow. Garden escape. Naturalized in hedge banks, ditches, etc., mostly S.W. England. Flo. July–Sept.

Artemisia absinthium L. **Wormwood.** ¶Stem silky, 2 ft; leaf segments blunt, silky both sides; bracts silky; heads hemispherical. In waste places, especially by the sea. Flo. July. ✵.

Artemisia maritima L. **Sea Wormwood.** ¶Aromatic; stem 15 in., downy; leaf segments blunt, woolly above and beneath. On sandy seasides, chiefly in S. and E. England and S. Wales. Flo. Aug.–Sept. ✵.

Artemisia campestris L. **Breckland Wormwood.** ¶Scentless; stem 18 in., glabrous; leaf segments narrow, linear, acute; bracts reddish. On sandy heaths of E. Anglia only. Flo. Aug.–Sept. ✵.

Tussilago farfara L. **Coltsfoot.** ¶Perennial with deep rhizomes; flo. rays very many, female, bright yellow. Common on basic soils, a troublesome weed. Flo. March. ✤.

*Petasites albus (L.) Gaertn. **White Butterbur.** ¶Perennial with thick rhizomes; leaves roundish, cordate, up to 1 ft wide, glabrous above, white pubescent beneath; leaf stems hairy; flo. heads many, white, scented, long stalked, appearing before the leaves; bracts narrow, pale green, glabrous. Garden escape. Naturalized in woods and plantations, by roadsides, etc., mostly in N.E. Scotland. Flo. March–May.

*Petasites japonicus (Sieb. & Zucc.) F. Schmidt. ¶Low creeping perennial; leaves roundish, cordate, deeply toothed, glabrous, bright green, up to 3 ft wide; flo. heads many, whitish, in dense corymbs, appearing before the leaves; bracts broad, oblong, pale green. Garden escape. Naturalized by lakes, etc., chiefly in S. England, rare. Flo. March–April.

*Petasites fragrans (Vill.) C. Presl. **Winter Heliotrope.** ¶Perennial with deep rhizomes; scapes with 6–8 heads of pale lilac flo.; leaves surviving winter. Established in hedge banks. Flo. Feb. ✤.

Petasites hybridus (L.) Gaertn., Mey. & Scherb. **Butterbur.** ¶Perennial with deep thick rhizomes; leaves 2 ft wide; flo. heads many, pink. Native, streamsides and wet meadows, mostly male except in N.W. Flo. April. ✤.

*Homogyne alpina (L.) Cass. ¶Leaves 1 in. across, reniform, dark green above, paler beneath; leaf stalks hairy; flo. heads similar to those of *Tussilago farfara*, solitary, purplish, on stem up to 6 in. Introduced. Naturalized in mountains in Clova and Outer Hebrides. Flo. May–Aug.

Doronicum pardalianches L. **Leopard's Bane.** ¶Leaves ovate amplexicaul; scape 18 in., with several heads, 1½–2 in., yellow. Introduced in a few plantations. Flo. May–July.

A similar plant with leaves narrowed into petiole and solitary heads 2½ in. wide is *D. plantagineum* L., sometimes found outcast from gardens.

PLATE 47

Senecio vulgaris L. **Groundsel.** ¶Flo. heads with involucre cylindrical; bracts linear, outer black tipped; rays none. Abundant in cultivated ground. Flo. all the year. ✤. Some varieties have a few ray florets. The figure is labelled var. *radiatus*. ✤.

Senecio sylvaticus L. **Wood Groundsel.** ¶Leaves softly pubescent; flo. heads with involucre conical, glandular; rays revolute. Common in woods on sandy soils. Flo. July–Sept. ✤.

Senecio × viscidulus Scheele. (*S. sylvaticus × viscosus*). ¶Intermediate between the parents, sometimes occurs where the two grow together.

Senecio viscosus L. **Sticky Groundsel.** ¶Stem stout, very glandular; heads with involucre ovoid, conical; rays revolute. In waste ground, locally common. Flo. July–Sept. ✤.

*Senecio squalidus L. **Oxford Ragwort.** ¶Stem 1 ft; leaves glabrous, toothed or pinnatifid; heads ¾ in.; rays rather broad. Introduced, spreading on railways, etc., locally abundant, but rare in Scotland and N. Ireland. Flo. June–Sept. ✤.

*Senecio × londinensis Lousley. (S. squalidus × viscosus). ¶Intermediate between the parents, sometimes occurs where the two grow together.

*Senecios squalidus × vulgaris. ¶Intermediate between the parents, sometimes occurs where the two grow together.

Senecio erucifolius L. **Hoary Ragwort.** ¶Stem 2–3 ft; leaves with linear-acute lobes, cottony beneath. On calcareous and heavy soils, mainly in S. and E. England. Flo. July–Aug. �.

Senecio jacobaea L. **Ragwort.** ¶Stem 2–3 ft; leaves glabrous with lobes broadly toothed and blunt. Abundant on neglected pastures. Flo. July–Oct. ✢.

Senecio aquaticus Hill. **Marsh Ragwort.** ¶Stem 1–3 ft, purplish; upper leaves pinnatifid with forward pointing lobes, lower undivided or pinnatifid. Wet meadows. Flo. July–Aug. ✢.
Var. *pennatifidus* Gren. & Gódr. ¶Leaves with lobes at right angles.

Senecio × ostenfeldii Druce. (S. aquaticus × jacobaea). ¶Intermediate between the parents, often occurs where the two grow together, especially in Scotland and Wales.

*Senecio doria L. ¶3 ft; leaves elliptical, fleshy, glaucous, entire or toothed; heads ½ in.; rays few, 4–6. Established on a few streamsides. Flo. July–Sept.

*Senecio fluviatilis Wallr. **Broad-leaved Ragwort.** S. sarracenicus auct. ¶Stoloniferous; stem 3 ft; leaves elliptical, glabrous, 7 × 1½ in.; heads 1 in.; involucre pubescent. Introduced, streamsides. Flo. Aug.

Senecio paludosus L. **Great Fen Ragwort.** ¶Stem 4–5 ft; leaves long lanceolate, serrate, cottony beneath; rays many. Fen ditches, in E. England, very rare, almost extinct. Flo. May–July. ✢.

Senecio palustris (L.) Hook. **Marsh Fleawort.** S. congestus (R. Br.) DC. ¶Stem stout, woolly, 2–3 ft; leaves broadly lanceolate; involucre without shorter scales; heads ¾ in., crowded. Fen ditches, in E. England, apparently extinct. Flo. June.

Senecio integrifolius (L.) Clairv. **Field Fleawort.** S. campestris (Retz.) DC. ¶Stem 6–8 in., wiry, cottony; lower leaves lanceolate, narrowed to stalk. On chalk downs and limestone grassland, S. England to Lincolnshire, local. Flo. June–July. ✢.

Senecio spathulifolius Turcz. **Spathulate Fleawort.** ¶Stem 18 in., stout; lower leaves narrowed abruptly to stalk; stem leaves amplexicaul. Cliffs in Anglesey and Micklefell, Yorkshire. Flo. June–July. ✢.

*Senecio cineraria DC. ¶Stem shrubby and woolly; leaves pinnatifid, white felted beneath; heads many. Naturalized on sea cliffs, S. and S.W. Flo. June–Aug. ✢.

Carlina vulgaris L. **Carline Thistle.** ¶Leaves and outer bracts spinous; inner bracts whitish, spreading like rays; florets purple. On calcareous grassland, local. Flo. July–Sept. ✢.

Arctium lappa L. **Great Burdock.** A. majus Bernh. ¶Leaf petioles solid; heads few, 1½–2 in., long stalked, open in fruit; bracts green. Scattered in waste places mostly in S. and mid Britain. Flo. July–Sept. ✢.

Arctium pubens Bab. **Common Burdock.** A. nemorosum auct. A. vulgare auct. ¶Petioles hollow; heads 1–1½ in., stalked and webbed, wide open in fr.; all bracts subulate, equalling the flo. In woods, scrub, etc., local. Flo. July–Sept. ✢.

Arctium minus Bernh. **Lesser Burdock.** ¶Smaller plant; heads short stalked or sessile, ¾–1 in., ovate, closed in fr.; bracts distinctly shorter than flo., subulate. In waste places, by roadsides, etc., common. Flo. July–Sept. ❀.

PLATE 48

Carduus pycnocephalus L. **Plymouth Thistle.** ¶Wings on stems interrupted below heads; leaves cottony beneath; heads ¾ in., florets exceeding bracts. Long established on Plymouth Hoe. Flo. June–August.

Carduus tenuiflorus Curt. **Slender-flowered Thistle.** ¶Stem winged and spinous throughout; leaves less cottony; heads ½ in.; florets not exceeding bracts. On sea cliffs, rare inland. Flo. June–Aug. ❀.

Carduus nutans L. **Nodding Thistle.** ¶Stem wings interrupted; heads 2 in., nodding; inner bracts contracted above base. On calcareous soils, local in N. England and rare in Scotland and Ireland. Flo. May–Aug. ❀.

Carduus acanthoides L. **Welted Thistle.** *C. crispus* auct. ¶Stem wings almost continuous; heads ¾ in., erect; inner bracts not contracted above base. Waste places, rare in Scotland and W. Ireland. Flo. June–Aug. ❀.

Cirsium vulgare (Savi) Ten. **Spear Thistle.** *Carduus lanceolatus* L. ¶Stem leaves ½–1 ft, decurrent, with few lobes; heads 1–1½ in.; involucre ovate, hairy. Common. Flo. July–Sept. ❀.

Cirsium eriophorum (L.) Scop.
Subsp. *britannicum* Petrak. **Woolly Thistle.** ¶Leaves 1–2 ft, not decurrent, lobes deep and bifid; heads 2–3 in., globose, woolly. On calcareous soil, mainly in S. and E. England and Midlands, local. Flo. Aug. ❀.

Cirsium palustre (L.) Scop. **Marsh Thistle.** *Carduus palustris* L. ¶Stem 3–5 ft; leaves decurrent, pinnatifid, spinous; heads ¾ in., clustered. Common in wet places. Flo. June–Sept. ❀.

Cirsium dissectum (L.) Hill. **Meadow Thistle.** *Carduus pratensis* Huds. ¶Stoloniferous; stem 2 ft, simple, cottony; leaves mostly basal, toothed or lobed, prickles soft. In wet meadows, mainly S. and mid Britain and Ireland. Flo. June–July. ❀.

Cirsium tuberosum (L.) All. **Tuberous Meadow Thistle.** ¶Similar to *C. dissectum*, but with tuberous roots and no stolons; basal leaves deeply lobed. In calcareous pastures, rare and local, Wiltshire, Gloucestershire, Glamorgan and Cambridgeshire. Flo. Aug.

Cirsium heterophyllum (L.) Hill. **Melancholy Thistle.** ¶Stoloniferous; stem 3 ft; leaves broad, cordate, not prickly, white beneath. In wet mountainous places, mid Wales to Scotland, very rare in Ireland. Flo. July–Aug. ❀.

Cirsium acaule Scop. **Ground Thistle.** *C. acaulon* auct. ¶Stemless or nearly so; flo. heads sessile on basal leaf rosette. On calcareous pastures from Yorkshire southwards. Flo. July–Aug. ❀.

Cirsium arvense (L.) Scop. **Creeping Thistle.** ¶Roots creeping and white; stem 2 ft without wings; heads dioecious, bracts appressed. In grass, abundant. Flo. July–Sept. ❀.

*Cirsium oleraceum (L.) Scop. ¶Stem 3 ft, wingless; leaves ovate, uppermost yellowish exceeding flo. heads. Locally established in plantations. Flo. July.

PLATE 49

Onopordon acanthium L. **Scottish Thistle.** ¶Stem 3–5 ft, broadly winged; leaves elliptic, woolly, spinous; heads nearly globose. Doubtfully native. By roadsides, in waste places, etc., mainly E. England. Flo. July–Aug. ✲.

*Silybum marianum (L.) Gaertn. **Milk Thistle.** ¶Stem 4 ft; leaves large, green, variegated with milk-white beside veins; heads 2 in. Naturalized locally. Flo. June–July.

Saussurea alpina (L.) DC. **Alpine Saw-wort.** ¶3–12 in.; stem and underside of leaves cottony; flo. scented, blue. On alpine rocks, Scotland to N. Wales and Ireland. Flo. Aug.–Sept. ✲.

Serratula tinctoria L. **Saw-wort.** ¶Stem 1–2 ft, slender, grooved; leaves mostly pinnate; margin finely toothed. In moist meadows and moors in England and Wales, very rare in Ireland and absent from Scotland. Flo. June–Aug. ✲.

*Centaurea jacea L. ¶Leaves lanceolate, mostly subentire; bract appendages pale brown, rounded and jagged. In pastures, S. England, introduced, rare. Flo. Aug.–Sept. ✲.

Centaurea nigra L. **Knapweed, Hardheads.** *C. obscura* Jord. ¶Stem swollen below the heads; bract appendages blackish, concealing base. Frequent in grassy places on heavy soils, especially in the N. Flo. July–Sept. ✲.

Centaurea nemoralis Jord. **Brown Knapweed.** ¶Stem slender, not swollen below heads; bract appendages brown; outer flo. often enlarged. Common in grassy places on calcareous and light soils, especially in S. England. Flo. July–Sept. ✲.

Centaurea scabiosa L. **Great Knapweed.** ¶Leaves pinnatifid; bracts pale green, not fully covered by dark fringe. Mostly on calcareous soils, but frequent by railways as an introduction. Flo. July–Sept. ✲.

Centaurea cyanus L. **Cornflower.** ¶Stem, and upper linear-lanceolate leaves cottony; bract fringe silvery; flo. blue. Cornfields and waste land. Flo. June–Aug. ✲.

**Centaurea paniculata* L. ¶Leaves pinnatifid, lobes linear cottony; bract teeth small pale; flo. purple. Established in Jersey. Flo. July.

Centaurea aspera L. ¶Leaves narrow; bract fringe reflexed yellowish, palmate, spinous. Channel Islands. Flo. July–Aug. ✲.

Centaurea calcitrapa L. **Star Thistle.** ¶Flo. red-purple; bracts ending in long spreading spurs and smaller spines. Gravelly and sandy places, mainly S. England, rare. Flo. July–Sept. ✲.

Centaurea solstitialis* L. **Yellow Star Thistle. ¶Stem broadly winged; bracts palmately spinous; terminal spine and flo. yellow. Introduced in cultivated land. Flo. July–Sept.

PLATE 50

Cichorium intybus L. **Chicory.** ¶Stem 3 ft, branched and tough; heads clustered in axils; flo. blue. In fields, by roadsides, etc., chiefly on calcareous and alluvial soils, probably introduced in Scotland and Ireland. Flo. July–Sept. ✲.

Arnoseris minima (L.) Schweigg. & Koerte. **Swine's Succory.** *A. pusilla* Gaertn. ¶Leaves radical; stems hollow, widening above; bracts united; flo. yellow. On sandy soils in S. and E. counties. Flo. June–Aug. ✲.

Lapsana communis L. **Nipple-wort.** ¶Stem 2 ft, branched and leafy; bracts linear, erect; florets few in each head, pale yellow. Common, except in N. Scotland. Flo. July–Sept. �֍.

Picris hieracioides L. **Hawkweed Ox-tongue.** ¶Stem 2 ft, with hooked bristles; stiff bristles on leaves; beak of fr. short. Mostly on calcareous soils in S. Britain, very rare in Ireland. Flo. July–Sept. ✖.

Picris echioides L. **Bristly Ox-tongue.** *Helmintia echioides* (L.) Gaertn. ¶Stem 2 ft; leaves and bracts with hairs on white tubercles; fr. long beaked. On calcareous soils and sea cliffs mostly in S. and E. England and Wales, very rare in Ireland, and introduced in Scotland. Flo. June–Sept. ✖.

Crepis foetida L. **Stinking Hawk's-beard.** ¶Stem 2 ft, branched and leafy below; buds drooping; bracts downy; inner fr. long beaked. Mostly on chalk, S. England, rare. Flo. June–Aug. ✖.

*Crepis vesicaria.

Subsp. *taraxacifolia* (Thuill.) Thell. **Beaked Hawk's-beard.** *C. taraxacifolia* Thuill. ¶Stem 1½ ft, branched above; heads many, erect in bud; fr. beaked. In waste ground, fields, by roadsides, etc., common in S. and E. England and the Midlands, local in Wales and Ireland, and rare, but increasing in N. England and Scotland. Flo. June–July. ✖.

*Crepis setosa Haller f. **Bristly Hawk's-beard.** ¶Stem 2 ft; leaves pinnate, hispid; bracts bristly; flo. pale yellow; fr. beaked. Introduced, mostly in clover fields, rare. Flo. July–Aug.

Crepis capillaris (L.) Wallr. **Smooth Hawk's-beard.** *C. virens* L. ¶Stem 2 ft; leaves pinnate, upper sagittate, glabrous; heads ½ in.; fr. 10 ribbed. Common. Flo. June–Sept. ✖.

*Crepis nicaeensis Balb. **French Hawk's-beard.** ¶Leaves pinnate or sagittate, roughly hairy; heads 1 in.; bracts glandular; disk ciliate. Introduced in cultivated land, rare. Flo. June–July.

Crepis biennis L. **Greater** or **Rough Hawk's-beard.** ¶Stem 3 ft; leaves hispid, pinnate, broad; heads 1½ in.; inner bracts downy within. On calcareous soils, native in S. and E. England, probably introduced elsewhere, local. Flo. June–July. ✖.

Crepis mollis (Jacq.) Aschers. **Soft Hawk's-beard.** ¶Stem 1½ ft; leaves entire; outer bracts short, appressed, glandular; fr. with 20 ribs. In woods in the N., local. Flo. July–Aug. ✖.

Crepis paludosa (L.) Moench. **Marsh Hawk's-beard.** ¶Stem 2 ft; leaves tapering to point; bracts woolly, glandular; pappus brown. In wet meadows from S. Wales to N. Scotland and Ireland. Flo. July–Sept. ✖.

Hypochoeris glabra L. **Smooth Cat's-ear.** ¶Stem 3–10 in.; leaves radical; heads ½ in., bracts glabrous; inner fr. beaked. Sandy heaths and dunes, mostly in the southern half of Britain, local; rare in Scotland and Ireland, opening in morning sun only. Flo. June–Oct. ✖.

Hypochoeris radicata L. **Common Cat's-ear.** ¶Stem 1½ ft; forked and bracteate; leaves radical, hispid; heads 1½ in. across. Very common. Flo. May–July. ✖.

Hypochoeris maculata L. **Spotted Cat's-ear.** ¶Stem 1½ ft; leaves hispid, purple spotted; heads broad; involucre blackish, hispid. On calcareous banks and cliffs, mostly E. England, very local; very rare in the Channel Islands, Cornwall, N. Wales and Lancashire. Flo. July–Aug. ✖.

Genus HIERACIUM **PLATE 51**

Botanists who wish to identify *Hieracia* should study H. W. Pugsley's 'Prodromus of the British Hieracia' in the *Journal of the Linnean Society of London* (Botany), vol. 54. This is sold at the Society's rooms at Burlington House, Piccadilly, London W.1. Mr Pugsley has given us a clear picture of the genus with descriptions of 260 species and their distribution. The following notes are only abbreviated extracts from Mr Pugsley's summary of sections, together with short descriptions of 23 sample species, 15 of them figured, in order to show the kind of gradation which may be recognized among them.

Section 1. *Amplexicaulia.* ¶Leaves mostly in a radical rosette, densely clothed with many stalked glands; stem with a few amplexicaul leaves; heads large; ligules with pilose tips. Unlike the rest of the genus the 3 species in this section seem to be fairly recently introduced, e.g. *Hieracium amplexicaule* L.

Section 2. *Alpina.* ¶Leaves in a radical rosette, with long pilose hairs and sparingly clothed with stalked glands; stem leaves o or bract-like; heads solitary, rather large; involucre (floral bracts) incumbent in bud, densely clothed with long pilose hairs; ligules (strap-shaped corolla) pilose at tip. 15 species including:

Hieracium holosericeum Backh. ¶Leaves light green, narrow, obtuse, subentire, all clothed with long silky pilose hairs. Chiefly in N. Scotland. ✵.
The scarcer *H. alpinum* L. has leaves darker green, more obovate, with less silky heads.

Section 3. *Subalpina.* ¶Leaves in a radical rosette, pilose, and with a few fine yellow glands; stem leaves 1–few, small, lanceolate; inflo. of 2–5 large heads, often very glandular or pilose. 22 species including:

Hieracium lingulatum Backh. ¶Radical leaves long, lanceolate, subentire, rough with stiff pilose hairs; head large, blackish, pilose; flo. bracts broad, erect in bud. Central to N. Scotland. ✵.

Section 4. *Cerinthoidea.* ¶Stem and leaves without glands, in rosette, clothed with long denticulate hairs, rather glaucous; stem leaves semi-amplexicaul; heads large, with densely pilose incumbent bracts; ligules with pilose tips. 14 species including:

Hieracium anglicum Fr. ¶Radical leaves ovate, denticulate, narrowed below to petiole; stem leaves 2, upper bract-like; heads 1–4 with long glandular penduncles; flo. bracts densely clothed with long black-based hairs and few glands; styles livid. Widely distributed in Scotland, N. England and Ireland. ✵.

Section 5. *Oreadea.* ¶Leaves in rosette, narrowed below (except nos. 1–3), often glaucous, without glands but with long rigid hairs (setae); stem leaves not amplexicaul; heads less pilose than in sections 2–4; flo. bracts erect; ligules mostly glabrous tipped; styles yellow. 19 species including:

Hieracium lasiophyllum Koch. ¶Leaves oblong, obtuse, little toothed, rounded below, upper surface rough with setae; flo. bracts greyish green. England (W. Midlands), Wales, Scotland and Ireland.

Hieracium eustomon (E. F. Linton) Roffey. ¶Leaves broadly oval, rounded below, toothed, with setae on margin only; flo. bracts dark green. In Devon, W. Somerset and Wales.

Hieracium schmidtii Tausch. ¶Leaves oval, toothed, usually tapering below, with stiff hairs on margin only; 1 stem leaf; flo. bracts dark green. England, Wales, Scotland, Ireland. ❋.

Hieracium argenteum Fr. ¶Plant more slender; leaves narrower, lanceolate, glaucous, toothed, with fewer stiff hairs; 2 stem leaves; flo. bracts dark green. In N. England, Wales, Scotland and Ireland.

Section 6. *Suboreadea.* ¶Leaves in rosette, glaucous, sometimes purple spotted, rather board, rounded or angled below; stem leaves 0–3, narrowed below, with hairs less rigid than in section 5; bracts usually erect in bud; styles yellow. 17 species including:

Hieracium britannicum F. J. Hanb. ¶Leaves ovate-lanceolate, scarcely glaucous, unspotted, sharply toothed; stem leaf 0 or 1; flo. bracts long, narrow, greyish green; ligules glabrous. Wales, and from Cheddar, Derby dales, Teesdale to Scotland and Ireland. ❋.

Section 7. *Vulgata.*

Subsection *Bifida.* ¶Leaves in rosette, mostly glabrous above; peduncles and flo. bracts not very glandular, but more or less pilose and with stellate hairs. 13 species of limited distribution in N. England and Scotland.

Subsection *Stellatifolia.*¶Leaves in a rosette, these and the flo. bracts clothed with stellate hairs. 2 species of limited distribution in England and Wales.

Subsection *Glandulosa.* ¶Leaves in rosette, usually more or less clothed with long pilose hairs; flo. bracts clothed with dark, strong glandular hairs; stem leaves 0–1. 21 species including:

Hieracium pellucidum Laest. ¶Leaves dark green, subglabrous above, purplish beneath, broadly oval, with broad toothed base; heads small; flo. bracts blackish green; styles livid. In England, Wales and Ireland.

Hieracium exotericum Jord. ex Bor. ¶Leaves light green, softly pilose on both surfaces, oval with broad toothed base; styles yellow. England, Wales, Ireland, rare in Scotland.
Forma *grandidens* (Dahlst.) Pugsl. ¶Leaves more deeply toothed; styles livid. ❋.

Subsection *Sagittata.* ¶Leaves mostly in rosette, pilose, with spreading teeth at base; flo. bracts densely glandular and sometimes with long or stellate hairs. 12 species in Scotland, N. England, Wales.

Subsection *Caesia.* ¶Plants with more stem leaves, glaucous, narrowed below flo. bracts with dense stellate hairs and a few glandular. 23 species mostly in Scotland and N. England.

Subsection *Eu-vulgata.* ¶Plants with several stem leaves, tapering to petiole; flo. bracts densely glandular and with stellate hairs. 22 species, mostly in England and Wales, including:

Hieracium vulgatum Fr. ¶Radical leaves narrow with sharp ascending teeth, purplish beneath; stem leaves 2–5; flo. bracts greyish green, incumbent in bud, with pilose hairs and a few short glands. In Scotland, N. and mid England, Wales, Ireland. ❋.

PLATE 52

Hieracium maculatum Sm. ¶Radical leaves narrow, dark green, spotted, dentate, with stiff hairs on both surfaces; stem leaves 3–5; flo. bracts greyish green, with short glandular and few longer pilose hairs. In England. ❋.

Hieracium diaphanum Fr. *H. anglorum* (Ley) Pugsl. ¶Plant robust; radical leaves often few, ovate, dentate; stem leaves 3–5; heads small; flo. bracts with dense, dark glandular hairs and a few stellate. In many counties of England, rare in Ireland.

Hieracium lachenalii C. C. Gmel. ¶Plant robust; radical leaves few, with rough hairs, ovate, sharply dentate; stem leaves 4–12; flo. bracts deep olive-green, with stellate hairs; ligules with pilose tips. In 47 counties of England and Wales. �.

Section 8. *Alpestria*. ¶Stem leaves numerous, rounded below, amplexicaul; heads few, often on branches from upper leaf axils; flo. bracts dark, obtuse, finely glandular, without stellate hairs; ligules glabrous. 18 species in N. Scotland.

Section 9. *Prenanthoidea*. ¶Radical leaves 0; stem leaves numerous, green reticulate below, semi-amplexicaul; heads many, small; peduncles and flo. bracts densely clothed with dark glandular hairs; styles livid. 2 species.

Section 10. *Tridentata*. ¶Plants often tall; stem leaves many, green, serrate, with thickened edges and narrowed base; flo. bracts incumbent in bud, less clothed than in sections 1–9, often microglandular; ligules glabrous. 32 species mostly of very limited distribution, but including:

Hieracium trichocaulon (Dahlst.) Johans. *H. tridentatum* Fr. ¶Leaves elliptic-lanceolate with sharp erect teeth, subglabrous; heads many, small, pale; flo. bracts olive-green with pale edges, with some pilose hairs and some glandular. In 27 counties of England and Wales. ✶.

Section 11. *Foliosa*. ¶Leaves all on the stem, numerous, paler and reticulate beneath; upper semi-amplexicaul, margins thickened; heads rather large, numerous; flo. bracts with glandular hairs and some pilose. 16 species, mostly in Scotland and N. England, including:

Hieracium latobrigorum (Zahn) Roffey. ¶Leaves dull or yellowish green, shortly or sparingly dentate, lower tapering below, upper rounded; peduncles with stellate hairs; flo. bracts dark olive-green, with dark glandular hairs and micro-glands; styles yellow. In 19 counties of Scotland, 4 of England. ✶.

Section 12. *Umbellata*. ¶Leaves numerous, not reticulate beneath, margins recurved, base narrow, attentuate; inflo. subumbellate; outer flo. bracts with reflexed tips, nearly glabrous. 3 species including:

Hieracium umbellatum L. subsp. *umbellatum*. ¶Leaves numerous, dark green, paler beneath, linear-lanceolate with few small spreading teeth; flo. bracts blackish green; styles yellow. In 63 counties of England, Wales and Scotland, 11 in Ireland. ✶.

Hieracium umbellatum L. subsp. *bichlorophyllum* (Druce & Zahn) P. D. Sell & C. West. *H. bichlorophyllum* (Druce & Zahn) Pugsl. ¶Leaves numerous, clear green, paler beneath, oblong-lanceolate subentire or with 1–2 broad shallow teeth; inflo. with longer branches; flo. bracts olive-green; styles yellow. In S.W. England, Wales and Ireland.

Section 13. *Sabauda*. ¶Stems hirsute; leaves numerous, lower lanceolate, upper ovate, often densely pilose beneath, not reticulate; flo. bracts appressed or the outer lax, dark green with fine glands and pilose or subglabrous; styles livid. 11 species mostly in England and Wales.

Hieracium perpropinquum (Zahn) Druce. *H. bladonii* Pugsl. ¶Lower stem clothed with long whitish hairs; leaves dark green, broadly lanceolate, with sharp ascending teeth; peduncles with stellate and pilose hairs; flo. bracts with some glandular hairs and long whitish hairs at base; outer bracts loose. In 36 counties of England and Wales, 7 of Scotland. ❀.

Section 14. *Pilosellina*. ¶Plants with stolons, basal rosettes and 1-headed flo. stems; ligules pale yellow, red beneath.

Pilosella officinarum C. H. & F. W. Schultz. **Mouse-ear Hawkweed.** *Hieracium pilosella* L. ¶Stolons long and creeping; leaves setose above and on the margins, white beneath with soft hairs; flo. bracts clothed with dense stellate, glandular and pilose hairs. Generally distributed and common. ❀ on plate 51.

Pilosella peleteriana (Mérat) C. H. & F. W. Schultz. *Hieracium peleterianum* Mérat. ¶Stolons short and thick; leaves deep green, with dense pilose hairs above, grey beneath with stellate hairs; flo. bracts tapering, clothed with long, pale black-based hairs. Channel Islands and Cornwall to Merioneth and Derbyshire, very local. ❀.

Section 15. *Pratensina*. ¶Plants with stolons and few stem leaves; leaves entire with long stiff hairs; heads many.

Pilosella aurantiaca (L.) C. H. & F. W. Schultz. **Orange Hawkweed.** *Hieracium aurantiacum* L.
Subsp. *aurantiaca*. ¶Plant with few stolons; leaves obovate; flo. brick-red or reddish orange. Garden escape. Naturalized in grassy places, rare.
Subsp. *brunneocroceum* (Pugsl.) P. D. Sell & C. West. *Hieracium brunneocroceum* Pugsl. ¶Plant with many long quick-growing stolons; leaves oblong or oblanceolate; flo. smaller than those of subsp. *aurantiaca*, brownish orange. Garden escape. Naturalized in grassy places, rather common.

Pilosella caespitosa (Dumort.) P. D. Sell & C. West. subsp. *colliniformis* (Naeg. & Peter) P. D. Sell & C. West. *Hieracium colliniforme* (Naeg. & Peter) Roffey. ¶Stem hairy; heads 12–30 in a compact corymb; flo. yellow with dark styles. Naturalized in a few scattered localities from the W. Midlands to N. Scotland, rare.

PLATE 53

Leontodon taraxacoides (Vill.) Mérat. **Hawkbit.** *L. leysseri* (Wallr.) Beck. ¶Stem slender, subglabrous; head solitary, drooping in bud; outer fr. with crown of scales, inner with pappus. Locally common in dry grassy places, but rare in N. England and very rare in Scotland. Flo. June–Sept. ❀.

Leontodon hispidus L. **Rough Hawkbit.** ¶Stem hairy; head solitary, densely hairy, drooping in bud; fr. with 2 rows of pappus. Locally common in grassy places, especially on calcareous soils, but very rare in Scotland and N. Ireland. Flo. June–Sept. ❀.

Leontodon autumnalis L. **Smooth Hawkbit.** ¶Stem glabrous, branched, scaly; leaves usually glabrous, often pinnatifid; fr. with 1 row of pappus. Common in grassy places. Flo. July–Oct. ❀.
Var. *pratensis* Koch. ¶Involucre clothed with black hairs. Mostly on mountains.

Taraxacum officinale Weber. **Dandelion.** ¶Leaves with tooth-like lobes; outer flo. bracts long, recurved; heads large; fr. light brown. Very common in fields, lawns, waste places, by roadsides, etc. Flo. March–July. ❀.

Taraxacum palustre (Lyons) DC. **Little Marsh Dandelion.** *T. paludosum* (Scop.)

Schlecht. ex Crep. ¶Leaves narrow, subentire or teeth few; heads small; flo. bracts broadly ovate, closely appressed. In marshes, fens, wet meadows, etc., local. Flo. May–July. ✲.

Taraxacum spectabile Dahlst. **Bog Dandelion.** ¶Leaves large, dark green, midrib red; flo. bracts loosely appressed; ligules red at back. In marshes, wet meadows, by streamsides, on mountains, etc., local. Flo. May–July.

Taraxacum laevigatum (Willd.) DC. **Lesser Dandelion.** *T. erythrospermum* Andrz. ex Bess. ¶Leaves deeply divided, segments narrow, with intermediate smaller ones; outer flo. bracts spreading, inner with a dorsal appendage at apex; fr. red. In dry places, common. Flo. May–July. ✲.

Taraxacum obliquum (Fr.) Dahlst. ¶Has fr. pale brown and brighter yellow flo.

Lactuca virosa L. **Acrid Lettuce.** ¶Stem 3 ft; lower leaves with broad segments; beak equalling smooth black fr. On waste ground, banks, etc., especially near the sea, mainly E. England, locally common. Flo. July–Aug. ✲.

Lactuca serriola L. **Prickly Lettuce.** *L. scariola* L. ¶Stem 4 ft; lower leaves with narrow distant curved segments; beak equalling fr. On sand dunes and waste places, mostly S. and E. England. Flo. July–Aug. ✲.

Lactuca saligna L. **Least Lettuce.** ¶Stem 2 ft; upper leaves linear, lower pinnate, segments narrow, acute; inflo. narrow; beak long. On banks near S. and E. coasts, local. Flo. July–Aug.

Mycelis muralis (L.) Reichb. **Wall Lettuce.** *Lactuca muralis* (L.) Gaertn. ¶Stem 2 ft; leaves thin, lobes irregular; inflo. wide spreading; beak of fr. very short. On calcareous rocks, walls and in woods, local in N. England and rare in Scotland and Ireland. Flo. July–Aug. ✲.

Cicerbita alpina (L.) Wallr. **Alpine Lettuce.** *Lactuca alpina* (L.) A. Gray. ¶Stem 3–4 ft, glandular above; leaves with large terminal lobe; involucre glandular; flo. blue. Clova Mountains, very rare. Flo. July–Aug. ✲.

*Cicerbita macrophylla (Willd.) Wallr. **Blue Sowthistle.** *Lactuca macrophylla* (Willd.) A. Gray. ¶Stem up to 3 ft, with creeping rhizome; glabrous below, glandular above; lower leaves large, lyrate, with triangular terminal lobe; upper leaves smaller, often sessile; involucre glandular, hairy; flo. lilac-blue in a simple or compound terminal raceme. Garden escape. Naturalized in grassy places and established on waste ground, widespread throughout Britain and Ireland. Flo. July–Aug.

Sonchus oleraceus L. **Common Sowthistle.** ¶Leaves not spinous, basal auricles acute, spreading; involucre glabrous; fr. 6 ribbed, rugose. On cultivated land, common. Flo. June–Aug. ✲.

Sonchus asper (L.) Hill. **Prickly Sowthistle.** ¶Leaves spinous, basal auricles round and clasping; involucre glabrous; fr. 6 ribbed, smooth. On cultivated land, common. Flo. June–Aug. ✲.

Sonchus arvensis L. **Corn Sowthistle.** ¶Stoloniferous; leaf spines soft, basal auricles round; inflo. with yellow glands; fr. 10 ribbed; flo. golden. Cultivated land, common. Flo. Aug.–Sept. ✲.

Sonchus palustris L. **Fen Sowthistle.** ¶Stem 6 ft; lower leaves deeply pinnatifid, basal lobes acute; inflo. with blackish glands; flo. lemon colour. Fens and ditches, E. England, rare. Flo. July–Aug. ✲.

Tragopogon pratensis L. **Goat's-beard.**
Subsp. *pratensis.* ¶Flo. rather pale yellow, equalling pale-edged involucre; anthers yellow; outer fr. smooth, 15–20 mm. Rare in waste places in Britain, common on Continent.
Subsp. *minor* (Mill.) Wahlenb. **Lesser Goat's-beard.** *Tragopogon minor* Mill. ¶Flo. bright yellow, shorter than red-edged involucre; anthers brownish; outer fr. rugose, 10–12 mm. Locally common in grassy places, waste places, etc., but rare in Scotland and Ireland. Flo. June–July. ✻.

* *Tragopogon porrifolius* L. **Salsify.** ¶Stem much thickened at top; flo. purple. Escape from cultivation. Naturalized in rough grassy places, etc., chiefly S. England. Flo. June–Aug.

Scorzonera humilis L. ¶Leaves lanceolate acuminate; flo. pale yellow, exceeding involucre, woolly below. Marshy fields in Dorset and meadow in Warwickshire. Flo. May–July.

LOBELIACEAE

Lobelia dortmanna L. **Water Lobelia.** ¶Aquatic; leaves radical submerged, linear, of 2 tubes; flo. pale lilac. In gravelly lakes, Wales, Lake District, Scotland and Ireland. Flo. July. ✻.

Lobelia urens L. **Blue Lobelia.** ¶Terrestrial; stem 1–2 ft, angular, leafy, with acrid juice; flo. blue. In heathy fields and woods, local. Cornwall, S. Devon, Hampshire, Sussex and formerly in S. Wales. Flo. Aug. ✻.

CAMPANULACEAE

Jasione montana L. **Sheep's-bit.** ¶Stem 1 ft, base leafy, pilose; heads solitary; flo. blue, petals narrow. On dry sandy and acid soils, especially in the W. Flo. May–Aug. ✻.

Wahlenbergia hederacea (L.) Reichb. **Ivy-leaved Bell-flower.** *Campanula hederacea* L. ¶Stems slender, trailing; leaves thin, glabrous; flo. pale blue; capsule opening at top. Acid moors and peat bogs, chiefly in the W. Flo. July–Aug. ✻.

Phyteuma tenerum R. Schulz. **Round-headed Rampion.** *P. orbiculare* auct., non L. ¶Lower leaves ovate; bracts triangular; flo. deep blue-purple, in globose heads. On chalk pastures mainly in S.E. England. Flo. July. ✻.

Phyteuma spicatum L. **Spiked Rampion.** ¶Lower leaves cordate; bracts linear; flo. cream colour, in oblong spike. Very local in woods, E. Sussex. Flo. July. ✻.

Campanula glomerata L. **Clustered Bell-flower.** ¶Stem 6–8 in., downy; leaves rounded below; flo. sessile, terminal, deep blue-purple. On calcareous downs, alluvial grassland and railway banks, chiefly S. and E. England, rare in S.W. England, Wales and Scotland. Flo. May–Sept. ✻.

Campanula trachelium L. **Nettle-leaved Bell-flower.** ¶Stem 2–3 ft, hispid; upper leaves shortly petioled, teeth coarse and blunt; peduncles 2–3 flowered. In shady places and woods on calcareous and stiff soils chiefly in the S. half of Britain. Flo. July–Sept. ✻.

Campanula latifolia L. **Greater Bell-flower.** ¶Stem 3–4 ft; upper leaves sessile, serrate; peduncles with 1 large blue-purple flo. In open woods and hedge banks, chiefly in the N. Flo. July. ✳.

Campanula rapunculoides L. **Creeping Bell-flower.** ¶Stoloniferous; stem 1½ ft; calyx tube with stiff appressed hairs; flo. blue-purple. Garden escape. Naturalized in grassy places, on hedge and railway banks and established in waste ground. Flo. July–Aug. ✳.

Campanula lactiflora Bieb. ¶Stem hispid, 3–5 ft, branched above; leaves sessile, ovate-lanceolate, deeply serrate, pale beneath; flo. large, open-campanulate, variable in colour from milky white tinged with blue to pale and dark blue, in loose leafy panicles; calyx lobes broad-ovate, acute, about half as long as the corolla. Garden escape. Naturalized by rivers, chiefly in Scotland. Flo. June–Sept.

Campanula rotundifolia L. **Harebell, Bluebell** (in Scotland). ¶Stoloniferous; stem 1 ft, decumbent below; radical leaves orbicular, upper linear. In dry grassy places, common except in S.W. England and Ireland where it is local. Flo. July–Sept. ✳.

Campanula persicifolia L. ¶Leaves long, linear-lanceolate, glabrous; flo. few, a broad open cup 1½ in. wide. Naturalized in a few shady places. Flo. June–Aug.

Campanula rapunculus L. ¶Tall, 3 ft; lower leaves truncate at base; flo. small, ½ in.; upper peduncles 1 flowered, lower 2–3 flowered. Locally naturalized on sandy soil, rare. Flo. July–Aug. ✳.

Campanula patula L. **Spreading Bell-flower.** ¶2 ft; lower leaves narrowed into petiole; flo. large, 1–1½ in., calyx lobes toothed at base. Shady places in England and Wales, local. Flo. July–Aug. ✳.

Campanula alliariifolia Willd. ¶Stem downy, 3–4 ft; radical leaves large, ovate-cordate to reniform, pubescent above, densely grey tomentose beneath, coarsely and ir-regularly toothed; upper leaves much smaller; flo. creamy white, 1–2 in. long, borne singly on short pedicels in the axils of the leaf-like bracts, the whole forming a loose terminal 1-sided raceme; calyx teeth separated by oblong to lanceolate appendages; stigmas 3. Garden escape. Naturalized on railway banks, chiefly in Devon and Cornwall. Flo. July–Sept.

Campanula medium L. **Canterbury Bell.** ¶Stem hispid, 1–3 ft; leaves sessile, ovate-lanceolate, crenate; flo. large, inflated-campanulate, dark blue to white; calyx teeth separated by broad reflexed appendages. Garden escape. Naturalized in chalky railway cuttings, chiefly S. England and Midlands. Flo. May–July.

Legousia hybrida (L.) Delarb. **Venus' Looking-glass.** *Specularia hybrida* (L.) A.DC. ¶8–10 in. hispid; leaves oblong, wavy; flo. small, erect, purple; capsule long. On cultivated land, chiefly S. and E. England, local. Flo. June–Sept. ✳.

ERICACEAE   **PLATE 55**

Vaccinium vitis-idaea L. **Cowberry.** ¶Leaves evergreen, leathery, dotted beneath, margins revolute; flo. pale pink; berries scarlet. On peat moors, common in N., local in Wales and Ireland. Flo. May–July. ✳.

Vaccinium myrtillus L. **Bilberry, Whortleberry.** ¶Leaves deciduous, ovate, acute, serrate, green; flo. subglobose; berry black. Common on moors though rare in S.E. England, E. Anglia and Midlands. Flo. April–June. ✳.

Vaccinium × intermedium Ruthe. (*V. myrtillus × vitis-idaea*). ¶Semi-evergreen; leaves elliptic, slightly serrate, with faint glandular dots beneath; fr. purplish, rarely produced. Occurs with the parents on Cannock Chase, Staffordshire and in Derbyshire, and probably elsewhere.

Vaccinium uliginosum L. **Bog Whortleberry.** ¶Leaves deciduous, oval, obtuse, entire, bluish green, net veined; berry black. On moors in Scotland and N. England, local. Flo. May–June. ✲.

Vaccinium oxycoccus L. **Cranberry.** *Oxycoccus palustris* Pers. ¶Stems slender; leaves small, ovate, with sides parallel; pedicels downy; fr. subglobose, red. Wet boggy heaths, chiefly in the N. half of Britain, local. Flo. June–Aug. ✲.

Vaccinium microcarpum (Rupr.) Hook. f. **Small Cranberry.** *Oxycoccus microcarpus* Turcz. ex Rupr. ¶Leaves triangular ovate, widest near base; pedicels glabrous; fruit more elongate. Bogs in central Scotland. Flo. July.

*_Vaccinium macrocarpon_ Ait. *Oxycoccus macrocarpos* (Ait.) Pursh. ¶Similar to *V. oxycoccus* but leaves oblong, up to twice as long and less glaucous beneath; flo. up to twice as large and up to 10 in a raceme (up to 4 in *V. oxycoccus*); fr. twice as large, red, edible. Bird-sown from gardens, etc., and naturalized on moors and heaths, chiefly N. England and Scotland. Flo. June–Aug.

Arbutus unedo L. **Strawberry Tree.** ¶Shrub 10–25 ft; leaves leathery, glabrous; flo. cream; fr. a warty berry. Native in S.W. Ireland. Flo. Sept.–Oct. ✲.

Arctostaphylos uva-ursi (L.) Spreng. **Bear Berry.** ¶Stem trailing; leaves thick, shining, evergreen; flo. pink-tipped; berry red. Common on stony moors in Scotland, N. England and W. Ireland. Flo. June. ✲.

Arctous alpinus (L.) Nied. **Alpine Bear Berry.** *Arctostaphylos alpinus* (L.) Spreng. ¶Stem trailing; leaves thin, wrinkled, not evergreen; flo. white; fr. black. On moors in N. Scotland. Flo. May. ✲.

Andromeda polifolia L. **Marsh Andromeda.** ¶Stem woody, prostrate below; leaves evergreen, glaucous beneath; fr. a subglobose capsule. Peat bogs, mid Scotland to mid England, mid Wales and Ireland. Flo. May–Sept. ✲.

*_Gaultheria shallon_ Pursh. ¶Evergreen shrub, up to 3 ft, spreading by underground stems; leaves alternate, ovate, acute, toothed; flo. urceolate, ¼ in., pinkish, in panicles; berry ¼ in., black, hairy. Planted for pheasant cover and naturalized on sandy heaths and peaty bogs. Flo. May–June.

*_Pernettya mucronata_ (L. f.) Gaudich. ex Spreng. ¶Erect evergreen shrub, up to 5 ft, stems freely suckering; leaves alternate, ovate, acute, mucronate, leathery, toothed; flo. campanulate, ¼ in., white, axillary, nodding; berry ½ in., white, pink, crimson, deep purple or black. Garden escape. Naturalized on heaths and banks, especially in Ireland. Flo. May–June.

Calluna vulgaris (L.) Hull. **Ling.** ¶Leaves minute, evergreen; calyx large, pink like corolla, with 4 ovate bracteoles. Common on moors and woodland banks. Flo. Aug.–Sept. ✲.

Erica ciliaris L. **Ciliate Heath.** ¶Leaves 3 in whorl, glandular, white beneath; stamens included; anthers not awned. Local in Cornwall, Devon and Dorset. Flo. Aug.–Sept. ✲.

Erica × watsonii Benth. (*R. ciliaris × tetralix*). ¶Intermediate between the parents, occurs commonly where they grow together.

Erica tetralix L. **Cross-leaved Heath.** ¶Leaves 4 in whorl, glandular, margins revolute to midrib; anthers awned. Common on boggy heaths. Flo. July–Aug. ❋.

Erica mackaiana Bab. **Mackay's Heath.** ¶Leaves wider, margin revolute, glabrous above, white beneath; calyx glabrous except apex; anthers awned. Wet moors in Galway and Donegal. Flo. Aug.–Sept. ❋.

Erica × praegeri Ostenf. (*E. mackaiana × tetralix*). ¶Intermediate between the parents, sometimes occurs where they grow together.

Erica cinerea L. **Purple Heather, Fine-leaved Heath.** ¶Stem with short leafy shoots; leaves 3 in whorl; stamens included; anthers awned. Common on dry heaths. Flo. July–Aug. ❋.

Erica vagans L. **Cornish Heath.** ¶Leaves 4–5 in whorl; flo. pale; pedicels long; stamens exerted; anthers not awned. Abundant on Lizard Head, Cornwall, perhaps also native in Fermanagh. Flo. Aug.–Sept. ❋.

Erica hibernica (Hook. & Arn.) Syme. **Irish Heath.** *E. mediterranea* auct. ¶Stem 3–5 ft; leaves 4–5 in whorl; flo. pale pink; anthers ½ exserted, not awned. On heaths in W. Ireland. Flo. April–May. ❋.

Ledum palustre L. ¶Stem 2 ft; leaves brown felted beneath, margin revolute; pedicels glandular; flo. white, petals free. In bogs, Stirlingshire and W. Perthshire, introduced elsewhere. Flo. June–July. ❋.

*Ledum groenlandicum Oeder. *L. latifolium* Jacq. ¶Similar to *L. palustre* but leaves elliptic, more densely felted beneath; pedicels slightly pubescent; capsule a little larger. Garden escape. Naturalized in bogs, etc., chiefly N. Britain, rare. Flo. June–July.

*Rhododendron ponticum L. ¶Large evergreen shrub; leaves elliptic to oblong; dark green; flo. large, widely campanulate, purple flecked with brown. Naturalized in woods and on heaths on peaty and sandy soils. Flo. May–June.

Phyllodoce caerulea (L.) Bab. **Scottish Menziesia.** *Bryanthus caeruleus* (L.) Dippel. ¶Stem 5–6 in., hairy above; leaves evergreen, linear; flo. purple. On a moorland in Perthshire. Flo. June–July. ❋.

Daboecia cantabrica (Huds.) C. Koch. **St Dabeoc's Heath.** *Boretta cantabrica* (Huds.) Kuntz. ¶Stem 1–2 ft, glandular above; leaves alternate, evergreen, white beneath; flo. rose-purple. On heaths in Mayo and W. Galway. Flo. Aug. ❋.

Loiseleuria procumbens (L.) Desv. **Trailing Azalea.** *Azalea procumbens* L. ¶Procumbent cushion-like shrubs; leaves evergreen, leathery; calyx reddish; corolla pink. On mountains in Scotland. Flo. May–July. ❋ on plate 56.

EMPETRACEAE

Empetrum nigrum L. **Crowberry.** ¶Stem prostrate; leaves 3–4 times as long as broad; flo. mostly dioecious. On moors in Scotland, N. and W. England to Devon. Flo. May–June. ❋.

Empetrum hermaphroditum Hagerup. ¶Stem not prostrate; leaves 2–3 times as long as broad; flo. hermaphrodite. On mountains, mostly in Scotland.

PYROLACEAE

PLATE 56

Pyrola rotundifolia L. **Large Wintergreen.**

Subsp. *rotundifolia*. ¶Flo. white, ½ in. across; pedicels 4–6 mm.; calyx lobes triangular, lanceolate, acute; style 7–8 mm., curved; stigma with 5 small erect lobes. In fens and damp woods, on rock ledges, etc., local in mid Scotland; very rare in England, S. Wales and Ireland. Flo. July–Sept. ❀.

Subsp. *maritima* (Kenyon) E. F. Warb. ¶Similar to subsp. *rotundifolia*, but pedicels shorter; calyx lobes ovate; style smaller and more curved. On dune slacks in N. Wales and Lancashire, rare.

Pyrola media Sw. **Medium Wintergreen.** ¶Flo. pinkish white, ⅜ in. (10 mm.); style straight, with 5 lobes above a thick ring. In woods and moors, mostly N. England, Scotland and N. Ireland, very local. Flo. June–Aug. ❀.

Pyrola minor L. **Lesser Wintergreen.** ¶Flo. pink, globose, ¼ in.; style very short; stigma with 5 spreading lobes. In woods, moors and dunes, mostly in the N. half of Britain, local. Flo. June–Aug. ❀.

Orthilia secunda (L.) House. *Pyrola secunda* L. *Ramischia secunda* (L.) Garcke. ¶Flo. greenish white, secund; style exserted; stigma with 5 spreading lobes. Woods and damp rocks, Scotland, N. England, Wales and Ireland, very local except in N. Scotland. Flo. July–Aug. ❀.

Moneses uniflora (L.) A. Gray. **One-flowered Wintergreen.** *Pyrola uniflora* L. ¶Flo. solitary, white, drooping; disk large; stigma with 5 spreading lobes. Pine woods in Scotland, local and rare. Flo. June–Aug. ❀.

MONOTROPACEAE

Monotropa hypophegea Wallr. **Yellow Bird's-nest.** ¶Saprophyte, without green colour; flo. glabrous inside; fr. subglobose. The name means 'under beech wood', also on dunes mostly S. England, local. Flo. June–Aug.

Monotropa hypopitys L. ¶Similar saprophyte; flo. many, clothed inside with stiff hairs; fr. ovoid. The name means 'under pine wood', mostly S. England, local. Flo. June–Aug. ❀.

For other saprophytes—cf. plates 66 and 81.

PLUMBAGINACEAE

Limonium vulgare Mill. **Sea Lavender.** *Statice limonium* L. ¶Leaves large, pinnately veined; spikelets crowded; calyx lobes with teeth between them. In muddy salt marshes, locally common in S. and E. England, rather rare in Wales and the N. Flo. July–Sept. ❀.

Limonium humile Mill. **Lax-flowered Sea Lavender.** *Statice rariflora* Drej. ¶Leaves pinnately veined; flo. separated on branches; calyx lobes with teeth between them. In muddy salt marshes, rather local. Flo. July–Aug. ❀.

Limonium bellidifolium (Gouan) Dumort. ¶Leaves small, obovate; stems spreading with many barren branches; calyx without teeth between. Drier saltings, Norfolk and Suffolk, and formerly in Lincolnshire. Flo. July. ❀.

Limonium auriculae-ursifolium (Pourr.) Druce. *Statice lychnidifolia* Girard. ¶Plant robust; leaves large, obovate, glaucous, 5 veined; calyx without teeth between. On seaside rocks, Jersey and Alderney. Flo. June–Sept.

Limonium binervosum (G. E. Sm.) C. E. Salmon. **Rock Sea Lavender.** ¶Leaves obovate or oblanceolate, 3 veined below; calyx without teeth between; spikelets in 2 rows. On sea cliffs, England and Wales. Flo. July–Sept. ✲.

Limonium recurvum C. E. Salmon. ¶Leaves obovate; petiole 3 veined; barren branches o; spikes dense; calyx teeth shallow, blunt. On cliffs at Portland, very rare. Flo. July–Sept.

Limonium transwallianum (Pugsl.) Pugsl. ¶Leaves narrow, oblanceolate, 1 veined; flo. small, 4 mm.; calyx teeth deep; petals narrow, blue. Sea cliffs, Pembrokeshire. Flo. July–Sept. ✲.

Limonium paradoxum Pugsl. ¶Branches short, erect, from near base; leaves 1 veined; flo. in small round heads. St David's Head, Wales and Donegal. Flo. July–Sept.

Armeria maritima (Mill.) Willd. **Thrift, Sea Pink.** *Statice armeria* L.
Subsp. *maritima.* ¶Leaves narrow, linear, 1 veined; calyx teeth acute or very shortly awned. Common on sea cliffs. Flo. March–Sept. ✲.
 Var. *planifolia* Syme. ¶Leaves a little broader, often 3 veined. Scottish mountains.
Subsp. *elongata* (Hoffm.) Bonnier. ¶Leaves 4 in.; scape tall, 18 in. On heaths, around Grantham, Lincolnshire and Leicestershire.

Armeria arenaria (Pers.) Schult. **Jersey Thrift.** *A. plantaginea* Willd. ¶Leaves 3–5 veined, margin membranous; calyx teeth with long awns equal to ½ their length. On sand dunes in Jersey. Flo. June–July.

DIAPENSIACEAE   **PLATE 57**

Diapensia lapponica L. ¶Stems forming a mat; leaves mostly in rosette, nearly linear; flo. pale yellow. Hill-tops at 2600 ft in Inverness-shire, discovered in 1951. Flo. July. ✲.

PRIMULACEAE

Hottonia palustris L. **Water Violet.** ¶Stems and leaves submerged; pedicels glandular; flo. lilac with yellow eye; fr. globose. In ponds and ditches, mostly in E. England. Flo. May–June. ✲.

Primula vulgaris Huds. **Primrose.** ¶Scape short or o; pedicels long; leaves narrowed gradually below; throat of corolla narrow. Common in woods and shady banks. Flo. Feb.–May. ✲.

Primula veris L. **Cowslip.** ¶Scape 8–10 in.; pedicels short; leaves abruptly narrowed below; flo. small. Locally common in meadows on basic and calcareous soils, but rare in Scotland and N. Ireland. Flo. April–May. ✲.

Primula veris × vulgaris. ¶This hybrid occurs with parent species. Variable and compared with *P. elatior* more hairy; flo. larger, yellower, with narrower throat.

Primula elatior (L.) Hill. **Oxlip.** ¶Leaves abruptly narrowed below; flo. facing one way; throat without folds, more open than in the hybrid. In woods on boulder clay, Essex, Hertfordshire, Bedfordshire, Huntingdonshire and E. Anglia. Flo. April–May. ❀.

Primula × media Petermann. (*P. elatior × veris*). ¶Intermediate between the parents, sometimes occurs where they grow together.

Primula × digenea Kerner (*P. elatior × vulgaris*). ¶A very variable hybrid; leaves usually intermediate between the parents; flo. similar to *P. vulgaris*, but usually paler yellow, and often with an orange eye; pedicels long, erect, pubescent; peduncle and calyx with long woolly hairs. Frequent where the parents grow together.

Primula farinosa L. **Bird's-eye Primrose.** ¶Leaves crenulate, mealy beneath; flo. petals not contiguous, lobes oblong, pale lilac, heterostylous. In damp meadows, N. England and S. Scotland. Flo. May–July. ❀.

Primula scotica Hook. ¶Leaves not crenulate, mealy beneath; petals contiguous, obcordate; red-purple styles all alike. In damp meadows, N. Scotland. Flo. May–June. ❀.

*Cyclamen hederifolium Ait. *C. neapolitanum* Ten. ¶Root a corm; leaves angled; peduncles erect and nodding in flo., coiled in fr.; corolla lobes reflexed. Locally naturalized, mostly in woods in S. England. Flo. Aug.–Sept. ❀.

Lysimachia thyrsiflora L. *Naumbergia thyrsiflora* (L.) Reichb. ¶Stem erect 2 ft; leaves glandular; flo. small, yellow; peduncles axillary at middle of stem. At edge of ponds and canals, mostly N. England, S. Scotland. Flo. June. ❀.

Lysimachia vulgaris L. **Yellow Loosestrife.** ¶Rhizomes stout; stem erect 3 ft; leaves glandular; flo. not glandular. In ditches, fens and riversides. Flo. July–Aug. ❀.

*Lysimachia punctata L. ¶Stem 2 ft; leaves ovate, margins ciliate; calyx and 1 in. corolla glandular, ciliate. Garden escape. Naturalized in wet places. Flo. July–Sept.

*Lysimachia ciliata L. ¶Stem 2 ft; leaves ovate-acuminate; petiole ciliate; petals very glandular at base; spreading by rhizomes. Garden escape. Naturalized by streams, ditches, etc., and established on waste ground. Flo. June–July. ❀.

*Lysimachia terrestris (L.) Britton, Sterns & Poggenb. ¶Stem erect, bearing bulbils in axils of narrow leaves; flo. yellow and purple. On shores of Lake Windermere.

Lysimachia nemorum L. **Yellow Pimpernel.** ¶Stems weak and prostrate; leaves ovate, glabrous; flo. pedicels slender. Common in woods, especially on stiff soils. Flo. May–Sept. ❀.

Lysimachia nummularia L. **Creeping Jenny.** ¶Stems matted; leaves suborbicular; gland dotted; flo. large; calyx ovate. On damp grassy places, in wet woods, etc., local, but rare in Ireland and a garden escape in S.W. England and N. Scotland.

Trientalis europaea L. **Chickweed Wintergreen.** ¶Rhizomes slender; stem 8 in.; leaves mostly in whorl at top; flo. white. High moors and pine woods, mostly Scotland and N. England, very rare in Suffolk. Flo. June–July. ❀.

PLATE 58

Glaux maritima L. **Saltwort, Sea Milkwort.** ¶Stems trailing; flo. small, axillary, sessile; corolla 0; calyx petaloid pink. On estuary mud and seaside rocks. Flo. June–Aug. ❀.

Anagallis arvensis L. **Scarlet Pimpernel.**
Subsp. *arvensis.* ¶Flo. petals overlapping, fringed with gland hairs, usually scarlet, rarely pink or blue; fr. pedicels longer than leaves. Common on cultivated and waste land, dunes, etc., but rare in mid and N. Scotland. ❀.
Subsp. *foemina* (Mill.) Schinz & Thell. ¶Petals obovate, not overlapping, glands few; fr. pedicels not longer than leaves. On cultivated land, S. England, rare. ❀.

Anagallis tenella (L.) L. **Bog Pimpernel.** ¶Stem prostrate; leaves nearly orbicular; flo. erect, funnel shaped, pink. On wet peaty heaths mostly in S. half of England, W. Scotland and W. Ireland. Flo. June–Aug. ❀.

Anagallis minima (L.) E. H. L. Krause. **Chaff Weed.** *Centunculus minimus* L. ¶Stem 1–3 in.; flo. sessile, axillary, minute, pinkish, chaff-like. On bare sandy ground, mostly S. England, W. Wales and W. Scotland. Flo. June–July. ❀.

Samolus valerandi L. **Brook Weed.** ¶Stem erect, 1 ft; leaves obtuse, glabrous; flo. white, pedicels bent. On wet ground, mostly near the sea, locally common, but very rare in E. Scotland. Flo. June–Aug. ❀.

OLEACEAE

Fraxinus excelsior L. **Ash.** ¶Tall tree; flo. in small racemes, without sepals or petals; stamens crimson; fr. winged. Native in woods, mostly on calcareous soils, but frequently planted elsewhere, and readily regenerating. ❀.

Ligustrum vulgare L. **Privet.** ¶Shrub, up to 10 ft; young shoots puberulous; leaves lanceolate; corolla limb equalling tube. Common on calcareous soils in S. England. Flo. June–July. ❀.
The commonly planted shrub with glabrous shoots, ovate leaves and longer corolla limb is *L. ovalifolium* Hassk.

BUDDLEJACEAE

*Buddleja davidii Franch. **Butterfly Bush.** ¶Shrub, up to 15 ft; branchlets downy; leaves lanceolate, acuminate, serrate, up to 1 ft long, green above, white felted below; flo. small, campanulate, lilac to deep purple with an orange eye, in dense long narrow drooping spikes, up to 1 ft long. The flowers are very attractive to butterflies. Garden escape. Naturalized in chalk pits, and established on waste ground, old walls, etc., mostly S. half of Britain and S. Ireland. Flo. June–Oct.

APOCYNACEAE

Vinca minor L. **Lesser Periwinkle.** ¶Stems rooting freely; leaves lanceolate, 1½ in.; calyx lobes glabrous; flo. 1 in., blue-mauve, solitary. In woods, local, fr. rarely found. Flo. March–May and autumn. ❀.

*Vinca major L. **Greater Periwinkle.**
Subsp. *major.* ¶Plant larger than *V. minor*; flo. stems not rooting; leaves ovate, 2 in.; calyx lobes ciliate; flo. 2–3, 1½–2 in. wide, blue-mauve. Garden escape. Naturalized in hedge banks, woods, etc., mostly in S. half of Britain. Flo. April–June.

Subsp. *hirsuta* (Boiss.) Stearn. *Vinca herbacea* auct., non Waldst. & Kit. ¶Similar to subsp. *major*, but leaves narrower, lanceolate; flo. deep violet, with much narrower lobes. Garden escape. Naturalized in woods and plantations, etc., in Devon, Essex, Kent and Glamorgan.

GENTIANACEAE

Cicendia filiformis (L.) Delarb. **Yellow Gentianella.** *Microcala filiformis* (L.) Hoffmans. & Link. ¶Slender, erect, 1–4 in.; leaves small; flo. small, ⅛ in., yellow. In sandy places, especially near the sea, S. England, W. and N. Wales and S.W. Ireland, rare. Flo. Aug.–Sept. ❀.

Exaculum pusillum (Lam.) Caruel. *Cicendia pusilla* (Lam.) Griseb. ¶Stems several, short, slender; leaves linear; flo. small, ⅛ in., pink. Sandy places in Guernsey, very rare. Flo. July–Sept. ❀.

Centaurium pulchellum (Sw.) Druce. **Lesser Centaury.** *Erythraea pulchella* (Sw.) Fr. ¶Plant erect, without basal rosette; flo. pedicelled, not clustered; lobes 3–4 mm., deep pink. Damp grassy places on stiff soils, often near the sea in S. England. Flo. June–Sept. ❀.

Centaurium tenuiflorum (Hoffmans. & Link) Fritsch. ¶Similar to *C. pulchellum* but branches more strict and erect. Corolla tube constricted above, petals narrower. I. of Wight and Dorset.

Centaurium erythraea Rafn. **Common Centaury.** *C. umbellatum* auct. ¶Erect from basal rosette; flo. subsessile; clusters subumbellate; stamens inserted at top of tube. Common in dry grassy places, wood borders, etc., especially on calcareous soil, also on dunes. Flo. June–Oct. ❀.
Sometimes found, var. *subcapitatum* (Corb.) Gilmour, with dwarf capitate growth rather resembling the following species, but with stamens inserted at top of corolla tube. ❀.

Centaurium capitatum (Willd.) Borbás. **Tufted Centaury.** ¶Dwarf plant branched from basal rosette; flo. capitate; stamens inserted at base of corolla tube. Dry calcareous downs near sea, mostly S. England and S. Wales, rare. Flo. July–Aug. ❀.

Centaurium littorale (D. Turner) Gilmour. **Sea Centaury.** ¶Erect from rosette; leaves linear, basal spathulate; flo. few, sessile, lobes 6–7 mm. Sand dunes near the sea, mostly N. and N.W. coasts. Flo. July–Aug. ❀.

Centaurium scilloides (L. f.) Samp. *C. portense* (Brot.) Butcher. ¶Stems decumbent, often barren; leaves obovate; flo. pedicelled; corolla lobes 8–9 mm. Cliffs in Pembrokeshire and W. Cornwall. Flo. July–Aug. ❀.

Blackstonia perfoliata (L.) Huds. **Yellow-wort.** *Chlora perfoliata* L. ¶Erect, 1 ft; very glaucous; cauline leaves connate in pairs; flo. bright yellow. On calcareous pastures and dunes, mostly England and Ireland. Flo. June–Oct. ❀.

PLATE 59

Gentiana pneumonanthe L. **Marsh Gentian.** ¶Stems suberect, 1 ft; leaves linear; flo. large, 1¼–1½ in., blue, narrowed below. On wet heaths, mostly S. and E. England, very local. Flo. July–Sept. ❀.

Gentiana verna L. **Spring Gentian.** ¶Leaves ovate, in rosettes; flo. solitary, ¾ in., deep blue, lobes spreading; tube cylindric. In grassy places on limestone, N. England and W. Ireland. Flo. April–June. ⚥.

Gentiana nivalis L. **Small Alpine Gentian.** ¶Annual; erect, 1–6 in.; leaves ¼ in.; flo. small, deep blue; tube cylindric. On rocks in Perthshire and Angus at about 3000 ft. Flo. July–Sept. ⚥.

Gentianella campestris (L.) Börner. **Field Felwort.** *Gentiana campestris* auct. ¶Stem 2–8 in.; sepals 4, 2 outer larger overlapping inner; flo. purple. In meadows, on dunes, etc., chiefly on acid soils in Ireland, Scotland, N. England to Berkshire and Devon. Flo. July–Oct. ⚥.
Var. *baltica* (Murb.) H. Sm. *Gentiana baltica* auct. ¶Annual; stem subsimple; cotyledons persisting; is, now, no longer regarded as distinct. ⚥.

Gentianella germanica (Willd.) Börner. **Scarce Autumn Felwort.** *Gentiana germanica* Willd. ¶Stem 6–10 in., branched; calyx lobes 5, lanceolate unequal; corolla 1 in., lilac, tapering below. Grassy places on calcareous soil, S. England, local. Flo. Aug.–Sept. ⚥.

Gentianella amarella (L.) Börner. **Autumn Felwort.** *Gentiana amarella* L.
Subsp. *amarella.* ¶Stem 3–9 in., subsimple; stem leaves ovate-lanceolate; calyx lobes 5 subequal; corolla ½–¾ in., cylindric, purple. On pastures and downs on calcareous soil, dunes, chiefly in England, Wales, N. and E. Scotland. Flo. Aug.–Oct. ⚥.
Subsp. *hibernica* Pritchard. ¶Similar to subsp. *amarella,* but basal leaves usually linear-lanceolate; corolla slightly larger, dull purple, rarely pale blue or white. In pastures on calcareous soil, Ireland. Flo. Aug.–Oct.
Subsp. *septentrionalis* (Druce) Pritchard. **Northern Felwort.** *Gentianella septentrionalis* (Druce) E. F. Warb., *Gentiana septentrionalis* (Druce) Druce. ¶Annual; 2–3 in.; calyx lobes unequal; corolla creamy white suffused with purplish red outside, whitish within. Dunes by the sea and limestone meadows near the sea, Scotland. Flo. July–Aug.
Subsp. *druceana* Pritchard. ¶Similar to subsp. *amarella* and subsp. *septentrionalis,* but middle and upper stem leaves ovate-lanceolate to lanceolate; flo. colour and shape similar to subsp. *septentrionalis.* Shell-sand dune slacks and limestone pastures, mid and N. Scotland, local. Flo. Aug.–Oct.

Gentianella × pamplinii (Druce) E. F. Warb. (*Gentianella amarella × germanica*) *Gentiana × pamplinii* Druce. ¶Intermediate between the parents and occurs rarely where they grow together.

Gentianella amarella × uliginosa. ¶Intermediate between the parents often occurs where they grow together.

Gentianella anglica (Pugsl.) E. F. Warb. **Dwarf English Felwort.** *Gentiana anglica* Pugsl.
Subsp. *anglica.* ¶2–4 in., branched from base; basal leaves narrowly spathulate, obtuse; stem leaves lanceolate, acute; corolla ½ in. long, about 1½ times as long as calyx teeth; calyx teeth unequal. Chalk grassland from Devon to Lincolnshire, local. Flo. April–June. ⚥.
Subsp. *cornubiensis* Pritchard. ¶Similar to subsp. *anglica,* but slightly smaller; basal leaves broadly spathulate; stem leaves linear or linear-lanceolate, obtuse; corolla slightly larger; calyx teeth subequal. Sea cliffs, W. Cornwall, local. Flo. March–June.

Gentianella uliginosa (Willd.) Börner. **Dune Felwort.** *Gentiana uliginosa* Willd. ¶Annual; 3–4 in.; often branched from base; cotyledons persisting; calyx lobes unequal; leaves lanceolate; flo. 4–5-merous. Sand dunes, S. Wales. Flo. July–Oct.

Menyanthes trifoliata L. **Bogbean.** ¶Aquatic; leaves large, tri-foliate and flo. pale pink, fimbriate, both held above water. Common in watery bogs. Flo. May–July. ❀.

Nymphoides peltata (S. G. Gmel) Kuntze. *Limnanthemum peltatum* S. G. Gmel. ¶Leaves orbicular, floating; petioles long; flo. yellow, fringed, fimbriate at base. In slow streams and ponds, mainly E. England, local. Flo. July–Aug. ❀.

POLEMONIACEAE

Polemonium caeruleum L. **Jacob's Ladder.** ¶2–3 ft; leaves pinnate; lower petioles winged; flo. deep blue; filaments hairy below. In woods and by streams, N. half of England, occurs elsewhere as a naturalized garden escape. Flo. June–July. ❀.

BORAGINACEAE

Cynoglossum officinale L. **Hound's Tongue.** ¶Stem woody; leaves softly hairy; fr. with hooked bristles and thickened border. Downs, wood borders, etc., on dry soils, especially near the sea, mainly in the S. half of Britain. Flo. June–Aug. ❀.

Cynoglossum germanicum Jacq. **Green Hound's Tongue.** *C. montanum* auct. ¶Stem slender, green; leaves subglabrous above; fr. bristly without a thickened border. Shady places in mid S. and E. England, rare. Flo. May–July. ❀.

*Omphalodes verna Moench. ¶Stoloniferous perennial; stem pubescent, up to 6 in.; basal leaves cordate; stem leaves broadly lanceolate to ovate; flo. sky-blue, ½ in. across, similar to a large forget-me-not, but throat closed by obtuse scales, in few-flowered cymes on erect stems; calyx 5-toothed, hairy; nutlets smooth with ciliate margins. Garden escape. Naturalized in hedge banks and woods. Flo. March–May.

*Asperugo procumbens L. **Madwort.** ¶Stems procumbent and bristly; leaves oblong, hispid; flo. small, axillary, becoming blue. Introduced, in fields and waste places, rare. Flo. May–July.

PLATE 60

Symphytum officinale L. **Comfrey.** ¶Stem winged with decurrent leaves; calyx teeth twice as long as tube; flo. cream or purple. Common by rivers and canals. Flo. May–June. ❀.

*Symphytum asperum Lepech. **Rough Comfrey.** ¶Stems covered with short hooked bristles; upper leaves shortly stalked; flo. becoming blue. Garden escape. Established in waste places, rare. Flo. June–July. ❀.

*Symphytum × uplandicum Nyman (*S. asperum × officinale*). **Blue Comfrey.** *S. peregrinum* auct. ¶Stem tall, branched, bristly, not winged; calyx teeth acuminate, twice length of tube; flo. blue. Naturalized in rough grassy places in waste places, by roadsides, etc. Flo. June–Aug.

Symphytum orientale L. ¶Leaves ovate, softly pubescent, petioled; calyx teeth obtuse, $\frac{1}{2}$ length of tube; flo. white. Garden escape. Naturalized in grassy places, by roadsides, etc., mainly S. England. Flo. April–May.

Symphytum caucasicum Bieb. ¶Stems rough, hairy, angular, $1\frac{1}{2}$–2 ft; leaves ovate-lanceolate, acuminate, slightly decurrent, softly hairy above, grey felted beneath; flo. blue, campanulate, in terminal twin racemes; calyx teeth obtuse, hispid. Garden escape. Naturalized in woods and plantations. Flo. May–June.

Symphytum tuberosum L. **Tuberous Comfrey.** ¶Root tuberous; stems 1–1$\frac{1}{2}$ ft; calyx teeth acute, 3 times length of tube; flo. cream. In woods, mainly N. England and Scotland, introduced elsewhere. Flo. June–July. ✂.

Symphytum grandiflorum DC. ¶Similar to *S. tuberosum* but with slender rhizomes and smaller leaves; calyx deeply divided; teeth linear-lanceolate, obtuse; flo. cream or yellowish white. Garden escape. Naturalized in woods and hedge banks, chiefly S. England and Midlands. Flo. April–May.

Borago officinalis L. **Borage.** ¶Leaves large, ovate, hispid; flo. $\frac{3}{4}$ in., deep blue; anthers exserted, black. Garden escape. Established on waste ground, etc. Flo. June–July.

Pentaglottis sempervirens (L.) Tausch. **Alkanet.** *Anchusa sempervirens* L. ¶Leaves broad, ovate, hispid; peduncles axillary, forked; flo. bright blue. Garden escape. Naturalized in woods, grassy places, by roadsides, etc., widespread. Flo. May–Aug. ✂.

Trachystemon orientalis (L.) G. Don. ¶Stem hispid, thick, up to 1 ft; radical leaves ovate, long stalked; flo. bluish violet, similar to those of *Borago officinalis*, but smaller with a longer corolla tube. Garden escape. Naturalized in hedge banks and woods, mainly S. England, rare. Flo. March–May.

Lycopsis arvensis L. **Lesser Bugloss.** ¶Leaves oblong, hispid with tuberous hairs; inflo. forked; flo. bright blue; corolla tube with double bend. Arable land, cornfields, etc., chiefly on light soils, especially near the sea, widespread but very rare in W. Ireland. Flo. June–July. ✂.

Pulmonaria longifolia (Bast.) Bor. **Narrow-leaved Lungwort.** *P. angustifolia* auct., non L. ¶Leaves narrow, lanceolate, not always blotched; flo. pink then bright blue. In woods on clay soil in Hampshire, Dorset and I. of Wight, rare. Flo. April–June. ✂.

Pulmonaria officinalis L. **Lungwort.** ¶Leaves broadly ovate, always with pale blotches; flo. pale purple. Garden escape. Naturalized in woods, chiefly in S. half of Britain, rare. Flo. April–May. ✂.

Mertensia maritima (L.) Gray. **Northern Shore-wort.** ¶Stem procumbent; leaves fleshy, glaucous, rough with hard points; flo. pink becoming bluish. On northern sea-shores. Flo. June–July. ✂.

Myosotis scorpioides L. **Water Forget-me-not.** *M. palustris* (L.) Hill. ¶Cyme not bracteate; calyx hairs appressed; teeth short, triangular; flo. $\frac{1}{4}$ in., style equalling calyx tube. Common by ponds and streams. Flo. May–Oct. ✂.

Myosotis secunda A. Murr. **Marsh Forget-me-not.** *M. repens* auct. ¶Stoloniferous; cyme bracteate; calyx hairs appressed; teeth $\frac{1}{2}$ calyx length; fr. pedicels long, 3–5 times calyx. Wet places on heaths, etc., particularly on peaty soils, widespread, but very rare in E. Anglia. Flo. May–Aug. ✂.

Myosotis stolonifera Gay. **Short-leaved Forget-me-not.** *M. brevifolia* C. E. Salmon.

¶Leaf length not exceeding twice its breadth, bluish green; calyx teeth obtuse; flo. paler. Wet hilly places, N. England, S. Scotland. Flo. June–Aug. ✳.

Myosotis caespitosa K. F. Schultz. **Lesser Water Forget-me-not.** ¶Stems, leaves and calyx with appressed hairs; cyme bracteate; flo. small, $\frac{1}{6}$ in.; style short, $\frac{1}{2}$ calyx tube. Common in watery places. Flo. May–Aug. ✳.

Myosotis sicula Guss. **Jersey Forget-me-not.** ¶Stem 2–6 in., subglabrous below; calyx subglabrous; teeth oblong, obtuse, $\frac{1}{2}$ length of calyx. On dunes in Jersey, rare. Flo. April–June.

Myosotis alpestris Schmidt. **Alpine Forget-me-not.** ¶Stem and leaves with spreading hairs; flo. large, $\frac{1}{4}$ in.; calyx with spreading and few hooked hairs. Mountain rocks, Teesdale and Perthshire, rare. Flo. July–Aug. ✳.

Myosotis sylvatica Hoffm. **Wood Forget-me-not.** ¶Stems and leaves with spreading hairs; calyx $\frac{3}{4}$ cleft, with straight and hooked hairs; flo. $\frac{1}{4}$–$\frac{3}{8}$ in. In woods except S.W. England, S. Wales, N. Scotland and Ireland, occurs also in grassy places, etc., as a naturalized garden escape. Flo. May–July. ✳.

Myosotis arvensis (L.) Hill. **Common Forget-me-not.** ¶Stem and leaves with spreading hairs; calyx with many hooked hairs; flo. $\frac{1}{8}$–$\frac{3}{16}$ in.; style short. Woods, cultivated lands, dunes, etc., common and widespread. Flo. April–Sept. ✳.

Myosotis discolor Pers. **Yellow Forget-me-not.** *M. versicolor* Sm. ¶Inflo. in fr. not much longer than leafy stem; calyx closed in fr.; flo. yellow becoming blue. Grassy places on light soils, widespread. Flo. May–June. ✳.

Myosotis ramosissima Rochel. **Early Forget-me-not.** *M. hispida* Schlecht., *M. collina* auct. ¶Inflo. in fr. much longer than leafy stem; calyx open in fr.; flo. bright blue. Common on dry banks and wall tops, mainly S. half of Britain. Flo. April–June. ✳.

PLATE 61

Lithospermum purpurocaeruleum L. **Blue Gromwell.** ¶Stems long, creeping and trailing, flo. portion erect, forked, supported by shrubs; flo. deep blue. Thickets on chalk and limestone, mostly S.W. England and S. Wales, rare, occurs elsewhere as a garden escape. Flo. May–July. ✳.

Lithospermum officinale L. **Gromwell.** ¶Perennial; $1\frac{1}{2}$ ft; leaves acute, lateral nerves obvious; nutlets smooth and white. Bushy places, mostly on calcareous soil. Flo. June–July. ✳.

Lithospermum arvense L. **Corn Gromwell.** ¶Annual; 1 ft; leaves obtuse, lateral nerves obscure; nutlets rugose, grey or brownish. Locally common on cultivated land in S. and E. England, rare elsewhere. Flo. May–July. ✳.

Echium vulgare L. **Viper's Bugloss.** ¶Upper leaves rounded at base; lower with no obvious lateral veins; flo. blue, 4 stamens exserted. Calcareous downs, dry pastures, dunes, sea cliffs, etc., widespread in England and Wales, local in Scotland and Ireland. Flo. June–Aug. ✳.

Echium lycopsis L. **Purple Bugloss.** *E. plantagineum* L. ¶Upper leaves cordate at base; lower with obvious lateral veins; flo. purple, 2 stamens exserted. Sea cliffs and dunes, Cornwall and Jersey, occurs elsewhere as a garden escape. Flo. June–Aug.

CONVOLVULACEAE

Calystegia sepium (L.) R. Br. **Bindweed.**
Subsp. *sepium*. ¶Stems long, glabrous, climbing; flo. white, rarely pink (f. *colorata* Lange); flo. bracts ½ in. long, cordate, not inflated. On hedges, in marshes, ditches and gardens, etc., widespread, but less common in Scotland. Flo. June–Aug. ✲.

Subsp. *roseata* Brummitt. ¶Stems usually hairy; leaf apex often more attenuate; flo. pink. On hedges, in marshes and ditches in coastal and subcoastal areas in the west from Cornwall to mid Scotland. Flo. June–Aug.

Calystegia × *lucana* (Ten.) G. Don. (*C. sepium* × *silvatica*). ¶Intermediate between the two parents and often frequent where they grow together, especially in S. England and Midlands.

*Calystegia pulchra Brummitt & Heywood. *C. dahurica* auct., non (Herbert) G. Don. ¶Stems long, climbing; peduncles hairy; bracteoles slightly inflated; flo. bright pink, usually with white bands on the throat, intermediate in size between *C. sepium* and *C. silvatica*. Garden escape. Naturalized in hedge banks and thickets, etc., usually near habitation, rather common. Flo. June–Aug.

*Calystegia silvatica (Kit.) Griseb. **Great Bindweed.** *C. sylvestris* (Willd.) Roem. & Schult. ¶Stems very long, climbing; flo. bracts 1 in. long, triangular, inflated. Garden escape. Naturalized in hedges and thickets and established on waste ground, widespread. Flo. June–Aug.

Calystegia soldanella (L.) R. Br. **Sea Bindweed.** ¶Stem short, 6–12 in., procumbent; leaves reniform; flo. bracts ½ in.; flo. pink. On sandy sea-shores, widespread, but rare in Scotland. Flo. June–Aug. ✲.

Convolvulus arvensis L. **Lesser Bindweed.** ¶Stem climbing; flo. bracts very small, low on peduncle; flo. 1 in., pink and white. Common in cultivated soil, but rare in N. Scotland. Flo. June–Aug. ✲.

Cuscuta europaea L. **Greater Dodder.** ¶Parasitic, string-like, climbing; heads ½–¾ in.; corolla scales small; styles shorter than ovary. On nettles and hops, S. England, rare. Flo. July–Sept. ✲.

Cuscuta epithymum (L.) L. **Lesser Dodder.** ¶Parasitic, thread-like, red; heads smaller, pink; corolla scales nearly closing tube; styles longer than ovary. On heather and gorse (sometimes white flo. on clover, *Lotus*, etc.), chiefly S. and E. England. Flo. July–Sept. ✲.

SOLANACEAE

Solanum dulcamara L. **Woody Nightshade.** ¶Perennial; shrubby; leaves cordate, upper hastate; flo. ½ in., blue-purple; berry scarlet. Common in hedgerows, copses and marshes, but local in Scotland. Flo. June–Aug. ✲.

Solanum nigrum L. **Black Nightshade.** ¶Annual; stem herbaceous, angled; leaves ovate; flo. ¼ in., white; berry black. On sea cliffs and cultivated land in England and Wales, introduced in Scotland and Ireland. Flo. July–Sept. ✲.

*Lycium barbarum L. *L. halimifolium* Mill. ¶Stem with a few straight spines; leaves lanceolate, grey-green; petals short. Garden escape. Naturalized in hedges and thickets and established on waste ground. Flo. June–Aug.

Lycium chinense Mill. **Duke of Argyle's Tea-tree.** *L. barbarum* auct. ¶Usually without spines; leaves a little wider, bright green; corolla lobes equalling tube. Garden escape. Naturalized in hedges, etc., especially near the sea. Flo. Aug.–Oct. ✼.

Atropa bella-donna L. **Deadly Nightshade.** ¶Stem 3 ft; leaves in unequal pairs; flo. dull purple; berries black; very poisonous. Native in woods and thickets on calcareous soil in England and Wales; elsewhere on waste ground, etc., as an introduction. Flo. June–Aug. ✼.

Datura stramonium L. **Thorn-apple.** ¶Leaves very broad, coarsely toothed; flo. erect, 2 in., funnel shaped, white; fr. covered with spines, very poisonous. Introduced. Flo. June–July.

Hyoscyamus niger L. **Henbane.** ¶Stem 2 ft; leaves downy; flo. with many dark purple veins; fr. enclosed in calyx. In sandy waste places especially near the sea, chiefly in the S. half of Britain. Flo. May–Aug. ✼.

Physalis alkekengi L. **Winter Cherry.** ¶Perennial with a creeping root; stem pubescent, 1–1½ ft; leaves in pairs, entire, variable in shape from ovate-acute to ovate-deltoid, acuminate, on long stems; flo. rotate, dirty white, solitary, **axilla**ry; calyx ovate, inflated reddish yellow, enclosing the orange-red berry which resembles a small cherry. Garden escape. Established on waste ground. Flo. June–Aug.

SCROPHULARIACEAE

PLATE 62

Verbascum thapsus L. **Common Mullein.** ¶Leaves decurrent, clothed with soft wool; sepals ovate, upper filaments with white hairs, lower subglabrous. Common on dry soil, chiefly in England and Wales, mostly casual in Scotland and Ireland. Flo. June–Aug. ✼.

Verbascum thapsiforme Schrad. ¶Similar to *V. thapsus*, but corolla larger, and flat; filaments shorter with decurrent anthers. Naturalized on banks, etc., rare. Flo. June–Aug.

Verbascum phlomoides L. ¶Similar to *V. thapsiforme*, but leaves non-decurrent. Garden escape. Established on waste ground, chiefly in S. England. Flo. June–Aug.

Verbascum pulverulentum Vill. **Hoary Mullein.** ¶Leaves not decurrent, clothed with mealy white wool; sepals lanceolate; all filaments with white hairs. Norfolk and Suffolk, introduced elsewhere. Flo. July–Aug. ✼.

Verbascum speciosum Schrad. ¶Plant clothed with thick white wool; corolla yellow, larger than in *V. pulverulentum*; sepals lanceolate; all filaments with white hairs. Introduced. Naturalized on banks, waste ground, etc. Flo. July–Aug.

Verbascum lychnitis L. **White Mullein.** ¶Leaves green above, white woolly beneath; sepals linear; all filaments with white hairs; flo. white or yellow. Calcareous banks and quarries, chiefly in S. England. Flo. July–Aug. ✼.

Verbascum nigrum L. **Dark Mullein.** ¶Leaves dark green above, pubescent beneath; filaments with purple hairs. Calcareous banks, chiefly in S. England, rare in Wales, and introduced in Scotland and Ireland. Flo. June–Sept. ✼.

Verbascum chaixii Vill. Similar to *V. nigrum*, but leaves rounded at base; flo. 2–4 in axils of branches. Established on waste ground, etc. Rare.

Verbascum virgatum Stokes. **Slender Mullein.** ¶Stem and leaves green but glandular;

flo. large, clustered in axils; subsessile filaments with purple hairs. Native in Cornwall and Devon, introduced elsewhere. Flo. June–Sept. ❀.

Verbascum blattaria L. **Moth Mullein.** ¶Plant green, glandular above; flo. solitary, axillary, pedicelled; filaments with purple hairs. In waste places, chiefly S. and E. England. Flo. June–Sept.

The following hybrids have been noted in Britain:
Verbascum lychnitis × *thapsus* = *V.* × *thapsi* L.; *V. lychnitis* × *pulverulentum* = *V.* × *regelianum* Wirtg.; *V. lychnitis* × *nigrum* = *V.* × *schiedeanum* Koch; *V. pulverulentum* × *thapsus* = *V.* × *godronii* Bor.; *V. nigrum* × *thapsus* = *V.* × *semialbum* Chaub.; *V. nigrum* × *pulverulentum* = *V.* × *wirtgenii* Franch.

*Cymbalaria muralis Gaertn., Mey. & Scherb. **Ivy-leaved Toadflax.** *Linaria cymbalaria* (L.) Mill. ¶Stems weak, trailing; leaves 5 lobed, glabrous; flo. mauve, lip white and yellow. Introduced, common on old walls. Flo. May–Sept. ❀.

Kickxia elatine (L.) Dumort. **Fluellen.** *Linaria elatine* (L.) Mill. ¶Stem prostrate; leaves with basal lobes; pedicels glabrous; flo. spur straight. Cornfields and arable land in England and Wales, rare in Ireland. Flo. July–Oct. ❀.

Kickxia spuria (L.) Dumort. **Round-leaved Fluellen.** *Linaria spuria* (L.) Mill. ¶Stem prostrate; leaves ovate or orbicular; pedicels hairy; flo. spur curved. Cornfields and arable land in mid, S. and E. England, very rare in Wales, and casual elsewhere. Flo. July–Oct. ❀.

Chaenorhinum minus (L.) Lange. **Small Toadflax.** *Linaria minor* (L.) Desf. ¶Stem erect, 6 in., glandular; flo. solitary, axillary, mauve; spur short. On cultivated land, railways, in chalk pits, rather common, but rare in Scotland. Flo. May–Sept. ❀.

Linaria pelisseriana (L.) Mill. **Jersey Toadflax.** ¶Stem erect, ½–1 ft; flo. few, violet with white lip; spur long and straight. On heaths in Jersey. Flo. May–July.

*Linaria purpurea (L.) Mill. **Purple Toadflax.** ¶Perennial; erect, 2–3 ft; flo. dense, violet; spur long and curved. Introduced, rather common on old walls, waste ground, etc. Flo. June–Sept. ❀.

Linaria repens (L.) Mill. **Pale Toadflax.** ¶Stem from rhizome erect, 1–2 ft; flo. pale mauve with purple veins; spur short. On stony or calcareous land, railway tracks, local. Flo. June–Sept. ❀.

Linaria repens × *vulgaris* = *L.* × *sepium* Allman. ¶Flo. yellowish, striped with purple; foliage intermediate between the parents; variable. Sometimes occurs where the parents grow together.

Linaria vulgaris Mill. **Common Toadflax.** ¶Stem from rhizome erect, 2 ft; leaves linear, rarely lanceolate; flo. large, yellow, lip orange. Common in England, Wales and S. Scotland, local in N. Scotland and Ireland. Flo. July–Oct. ❀.

*Linaria supina (L.) Chazelles. ¶Stem glaucous; branches prostrate and ascending; flo. ½ in., few, close, yellow with orange lip. Sandy places near Par, Cornwall and Plymouth. Flo. June–Sept.

*Linaria arenaria DC. **Sand Toadflax.** ¶Stems 4–6 in., much branched, sticky with glands; flo. small, bright yellow; spur slender. Naturalized on sand dunes, N. Devon. Flo. May–Sept. ❀.

*Antirrhinum majus L. **Snapdragon.** ¶Bracts short, ovate; calyx lobes ovate, much shorter than corolla. Plentifully naturalized on old walls and rock cuttings. Flo. July–Sept.

Misopates orontium (L.) Raf. **Weasel's Snout.** *Antirrhinum orontium* L. ¶Bracts linear; calyx lobes long, linear, equalling pink corolla. On cultivated land, mostly in S. and E. England and Wales. Flo. July–Sept. ⚘.

PLATE 63

Scrophularia auriculata L. **Water Figwort.** *S. aquatica* auct. ¶Stems narrowly 4 winged; leaves crenate; bracts small; staminode orbicular. Common by ponds and wet ditches in England, local in Wales and Ireland, rare in Scotland. Flo. June–Sept. ⚘.

Scrophularia umbrosa Dumort. **Scarce Water Figwort.** *S. ehrhartii* Stevens., *S. alata* Gilib. ¶Stem broadly 4 winged; leaves serrate; bracts leafy; flo. fewer; staminode 2 lobed. In wet shady places, rare. Flo. July–Sept. ⚘.

Scrophularia nodosa L. **Figwort.** ¶Root knobbed; stem 4 angled, not winged; leaves coarsely serrate at base. Common in woods and hedge banks. Flo. June–Sept. ⚘.

Scrophularia scorodonia L. **Balm-leaved Figwort.** ¶Stem and leaves pubescent; leaves very rugose, doubly serrate; teeth mucronate. In Cornwall, S. Devon and Channel Islands. Flo. June–Aug. ⚘.

*Scrophularia vernalis L. **Yellow Figwort.** ¶Glandular, hairy; sepals subacute, without a border; flo. greenish yellow; staminode o. Naturalized in a few shady places. Flo. April–June.

*Mimulus guttatus DC. **Monkey Flower.** ¶Glabrous excepting pubescent calyx; flo. yellow with red spots; lower lip much the longest. Garden escape. Naturalized by streams in many places. Flo. June–Aug. ⚘.

*Mimulus luteus L. **Blotched Monkey Flower.** ¶Glabrous throughout; flo. with large red blotches; lower lip but little longer than upper. Garden escape. In similar places, mainly northern. Flo. June–Sept.

* Mimulus moschatus Dougl. ex Lindl. **Musk.** ¶Plant glandular, hairy; formerly fragrant; calyx teeth subequal; flo. ¼–½ in., yellow. Garden escape. Naturalized by sides of streams, etc. Flo. July–Aug.

Limosella aquatica L. **Mudwort.** ¶Leaves spathulate; calyx longer than corolla tube; corolla white or mauve; lobes triangular. On mud at margin of pools, rare and decreasing. Flo. June–Oct. ⚘.

Limosella subulata Ives. ¶Leaves all subulate; calyx short; corolla white with longer orange tube; lobes ovate. In Wales at margin of pools, very rare. Flo. June–Oct.

Sibthorpia europaea L. **Cornish Moneywort.** ¶Very slender; stems and leaves hairy; upper lobes of corolla yellowish, lower pink. On shady stream banks, very rare in S. England, and local in S.W. England and Wales. Flo. July–Oct. ⚘.

Digitalis purpurea L. **Foxglove.** ¶Stems 3–6 ft; leaves 6–12 in.; flo. pink-purple, pollinated by humble bees. Common in woodland clearings and heaths. Flo. July–Sept. ⚘.

*Erinus alpinus L. ¶Perennial; plant small, tufted; stems many; leaves obovate, the basal ones forming a rosette; corolla slender, tubular, purple; capsule ovoid. Garden escape. Naturalized in rocky woods and established on old walls, particularly in N. England and Scotland. Flo. April–Oct.

*_Veronica filiformis_ Sm. **Round-leaved Speedwell.** ¶Stems slender, creeping; leaves suborbicular, pubescent; pedicels long; flo. blue. Garden escape, spreading without setting fr. Locally abundant in meadows, by streams, also as a pest of lawns in many places. Flo. Mar.–May. �.

Veronica hederifolia L. **Ivy-leaved Speedwell.** ¶Stems decumbent, hairy; leaves with basal lobes; sepals cordate; flo. small, lilac. Common on hedge banks, cultivated ground, by streamsides and as a garden weed. Flo. March–May. ✻.

Veronica polita Fr. **Grey Speedwell.** ¶Leaves grey-green, pubescent, equalling pedicels; sepals ovate; capsule lobes erect. Common in cultivated ground. Flo. March–Nov. ✻.

Veronica agrestis L. **Field Speedwell.** ¶Leaves yellow-green; sepals oblong, spreading beside capsule lobes; flo. blue and white or pink. In cultivated land, less common. Flo. March–Nov. ✻.

*_Veronica persica_ Poir. **Persian Speedwell.** _V. buxbaumii_ Ten. ¶Leaves bright green; flo. large; pedicels long; capsule lobes divergent, keeled. An old introduction, now the commonest species. Flo. all months. ✻.

*_Veronica praecox_ All. ¶Stem erect; leaves conspicuously dentate; pedicels not twice as long as calyx; fr. longer than broad. Chiefly in sandy fields in E. Anglia.

Veronica triphyllos L. **Fingered Speedwell.** ¶Leaves with 3–7 fingerlike lobes; sepals spathulate; flo. deep blue. On sandy fields, chiefly in E. Anglia. Flo. April–June. ✻.

Veronica verna L. **Spring Speedwell.** ¶Stems erect, 2–4 in.; leaves pinnate, 3–7 lobed; sepals linear-lanceolate, unequal; flo. lilac, small. Dry pastures, Norfolk and Suffolk, rare. Flo. May–June. ✻.

*_Veronica peregrina_ L. **American Speedwell.** ¶Erect, 2–8 in.; leaves ovate, subentire; bracts longer than blue flo.; style almost wanting. Cultivated land in Scotland, N.W. Ireland, and elsewhere. Flo. April–July.

*_Veronica repens_ Clarion ex DC. **Corsican Speedwell.** ¶Stems creeping; leaves broadly ovate, subentire; flo. few, 3–6, pink; pedicels longer than bracts. Garden escape. N. England. Flo. April–May.

PLATE 64

Veronica arvensis L. **Wall Speedwell.** ¶Leaves ovate, pubescent; bracts mostly leaf-like; spike elongating; flo. bright blue. Common on dry soils, banks and walls. Flo. March–Sept. ✻.

Veronica serpyllifolia L. **Thyme-leaved Speedwell.**

Subsp. _serpyllifolia_. ¶Stem creeping; leaves ovate, glabrous; spike erect; flo. whitish; fr. shorter than calyx. Common on cultivated land and heaths. Flo. March–Oct. ✻.

Subsp. _humifusa_ (Dickson) Syme. ¶Leaves suborbicular; inflo. glandular; flo. blue. On mountains.

Veronica alpina L. **Alpine Speedwell.** ¶Leaves subglabrous; flo. few, small, dull blue; fr. longer than broad. On mountain rocks in Scotland, local. Flo. July–Aug. ✻.

Veronica fruticans Jacq. **Shrubby Speedwell.** _V. saxatilis_ Scop. ¶Stem wiry; leaves glabrous; corolla large, bright blue with red eye; fr. longer than calyx. On high mountain rocks, mid Scotland. Flo. July–Aug. ⚘⚘.

Veronica spicata L. **Spiked Speedwell.**
Subsp. *spicata.* ¶Stem 1 ft, slender; leaves gradually narrowed to petiole; flo. deep blue-purple. On dry grassland in E. Anglia, rare. Flo. July–Sept. ⚘⚘.
Subsp. *hybrida* (L.) E. F. Warb. ¶Plant stouter, 1–2 ft; leaves abruptly narrowed to broader petiole, and more crenate. On limestone rocks, Avon Gorge, Wales, Yorkshire, and Westmorland, rare. Flo. July–Sept.

Veronica officinalis L. **Common Speedwell.** ¶Stem creeping; leaves ovate, hairy; flo. lilac; spike rather dense; pedicels short. Common on dry heaths and banks. Flo. May–Aug. ⚘⚘.

Veronica chamaedrys L. **Germander Speedwell.** ¶Stem hairy on 2 sides; leaves hairy; flo. large and blue; ft. shorter than calyx. Common on cultivated ground, in grassy places, etc. Flo. March–Aug. ⚘⚘.

Veronica montana L. **Wood Speedwell.** ¶Stem hairy all round; leaves yellow-green; flo. lilac; capsule exceeding calyx. In woods on damp or stiff soils. Flo. April–July. ⚘⚘.

Veronica scutellata L. **Marsh Speedwell.** ¶Leaves linear-lanceolate; flo. spikes lax, alternate; flo. pale lilac. On wet meadows and moors. Flo. June–Aug. ⚘⚘.

Veronica anagallis-aquatica L. **Water Speedwell.** ¶Stem green; leaves long; spikes long; flo. blue; fruiting pedicels ascending. In edges of ponds and watery places, mostly S. and E. England, rare elsewhere. Flo. June–Aug. ⚘⚘.

Veronica catenata Pennell. **Pink Water Speedwell.** *V. aquatica* Bernh., non Gray. ¶Stem purple; leaves and spikes shorter; flo. pink; fruiting pedicels spreading. In similar watery places, mostly S. and E. England, local in Wales and Ireland, very rare in Scotland. Flo. June–Aug. ⚘⚘.

Veronica beccabunga L. **Brooklime.** ¶Stems creeping, fleshy; leaves obtuse; spikes opposite; flo. bright blue; capsule suborbicular. In small streams and watery places. Flo. May–Sept. ⚘⚘.

Euphrasia micrantha Reichb. **Common Slender Eyebright.** ¶Slender, erect, subsimple; leaves many, small; flo. coloured, lower lip longer; capsule narrow. From Cornwall and Devon to Shetland. Flo. July–Sept. ⚘⚘.

Euphrasia scottica Wettst. **Slender Scottish Eyebright.** ¶Stem slender, erect, subsimple; leaves fewer, wider; flo. white; lower lip equalling upper. On moors and mountains, S. Wales to Shetland. Flo. July–Aug. ⚘⚘.

Euphrasia rhumica Pugsl. ¶Stem slender, erect, purplish; leaves narrow, with fine white bristles on both surfaces; flo. small, white, tinged with blue; capsule ovate-oblong. Isle of Rhum (Inner Hebrides). Flo. Aug.

Euphrasia frigida Pugsl. ¶Plant suberect, lax; lower leaves distant, obtuse; flo. white, lower lip longer; capsule large, broad, deeply cut. Teesdale to Shetland. Flo. July–Aug.

Euphrasia foulaensis Townsend ex Wettst. ¶Shorter, less slender; leaves broad, obtuse; flo. violet (or white), lip not much longer; capsule broad. N. Scotland to Shetland. Flo. July–Aug.

Euphrasia eurycarpa Pugsl. ¶Plant suberect, slender, purplish; leaves small, broad, oval; flo. white with bluish upper lip; capsule small, as broad as long. Isle of Rhum (Inner Hebrides). Flo. Aug.

Euphrasia campbelliae Pugsl. ¶Plant erect, slender, purplish; leaves with thick white bristles on margins and nerves; flo. white with purplish upper lip; capsule medium, oblong. Isle of Lewis (Outer Hebrides). Flo. July.

Euphrasia rotundifolia Pugsl. ¶Erect with short branches; leaves rounded, crenate, hirsute; flo. small, white; capsule large and broad. On sea cliffs in Sutherland, etc. Flo. July.

Euphrasia marshallii Pugsl. ¶Erect and branched; leaves broad, obtuse, hirsute; flo. medium, white; capsule large and broad. Sea cliffs in W. Sutherland and Caithness. Flo. July–Aug.

Euphrasia curta (Fr.) Wettst. **Hairy-leaved Eyebright.** ¶Erect with basal branches; leaves small, acute, hirsute; flo. small, white; capsule small and narrow. Local on grassy mountain slopes and seasides. Flo. June–Sept.

Euphrasia cambrica Pugsl. **Dwarf Welsh Eyebright.** ¶Very dwarf, $\frac{1}{2}$–1 in.; leaves obtuse, sparingly hirsute; flo. small, whitish, lips subequal; capsule large and broad. High Welsh mountains and Kirkstone Pass. Flo. July.

Euphrasia tetraquetra (Bréb.) Arrondeau. **Broad-leaved Eyebright.** *E. occidentalis* Wettst. ¶Dwarf, 2–4 in.; branches basal, stout; leaves large, hiding internodes; flo. small, white; capsule 6–8 mm. Sea cliffs, especially in S.W. Flo. May–Aug.

Euphrasia nemorosa (Pers.) Wallr. **Common Eyebright.**¶Stem erect, 5–10 in.; branches several, suberect; leaves glabrous, teeth acute or aristate; flo. white or purplish above, lower lip longer. Common. Flo. July–Sept. ✲.
Var. *calcarea* Pugsl. ¶Dwarf but coarse, with small flo. On chalk downs.
Var. *collina* Pugsl. ¶Small but coarse, with flo. larger. On hills in W.
Var. *sabulicola* Pugsl. ¶Small, with flo. very small, white. Sands in Scotland.

Euphrasia heslop-harrisonii Pugsl. ¶Plant suberect, slender, flexuous; leaves small, with blunt shallow teeth; flo. small, white with pale blue upper lip; capsule narrow, oblong. Isle of Rhum (Inner Hebrides) and West Ross.

Euphrasia confusa Pugsl. **Little Kneeling Eyebright.** ¶Dwarf, 1–4 in.; many slender kneeling branches; leaves many, small; flo. small; capsule small but broad. Grassy cliffs and moors, W. England to N. Scotland. Flo. July–Sept. ✲.

Euphrasia pseudokerneri Pugsl. **Chalk Hill Eyebright.** ¶Erect; branches many, spreading; leaves small, paler below; flo. large, white; capsule small, 5 mm., not exceeding calyx. Chalk downs. Flo. June–Sept.

Euphrasia arctica Lange ex Rostrup. **Greater Eyebright.** *E. borealis* auct. ¶Plant large, with coarse growth; leaves large, thick, dark green; flo. large, white; capsule large. Scotland and N. England, rare in S. Flo. July–Aug.

Euphrasia brevipila Burnat & Gremli. **Short-haired Eyebright.** ¶Plant large, growth coarse; leaves more yellowish, with short glands and bristles; flo. large, lilac or white. Common in Scotland, local in England. Flo. June–Aug. ✲.

Euphrasia rostkoviana Hayne. **Large-flowered Sticky Eyebright.** ¶Basal branches many, slender; leaves rather small, clothed with glandular hairs; flo. large, lower lip much the larger. Meadows in W., local. Flo. July–Aug.

Euphrasia montana Jord. **Mountain Sticky Eyebright.**¶Stem simple or little branched;

leaves clothed with glandular hairs; flo. white, large, elongating from 10 to 13 mm. Mountain pastures, N. England. Flo. June–July.

Euphrasia rivularis Pugsl. **Snowdon Eyebright.** ¶Stem slender, subsimple; leaves small, glandular, hairy; flo. large, 8–9 mm., lilac; capsule broad and short. On Snowdon range only. Flo. early summer.

Euphrasia anglica Pugsl. **English Sticky Eyebright.** ¶Whole plant densely clothed with glandular hairs; leaves broad; flo. large, whitish. On moist heaths and meadows, common in S.W. England. Flo. May–Sept. ❀.

Euphrasia vigursii Davey. ¶Plant erect, robust; leaves covered with glandular hairs of varying sizes; flo. large, purplish to lilac; capsule elliptic. Heaths, Cornwall and S. Devon, local. Flo. June–Sept.

Euphrasia hirtella Jord. ex Reut. **Small-flowered Sticky Eyebright.** ¶Stem subsimple; upper internodes crowded, densely glandular; leaves large, with deep teeth; flo. small. In Wales. Flo. early summer.

Euphrasia salisburgensis Funck. **Narrow-leaved Eyebright.** ¶Leaves very small, less than half as broad as long, upper linear; flo. small. On limestone, mid Yorkshire and in Ireland. Flo. July–Aug. ❀.

PLATE 65

Odontites verna (Bellardi) Dumort. **Red Bartsia.** *Bartsia odontites* (L.) Huds.
Subsp. *verna.* ¶Branches ascending; leaves lanceolate, toothed; bracts exceeding pink flo. Common in Scotland, less so in England. Flo. June–July. ❀.
Subsp. *serotina* Corb. ¶Branches horizontal; leaves narrow, subentire; bracts not longer than flo. Common in arable fields in S. England. Flo. July–Aug.

Parentucellia viscosa (L.) Caruel. **Yellow Bartsia.** *Bartsia viscosa* L. ¶Plant 6–18 in.; viscid with glandular hairs; flo. yellow, lower lip longer. In damp grass, mostly near S. and W. coasts. Flo. June–Sept. ❀.

Bartsia alpina L. **Alpine Bartsia.** ¶Rhizome short; plant pubescent; bracts purplish; flo. dull purple, lips subequal. In mountain pastures, Yorkshire to Perthshire. Flo. June–Aug. ❀.

Pedicularis palustris L. **Red Rattle.** ¶Annual 8–18 in., much branched below; leaf pinnae many; calyx pubescent; flo. pink and crimson. Watery places on heaths and moors. Flo. May–Sept. ❀.

Pedicularis sylvatica L. **Lousewort.** ¶Perennial, 3–6 in.; branches few basal; leaf pinnae few; calyx glabrous outside; flo. few. Common on heaths and hill pastures. Flo. April–July. ❀.

Rhinanthus serotinus (Schönh.) Oborny. **Greater Hayrattle.** *R. major* Ehrh., non L.
Subsp. *aperus* (Fr.) Hyland. ¶Plant robust; leaves long, teeth many, acute; bracts acuminate; inflo. crowded; corolla 20–22 mm., tube slightly curved; purple teeth longer than broad. In cornfields, arable ground, grassy places, etc., rare. Flo. June–Sept. ❀.

Rhinanthus minor L. **Hayrattle.**
Subsp. *minor.* ¶Less robust; branches short; leaves crenate, intercalary none; corolla 15 mm., straight; purple teeth broader than long; lowest bract teeth less deep. Common in pastures on basic soils. Flo. May–June. ❀.

Subsp. *stenophyllus* (Schur.) Swartz. *Rhinanthus stenophyllus* (Schur.) Druce. ¶Flo. branches many; intercalary leaves 2–4, linear-lanceolate, teeth often prominent. Common in Scotland and W. England, often on limestone. Flo. June–Aug. ✳.

Subsp. *calcareus* (Wilmott) E. F. Warb. *Rhinanthus calcareus* Wilmott. ¶Flo. branches many, slender; intercalary leaves 2–4, small, linear, teeth appressed. On chalk and limestone, S. England and Scotland. Flo. July–Aug.

Subsp. *monticola* (Sterneck) Swartz. *Rhinanthus monticola* Sterneck. *R. spadiceus* Wilmott. ¶Lower internodes crowded, bearing short flowerless branches; calyx often violet tinted. On lower mountain pastures, N. England and Scotland. July–Aug. ✳.

Subsp. *borealis* (Sterneck) P. D. Sell. *Rhinanthus borealis* (Sterneck) Marshall. ¶Stem simple, 4–8 in., leaves broad, blunt, pubescent; calyx hairy. On mountains in Scotland and Kerry. Flo. July–Aug. ✳.

Subsp. *lintoni* (Wilmott) P. D. Sell. *Rhinanthus lintoni* Wilmott. *R. drummond-hayi* auct. ¶Stem 4–8 in., subsimple, slender; leaves narrow, tapering; calyx pubescent, elongate. On mountains in Scotland. Flo. July–Aug. ✳.

Melampyrum cristatum L. **Crested Cow-wheat.** ¶Flo. in dense spike, yellow and purple tinted; bracts with wider, pink, finely pectinate base, lower with long points. Woods, S. and E. England, local. Flo. June–Sept. ✳.

Melampyrum arvense L. **Field Cow-wheat.** ¶Flo. pink and yellow in lax spike; bracts finely pinnate, points less long. In cornfields, S. and E. England, local and rare. Flo. June–Sept. ✳.

Melampyrum pratense L. **Common Cow-wheat.** ¶Flo. in separate leaf axils; calyx small; corolla $\frac{3}{4}$ in., yellow in woods, or white splashed with pink on moors. Common. Flo. June–Aug. ✳.

Melampyrum sylvaticum L. **Wood Cow-wheat.** ¶Flo. in separate leaf axils; calyx lobes long, equalling smaller yellow corolla. Mountain woods, chiefly in Scotland, local. Flo. June–Aug. ✳.

OROBANCHACEAE   **PLATE 66**

Orobanche purpurea Jacq. **Purple Broomrape.** *O. caerulea* Vill. ¶Stem simple, bluish; flo. dull bluish purple, with 1 bract and 2 bracteoles; stigma lobes white, united. On *Achillea*, Channel Islands, common; S. and E. England, rare. Flo. June–July. ✳.

Orobanche ramosa L. **Branched Broomrape.** ¶Stem with a few basal branches; flo. $\frac{1}{2}$ in., cream with purple edges; 1 bract and 2 bracteoles. Channel Islands, introduced in S.E. England. Flo. July–Sept. ✳.

Orobanche rapum-genistae Thuill. **Greater Broomrape.** ¶Stem 2 ft; flo. large, yellowish; bract 1 only; stamens basal; stigma lobes yellow, distant. On gorse and broom, chiefly in England and Wales, rare and decreasing. Flo. May–July. ✳.

Orobanche alba Steph. ex Willd. **Red Broomrape.** ¶Stem 3–6 in., red; flo. deep red (in Britain); stigma lobes red, contiguous. On thyme, chiefly near the S. coast of Cornwall, W. coast of Scotland and N.E. and W. coasts of Ireland. Flo. June–Aug. ✳.

Orobanche caryophyllacea Sm. **Clove Scented Broomrape.** ¶Flo. large, yellowish, purple tinted, densely glandular; stamens sub-basal; stigma lobes distant, purple. On *Galium*, coast of E. Kent, rare. Flo. July. ✳.

Orobanche elatior Sutton. **Tall Broomrape.** *O. major* auct. ¶Stem 1–2 ft; flo. pale yellow, tinted purple, glandular; stigma lobes yellow; stamens inserted 5 mm. above base. On *Centaurea scabiosa*, S. and E. England, local. Flo. July. ❀.

Orobanche reticulata Wallr.
Subsp. *pallidiflora* (Wimm. & Grab.) Hegi. **Thistle Broomrape.** ¶Stem 1 ft, glandular; flo. yellowish with purple edges; stamens 3–4 mm. above base; stigmas purple. On thistles, mostly in Yorkshire, rare. Flo. June–Aug.

Orobanche minor Sm. **Lesser Broomrape.** *O. apiculata* Wallr. ¶Spike lax, yellow tinted purple; corolla curved and equal throughout; stigma lobes purple, contiguous; filaments subglabrous. On Leguminosae, mostly S. and E. England, S. Wales and S. Ireland. ❀.
Var. *flava* Regel. ¶Stems, flo. and stigma lobes yellow. In Channel Islands.
Var. *compositorum* Pugsl. ¶Corolla long and narrow; filaments hairy. On *Crepis*.

Orobanche picridis F. W. Schultz ex Koch. **Picris Broomrape.** ¶Flo. pale, whitish yellow, tinted purple, glandular; filaments very hairy below, inserted 4 mm. above base. On *Picris* and *Crepis*, S. England, rare. Flo. June–July. ❀.

Orobanche hederae Duby. **Ivy Broomrape.** ¶Corolla straight, cream veined purple; stamens inserted 3 mm. above base; stigma lobes yellow, united. On ivy, S. England, Wales, and Ireland, mainly coastal. ❀.

Orobanche maritima Pugsl. **Carrot Broomrape.** *O. amethystea* auct. ¶Flo. many, dull yellow veined purple; central lobe larger; stigma lobes purple, partly united. Chiefly on *Daucus*, S. coasts of England and Wales, rare. Flo. June–July.

Lathraea squamaria L. **Toothwort.** ¶Root parasite without green colour; stem 6 in.; calyx glandular; flo. cream. On roots of hazel and elm in woods, copses and shady places. Flo. March–May. ❀.

LENTIBULARIACEAE

Utricularia vulgaris L. **Common Bladderwort.** ¶Aquatic with bladders on green capillary leaves; upper lip of flo. equalling palate, lower lip deflexed. In ponds, local and decreasing. Flo. July–Aug. ❀.

Utricularia neglecta Lehm. **Western Bladderwort.** *U. major* auct. ¶Aquatic with bladders on green leaves; upper lip of flo. longer than palate, lower lip margins flat. In ponds, chiefly in W. England. Flo. July–Aug. ❀.

Utricularia intermedia Hayne. ¶Aquatic with bladders mostly on colourless leaves under mud; flo. bright yellow streaked red. In peaty water, chiefly in N. England, Scotland and W. Ireland, very local. Flo. rare, July–Sept. ❀.

Utricularia minor L. **Lesser Bladderwort.** ¶Aquatic with bladders on small colourless and green leaves; flo. pale and small, 6–8 mm. In boggy pools and ditches, chiefly N.W. England, Scotland and Ireland, local. Flo. July–Sept. ❀.

Pinguicula vulgaris L. **Common Butterwort.** ¶Flo. $\frac{1}{2}$–$\frac{3}{4}$ in., violet with white throat; lobed of lip spreading; spur 5–6 mm., acute. On wet rocks and bogs, chiefly N. England, Scotland and N. Ireland. Flo. May–June. ❀.

Pinguicula grandiflora Lam. **Greater Butterwort.** ¶Flo. large, 1 in., violet with white throat; lobes of lip broad, overlapping spur 10 mm. Bogs in S.W. Ireland, naturalized in S.W. England. Flo. May–June. ❀.

Pinguicula alpina L. ¶Flo. $\frac{3}{8}$ in., white with yellow mouth; spur conical, 2–3 mm.; capsule oval. Ross, probably extinct. Flo. June.

Pinguicula lusitanica L. **Pink Butterwort.** ¶Flo. $\frac{1}{4}$ in., pinkish lilac and yellow; spur cylindrical; capsule globose. In wet heaths and peaty bogs, mostly S.W. England, W. Scotland, and W. Ireland. Flo. June–Sept. ✳✳.

VERBENACEAE   **PLATE 67**

Verbena officinalis L. **Vervain.** ¶Stem 18 in., tough, hispid; branches few, spreading; flo. few, pale lilac. In England and Wales, rather local. Flo. July–Sept. ✳✳.

LABIATAE

Mentha suaveolens Ehrh. **Round-leaved Mint.** *M. rotundifolia* auct., non (L.) Huds. ¶Leaves nearly round, much wrinkled; bracts lanceolate; flo. in compact spike. Near S.W. coasts and local elsewhere, England and Wales. Flo. late summer. ✳✳.

Mentha spicata × suaveolens. **French Mint.** *M. alopecuroides* Hull. ¶Very robust; leaves large, broadly ovate, softly wrinkled; bracts subulate; flo. in a spike. Commonly naturalized from gardens. Flo. late summer.

Mentha longifolia (L.) Huds. **Horse Mint.** ¶Leaves lanceolate, woolly white beneath; bracts subulate; flo. spike dense. Commonly naturalized from gardens. Now regarded as merely a hairy form of *M. spicata*. Flo. late summer. ✳✳.

*Mentha spicata L. **Spear Mint.** ¶Leaves sessile, lanceolate, glabrous; flo. in spike; bracts linear; lower stamens exserted. Commonly naturalized from gardens. Flo. Aug. ✳✳.

Mentha × piperita L. = *M. aquatica × spicata.* **Pepper Mint.** ¶Stem red; leaves ovate, stalked, subglabrous, purple tinted; spike interrupted below; stamens included. In ditches, local. Flo. late summer. ✳✳.

Mentha aquatica L. **Water Mint.** ¶Stem and ovate leaves robust, hairy; inflo. of 2–3 whorls, lower separate; stamens exserted. In ditches and wet places. Flo. late summer. ✳✳.

Mentha × smithiana R. A. Graham = *M. aquatica × arvensis × spicata.* *M. rubra* Sm., non Mill. ¶Stems often red; leaves broadly ovate, obtuse, subglabrous; bracts leaf-like; calyx teeth twice as long as broad; stamens exserted. Flo. late summer. ✳✳.

Mentha × gentilis L. = *M. arvensis × spicata.* ¶Leaves ovate-lanceolate, hairy; bracts leaf-like; pedicels and calyx subglabrous; teeth twice as long as broad; flo. small, 3 mm.; stamens not exserted. ✳✳.

Mentha × verticillata L. = *M. aquatica × arvensis.* *M. sativa* L. ¶Robust; leaves ovate, hairy; bracts leaf-like; pedicels and calyx hairy; teeth twice as long as broad; stamens not exserted. Common. Flo. late summer.

Mentha arvensis L. **Corn Mint.** ¶Leaves ovate, hairy; whorls axillary, distant; bracts leaf-like; calyx teeth triangular, hairy, as long as broad; stamens exserted. Common in cornfields. Flo. late summer. ✳✳.

Mentha pulegium L. **Penny Royal.** ¶Stem prostrate below; leaves small, oval, $\frac{1}{4}$–$\frac{1}{2}$ in.;

whorls distant; bracts leaf-like; flo. swollen below mouth. Damp sandy places, local. Flo. late summer. ❀.

Lycopus europaeus L. **Gipsy-wort.** ¶Stem 2–3 ft; leaves lobed or dentate; calyx spine pointed; flo. white, spotted purple. Common in ditches and river banks. Flo. June–Sept. ❀.

Origanum vulgare L. **Marjoram.** ¶Stem wiry, branched as shown; bracts leaf-like, small; bracteoles purple; flo. pale rose. Common on calcareous soils. Flo. July–Sept. ❀.

PLATE 68

Thymus serpyllum L. **Wild Thyme.** ¶Creeping stems many, long; flo. stems hairy all round; leaves 4–6 mm.; flo. in 1 head. In E. England. Flo. June–Aug. ❀.

Thymus drucei Ronn. **Common Wild Thyme.** ¶Creeping stems many, dense; flo. stems hairy on 2 sides only; leaves 5–8 mm.; flo. in 1 head. Common on dry banks and heaths. Flo. June–Aug.

Thymus pulegioides L. **Larger Wild Thyme.** *T. chamaedrys* Fr. ¶Creeping stems few; stem angles sharp and hairy; leaves up to 10 mm.; inflo. with separate whorl below. Calcareous and dry soils, S. and E. England. Flo. July–Aug. ❀.

Clinopodium vulgare L. **Cushion Calamint.** *Calamintha clinopodium* Benth. ¶Stems 1½ ft; flo. rose-red in terminal and axillary heads; bracteoles subulate, ciliate. Common in England. Flo. July–Sept. ❀.

Acinos arvensis (Lam.) Dandy. **Basil Thyme.** *Calamintha acinos* (L.) Clairv. ¶Stem 6–8 in., ascending; flo. blue in small whorls; calyx curved, swollen below. Fairly common, especially on calcareous soils. Flo. Aug.–Sept. ❀.

Calamintha nepeta (L.) Savi. **Lesser Calamint.** ¶Stem 1 ft; leaves small, greyish, hairy; calyx teeth nearly alike, internal hairs protruding; flo. mauve. Mainly S. England, rare. Flo. July–Aug. ❀.

Calamintha ascendens Jord. **Common Calamint.** *C. officinalis* auct. ¶Stem 1 ft; leaves larger, green; calyx with lower teeth much longer; flo. pale lilac, spotted. On basic or calcareous banks, England. Flo. July–Sept. ❀.

Calamintha sylvatica Bromf. **Wood Calamint.** *C. intermedia* auct. ¶Stem 2 ft; leaves large; flo. large, 15–20 mm., deeply purple blotched. Very local on chalk, I. of Wight. Flo. Aug.–Sept. ❀.

*Melissa officinalis L. **Balm.** ¶Stems many, 2 ft; leaves ovate, wrinkled; calyx with 2 unequal lips; flo. white. Naturalized, mainly in S. England. Flo. May–July. ❀.

Salvia horminoides Pourr. **Wild Sage, Clary.** ¶Leaves coarsely toothed or lobed; upper teeth of calyx united; flo. often shorter than calyx, violet with 2 white spots. Mostly S. England. Flo. May–July. ❀.

Salvia verbenaca L. ¶Leaves coarsely toothed or lobed; upper teeth of calyx united; flo. usually longer than calyx, purple unspotted. Vazon Bay, Guernsey. Flo. June–Aug.

Salvia pratensis L. **Meadow Clary.** ¶Upper leaves and bracts ovate; corolla large, up to 1 in., 3 times length of calyx, deep violet. On calcareous pastures, very local. Flo. June–July. ❀.

Salvia verticillata L. ¶Bracts small, brown, reflexed; clayx with 3 upper teeth distinct; flo. ½ in., violet, with a ring of hairs within. In waste places. Flo. June–July.

Nepeta cataria L. **Cat Mint.** ¶Stem 2–3 ft; leaves pubescent, white beneath; inflo. dense; flo. white. Mostly on calcareous soil, local. Flo. July–Sept. ✿.

Glechoma hederacea L. **Ground Ivy.** *Nepeta glechoma* Benth. ¶Stem creeping; leaves reniform, soft; flo. blue-purple, sometimes small and female. Common. Flo. April–June. ✿.

Scutellaria galericulata L. **Skull-cap.** ¶Stem 1 ft, from rhizome; leaves rounded or cordate below; flo. ½–¾ in., blue-violet. Edges of ponds and streams. Flo. July–Sept. ✿.

Scutellaria hastifolia L. ¶Stem 1 ft, from rhizome; leaves hastate below; flo. in terminal spike, ¾–1 in., blue-violet. In a wood, W. Norfolk, introduced. Flo. July–Sept.

Scutellaria minor L. **Lesser Skull-cap.** ¶Stem 6 in., from rhizome; leaves round below; flo. in leaf axils ⅜ in., pale pink. Common on wet heaths. Flo. July–Sept. ✿.

PLATE 69

Prunella vulgaris L. **Self-heal.** ¶Leaves ovate, subentire, rounded below; upper teeth of calyx united; flo. blue-violet, rarely pink. Flo. June–Sept. ✿.

Prunella laciniata (L.) L. ¶Upper leaves lobed or pinnate, cuneate below; upper teeth of calyx more distinct; flo. creamy white. On chalk downs in S. England, local. Flo. June–Aug. ✿.

Melittis melissophyllum L. **Bastard Balm.** ¶Stem 1–2 ft; leaves strong smelling; flo. large, white blotched red-purple. In woods and banks, S.W. England and S. Wales. Flo. May–June. ✿.

Marrubium vulgare L. **White Horehound.** ¶Stem and leaves hoary or woolly; calyx with 10 subulate hooked teeth; flo. whitish. On downs and chalk cliffs. Flo. July–Oct. ✿.

Betonica officinalis L. **Betony.** *Stachys betonica* Benth. ¶Stem 1 ft; leaves distant; flo. mostly in dense head, red-purple, without internal hairs. In hedge banks, common. Flo. June–Sept. ✿.

Stachys palustris L. **Marsh Woundwort.** ¶Stem 3 ft, from rhizome; leaves lanceolate; bracteoles equalling pedicels; flo. pale lilac. By ditches and streams, common. Flo. July–Sept. ✿.

Stachys sylvatica L. **Wood Woundwort.** ¶Leaves ovate; petioles long; bracteoles equalling pedicels; flo. claret colour. Common. Flo. July–Sept. ✿.

Stachys alpina L. **Alpine Woundwort.** ¶Stem 2 ft; leaves often purplish; bracteoles exceeding pedicels; flo. red with yellow eye, downy. In woods, Gloucestershire and Denbighshire, very rare. Flo. July–Aug. ✿.

Stachys germanica L. **Downy Woundwort.** ¶Plant stoloniferous, clothed with long white hairs; flo. in dense spike, pale rose. Calcareous soil in Oxfordshire, etc., very rare. Flo. July–Aug. ✿.

Stachys arvensis (L.) L. **Field Woundwort.** ¶Annual, 6–10 in., branched at base; flo. ¼ in., pale lilac. Cultivated fields, common in W. England. Flo. June–Aug. ✿.

Stachys annua (L.) L. ¶Annual, 6–10 in.; leaves oblong, 1–2 in.; flo. ½ in., pale yellow. On cultivated land, casual. Flo. June–Sept. ❀.

Galeopsis ladanum L. ¶Stem softly hairy, not thickened at nodes; leaf width ½–1 in., side 3–8 toothed; flo. small, lilac. Cultivated and waste land, casual. Flo. July–Sept.

Galeopsis angustifolia Ehrh. ex Hoffm. ¶Stem soft, not thickened at nodes; leaves linear-lanceolate, ¼–½ in. wide; teeth few; flo. large, ¾–1 in., pale rose. Cultivated land. Flo. July–Sept. ❀.

Galeopsis segetum Neck. *G. dubia* Leers. ¶Stem not thickened at nodes; leaves very soft, downy; flo. large, pale yellow. On sandy cornfields, rare. Flo. July–Aug. ❀.

Galeopsis tetrahit L. **Common Hemp-nettle.** ¶Stem thickened at nodes, hispid; flo. ¾ in., rose-purple and yellow; mid lobe of lip flat, entire, margin pale. Woods and hedge banks. Flo. July–Sept. ❀.

Galeopsis bifida Boenn. ¶Thickened at nodes, more evenly hispid; flo. ½ in., mid lobe of lip convex notched, deeply coloured to margin. Probably hybrid. Arable land. Flo. July–Sept.

Galeopsis speciosa Mill. **Large-flowered Hemp-nettle.** ¶Thickened at nodes, evenly hispid; flo. ¾ in., pale yellow, and lip mostly violet. Arable land, especially on peaty soil of Fen district. Flo. July–Sept. ❀.

Leonurus cardiaca L. **Motherwort.** ¶Stem 3 ft; lower leaves 5 lobed, upper 3 lobed; flo. in dense whorls, white or pink, purple spotted. Introduced, rare. Flo. July–Sept.

PLATE 70

Lamium amplexicaule L. **Henbit.** ¶Bract leaves sessile, like an involucre; calyx short and closing; corolla pink with crimson hood. In cultivated ground, chiefly S. and E. Britain. Flo. April–Aug. ❀.

Lamium moluccellifolium Fr. **Intermediate Dead-nettle.** *L. intermedium* F. ¶Upper bracts sessile; calyx deeply cut, spreading; corolla ½ in., pale pink. Cultivated ground in N. England and Scotland, rare elsewhere. Flo. June–Sept. ❀.

Lamium hybridum Vill. **Cut-leaved Dead-nettle.** *L. incisum* Willd. ¶Leaves all stalked, truncate at base, teeth deeply cut; corolla short, ring of hairs within faint or o. In cultivated ground, local. Flo. April–June. ❀.

Lamium purpureum L. **Purple Dead-nettle.** ¶Leaves cordate at base, teeth rounded; corolla pink, with ring of hairs inside. Very common. Flo. April–Aug. ❀.

Lamium maculatum L. **Spotted Dead-nettle.** ¶Leaves usually blotched with white; corolla pink with ring of hairs. Introduced. Flo. May–Aug.

Lamium album L. **White Dead-nettle.** ¶Flo. large and white, lateral lobes of lower lip with small teeth. Waste ground and roadsides. Flo. April–June and autumn. ❀.

Lamiastrum galeobdolon (L.) Ehrend. & Polatschek. **Yellow Archangel.** *Galeobdolon luteum* Huds., *Lamium galeobdolon* (L.) L. ¶Stolons widely spreading; flo. yellow, lower lip with 3 subequal lobes. In woods, especially on stiff soils, chiefly in S. England and Midlands. Flo. May–July. ❀.

Ballota nigra L. **Horehound.**
*Subsp. *nigra*. ¶Stem 1–2 ft, hairy, strong smelling; calyx tube short; calyx teeth

lanceolate, 2–4 mm. long; flo. pale purple. Introduced, waste ground, etc., very rare. Flo. June–Sept.

Subsp. *foetida* Hayek. ¶Differs from subsp. *nigra* in its longer calyx tube and broadly ovate calyx teeth, becoming abruptly acuminate, 1–2 mm. long; flo. pale purple. Common in hedge banks, waste ground, etc., in England and Wales, local in Scotland and Ireland. Flo. June–Sept. ✂.

Teucrium botrys L. **Cut-leaved Germander.** ¶Stem 8 in., leaves all pinnatifid; calyx gibbous; flo. pale purple. On chalk in S. England, rare. Flo. July–Sept. ✂.

Teucrium scordium L. **Water Germander.** ¶Plant 1 ft, stoloniferous; stems and leaves softly hairy; flo. pale purple. Wet places, and hollows on sand dunes. S. and E. England and Ireland, very local. Flo. July–Sept. ✂.

*Teucrium chamaedrys L. **Wall Germander.** ¶Stem 1 ft; leaves dark green, cuneate below, uppermost smaller; flo. purple. Introduced, on walls and ruins, rare. Flo. July–Sept. ✂.

Teucrium scorodonia L. **Wood Sage.** ¶Stem 1 ft; leaves wrinkled; flo. yellowish green, in pairs. Common. Flo. July–Sept. ✂.

Ajuga reptans L. **Bugle.** ¶Stolons leafy; stem hairy on 2 sides; uppermost leaves shorter than blue flo. Common on damp ground. Flo. May–July. ✂.

Ajuga pyramidalis L. **Pyramidal Bugle.** ¶Stem 6 in., hairy all round; upper leaves longer than pale mauve flo. Rock crevices in Scotland, N. England, Ireland, scarce. Flo. May–July. ✂.

Ajuga genevensis L. ¶Rhizomatous; stem hairy all round; upper leaves shorter than deep blue flo. Chalk pastures in Berkshire, perhaps introduced. Flo. May–July. ✂.

Ajuga chamaepitys (L.) Schreb. **Ground-pine.** ¶Stem 6 in.; leaves of 3 narrow lobes; flo. short, in pairs, yellow. In chalky fields, S.E. England, local. Flo. May–Sept. ✂.

PLANTAGINACEAE   **PLATE 71**

Plantago major L. **Great Plantain.** ¶Leaves abruptly contracted below to a petiole; spike of flo. brownish; capsule many seeded. Common. Flo. May–Sept. ✂.

Plantago media L. **Hoary Plantain, Lamb's-tongue.** ¶Leaves gradually narrowed below, subsessile, pubescent; flo. whitish; stamens purple. On basic and chalky soils, chiefly in England. Flo. June–Sept. ✂.

Plantago lanceolata L. **Ribwort Plantain.** ¶Leaves lanceolate, ribbed; scape furrowed; spike ovate; flo. brown. Common in pastures. Flo. April–Aug. ✂.

Plantago maritima L. **Sea Plantain.** ¶Leaves long, linear, fleshy; flo. brown; stamens pale yellow. In salt marshes and on mountains. Flo. June–Aug. ✂.

Plantago coronopus L. **Buck's-horn Plantain.** ¶Leaves pinnatifid and pubescent, but very variable. In gravelly places, commonest near the sea. Flo. May–Aug. ✂.

*Plantago indica L. *P. psyllium* L. ¶Stem long, leafy and branched; leaves linear, opposite. Introduced in cultivated ground and sand dunes. Flo. July–Aug.

Littorella uniflora (L.) Aschers. **Shore-weed.** *L. lacustris* L. ¶Submerged, with slender stolons; male flo. stalked, female sessile with long slender stigmas. On gravel in lakes and reservoirs, local. Flo. June–Aug. ✂.

ILLECEBRACEAE

Illecebrum verticillatum L. **Knot-grass.** ¶Branches prostrate; sepals thick, white, hooded and awned; petals minute, white. On moist sand in S. England, introduced elsewhere, very local. Flo. July–Sept. ⚘.

Herniaria glabra L. **Rupture-wort.** ¶Leaves narrowed below; fr. acute, longer than sepals, which are glabrous. Dry sandy places, mostly in E. Anglia, rare. Flo. July–Sept. ⚘.

Herniaria ciliolata Melderis. **Ciliate Rupture-wort.** *H. ciliata* Bab., non Clairv. ¶Leaves ovate, usually ciliate; sepals tipped with a bristle; fr. obtuse, equalling sepals. Lizard Head and Channel Islands. Flo. July–Aug.

**Herniaria hirsuta* L. ¶Branches and leaves clothed with spreading hairs; leaves lanceolate, narrowed at both ends. Casual, Hampshire and S. Devon. Flo. July–Sept.

Corrigiola litoralis L. **Strap-wort.** ¶Plant glaucous or reddish; leaves tapering below, stipulate; flo. clustered, white tipped with red. Gravelly bank of Slapton Ley and in Channel Islands, elsewhere adventive on railway tracks. Flo. July–Aug. ⚘.

Scleranthus annuus L. **Knawel.** ¶Stems erect; calyx lobes acute, with narrow white margin, spreading in fr. In sandy fields. Flo. June–Aug. ⚘.

Scleranthus perennis L. **Perennial Knawel.** ¶Stem procumbent; calyx lobes rounded with broad white margins, closed in fr. Sandy fields in Norfolk and Suffolk, and in Radnorshire. Flo. June–Aug.

Subsp. *perennis.* ¶Stems ascending to erect, woody below; sepals oblong, blunt, with broad white margins; closed in fr. On rocks in Radnorshire only. Flo. June–Aug.

Subsp. *prostratus* P. D. Sell. ¶Similar to subsp. *perennis* but with long procumbent or slightly ascending stems and smaller leaves and fr. Sandy heaths in Norfolk and Suffolk. Flo. June–Aug. ⚘.

AMARANTHACEAE

**Amaranthus retroflexus* L. ¶Stout, erect, pubescent, leafless above; leaves ovate; flo. in dense spikes; sepals 5. Casual; alien, in cultivated land. Flo. July–Sept.

CHENOPODIACEAE

Chenopodium polyspermum L. **Many-seeded Goose-foot.** ¶Leaves ovate, green; flo. spikes small, leafless; sepals 5, not keeled; testa of seed has pit with sinuous margin. Cultivated ground, chiefly S. England. Flo. July–Sept. ⚘.

Chenopodium vulvaria L. **Stinking Goose-foot.** *C. olidum* Curt. ¶Leaves rhomboid-oval, mealy; flo. spikes dense; sepals not keeled; seed testa with faint furrows. Waste places, chiefly S. England. Flo. Aug.–Sept. ⚘.

Chenopodium album L. **Fat Hen.** ¶Stem often reddish; leaves thick, variable, dentate, mealy; inflo. branched; sepals keeled; testa of seed faintly striate or reticulate. Arable land, common. Flo. July–Aug. ⚘.

Chenopodium suecicum. J. Murr. *C. viride* auct. ¶Similar to *C. album*, but stem green; leaves thin, bright glaucous green; seed testa regularly pitted, obtusely keeled.

Chenopodium pratericola Rydb. ¶Leaves linear oblong, glaucous beneath; sepals strongly keeled; seed testa with small network. Casual on rubbish tips.

Chenopodium opulifolium Schrad. ex Koch & Ziz. ¶Stem 2 ft; leaves broad, obtuse, dentate, mealy below; sepals keeled; testa furrowed and finely papillose. Waste places. Flo. Aug.–Sept.

PLATE 72

Chenopodium ficifolium Sm. **Fig-leaved Goose-foot.** ¶Lower leaves with pair of ascending lobes; sepals white with green keel; seed testa furrowed. Cultivated and waste land, locally common in S. and E. England, rare elsewhere. Flo. July–Sept. ⅜.

Chenopodium berlandieri Moq. ¶Leaves 3 lobed, mealy; flo. clusters in lax spikes; seed testa with honeycomb pattern. In docks and rubbish tips.

Chenopodium hircinum Schrad. ¶Leaves 3 lobed, mealy, white and smelling; flo. clusters in short dense spikes; testa with furrows and pits. In docks and rubbish tips. Flo. late summer.

Chenopodium murale L. **Sowbane, Nettle-leaved Goose-foot.** ¶Stem leafy almost to top; leaves sharply toothed; flo. branches short; testa with dense, minute pits. In cultivated and waste ground. Flo. Aug. ⅜.

Chenopodium hybridum L. **Sowbane.** ¶Lower leaves subcordate, teeth few and large; flo. spikes spreading; sepals hardly keeled; testa with large pits. Cultivated land, chiefly S. and E. England, rare. Flo. late summer.

Chenopodium urbicum L. ¶Leaves glabrous, triangular, dentate; flo. spikes short, erect; clusters small; seeds black; testa reticulate. Cultivated land. Flo. late summer.

Chenopodium rubrum L. **Red Goose-foot.** ¶Stem often red; leaves rhomboidal, coarsely toothed; sepals of lateral flo. 3–4, free to middle; seed red-brown; testa pitted. Cultivated and waste ground, pond verges, etc., common in S. and E. England. Flo. Aug. ⅜.

Chenopodium botryodes Sm. ¶Leaves subentire, triangular; sepals of lateral flo. 2–4, united almost to apex, keeled at top. Salt marshes, S. and E. England. Flo. Sept. ⅜.

Chenopodium glaucum L. **Oak-leaved Goose-foot.** ¶Leaves small, oak shaped, green above, white beneath; flo. spikes many, small; seeds reddish. In rich ground, chiefly S. England. Flo. Sept. ⅜.

Chenopodium bonus-henricus L. **Good King Henry.** ¶Perennial, 1½ ft; leaves broad, green; inflo. pyramidal; stigmas long. In rich soils and farmyards, not native. Flo. May–Aug. ⅜.

Beta vulgaris
Subsp. *maritima* (L.) Arcangeli. **Sea Beet.** *B. maritima* L. ¶Stems mostly decumbent; leaves thick, green and glossy; fruiting sepals corky. On sea-shores. Flo. July–Sept. ⅜.
Cultivated forms of *B. vulgaris*, with erect stem and thick root, sometimes occur as outcasts.

Atriplex littoralis L. **Grass-leaved Orache.** ¶Leaves linear, entire or toothed; flo. spike long, leafless above; fruiting sepals rhomboid, tuberculate. On sea-shores. Flo. July–Aug. ⅜.

Atriplex patula L. **Common Orache.** ¶Leaves tapering to pedicel, lobes ascending; sepals smooth or little tuberculate. In cultivated and waste ground, common. Flo. Aug.–Sept. �֎.

Atriplex hastata L. **Hastate Orache.** ¶Leaves triangular, abruptly contracted below; sepals mostly truncate below, less than half united. Waste ground, common, especially near the sea. Flo. Aug.–Sept. ✢.

Atriplex glabriuscula Edmondst. **Babington's Orache.** ¶Stems spreading; leaves triangular, subentire; inflo. leafy; sepals 5–10 mm., tubercled, united along the base.
Var. *babingtonii* (Woods) Moss. ¶Leaves much toothed; sepals 5 × 5 mm. On sea-shores, common. Flo. July–Sept. ✢.

Atriplex laciniata L. **Frosted Orache.** *A. sabulosa* Rouy. ¶Plant silvery white, decumbent; leaves rhomboid-ovate, very mealy; flo. spikes short. Sandy sea-shores, local. Flo. July–Sept. ✢.

Halimione portulacoides (L.) Aellen. **Sea Purslane.** *Atriplex portulacoides* L. ¶Perennial, dense, shrubby plants; leaves mostly opposite, entire; sepals 3 lobed. Locally abundant in salt marshes. Flo. July–Sept. ✢.

Halimione pedunculata (L.) Aellen. *Atriplex pedunculata* L. ¶Annual, erect; leaves alternate, entire; sepals 3 lobed; fr. pedicelled. In salt marshes, E. England, very rare. Flo. July–Sept. ✢.

Salicornia perennis Mill. **Perennial Glasswort.** ¶Perennial, much branched, in large tussocks; fertile segments 4–8; central separating 2 lateral. Salt marshes, S. England. Flo. Aug.–Sept.

Salicornia dolichostachya Moss. ¶Annual; spikes long, 3–5 in.; segments 15–30; central flo. larger, almost separating the lateral. Tidal salt marshes. Flo. Aug.–Sept.

Salicornia europaea L. *S. stricta* Dumort. ¶Bright green; spikes long, blunt, segments 6–16; flo. nearly equal, central, not separating the lateral. In muddy, tidal marshes. Flo. Aug.–Sept. ✢.

Salicornia ramosissima Woods. **Prostrate Glasswort.** *S. prostrata* auct. ¶Stems usually becoming prostrate and reddish; flo. branches short and tapering, segments 2–6, oval; central flo. large but not separating lateral ones; young plants sometimes erect and variable in angle of branching. Flo. Aug.–Sept. ✢.

Salicornia pusilla Woods. **Fragile Glasswort.** *S. disarticulata* Moss. ¶Stems erect; flo. branches very short, segments 1–2, all separating when ripe; flo. solitary not in threes. Drier parts of salt marshes, S. and E. coasts. Flo. Aug.–Sept.

PLATE 73

Suaeda fruticosa Forsk. **Shrubby Sea-blite.** ¶Perennial shrub, 2–3 ft; leaves rounded at ends; stigmas 3; seeds smooth. On shingle, S. and E. coasts. Flo. July–Sept. ✢.

Suaeda maritima (L.) Dumort. **Annual Sea-blite.** ¶Annual, mostly spreading or prostrate, glaucous and reddish; leaves acute; stigmas 2; seeds reticulate. Common on sea-shores. Flo. July–Sept. ✢.

Salsola kali L. **Saltwort.** ¶Prostrate and prickly; stems striped; leaves succulent, spinous; flo. axillary; sepals thick and green. On sandy sea-shores. Flo. July–Sept. ✢.

POLYGONACEAE

Polygonum convolvulus L. **Black Bindweed.** ¶Stem 3 ft, twining; flo. subsessile or pedicels 1–2 mm.; outer sepals keeled. On cultivated ground. Flo. July–Sept. ❀.

Polygonum dumetorum L. **Copse Buckwheat, Bindweed.** ¶Stem 5 ft, twining; flo. pedicels 8 mm. long; outer sepals broadly winged. In hedges and thickets, chiefly S. England, rare. Flo. July–Sept. ❀.

Polygonum aviculare L. **Common Knotgrass.** *P. heterophyllum* Lindm. ¶Stems mostly prostrate; leaves lanceolate, very unequal; ochreae silvery, torn; sepals pinkish, united at base only. In cultivated and waste ground, etc., common. Flo. July–Aug. ❀.

*Polygonum aubertii L. Henry. **Russian Vine.** *P. baldschuanicum* auct., non Regel. ¶Rampant woody climber; leaves cordate to hastate; flo. white in axillary and terminal panicles. Garden escape, or outcast, naturalized in hedges and thickets and on waste ground. Flo. Aug.–Nov.

Polygonum rurivagum Jord. ex Bor. ¶Leaves unequal, linear-lanceolate, acute; ochreae long, 8–10 mm.; fr. 2 mm. On arable calcareous land, local.

Polygonum arenastrum Bor. *P. aequale* Lindm. ¶Stems matted; leaves small, blunt, nearly equal; sepals green and white, united halfway; fr. 2·5 mm. Paths and farm gateways. ❀.

Polygonum boreale (Lange) Small. ¶Leaves oblong-ovate to spathulate; petioles projecting from ochreae; fr. 3·5–4·5 mm. Arable land, Sutherland, Orkney and Shetland.

Polygonum oxyspermum Mey. & Bunge ex Ledeb. subsp. *raii* (Bab.) D. A. Webb & A. O. Chater. **Ray's Knotgrass.** *P. raii* Bab. ¶Stems prostrate, woody; leaf margins flat; ochreae silvery, torn, with simple veins; fr. 5–6 mm., exceeding sepals. On seashores. Flo. June–Sept. ❀.

Polygonum maritimum L. **Sea Knotgrass.** ¶Stems prostrate, woody; leaf margins revolute; ochreae with many-branched veins; fr. 4 mm. On sea-shores in S.W. England and Channel Islands, very rare. Flo. July–Sept.

Polygonum hydropiper L. **Water Pepper, Biting Persicaria.** ¶Stems suberect, 1–2 ft, nodding; flo. greenish; sepals with yellow glands. Common in damp places. Flo. July–Sept. ❀.

Polygonum mite Schrank. **Lax-flowered Persicaria.** *P. laxiflorum* Weihe. ¶Similar to *P. hydropiper* but not acrid, suberect; ochreae much fringed; flo. interrupted pink, without glands. In ditches and wet places, local. Flo. June–Sept. ❀.

Polygonum minus Huds. **Lesser Persicaria.** ¶Stem ½–1 ft; leaves narrow, 2–5 mm. wide; ochreae much fringed; flo. smaller, pink; fr. only 2–2·5 mm. Edges of pools and streams, local. Flo. Aug.–Sept. ❀.

Polygonum persicaria L. **Common Persicaria.** ¶Leaves often dark blotched; ochreae fringed; inflo. dense, obtuse; flo. pink, without glands. In cultivated and damp ground, common. Flo. June–Sept. ❀.

Polygonum lapathifolium L. **Pale Persicaria.** ¶Leaves often black blotched or downy; ochreae unfringed except uppermost; inflo. dense, obtuse; flo. greenish white, sometimes glandular. Flo. June–Sept. ❀.

Polygonum nodosum Pers. **Spotted Persicaria.** *P. maculatum* (Gray) Dyer ex Bab. ¶Undersides of leaves dotted with glands; ochreae shortly fringed; inflo. lax and acute; flo. pink; peduncle glandular. In damp ground, local. The specimen figured was exceptionally large, but determined by an expert. Flo. July–Sept. ✳.

Polygonum amphibium L. **Amphibious Persicaria.** ¶Aquatic; leaves usually ovate-oblong, floating; flo. in a stout spike, pink. In pools and slow streams. Flo. July–Sept. ✳.

Polygonum bistorta L. **Snakeweed, Bistort.** ¶Rhizome twisted; stem simple, erect; young leaves folded lengthwise; flo. pink. In moist meadows. Flo. June–Aug. ✳.

*Polygonum campanulatum Hook. f. ¶Plant superficially resembling *P. bistorta*, but leaves very tomentose, whitish to buff beneath. Garden escape, naturalized in ditches, wet places, etc., especially in Ireland, rare. Flo. June–Sept.

Polygonum viviparum L. **Alpine Bistort.** ¶Rhizome creeping; stem erect ½–1 ft; spike slender; flo. pink mixed with red bulbils. On mountain pastures in N. England and Scotland. Flo. June–Aug. ✳.

*Polygonum cuspidatum Sieb. & Zucc. **Japanese Polygonum.** ¶Rhizome deep; plant very large; leaves broadly ovate, truncate at base; inflo. of many-flowered axillary panicles; flo. white. Persistent garden escape, common on waste ground, etc. Flo. Aug.–Oct.

*Polygonum sachalinense F. Schmidt. ¶Resembling *P. cuspidatum* but taller and stouter; leaves ovate-acute, cordate at base; inflo. shorter and more compact; flo. white. Garden escape, established in waste ground, etc. Flo. Aug.–Oct.

*Polygonum polystachyum Wall. ex Meisn. ¶Rhizome creeping; stems stout, erect; leaves oblong-lanceolate, acuminate, truncate or cuneate at the base; sometimes hairy beneath, with red veins; flo. white in lax leafy panicles. Garden escape, established on waste ground, etc. Flo. Aug.–Oct.

*Polygonum amplexicaule D. Don. ¶Stems erect; leaves large, ovate, cordate; lower leaves stalked, upper leaves sessile, clasping stem; flo. dark red in dense cylindrical spikes. Garden escape, naturalized in thickets, hedge banks, etc. Flo. July–Sept.

*Polygonum sagittatum L. ¶Stems weak with many short hooked prickles; leaves oblong-sagittate, glabrous; flo. white in small spikes. Garden escape, naturalized in ditches in Ireland, etc. Flo. July–Sept.

PLATE 74

*Fagopyrum esculentum Moench. **Buckwheat.** *F. sagittatum* Gilib. ¶Stem 1–2 ft, branched; leaves cordate at base; flo. pink or white; fr. 6 mm., much exceeding sepals. Cultivated alien, casual. Flo. July–Aug.

Koenigia islandica L. ¶Annual; stem mostly 1–2 in.; leaves small, ¼ × ⅛ in., obovate; ochreae short; flo. small, clustered; fr. trigonous. Mountains of Skye. Flo. Aug.–Sept.

Oxyria digyna (L.) Hill. **Mountain Sorrel.** ¶Stem 6–10 in.; leaves radical, reniform; inflo. leafless; inner sepals enlarging in fr. On damp mountain rocks, chiefly in Scotland. Flo. July–Aug. ✳.

Rumex conglomeratus Murr. **Sharp Dock.** ¶Leaves oblong, sometimes narrowed centrally; fr. sepals oblong, entire, all with tubercles. Common on waste ground, etc. Flo. July–Aug. ⚥.

Rumex rupestris Le Gall. **Shore Dock.** ¶Leaves oblong, blunt, glaucous; fr. sepals oblong, entire, 4 mm., all with long tubercles, 2·5–3 mm. On sea cliffs in S.W. England, Wales and Channel Islands. Flo. June–Aug. ⚥.

Rumex sanguineus L. var. *viridis* Sibth. **Red-veined Dock.** ¶Leaves ovate-lanceolate, with green or with red veins; fr. sepals oblong, entire, only 1 with a globular tubercle. In woods and shady places. Common except in Scotland, where it is local or rare. Flo. June–Aug. ⚥.

Rumex maritimus L. **Golden Dock.** ¶Upper leaves linear-lanceolate; fr. sepals acute, with long, slender teeth and slender pedicels; plant golden in fruit. Wet ground near pools, chiefly in England, rare. Flo. June–Sept. ⚥.

Rumex palustris Sm. **Yellow Marsh Dock.** ¶Like above but fr. sepals and tubercles obtuse with shorter teeth; pedicels shorter, thicker. In wet ground near pools, chiefly S. and E. England, local. Flo. June–Sept. ⚥ (fr. only).

Rumex pulcher L. **Fiddle Dock.** ¶Branches nearly horizontal; leaves oblong or fiddle shaped; fr. sepals ovate, toothed, all tubercled. In grassy places, mainly S. and E. England. Flo. June–July. ⚥.

Rumex obtusifolius L. **Broad-leaved Dock.** ¶Lower leaves very broad, ovate-oblong; fr. sepals triangular, toothed, 1 with tubercle. Very common in cultivated and waste ground and field margins. Flo. July–Oct. ⚥.

Rumex crispus L. **Curled Dock.** ¶Branches erect; leaves oblong-lanceolate, margins crisped; fr. sepals ovate, subentire, 1 or all 3 tubercled. Common in cultivated and waste ground, etc. Flo. June–Oct. ⚥.

Rumex crispus × *obtusifolius* = *R.* × *acutus* L., *R. pratensis* Mert. & Koch. ¶Intermediate between the parents. Common.

Rumex longifolius DC. **Long-leaved Dock.** *R. domesticus* Hartm., *R. aquaticus* auct., non L. ¶Stem 1–4 ft; leaves very long, margin undulate; fr. sepals broadly cordate, entire; tubercles o. Wet places, N. England and Scotland. Flo. June–Aug. ⚥.

*Rumex patientia L. ¶Very tall; leaves ovate-acute; fr. sepals broadly ovate, subentire, 1 with tubercle. Introduced in waste places, mainly in S. England. Flo. June–July.

Rumex hydrolapathum Huds. **Great Water Dock.** ¶Stem stout, 5–6 ft; leaves ovate-lanceolate; fr. sepals 6–8 mm., triangular, shortly dentate and tubercled. Margins of canals and pools, common in S. England and Midlands, local in W. England, Wales and Ireland, and rare in Scotland. Flo. July–Sept. ⚥.

Rumex aquaticus L. **Scottish Water Dock.** ¶Stem 5–6 ft; leaves broad, cordate; fr. sepals ovate-triangular, entire, 5–8 mm.; tubercles o; pedicels slender. Watery places, W. Scotland, very rare. Flo. July–Aug.

*Rumex alpinus L. **Monk's Rhubarb.** ¶Rhizome creeping; leaves rounded, as broad as long; fr. sepals ovate, entire; tubercles o. Introduced, near buildings, mainly in N. Flo. July–Aug.

*Rumex scutatus L. **French Sorrel.** ¶Leaves 1–1½ in., rounded, as broad as long, basal lobes diverging; flo. bisexual. Introduced. Flo. June–July.

Rumex acetosa L. **Common Sorrel.** ¶Leaves oblong, hastate with downward lobes; flo. unisexual, outer sepals reflexed. Common in pastures. Flo. May–June. ⚥.

Rumex acetosella L. **Sheep's Sorrel.** ¶Smaller, 6–10 in.; leaves lanceolate, hastate, lobes spreading; flo. unisexual, outer sepals erect. Common on heaths and acid soils. Flo. May–Aug. ✳.

Rumex tenuifolius (Wallr.) Löve. ¶Like above, but leaves very narrow, margins inrolled; fr. 1 mm. On poorest soils. Flo. May–Aug.

ELAEAGNACEAE   **PLATE 75**

Hippophae rhamnoides L. **Sea Buckthorn.** ¶Thorny shrub, 6–8 ft; leaves clothed with silvery scales; flo. small, green; fr. globose, orange. Sand dunes mainly on E. and S.E. coasts. Flo. March–April. ✳.

LORANTHACEAE

Viscum album L. **Mistletoe.** ¶Shrubby parasite, 2 ft; leaves thick; flo. mostly unisexual; petals yellowish; fr. white. On branches of apple, poplar and other trees, mainly in S. and E. England, local. Flo. Feb.–April. ✳.

SANTALACEAE

Thesium humifusum DC. **Bastard Toadflax.** ¶Slender, prostrate, root parasite; flo. small, with 3 bracteoles, cream. On various roots in chalky soil in S. and E. England. Flo. June–Aug. ✳.

EUPHORBIACEAE

Euphorbia peplis L. **Purple Spurge.** ¶Procumbent, purple; leaves lopsided with narrow stipules; bracts leaf-like; glands entire, rounded. Sandy shores, mainly in S.W. England and Channel Islands, very rare. Flo. July–Sept. ✳.

Euphorbia helioscopia L. **Sun Spurge.** ¶Erect 1½ ft; leaves obovate, narrowed below; bracts leaf-like; glands entire, green; capsule smooth. Common in cultivated land. Flo. May–Oct. ✳.

Euphorbia platyphyllos L. **Broad-leaved Spurge.** ¶Leaves oblong, base cordate; upper bracts different, deltoid; glands oval; capsule with warts. Arable land, chiefly S. England, local. Flo. June–Aug. ✳.

Euphorbia stricta L. **Upright Spurge.** ¶Similar to *E. platyphyllos*; leaves smaller, clasping; bracts changing gradually to leaves; capsule smaller, 1·5–2 mm., warts more prominent, cylindrical. In limestone woods, W. Gloucestershire and Monmouthshire, very rare. Flo. June–Sept.

Euphorbia hyberna L. **Irish Spurge.** ¶Perennial; leaves large, 3 in.; bracts ovate, rounded below; glands entire; capsule 5–6 mm., with prominent warts. Locally common in woods in S.W. Ireland, and very rare in woods in S.W. England. Flo. April–July. ✳.

*Euphorbia dulcis L. **Sweet Spurge.** ¶Perennial; leaves oblanceolate; upper bracts deltoid, truncate below; glands entire, green becoming purple; capsule 2–3 mm., warts prominent. Alien. Flo. June–Aug.

* *Euphorbia corallioides* L. ¶Tall. 2–3 ft; leaves lanceolate, woolly; bracts pilose; glands entire; capsule woolly. Introduced in Sussex, and elsewhere. Flo. May–June.

* *Euphorbia pilosa* L. **Hairy Spurge.** ¶Rhizome stout; stems 2–3 ft; leaves large, oblong, pilose; upper bracts oval; glands entire; capsule nearly smooth. Woods near Bath, probably extinct. Flo. May–June.

Euphorbia amygdaloides L. **Wood Spurge.** ¶Stem 2 ft, pubescent; upper bracts yellowish, united in pairs; glands with horns. Common in S. England. Flo. March–June. ❀.

* *Euphorbia uralensis* Fisch. ex Link. **Russian Spurge.** *E. virgata* Waldst. & Kit., non Desf. ¶Rhizome creeping; branches long; leaves 2½ in., narrowly oblong; glands with long horns. Locally naturalized, mostly S. and E. England. Flo. May–July.

Euphorbia esula L. ¶Rhizome creeping; branches short; leaves 1½ in., oblanceolate, widest near apex; glands with short horns. In woods, rare, and much confused with *E. uralensis*. Flo. May–July.

Euphorbia cyparissias L. **Cypress Spurge.** ¶Rhizome creeping; leaves narrowly linear, numerous; bracts yellowish; glands with short horns. Perhaps native on calcareous soils in S.E. England, but mainly garden escape. Flo. June–Sept. ❀.

Euphorbia paralias L. **Sea Spurge.** ¶Leaves oblong, blunt, thick and fleshy; glands with short horns; seeds smooth. On sandy sea-shores, mainly S. and W. England, Wales and Ireland. Flo. Aug.–Sept. ❀.

Euphorbia portlandica L. **Portland Spurge.** ¶Leaves obovate-lanceolate, apiculate, glaucous; glands with long horns; seeds pitted. On sandy shores, S. and W. coasts of England and Wales, and N. and E. coasts of Ireland. Flo. June–Sept. ❀.

Euphorbia peplus L. **Petty Spurge.** ¶Stem 6–10 in.; leaves ovate, stalked; bracts ovate; umbel rays 3; glands with long horns. Common weed in cultivated ground. Flo. May–Oct. ❀.

Euphorbia exigua L. **Dwarf Spurge.** ¶Stem 4–8 in.; slender; leaves linear, tapering, acute; bracts lanceolate; glands with long horns. Common in cultivated ground, chiefly S. and E. England. Flo. June–Aug. ❀.

Euphorbia lathyrus L. **Caper Spurge.** ¶Stem 2–3 ft; leaves large, narrowly oblong; bracts ovate-acute; glands with horns; capsule large. In woods, local, mostly a garden weed, chiefly in S. half of Britain. Flo. June–July. ❀.

Mercurialis perennis L. **Dog's Mercury.** ¶Rhizome perennial; stem unbranched, hairy; female flo. long stalked. Very common in woods, in England, Wales, and S. Scotland, local in Ireland, and very rare in N. Scotland. Flo. March–April. ❀.

Mercurialis annua L. **Annual Mercury.** ¶Annual; stem branched, subglabrous; female flo. subsessile in leaf axils. In cultivated soil, common in S. and E. England, local or rare elsewhere. Flo. July–Sept.

ARISTOLOCHIACEAE   PLATE 76

Asarum europaeum L. **Asarabacca.** ¶Rhizome thick; stem very short, pubescent, bearing 2 leaves, 2 scales and 1 purplish flo. In woods, rare, perhaps native. Flo. May–Aug. ❀.

Aristolochia clematitis L. **Birthwort.** ¶Rhizome long; stem 2 ft, flo. tube dull yellow; fr. ¾ in., pear shaped. Naturalized in a few places. Flo. June–Sept. ❀.

THYMELAEACEAE

Daphne mezereum L. **Mezereon.** ¶Erect shrub, 2 ft; leaves thin, not evergreen; flo. red-purple; fr. scarlet. Calcareous woods, mainly in England, introduced elsewhere, rare. Flo. Feb.–March. ❀.

Daphne laureola L. **Spurge Laurel.** ¶Erect shrub, 2 ft; leaves evergreen, thick and glossy; flo. green; fr. black. Calcareous woods, mainly S. and E. England. Flo. Feb.–May. ❀.

ULMACEAE

Ulmus glabra Huds. **Wych Elm.** *U. montana* Stokes. ¶Leaves obovate, 2–6 in., with long tapering point, base of longer side rounded, hiding petiole. Common in hedges, etc. Flo. Feb.–March. ❀.

Ulmus procera Salisb. **English Elm.** *U. campestris* auct. ¶Tall spreading tree; leaves 2–3 in., suborbicular or ovate-acute, unequal at base, teeth curved. Widespread in England, Wales and Ireland, rare in Scotland. Flo. Feb.–March. ❀.

Ulmus angustifolia (Weston) Weston. **Cornish Elm.** *U. stricta* (Ait.) Lindl. ¶Smaller tree; branches erect; leaves narrowly ovate, with blunt teeth. In S.W. England. Flo. Feb.–March.

Ulmus coritana Melville. ¶Spreading tree, 60 ft; leaves narrowly or broadly ovate, biserrate, glabrous above, glandular beneath; base asymmetrical. Mid and E. England. Flo. Feb.–March.
The hybrid. *U. coritana × glabra* is fairly common.

Ulmus carpinifolia Gled. **Smooth Elm.** *U. nitens* Moench. ¶Leaves long, obovate-lanceolate, acuminate, shining, biserrate, base unequal, lower part of long side often straight. Fairly common in E. England. Flo. Feb.–March.
Var. *plotii* (Druce) Tutin. ¶Branches spreading; leaves elliptic, subglabrous, base nearly equal sided. In Midlands and E. England.

CANNABINACEAE

Humulus lupulus L. **Hop.** ¶Stems long, climbing; male inflo. much branched; female with broad bracts. Common in hedges, etc., in S. and E. England, the Midlands, local in N. England, Wales and Ireland, and rare in Scotland. Flo. July–Aug. ❀.

URTICACEAE

Urtica dioica L. **Stinging Nettle.** ¶Stoloniferous; stem 2–3 ft; leaves 2½ in., cordate; flo. spikes 2–3 in. Too common. Flo. June–Sept. ❀.

Urtica urens L. **Small Nettle.** ¶Annual; stem 1 ft; leaves 1½ in., ovate, all hairs stinging;

flo. spike ½ in. Cultivated ground, mostly on light soils, common in the E. half of Britain, local in the W. half of Britain, and in Ireland. Flo. June–Sept. �ло.

Parietaria judaica L. **Pellitory of the Wall.** *P. diffusa* Mert. & Koch, *P. officinalis* auct. ¶Red stems and leaves softly hairy; female flo. terminal, male lateral; filaments elastic. In crevices of old walls, etc., common in S. and E. England, the Midlands and Ireland, mainly coastal in Wales, local in N. England, and rare in Scotland. Flo. June–Sept. �ло.

*Soleirolia soleirolii (Req.) Dandy. **Mother of Thousands.** *Helxine soleirolii* Req. ¶Stems slender, creeping, matted; leaves small, round; flo. small. Spreading from rock gardens, common in hedge banks, walls, etc., in S.W. England. Flo. May–Sept.

MYRICACEAE

Myrica gale L. **Bog Myrtle, Sweet Gale.** ¶Stem 3 ft; leaves grey-green, with fragrant yellow glands; inflo. catkins; bracts and anthers red. In wet heaths and fens, chiefly in N.W. England, Scotland and W. Ireland. Flo. April–May. �ло.

BETULACEAE

Betula pendula Roth. **Silver Birch.** *B. verrucosa* Ehrh. ¶Bark white; twigs long, pendulous; leaves doubly serrate, glabrous; catkin scales reflexed. Common in woods, on heaths, etc. Flo. April–May. �ло.

Betula pubescens Ehrh. **Brown Birch.** ¶Stems more bushy, dark brown; leaves singly serrate, downy; catkin scales straight. Common on damp heaths, etc. Flo. April–May. �ло.

Subsp. *odorata* (Bechst.) E. F. Warb. ¶Young twigs and leaves have brown resinous warts, viscid buds and smaller leaves. Scottish Highlands. Flo. April–May.

Betula nana L. **Dwarf Birch.** ¶Dwarf shrub, 1–3 ft; leaves small, suborbicular, crenate; catkins short, oval. Locally common on mountains in Mid and N. Scotland, and very rare in a solitary locality in Upper Teesdale, N. England. Flo. May. �ло.

PLATE 77

Alnus glutinosa (L.) Gaertn. **Alder.** *A. rotundifolia* Stokes. Leaves blunt, green, veins few. In wet woods, by streamsides, etc., common. Flo. Feb.–March. �ло.

*Alnus incana (L.) Moench. ¶Leaves acute, pale below, veins many. Planted, particularly in Scotland. Flo. March.

CORYLACEAE

Carpinus betulus L. **Hornbeam.** ¶Leaves plaited, ovate, serrate; fr. subtended by a very large 3-lobed bract. Common in woods and hedges in England, particularly the S.E., local in Wales and rare in Scotland and Ireland. Flo. May. �ло.

Corylus avellana L. **Hazel.** ¶Leaves rounded, cordate, stipulate; female flo. small, enclosed in green bracts. In woods and hedges, common. Flo. March–April. ❋.

FAGACEAE

Quercus robur L. **Pedunculate Oak.** ¶Leaves subglabrous, mostly with a projecting auricle at base; flo. and fr. pedunculate. In woods, hedges, etc., common, especially on basic soils. Flo. April–May. ❋.

Quercus petraea (Mattuschka) Liebl. **Sessile Oak.** *Q. sessiliflora* Salisb. ¶Leaves with stellate hairs below, without auricle at base; flo. and fr. subsessile. In woods, hedges, etc., common, especially on acid soils. Flo. April–May. ❋.

Quercus petraea × *robur* = *Q.* × *rosacea* Bechst. ¶Intermediate between the two parents, it is sometimes found where they grow together.

*Quercus ilex L. **Evergreen Oak, Holm Oak.** ¶Leaves evergreen, dark green, glossy above, whitish-grey tomentose beneath, entire, or lightly toothed; fr. cup with small ovate scales. Planted in woods and hedges where it sometimes regenerates, chiefly S. and E. England. Flo. April–May.

*Quercus borealis Michx. f. var. *maxima* (Marsh.) Ashe. **Red Oak.** *Q. rubra* L. sec. Duroi, *Q. maxima* Marsh. ¶Leaves oblong, with 3–5 pairs of triangular-acute pointed lobes reaching half-way to midrib, glabrous except for reddish-brown tufts of hair on the primary veins beneath; fr. cup shallow, saucer shaped, enclosing only base of fr. which is light brown and smooth. Planted in woods where it sometimes regenerates. Flo. May.

*Quercus cerris L. **Turkey Oak.** ¶Leaves with many acute lobes; fr. cup with spreading scales. Often planted in woods and hedges, and regenerating freely. Flo. May.

*Castanea sativa Mill. **Spanish Chestnut.** ¶Tree 70 ft; leaves oblong-lanceolate, serrate; fr. 1–3 in a spinous involucre. Introduced, in woods, hedges, etc. Flo. May.

Fagus sylvatica L. **Beech.** ¶Leaves ovate, silky; male catkins tassel-like; fr. triquetrous in woody spinous involucre. Woods, especially on chalky soil. Flo. March–April. ❋.

SALICACEAE

Salix pentandra L. **Bay Willow.** ¶Stem 20 ft; leaves lanceolate, glossy; catkin scales yellowish; stamens 5; capsule glabrous. Wet places mainly in N. England, Scotland and N. Ireland, introduced elsewhere. Flo. May–June. ❋.

Salix triandra L. **Almond Willow.** ¶Stem 20 ft; leaves glabrous, paler below; catkin scales yellowish; stamens 3; capsule glabrous. Sides of streams and osier beds, chiefly in S. and E. England. Flo. April. ❋.

Salix fragilis L. **Crack Willow.** ¶Stem 50 ft; twigs fragile at joints; leaves long; catkins long, pendulous; scales yellowish; stamens 2. By streams, ponds, etc. Common. Flo. April. ❋.

Salix alba L. **White Willow.** ¶Stem 50 ft; leaves white and silky; catkin scales yellowish; stamens 2; stigma bifid. By streams, ponds, etc. Common. Flo. April–May. ❋.

Salix purpurea L. **Purple Willow.** ¶Stem 4–10 ft; leaves blue-green above, paler below; catkin scales dark at tip; stamens connate, purple. In fens and osier beds, local. Flo. March–April. ✿.

Salix viminalis L. **Common Osier.** ¶Stem 10–15 ft; twigs long and straight; leaves long, silky below; catkin scales dark at tip; anthers yellow. By streams and in osier beds, common. Flo. April–May. ✿.

Salix lapponum L. **Downy Willow.** ¶Stem 30 ft; leaves oblong, silky especially below; scales dark at tip; anthers yellow and brown. Wet mountain rocks, Scotland and N. England. Flo. July. ✿.

Salix aurita L. **Eared Willow.** ¶Stem 4–6 ft with raised striations under bark; leaves wrinkled, downy below, stipules large; scales dark at tip. In damp woods, on heaths, by moorland streams, etc., throughout the British Isles, but especially frequent in Scotland and N. Ireland. Flo. April–May. ✿.

PLATE 78

Salix caprea L. **Great Sallow.** ¶Stem 25 ft; twigs without striations; leaves ovate, grey tomentose beneath; catkin scales dark at tip. In woods and hedgerows. Flo. March–April. ✿.

Salix cinerea L. **Fen Sallow.**

Subsp. *cinerea.* ¶Stem 25 ft; twigs downy, with raised striations under bark; leaves obovate, grey beneath; anthers yellow. In fens, etc., in E. England, local. Flo. March–April.

Subsp. *oleifolia* Macreight **Common Sallow.** *S. atrocinerea* Brot., *S. cinerea* subsp. *atrocinerea* (Brot.) Silva & Sobrinho. ¶Stem 12–15 ft; twigs subglabrous, with raised striations under bark; leaves obovate, with rust-coloured hairs beneath; catkin scales dark at tip; anthers reddish. Common by streams. Flo. March–April. ✿.

Salix repens L. **Creeping Willow.** ¶Stems mostly prostrate; leaves oblong-lanceolate with silky hairs; catkin scales brown at tip. On wet heaths and sand dunes, common. Flo. April–May. ✿.

Salix nigricans Sm. **Dark-leaved Willow.** ¶Stems 6–12 ft, spreading, striate under bark; leaves deep green, paler pubescent below, black when dry; scales dark at tip. Mountains in the N. Flo. May. ✿.

Salix phylicifolia L. **Tea-leaved Willow.** ¶Stems 6–12 ft, striate under bark; leaves glabrous, glaucous below, not black when dry; scales dark tipped. Wet rocks in the N. Flo. April–May. ✿.

Salix hibernica Rech. f. ¶Similar to *S. phylicifolia* but not striate under bark; leaves broadly lanceolate to elliptical, almost entire, broadly cuneate at base, apex shortly acuminate (not tapering as in *S. phylicifolia*). Rocks, etc., in N.W. Ireland. Flo. April–May.

Salix arbuscula L. **Little Tree Willow.** ¶Low shrub; twigs striate; leaves glabrous above, glaucous beneath; scales brown tipped, with white hairs; anthers reddish. Mountains, Perthshire and Argyll. ✿.

Salix lanata L. **Woolly Willow.** ¶Large shrub; buds large, woolly; leaves silky above, woolly beneath; scales with long yellow hairs. Mountain rocks in Scotland, rare. Flo. June. ❀.

Salix myrsinites L. **Myrtle-leaved Willow.** ¶Low shrub; twigs not striate; leaves green and shining; scales purple, dark tipped, hairy; anthers purple. Wet mountain rocks, Scotland. Flo. May–June. ❀.

Salix herbacea L. **Least Willow.** ¶Plant small, from rhizome; leaves ½ in., suborbicular, bright green; catkins terminal. On mountain tops, plentiful in Scotland, local in N. England, Wales and Ireland. Flo. June–July. ❀.

Salix reticulata L. **Reticulate Willow.** ¶Stem creeping, rooting; leaves 1 in., becoming subglabrous, oval, glaucous and reticulate beneath. Rocks in Highlands of Scotland. Flo. June–July. ❀.

*Populus alba L. **Lobed** or **White Poplar.** ¶Buds downy; leaves suborbicular, snowy white beneath; catkin scales crenate; stigmas linear, cruciform. Planted, not native. Flo. March–April. ❀.

Populus canescens (Ait.) Sm. **Grey Poplar.** ¶Buds downy; leaves grey beneath, broadly ovate, with 4–5 blunt teeth each side; scales laciniate. Damp woods mainly in S. England. Flo. March. ❀ (leaf only).

Populus tremula L. **Aspen.** ¶Buds rather sticky; leaves glabrous, broader than long, petiole compressed; catkin scales deeply laciniate. In woods, on heaths, etc., common. Flo. March. ❀.

Populus nigra L. **Black Poplar.**

**Subsp. *nigra*. ¶Branches spreading; buds sticky; leaves glabrous, acuminate, with many small crenate teeth; catkin scales laciniate. Introduced, planted in woods, hedges, etc., not common. Flo. April. ❀.

Subsp. *betulifolia* (Pursh) W. Wettst. *P. betulifolia* Pursh. ¶Similar to subsp. *nigra* but with smaller leaves, and a delicate pubescence on petioles, inflo. and young shoots. Perhaps native by streamsides, in wet woods, etc., in S. and E. England and the Midlands, local. Flo. April.

Both subspecies are frequently confused with *P. × canadensis* var. *serotina* which is common.

Var. *italica* Duroi. **Lombardy Poplar.** *P. italica* (Duroi) Moench. ¶Branches and twigs all closely erect, fastigiate; leaf blades smaller. Often planted.

*Populus × canadensis Moench var. *serotina* (Hartig) Rehd. **Hybrid Black Poplar.** *P. serotina* Hartig. ¶Very similar to *P. nigra*; branches ascending; buds longer; leaves with teeth a little deeper, often with 2 glands at base of blade. Planted. Flo. April.

Monocotyledones

ALISMATACEAE   **PLATE 79**

Baldellia ranunculoides (L.) Parl. **Lesser Water Plantain.** *Alisma ranunculoides* L. ¶Stems 1 ft; leaves narrow, lanceolate; flo. whorled, lilac; fr. head spherical. Beside streams and ponds, local. Flo. May–Aug. ❀.
Var. *repens* Davies. ¶Has flo. larger, ¾ in., on creeping stems. Lakesides, Wales and Ireland.

Luronium natans (L.) Raf. **Floating Water Plantain.** *Alisma natans* L. ¶Stems long, floating; leaves long petioled, small obtuse; flo. solitary, white. In lakes and canals, chiefly in Wales, rare. Flo. Aug. ✼.

Alisma plantago-aquatica L. **Water Plantain.** ¶Leaves ovate, rounded at base; flo. pinkish white; anthers twice as long as broad; style lateral, long. Beside ponds and ditches, common, except in Scotland, where it is local. Flo. July–Aug. ✼✼.

Alisma lanceolatum With. **Lanceolate Water Plantain.** ¶Leaves lanceolate, narrowed below; anthers as long as broad; style short near top of ovary. Mainly in S. and E. England, less common. Flo. July–Aug. ✼✼.

Alisma lanceolatum × plantago-aquatica. ¶Intermediate between the parents, it often occurs where the two grow together.

Alisma gramineum Lejeune. ¶Leaves very long, strap-like, $\frac{1}{8}$–$\frac{1}{2}$ in. wide, submerged, or oblong, petiolate; flo. below or above water; stigma curled; fruit widest at top; stalk arcuate. River Glen and other streams in Lincolnshire and near Droitwich, Worcestershire. Flo. July–Sept.

Damosonium alisma Mill. **Thrumwort, Star-fruit.** *D. stellatum* Thuill. ¶Leaves floating, oblong, 5 veined; flo. white; carpels with long beak, star-like. In ponds and ditches, with gravelly or sandy bottoms in S. England, rare. Flo. June–July. ✼.

Sagittaria sagittifolia L. **Arrowhead.** ¶Stoloniferous; aerial leaves arrow-shaped; flo. white with purple centre. In mud by streams and ponds, common in S. and E. England and the Midlands, local in Ireland, rare in Wales, and introduced and very rare in S.W. England and Scotland. Flo. July–Aug. ✼.

BUTOMACEAE

Butomus umbellatus L. **Flowering Rush.** ¶Stem 3 ft; leaves linear, triquetrous; flo. pink. By ponds and dikes, local, but widespread in most of England except the N. where it is rare, rather rare in Wales and Ireland, and introduced and very rare in Scotland. Flo. July–Sept. ✼.

HYDROCHARITACEAE

Hydrocharis morsus-ranae L. **Frog-bit.** ¶Stems floating; leaves in tufts; flo. dioecious, white, springing from pellucid sheaths. In canals and ponds, locally common in S. and E. England and the Midlands, rare in Wales, N. England and Ireland and absent from Scotland. Flo. July–Aug. ✼.

Stratoites aloides L. **Water Soldier.** ¶Stem submerged, rising to surface for flo.; leaves spinous-serrate, aloe-like; flo. dioecious, white. Ponds and ditches in E. England, introduced elsewhere, rare. Flo. June–Aug. ✼.

Elodea nuttalii (Planch.) St John. *Hydrilla verticillata* auct. ¶Stems submerged, very long; leaves linear, acute, with small sharp teeth and small scales near the base. In Esthwaite Water, N. Lancs. and W. Galway, Ireland. Flo. not recorded from the British Isles.

*Elodea canadensis Michx. **Canadian Pondweed.** ¶Stem submerged, leaves oblong, dark green, 3 in whorl; flo. with long, slender tube, purplish. In still waters, introduced, common, except in N. Scotland. Flo. May–Sept. ✼.

*Elodea ernstae St John, *E. callitrichoides* auct., non (Rich.) Casp. ¶Stems submerged; leaves lanceolate, acute or acuminate, translucent, dark green, lightly toothed, usually in whorls of 3; flo. dioecious, small, solitary, whitish; male flo. on pedicels 20–30 mm. long; female flo. submerged with very long stigmas which reach the surface of the water. Introduced. Naturalized in ponds and streams, chiefly S. England. Female plants only have so far been found in Britain. Flo. Oct.–Nov.

*Lagarosiphon major (Ridl.) Moss. ¶Stems stout, rigid, submerged, long, leafy throughout, superficially resembling a robust, luxuriant form of *Elodea canadensis*; leaves thick, dark green, translucent, linear-acute, with short blunt triangular-shaped teeth; flo. dioecious, small, whitish, enclosed in long spathes; male spathe ovate, many flowered, flo. floating free on water on reaching the surface; female spathe ovate or oblong, 1 flowered. Introduced. Naturalized in ponds, lakes, slow streams, etc., chiefly S. England. Flo. June–Sept.

JUNCAGINACEAE

Triglochin palustris L. **Marsh Arrow-grass.** ¶Leaves filiform, semicylindrical to tip; fr. linear; carpels adhering at tip. In marshy places, local, but widespread. Flo. June–Aug. ❊.

Triglochin maritima L. **Sea Arrow-grass.** ¶Leaves linear, flattened at tip; fr. ovoid, carpels separating. Sea-shores and salt marshes. Flo. July–Sept. ❊.

SCHEUCHZERIACEAE

Scheuchzeria palustris L. ¶Stem 6 in.; leaves linear, semicylindrical, with a pore at top; flo. yellowish green. In wet moss, Perthshire and Argyll, Scotland and Offaly, Ireland, formerly known from Shropshire and elsewhere, very rare. Flo. June–Aug. ❊.

ORCHIDACEAE   **PLATE 80**

Hammarbya paludosa (L.) Kuntze. **Little Bog Orchid.** *Malaxis paludosa* (L.) Sw. ¶Stem 1–4 in.; leaves concave, bearing tiny bulbils; flo. green, with lip at back. In sphagnum bogs, mostly northern, very rare in S. Flo. Aug.–Sept. ❊.

Liparis loeselii (L.) Rich. **Fen Orchid.** ¶Stem 4–6 in.; flo. yellowish green, lip oblong, mostly upwards; leaves lanceolate or ovate (var. *ovata* Riddelsd. ex Godfery, Glamorgan and Carmarthen dunes). Mostly in fens in E. England. Flo. July. ❊.

Corallorhiza trifida Chatel. **Coral Root.** ¶Root fleshy with rounded lobes or branches; saprophyte with brown scales; flo. yellowish, lip white, purple spotted. Boggy woods in Scotland and N. England. Flo. June–Aug. ❊.

Neottia nidus-avis (L.) Rich. **Bird's-nest Orchid.** ¶Roots many, thick, interlaced; saprophyte with brown scales; flo. brown. In shady woods, especially of beech, chiefly in S. half of Britain. Flo. June–July. ❊.

Listera ovata (L.) R. Br. **Twayblade.** ¶Stem 18 in.; leaves 2, large, 4–6 in., ribbed;

flo. spike long and green. In damp woods and shady pastures, locally common except in N. Scotland. Flo. June–July. ⚥.

Listera cordata (L.) R. Br. **Lesser Twayblade.** ¶Stem 6–8 in.; leaves small, 1 in., opposite; flo. spike small, reddish. In sphagnum under heather and in woods, Scotland, N.W. England, rare in S.W. England, Wales and Ireland. Flo. July–Sept. ⚥.

Spiranthes spiralis (L.) Chevall. **Lady's Tresses.** *S. autumnalis* Rich. ¶Tubers ovate; leaves radical, ovate; flo. white in 1 spiral. In pasture, often calcareous, chiefly in S. half of Britain and S. Ireland, absent from Scotland. Flo. Aug.–Sept. ⚥.

Spiranthes aestivalis (Poir.) Rich. **Summer Lady's Tresses.** ¶Roots cylindrical; stem bearing lanceolate leaves; flo. white in 1 spiral. Formerly in marshy ground in the New Forest, Hampshire, and in the Channel Islands, but probably now extinct. Flo. July–Aug. ⚥.

Spiranthes romanzoffiana Cham. **Threefold Lady's Tresses.** ¶Roots cylindrical; leaves cauline; flo. in 3 spiral rows. Flo. Aug.–Sept.
Subsp. *gemmipara* (Sm.) Clapham. ¶Cauline leaves fairly broad, not acuminate; flo. close together, white. In S.W. Ireland and W. Devon, very rare.
Subsp. *stricta* (Rydb.) Clapham. ¶Leaves long, narrow, acuminate; flo. greenish white; spike long and lax. N.E. Ireland, Hebrides and Argyll, in boggy pastures.

Goodyera repens (L.) R. Br. **Creeping Lady's Tresses.** ¶Rhizome creeping; stem glandular; leaves net veined; flo. white; lip pouched. Pine woods in Scotland and N. England, also in E. Anglia where it may have been introduced. Flo. Aug. ⚥.

Epipogium aphyllum Sw. **Leafless Epipogium.** ¶Stem 3–7 in.; saprophyte with brown scales; flo. few; petals long, lanceolate, yellowish; lip upwards, cordate, white with purple spots. Woods in deep shade in S. England, formerly in Herefordshire and Shropshire, very rare.

Cephalanthera rubra (L.) Rich. **Red Helleborine.** ¶Leaves lanceolate-acute; flo. rose-red; lip white tipped with purple; ovary downy, shorter than bract. In calcareous woods, in Gloucestershire and Buckinghamshire, very rare. Flo. June–July. ⚥.

Cephalanthera longifolia (L.) Fritsch. **Long-leaved Helleborine.** *C. ensifolia* (Schmidt) Rich. ¶Leaves long and narrow; flo. white, petals acute; ovary glabrous, longer than bracts. Woods on calcareous soil, local and rare. Flo. May–July. ⚥.

Cephalanthera damasonium (Mill.) Druce. **White Helleborine.** *C. grandiflora* Gray. ¶Leaves ovate-oblong; petals white, oblong, blunt; lip with yellow spot. Woods, especially beech, on calcareous soil, chiefly in S. England. Flo. May–June. ⚥.

Epipactis phyllanthes G. E. Sm. ¶Flo. cernuous or hanging down, open or closed until fertilized, pale green; lip-like lateral petals, not fully differentiated. Woods and sand dunes on calcareous soil. Flo. July–Aug.
Var. *pendula* (C. Thomas) D. P. Young. ¶Lip more differentiated, depression at base (hypochile) as long as reflexed tip (epichile). Northern.
Var. *vectensis* (T. & T. A. Stephenson) D. P. Young. ¶Lip with small green hypochile and longer straight tip (epichile). Southern.
Var. *degenera* D. P. Young. ¶Lip with shallow, rudimentary depression at base.

Epipactis leptochila (Godfery) Godfery. **Narrow-lipped Helleborine.** ¶Flo. spreading and open, green; lip green with hypochile red spotted within, tip long, spreading. Shady woods mainly in S. England. Flo. June–Aug. ⚥.

Epipactis dunensis (T. & T. A. Stephenson) Godfery. ¶Flo. incompletely open; epichile as broad as long. Lancashire and Anglesey dunes.

Epipactis helleborine (L.) Crantz. **Broad Helleborine.** *E. latifolia* (L.) All. ¶Leaves broadly ovate; sepals green; lip purple, fully differentiated, tip recurved; ovary subglabrous. In woods, locally common, except in Scotland where it is rare. Flo. July–Sept. �له.

Epipactis purpurata Sm. **Violet Helleborine.** *E. sessilifolia* Peterm. ¶Leaves narrower, ovate-lanceolate, purple beneath; bracts long; sepals greenish; lip whitish with recurved tip; ovary hairy. Calcareous woods, mainly in S. England and Midlands, local. Flo. Aug.–Sept.

Epipactis atrorubens (Hoffm.) Schult. **Dark-red Helleborine.** *E. atropurpurea* Raf. ¶Leaves small, elliptic; petals dark red-purple; lip broad with rugose swellings and reflexed tip. Limestone rocks, N. Wales, N. England, N. Scotland and W. Ireland, local and rare. Flo. June–July. ✦.

PLATE 81

Epipactis palustris (L.) Crantz. **Marsh Helleborine.** ¶Rhizome creeping; outer sepals greenish, inner white flushed with pink; lip crenate, with red veins and yellow spots. In fens, marshes and dunes, widespread, but local. Flo. June–Aug. ✦.

Anacamptis pyramidalis (L.) Rich. **Pyramidal Orchid.** *Orchis pyramidalis* L. ¶Spike pyramidal; flo. rose; lip with 3 oblong lobes and 2 tubercles; spur long and slender. On calcareous soils, widespread, but local in England and Ireland, rare in Wales and Scotland. Flo. July. ✦.

Himantoglossum hircinum (L.) Spreng. **Lizard Orchid.** *Orchis hircina* (L.) Crantz. ¶Plant tall, 2–3 ft; flo. green and brown; lip with 3 linear lobes, central lobe very long and twisted. Wood margins and rough grassy places usually on calcareous soil, mainly S. and E. England, very rare. Flo. May. ✦.

Aceras anthropophorum (L.) Ait. f. **Man Orchid.** ¶Tubers ovoid; sepals green, forming a hood; lip yellowish with 4 linear lobes; spur o. On chalk mainly in S. and E. England, local. Flo. June–July. ✦ on plate 82.

Orchis simia Lam. **Monkey Orchid.** ¶Tubers ovoid; flo. pale or crimson, hooded; lip with 4 narrow crimson lobes; spur cylindrical. On chalk, in S. England, very rare. Flo. May. ✦.

Orchis militaris L. **Soldier Orchid.** ¶Tubers ovoid; flo. pale purple with darker veins; lip 4 lobed with upturned ends. In woods on chalk in S. and E. England, very rare. Flo. May. ✦.

Orchis purpurea Huds. **Lady Orchid.** ¶Tubers ovoid; sepals forming hood, veined dark purple; lip broad, whitish, spotted red. Woods and shady places on chalk, mainly in Kent. Flo. May. ✦.

Orchis ustulata L. **Dwarf Orchid.** ¶Tubers ovoid; stem 6 in.; flo. small; hood dark purple, becoming white; lip white, spotted red. On calcareous hills, mainly S. England, local. Flo. June. ✦.

Orchis morio L. **Green-winged Orchid.** ¶Tubers ovoid; flo. hood with dark green veins; lip crimson-purple with pale centre. In moist meadows, mainly in S. half of Britain, and mid Ireland, locally plentiful. ✦.

Orchis mascula (L.) L. **Early Purple Orchid.** ¶Tubers ovoid; leaves blotched; flo. rich red-purple; lip nearly flat, spotted on pale centre. In shady places, common. Flo. April–May. ❀.

Orchis laxiflora Lam. **Jersey Orchid.** ¶Tubers ovoid; leaves ribbed, not blotched; sides of lip recurved, centre not spotted. Wet meadows in Channel Islands. Flo. May–June. ❀.

Dactylorhiza incarnata (L.) Soó. *Dactylorchis incarnata* (L.) Vermeul. *Orchis strictifolia* Opiz. ¶Stem hollow; leaves yellow-green, unspotted; flo. flesh colour; sides of lip reflexed. Wet meadows and marshes, widespread, but local. Flo. May–July. ❀.
Subsp. *coccinea* (Pugsl.) Soó. ¶Flo. smaller, bright red. Dunes in N.W.
Subsp. *pulchella* (Druce) Soó. ¶Flo. reddish purple, lip nearly flat.

Dactylorhiza kerryensis (Wilmott) P. F. Hunt & Summerhayes. *Dactylorchis majalis* auct. ¶Stem 1 ft, hollow; 6 leaves, 2 × ⅞ in., with or without ring-shaped spots; flo. red-purple; lip 8 × 10 mm., mid lobe triangular; spur narrow, 2·5 mm. Marshy meadows, Ireland, etc. Flo. May–June.
Subsp. *occidentalis* (Pugsl.) P. F. Hunt & Summerhayes. ¶Stem 6–10 in.; leaves much spotted, often arcuate; flo. spike short, deep red-purple. W. Ireland and N.W. Scotland.

Dactylorhiza praetermissa (Druce) Soó. *Dactylorchis praetermissa* (Druce) Vermeul. *Orchis praetermissa* Druce. ¶Stem 18 in., hollow; 6 leaves, 6 × 1 in., mostly unspotted; flo. deep red-purple; lip 9 × 11 mm., mid lobe short; spur broad. Basic marshes, S. and E. England, Midlands and S. Wales. Flo. May–June. ❀.

Dactylorhiza purpurella (T. & T. A. Stephenson) Soó. *Dactylorchis purpurella* (T. & T. A. Stephenson) Vermeul. ¶Stem 8 in., slightly hollow; 6 leaves, 4½ × ¾ in., slightly spotted; flo. very deep red-purple; lip 6 × 8 mm., entire; spur broad. Mainly Wales, N. England, Scotland and N. Ireland. Flo. June–July. ❀.

Dactylorhiza traunsteineri (Sauter) Soó. *Dactylorchis traunsteineri* (Sauter) Vermeul. ¶Stem 1 ft, slightly hollow; 4 leaves, lanceolate, 4½ × ½ in., transversely marked; flo. deep red-purple; lip deltoid, mid lobe triangular. In calcareous fens from S. and E. England to Wales and S. Scotland, local and rare. Flo. May–July.

Dactylorhiza maculata (L.) Soó. *Dactylorchis maculata* (L.) Vermeul.
Subsp. *ericetorum* (E. F. Linton) P. F. Hunt & Summerhayes. ¶Stem solid; lower leaves acute, spotted; flo. pale lilac or whitish, spotted; outer lobes of lip broad, rounded; spur slender. Peat moors, heaths, etc. Flo. May–July. ❀.

Dactylorhiza fuchsii (Druce) Soó. *Dactylorchis fuchsii* (Druce) Vermeul. *Orchis fuchsii* Druce. ¶Stem solid; lower leaves blunt, spotted; flo. lilac or whitish; lip with 3 rather deep triangular lobes. In woods, meadows, marshes, etc., on basic soils, widespread, but local. Flo June–Aug. ❀.
Subsp. *hebridensis* (Wilmott) Soó. ¶Lobes of lip rounded, deep red. In Hebrides only.

PLATE 82

Ophrys apifera Huds. **Bee Orchid.** ¶Sepals pink or whitish, inner small; lip very convex with tip recurved and hidden; side lobes hairy. On calcareous and basic soils, chiefly S. and E. England and the Midlands, rare in N. England and Ireland, mainly coastal in Wales, and absent from S.W. England and Scotland. Flo. June–July. ✤.

Var. *trollii* (Heg.) Druce. ¶Lip more yellow, nearly flat, tip spreading. ✤.

Ophrys fuciflora (Crantz) Moench. **Late Spider Orchid.** *O. arachnites* (L.) Reichard. ¶Outer sepals pink; inner narrow, downy; lip broad, brown, velvety, becoming convex; tip upturned. On chalk downs, S.E. England, very rare. Flo. June–July. ✤.

Ophrys sphegodes Mill. **Early Spider Orchid.** *O. aranifera* Huds. ¶Outer sepals green, inner green or brown; lip broad, brown, velvet with green edges, without a point. On chalk downs, S. England. Flo. April–June. ✤.

Ophrys insectifera L. **Fly Orchid.** *O. muscifera* Huds. ¶Plant slender; outer sepals green, inner filiform; lip narrow, oblong, rich brown with pale blue centre. On chalky soil. Mainly in S. half of Britain. Flo. May–June. ✤.

Herminium monorchis (L.) R. Br. **Musk Orchid.** ¶Stem 4–6 in.; flo. very small; sepals greenish; lip narrow, green, 3 lobed, pouched below. On calcareous soil in S. England, rare. Flo. June–July. ✤.

Gymnadenia conopsea (L.) R. Br. **Sweet-scented Orchid.** *Habenaria conopsea* (L.) Benth. ¶Flo. many, rose-pink or variable, fragrant; lip with 3 equal lobes and long slender spur. On basic or calcareous soil, locally plentiful. Flo. June–July. ✤.

Neotinea intacta (Link) Reichb. f. ¶Leaves oblong, often slightly spotted; flo. pinkish white; lip with lateral lobes narrow; spur short. Limestone pastures in W. Ireland, and in a solitary locality in the I. of Man. Flo. April–June.

Leucorchis albida (L.) E. Mey. ex Schur. **Small White Orchid.** *Habenaria albida* (L.) R. Br. ¶Root of fleshy fibres; flo. small, pendulous, greenish white; lip 3 lobed; spur short. On hilly pastures, mainly in the N. Flo. June–July. ✤.

Coeloglossum viride (L.) Hartm. **Frog Orchid.** ¶Stem 3–8 in.; flo. green; lip linear, brownish green, tubercled; spur short. In upland pastures, widespread, but local. Flo. June–Aug. ✤.

Platanthera chlorantha (Custer) Reichb. **Butterfly Orchid.** *Habenaria chlorantha* Bab. ¶Stem 18 in.; flo. white, scented; pollinia diverging below; spur curved downwards. In moist woods on basic and chalky soils, widespread, but local. Flo. May–July. ✤.

Platanthera bifolia (L.) Rich. **Lesser Butterfly Orchid.** *Habenaria bifolia* (L.) R. Br. ¶Stem 10 in.; flo. white, scented; pollinia parallel; spur slender, horizontal. Open woods, pastures, heaths, etc., on basic and chalky soils. Flo. May–July. ✤.

Cypripedium calceolus L. **Lady's Slipper.** ¶Flower sepals maroon, lateral twisted, 2 lower often connate; lip large, inflated, yellow. Woods on limestone, Yorkshire and Durham, very rare. Flo. May–June. ✤.

IRIDACEAE   **PLATE 83**

Iris pseudacorus L. **Yellow Flag.** ¶Stem 3 ft; leaves stiff, swordlike; flo. large, bright yellow; seeds brown. In wet fields and marshes, common. Flo. May–July. ✤.

Iris foetidissima L. **Stinking Iris.** ¶Stem 2 ft; leaves weak; flo. mauve with dark veins, rarely yellow; seeds scarlet. Woods and thickets on dry calcareous soils, chiefly in S. half of Britain, elsewhere as an introduction. Flo. May–July. ✤.

Iris spuria L. ¶Stem 3 ft; leaves linear; flo. violet and whitish; capsule with long point. Naturalized in fen dikes in Lincolnshire. Flo. June–July. ✼.

Hermodactylus tuberosus (L.) Mill. *Iris tuberosa* L. ¶Tubers finger-like; stem 1 ft; leaves linear, 4 angled; flo. sepals dark purple, inner thread-like. Naturalized in Cornwall and Channel Islands. Flo. April.

Crocus nudiflorus Sm. **Naked Autumn Crocus.** ¶Corm stoloniferous; leaves in spring; flo. in autumn, purple; stigma finely divided. Meadows mainly in the Midlands, not native. Flo. Sept.–Oct.

Crocus purpureus Weston. **Purple Crocus.** *C. vernus* auct. ¶Corm not stoloniferous; leaves with the purple or white flo.; stigmas blunt, orange. In meadows, mainly in S. and E. England, local, not native. Flo. March–April. ✼.

Romulea columnae Seb. & Mauri. **Warren Crocus.** *R. parviflora* Bub. ¶Corm ¼ in.; leaves very narrow, recurved; flo. pale lilac, midribs darker; fr. recurved. Sand near the sea, S. Devon and Channel Islands. Flo. April. ✼.

Sisyrinchium bermudiana L. **Blue-eyed Grass.** *S. angustifolium* Mill. ¶Leaves grass-like; spathe 2–3 flowered; flo. blue, paler outside; filaments united. Wet meadows and hills, W. Ireland. Flo. July. ✼.

Gladiolus illyricus Koch. ¶Stem 2 ft; leaves glaucous; flo. sepals crimson-purple or paler with dark centres; anthers shorter than filaments. Bushy heaths, Hampshire, Dorset, and formerly in the I. of Wight. Flo. July. ✼.

Gladiolus segetum Ker-Gawl. ¶Flo. larger, crimson-purple; anthers longer than filaments. A garden escape.

AMARYLLIDACEAE

Narcissus pseudonarcissus L. **Wild Daffodil.** ¶Stem 6–9 in.; flo. petals pale; corona deep yellow, irregularly lobed. In damp woods and riversides, locally plentiful. Flo. March–April. ✼.

Narcissus obvallaris Salisb. **Tenby Daffodil.** ¶Stem 10–12 in.; flo. petals deep yellow; corona distinctly 6 lobed, spreading. In grass near Tenby, Pembrokeshire. Flo. April. ✼.

Narcissus hispanicus Gouan. **Spanish Daffodil.** *N. major* Curt. ¶Stem 18 in.; flo. petals deep yellow; corona spreading, obscurely lobed. A garden escape. Flo. April.

Narcissus majalis Curt. **Pheasant's Eye.** *N. poeticus* auct. ¶Flo. petals white; corona very short, yellow with red rim. Flo. May.

Narcissus × biflorus Curt. **Primrose Peerless.** ¶Stem with 2 flo.; petals white; corona short, yellow. A hybrid, garden escape, not fruiting. Flo. April–May. ✼.

Galanthus nivalis L. **Snowdrop.** ¶Leaves glaucous; flo. white, pendulous, with green spot on short inner petals. Perhaps native in damp woods in S.W. England, Wales and adjacent counties, elsewhere as an introduction. Flo. Jan.–March. ✼.

Leucojum aestivum L. **Summer Snowflake.** ¶Stem 18 in.; spathe green at apex, with 3–6 flo. white with green tips. In wet meadows and withy beds, chiefly S. England, elsewhere as an introduction, local. Flo. May. ✼.

Leucojum vernum L. **Spring Snowflake.** ¶Stem 8 in.; spathe green in middle, with 1 flo. white with green tips. In Dorset and Somerset, elsewhere as an introduction, very rare. Flo. Feb.–March. ✿.

DIOSCOREACEAE   **PLATE 84**

Tamus communis L. **Black Bryony.** ¶Root a tuber; stem very long, twining; flo. dioecious, yellow-green; berry red. In woods and hedgerows, common in England and Wales, except in the N., introduced and very rare in Scotland, and absent from Ireland. Flo. May–July. ✿.

LILIACEAE

Ruscus aculeatus L. **Butcher's Broom.** ¶Stem 2 ft; flo. small, greenish, in centre of leaf-like branch or cladode; berry red. In woods and on cliffs, mostly in S. and E. England and S. Wales, elsewhere as an introduction. Flo. Feb.–April. ✿.

Asparagus officinalis L.
Subsp. *prostratus* (Dumort.) E. F. Warb. **Wild Asparagus.** ¶Stems prostrate; leaves minute, scarious; cladodes clustered, rigid; flo. yellow-green; berry red. On sea cliffs and sand, S. and S.W. England, Channel Islands, Wales and E. Ireland. Flo. June–Aug. ✿.
*Subsp. *officinalis*. ¶Stems erect, tall; cladodes slender and flexuous; flo. yellow-green; berry red. Introduced. Garden escape. Naturalized in grassy places, etc., common in S. and E. England. Flo. July–Oct.

Polygonatum verticillatum (L.) All. **Whorled Solomon's Seal.** ¶Leaves whorled; flo. constricted in the middle; filaments papillose; berry red. Mountain woods in Northumberland, Dumfries-shire, Perthshire, rare. Flo. June–July. ✿.

Polygonatum odoratum (Mill.) Druce. **Lesser Solomon's Seal.** ¶Stem 6–8 in.; flo. cylindrical, often solitary; filaments glabrous; berry bluish black. In calcareous woods, W. and N. England and Wales, elsewhere as an introduction, very local. Flo. June–July. ✿.

Polygonatum multiflorum (L.) All. **Solomon's Seal.** ¶Stem 2 ft; flo. constricted in the middle; filaments downy; berry black. In woods, mostly S. England and Wales, local. Flo. May–June. ✿.

A hybrid of the last two species is sometimes found, outcast from gardens.

Maianthemum bifolium (L.) Schmidt. **May Lily.** ¶Stem 4–8 in.; leaves 2 only; flo. petals 4, whitish, fragrant; fr. red. In woods, N. Yorkshire and N. Lincolnshire, and formerly in Middlesex, very rare. Flo. May–June. ✿.

Convallaria majalis L. **Lily of the Valley.** ¶Stem 6–8 in., angular; leaves large; bracts scarious; flo. white, scented; berry red. In hilly calcareous woods, widespread, but local throughout Britain, introduced in Ireland. Flo. May. ✿.

Simethis planifolia (L.) Gren. & Godr. *S. bicolor* (Desf.) Kunth. ¶Stem 6–18 in.; leaves grass-like; flo. purple outside, whitish within; very rare. On a heath, Co. Kerry and introduced near Bournemouth. Flo. June–July. ✿.

Allium ampeloprasum L. **Wild Leek.** ¶Stem 3–4 ft; leaves 1½ in. wide; umbel compact;

flo. many; usually without bulbils. Rocky coasts, Cornwall, Steep Holm, Pembrokeshire, Guernsey. Flo. July–Aug.

Allium babingtonii Borrer. ¶Stem 3–4 ft; leaves broad; umbel irregular, with secondary heads and many large bulbils. Coasts of Cornwall and W. Ireland. Flo. August.

Allium scorodoprasum L. **Sand Leek.** ¶Stem 2–3 ft; leaves ¼–½ in. wide; spathes 2; flo. rose with purple bulbils. Dry soils mainly in N. England and Scotland. Flo. July–Aug. ✂.

Allium sphaerocephalon L. **Round-headed Leek.** ¶Leaves tubular; spathes 2; umbels without bulbils; flo. rose; stamens with lateral points shorter than anthers. St Vincent rocks, Bristol and Jersey. Flo. June–July.

Allium vineale L. **Crow Garlic.** ¶Stem 2 ft; leaves tubular; spathe 1; flo. rose with many bulbils; stamens with lateral points longer than anthers. Common in S. half of Britain, less frequent in N., becoming rare in Scotland, very local in Ireland. Flo. June–Aug. ✂.

PLATE 85

Allium oleraceum L. **Field Garlic.** ¶Leaves fleshy, solid; spathes 2, long; flo. few, pink or brownish, with bulbils; stamens not trifid, equalling petals. Field borders, etc., widely distributed but rare. Flo. July–Aug. ✂.

*Allium carinatum L. ¶Similar to *A. oleraceum*, but leaves flat, grooved; petals bright pink; stamens longer than petals. Introduced, mainly N. England and Scotland. Flo. Aug.

Allium schoenoprasum L. **Chives.** ¶Leaves cylindrical; spathes 2; flo. umbel dense, globose; stamens half as long as spreading pink petals. On limestone, W. and N. England, Wales, elsewhere as an introduction, rare. Flo. June–July. ✂.
A. sibiricum auct. of W. Cornwall and Pembrokeshire is now said to be only a form of *A. schoenoprasum*. ✂.

*Allium roseum L. ¶Leaves linear, flat; spathes 2–4, short; flo. pink, with bulbils. Locally naturalized. Flo. June.

*Allium triquetrum L. **Triangular-stalked Garlic.** ¶Stem triquetrous; leaves radical, linear, keeled; spathes 2, short; flo. large, white. Naturalized in woods, etc., in W. Cornwall, S. Wales, S.W. Ireland and Guernsey. Flo. April–June. ✂.

*Allium paradoxum (Bieb.) G. Don. ¶Similar to *A. triquetrum*, but smaller, with brighter green stem and leaves; inflo. 1–4 flowered with numerous bulbils; flo. small, white. Naturalized in woods, thickets, plantations, by roadsides, etc., widely distributed, and increasing, though as yet rather rare. Flo. April–May.

Allium ursinum L. **Ransoms, Wood Garlic.** ¶Stem triquetrous; leaves broad, elliptic; flo. white, petals acute. Common in moist woods. Flo. April–June. ✂.

Muscari atlanticum Boiss. & Reut. **Grape Hyacinth.** *M. racemosum* auct. ¶Stem 6 in.; leaves narrow, flaccid; bracts minute; flo. dark blue, uppermost smaller, sterile. Sandy fields in E. England. Flo. April–May. ✂.

Scilla autumnalis L. **Autumn Squill.** ¶Leaves autumnal; flo. pale purple, without bracts; anthers purple. Dry pastures, usually near the sea, in S. England, elsewhere as an introduction. Flo. July–Sept. ✂.

Scilla verna Huds. **Spring Squill.** ¶Leaves in spring; flo. pale blue, with bracts; anthers blue. Mainly in W. coastal pastures, locally plentiful. Flo. April–May. �.

Endymion non-scriptus (L.) Garcke. **Bluebell.** *Scilla nutans* Sm. ¶Flo. nodding, cylindrical, petal tips recurved; anthers yellow. Woods, abundant over most of Britain, less frequent in Ireland. Flo. May (April–June). ✤.

*Endymion hispanicus (Mill.) Chouard. ¶Flo. erect, paler; petals more open, tips not recurved; anthers purple. A garden escape. Flo. May.

*Endymion hispanicus × non-scriptus. ¶Intermediate between the parents, it is commonly grown in gardens, and occurs in scrub, fields, etc., as an outcast or escape. Flo. May.

Ornithogalum umbellatum L. **Star of Bethlehem.** ¶Leaves green with white midrib; flo. subumbellate, erect, large, white. Perhaps native in grassy places in S. and E. England, elsewhere as an introduction. Flo. April–June. ✤.

*Ornithogalum nutans L. ¶Leaves glaucous; flo. in a nodding raceme, greenish white, petals 1 in. long. Introduced. Naturalized in grassy places, mostly S. and E. England, rare. Flo. April–May. ✤.

Ornithogalum pyrenaicum L. **Spiked Star of Bethlehem, Bath Asparagus.** ¶Leaves in spring, fading early; flo. many in erect spike, petals spreading. In woods, local, common near Bath. Flo. June–July. ✤.

*Lilium pyrenaicum Gouan. **Pyrenean Lily.** ¶Leaves alternate, lanceolate; flo. nodding, yellow with black spots. Naturalized in woods and hedge banks, N. Devon, etc. Flo. June–July. ✤.

*Lilium martagon L. **Turk's-cap Lily.** ¶Stem 2–3 ft; leaves mostly whorled; flo. nodding, pale purple with dark warts. Naturalized in woods, mostly S. England, local. Flo. Aug.–Sept.

Fritillaria meleagris L. **Fritillary, Snake's-head.** ¶Leaves few, linear; flo. nodding, red-purple, chequered dark and light; fr. erect. Damp meadows in S. and E. England, and the Midlands, local. Flo. May. ✤.

Tulipa sylvestris L. **Wild Tulip.** ¶Leaves linear; flo. bright yellow; fr. oblong, trigonous. Naturalized in meadows, etc., mainly in S. and E. England. Flo. April–May. ✤.

PLATE 86

Gagea lutea (L.) Ker-Gawl. **Yellow Star of Bethlehem.** ¶Bulb small; stem 6–8 in. with 1 hooded radical leaf and 2 bracts; flo. greenish yellow. Woods and grassy places in Britain, widespread, but very local. Flo. March–May. ✤.

Lloydia serotina (L.) Reichb. **Mountain Spiderwort.** ¶Stem 3–6 in.; leaves slender, triquetrous; flo. white with red-purple veins. Snowdon, very rare. Flo. June–July. ✤.

Colchicum autumnale L. **Meadow Saffron.** ¶Leaves large, oblong, 8–12 in. in spring; flo. in autumn, pale purple, like crocus but with 6 stamens. Meadows, mainly in S. half of Britain, very local, and very rare in Ireland. Flo. Sept.–Oct. ✤.

Narthecium ossifragum (L.) Huds. **Bog Asphodel.** ¶Leaves radical, rigid, linear; flo. bright yellow; anthers orange. Common in bogs on acid moors, chiefly W. and N. Britain, widespread in Ireland. Flo. July–Sept. ✤.

Tofieldia pusilla (Michx.) Pers. **Scottish Asphodel.** ¶Leaves sword-shaped; spike dense; bracts small, 3 lobed; flo. greenish white. By mountain streams, Scotland and N. England. Flo. June–Aug. �.

Paris quadrifolia L. **Herb Paris.** ¶Leaves 4, whorled; flo. solitary; sepals 8, acute, green; fr. a black berry. Woods on chalky soil, widespread, but very local over most of England except the S.W., where it is rare; rare in Wales, very rare in Scotland, and absent from Ireland. Flo. May–July. ✺.

JUNCACEAE

Juncus bufonius L. **Toad Rush.** ¶Dwarf 1 in. or 6–8 in.; flo. solitary or 2–3 together; sepals long or short, acuminate, green with hyaline border. Ditches and muddy places, common. ✺.

Juncus trifidus L. **Three-leaved Rush.** ¶Rhizome creeping; stems crowded, with 1 leaf; flo. 1–3 between 2 long leafy bracts. Mountain tops in Scotland. Flo. June–Aug. ✺.

Juncus squarrosus L. **Heath Rush.** ¶Leaves rigid, pressed to ground; bracts broad; inflo. terminal; flo. brown. Acid heaths and moors, abundant. Flo. June–July. ✺.

Juncus compressus Jacq. **Round-fruited Rush.** ¶Stems tufted; inflo. terminal, shorter than bract; flo. about 30; anthers equalling filaments; capsule subglobose. On basic soils, widespread, but local, in England; rare in Wales and absent from Scotland and Ireland. Flo. June–July. ✺.

*Juncus subulatus Forsk. ¶Rhizomatous; stems leafy, 2–3 ft; leaves glaucous, hollow; bract short; flo. many, green; stamens 6, short; styles twisted; capsule trigonous. Spreading in new salt marsh, Berrow, Somerset.

Juncus gerardii Lois. **Salt Mud Rush.** ¶Rhizome creeping; inflo. terminal, few flowered, longer than bract; anthers 3 times length of filaments; capsule acute. Salt marshes, common. Flo. June–July. ✺.

*Juncus tenuis Willd. **Slender Rush.** *J. macer* S. F. Gray. ¶Leaves with long auricles; inflo. terminal, overtopped by long bracts; flo. straw coloured. Waysides, heaths and woodland tracts, spreading. Flo. Aug. ✺.

Juncus balticus Willd. **Baltic Rush.** ¶Rhizome widely creeping; leaf sheaths broad; inflo. lateral at $\frac{2}{3}$ height; flo. about 12, brown; stamens 3. Dune slacks in Scotland and Lancashire. Flo. June–Aug. ✺.

Juncus filiformis L. **Thread Rush.** ¶Rhizome creeping; stems slender; inflo. lateral at $\frac{1}{2}$ height; flo. 6–8, pale; stamens 6. Lakesides, etc., mostly N. England and S. Scotland, local. Flo. June–Sept. ✺.

Juncus inflexus L. **Hard Rush.** *J. glaucus* Sibth. ¶Stem 2 ft, glaucous, with 12–18 striae; pith interrupted; inflo. lateral, lax, with straight branches. Wet basic soils, common. Flo. June–Aug. ✺.

Juncus effusus L. **Soft Rush.** *J. communis* auct. ¶Stem $2\frac{1}{2}$ ft, glossy green; inflo. lateral; bract not expanded; flo. greenish; capsule yellowish, retuse, not apiculate. Wet meadows, common. Flo. June–Aug. ✺.

Juncus subuliflorus Drej. **Common Rush.** *J. conglomeratus* auct. ¶Stem $2\frac{1}{2}$ ft, greyish green; inflo. dense, subglobose; base of bract expanded; flo. brown; capsule retuse, apiculate. Wet heaths, fields, etc., locally common. Flo. May–July. ✺.

Juncus maritimus Lam. **Sea Rush.** ¶Stem and leaves wiry, pointed; inflo. shorter than bract, erect; sepals lanceolate, outer acute, pale straw coloured. Salt marshes, common. Flo. July–Aug. ✽.

Juncus acutus L. **Sharp Sea Rush.** ¶Stem tall, stout, sharply pointed; sepals ovate, blunt, reddish brown with scarious margins. On sea sands, England, Wales and S. Ireland, rare. Flo. June. ✽.

Juncus subnodulosus Schrank. **Blunt-flowered Rush.** *J. obtusiflorus* Ehrh. ex Hoffm. ¶Stem 2–3 ft; leaves septate; secondary branches on inflo. at a wide angle; sepals obtuse; capsule ovoid. Marshes on basic soil, locally abundant in E. England, widely distributed elsewhere though rather rare. Flo. July–Sept. ✽.

Juncus acutiflorus Ehrh. ex Hoffm. **Sharp-flowered Rush.** *J. sylvaticus* auct. ¶Stem 2½ ft; leaves septate; secondary branches of inflo. at acute angle; sepals very acute, shorter than acute tapering capsule. Marshes, especially on acid soils, common. Flo. July–Sept. ✽.

Juncus articulatus L. **Jointed Rush.** *J. lampocarpus* Ehrh. ex Hoffm. ¶1–2 ft; leaves curved, septate; inflo. branches few; sepals acute; capsule shining, blackish, ovoid-acuminate. Common, especially on acid soil. Flo. June–Aug. ✽.

Juncus alpinoarticulatus Chaix. **Alpine Rush.** *J. alpinus* Vill. ¶Leaves septate; inflo. small; sepals obtuse, outer mucronate; capsule obtuse, mucronate. Wet places on mountains, N. England and Scotland, rare. Flo. July–Aug.

Juncus nodulosus Wahlenb. ¶Similar to *J. alpinus* but with inflo. irregular, some flo. subsessile, others on long peduncles in small umbels. Shore of Loch Ussie, E. Ross and near Braemar, Aberdeenshire.

Juncus bulbosus L. **Bulbous Rush.** *J. supinus* Moench. ¶Stems and leaves slender, often prostrate or floating; inflo. irregular; stamens 3; anthers equalling filaments; flo. viviparous. Wet heaths, bogs, pond verges, etc., on acid soils, common. Flo. June–Sept. ✽.

Juncus kochii F. W. Schultz. ¶Similar to *J. bulbosus*, more upright; stamens 6; anthers shorter than filaments. Probably common, but confused with *J. bulbosus*. Flo. June–Sept. ✽.

Juncus castaneus Sm. **Chestnut Rush.** ¶Stem 6–12 in.; leaves and long bract tapering to blunt point; heads 1–3; flo. very large, rich brown; capsule ¼ in. On high mountains, Scotland. Flo. June–July. ✽.

Juncus triglumis L. **Three-flowered Rush.** ¶Stems 3–6 in.; terete; leaves of 2 tubes; auricles large; flo. usually 3, level, capsule ovate. Wet places on high mountains, N. England, Scotland. Flo. June–July. ✽.

Juncus biglumis L. **Two-flowered Rush.** ¶Stems 2–6 in., channelled; leaves of 1 tube; auricles small; flo. 2, 1 above; capsule retuse. High mountains in Scotland, very rare. Flo. June–July. ✽.

Juncus capitatus Weigel. **Capitate Rush.** ¶Annual, 1–4 in.; leaves setaceous, without auricles; flo. clusters terminal, sessile, overtopped by a bract. W. Cornwall, Anglesey, Hebrides. Flo. May–June. ✽.

Juncus mutabilis Lam. **Pigmy Rush.** *J. pygmaeus* Rich. ¶Annual, 1–2 in., purplish;

leaf sheath long, auricled; flo. cylindrical in purplish, sessile clusters. W. Cornwall and Hebrides. Flo. May–June. ❀.

Luzula forsteri (Sm.) DC. **Forster's Wood-rush.** ¶Branches suberect in flo. and fr.; leaves narrow; flo. reddish; capsule short, acuminate; seed appendage short. Basic soils, S. England and Wales. Flo. April–June. ❀.

Luzula pilosa (L.) Willd. **Hairy Wood-rush.** ¶Branches spreading, deflexed in fr.; flo. brown; leaves 4 mm. wide; capsule obpyriform to cover long seed appendages. Woods, common throughout Britain, except E. Anglia, where it is rare; local in Ireland. Flo. April–June. ❀.

Luzula sylvatica (Huds.) Gaudin. **Great Wood-rush.** *L. maxima* (Reichard) DC. ¶Large tussocks; leaves $\frac{1}{4}$–$\frac{1}{2}$ in. wide; inflo. broadly spreading; flo. brown. In woods, especially on acid soil, common over most of Britain, especially in the N., but rare in E. Anglia; local in Ireland. Flo. May–June. ❀.

*Luzula luzuloides (Lam.) Dandy & Wilmott. *L. albida* (Hoffm.) DC. ¶Similar to *L. sylvatica* but smaller; leaves $\frac{1}{4}$ in. wide; flo. dirty white or pinkish. Introduced in woods, chiefly in N. England, rare. Flo. June–July.

Luzula spicata (L.) DC. **Spiked Wood-rush.** ¶Stem 6 in.; leaves small; inflo. drooping, dense, spike-like; sepals finely pointed. On mountains, mainly Scotland. Flo. June–July. ❀.

Luzula arcuata Sw. **Curved Wood-rush.** ¶Dwarf, 2–3 in.; leaves narrow; flo. clusters on few arcuate branches; sepals exceeding capsule. On high mountains, N. Scotland. Flo. June–July. ❀.

Luzula campestris (L.) DC. **Field Wood-rush.** ¶6 in.; inflo. of 1 sessile and a few stalked clusters; anthers prominent, much longer than filaments; seeds subglobose. Common in grassy places, etc. Flo. April–May. ❀.

Luzula multiflora (Retz.) Lejeune. **Many-flowered Wood-rush.** *L. erecta* Desv. ¶1–1$\frac{1}{2}$ ft; inflo. dense, subspherical or of several short-stalked clusters; anthers equalling filaments; seeds oblong. Peaty moors, open woods on acid soils, etc., common. Flo. April–June. ❀.

Luzula pallescens Sw. **Fen Wood-rush.** ¶Stem 6–12 in.; inflo. subumbellate of several clusters; flo. small, pale; capsule obovoid; seeds oblong. In fens, Huntingdonshire, introduced elsewhere, very rare. Flo. April–May.

TYPHACEAE

PLATE 88

Typha latifolia L. **Bulrush, Reedmace.** ¶6–7 ft; leaves $\frac{1}{2}$–$\frac{5}{8}$ in. wide; male and female inflo. contiguous, female without bracteoles. Beside streams and ponds, common throughout most of England, but local in Wales and Ireland, and rare in Scotland. Flo. June–July. ❀.

Typha angustifolia L. **Narrow-leaved Reedmace.** ¶6–7 ft; leaves $\frac{1}{8}$–$\frac{1}{4}$ in. wide; male and female inflo. separated, female with slender bracteoles. Beside streams and ponds, chiefly in S. and E. England, local. Flo. June–July. ❀.

SPARGANIACEAE

Sparganium erectum L. **Branched Bur-reed.** *S. ramosum* Huds. ¶Stem branched, whitish below; leaves keeled; fr. ¼ in., angled, abruptly contracted to beak. Beside ponds and ditches, common. Flo. June–Aug. ✲.
Var. *neglectum* (Beeby) Fiori & Paol. *S. neglectum* Beeby. ¶Stem red below; fr. ⅜ in., terete, tapering to beak. More local.

Sparganium emersum Rehm. **Unbranched Bur-reed.** *S. simplex* Huds. ¶Stem unbranched; leaves keeled; male heads with elongate anthers; lowest fr. head stalked. By ponds and ditches on basic soils, common, but less frequent than *S. erectum*. Flo. June–July. ✲.

Sparganium angustifolium Michx. **Floating Bur-reed.** *S. natans* auct. ¶Leaves floating, base expanded; anthers small; fr. tapering above and below; lowest head stalked. Mostly in mountain lakes and streams in Wales, N. England, Scotland and Ireland. Flo. July–Sept. ✲.

Sparganium minimum Wallr. **Small Bur-reed.** ¶Leaves thin, floating, base not expanded; male flo. head usually solitary; fr. oval. Lakes and pools, especially on acid soils, mostly in Wales, N. England, Scotland and Ireland, local. Flo. June–July. ✲.

ARACEAE

Arum maculatum L. **Lords-and-Ladies, Cuckoo-pint.** ¶Leaves in early spring, spotted or not; midrib dark green; spadix usually purple, ½ length of erect spathe. Hedge banks, common throughout most of England, Wales and Ireland, local in Scotland. Flo. April–May. ✲.

Arum italicum Mill. ¶Leaves before winter, unspotted; midrib light green; spadix orange, ⅓ length of pale green, drooping spathe. Mostly near S. coast of England, local. Flo. April–May. ✲.

*Acorus calamus L. **Sweet Flag.** ¶Stem 4 ft; spathe stem-like; leaves with wavy edges, scented when crushed; flo. crowded. Introduced, margins of pools, mostly in England. Flo. June–July. ✲.

*Calla palustris L. ¶Stem creeping; leaves broadly cordate or rounded; spathe oval, whitish; spadix crowded with flo. Introduced, swamps and pond sides, Surrey and elsewhere. Flo. June.

LEMNACEAE

Lemna trisulca L. **Ivy Duckweed.** ¶Frond thin, stalked, mostly submerged, branching at right angles; 1 root to each frond. In ponds, etc., locally common in England and Ireland, rare in Wales and Scotland. Flo. June–July. ✲.

Lemna minor L. **Lesser Duckweed.** ¶Frond ovate, budding freely, with single root. In ponds, etc., common, except in N. Scotland. Flo. June–July. ✲.

Lemna gibba L. **Gibbous Duckweed.** ¶Frond hemispherical, flattish above, rounded below, with single root. In ponds, etc., mainly S. and E. England and the Midlands, local. Flo. rare, summer. ✲.

Spirodela polyrhiza (L.) Schleid. **Great Duckweed.** *Lemna polyrhiza* L. ¶Frond ¼–⅜ in. wide; roots many. In ponds, mostly S. and E. England and the Midlands, local. Flo. very rare, July. ✻.

Wolffia arrhiza (L.) Hork. ex Wimm. ¶Frond only 1 mm., ovoid, rootless. In still waters, mainly S. England.

POTAMOGETONACEAE   **PLATE 89**

Groenlandia densa (L.) Fourr. **Opposite-leaved Pondweed.** *Potamogeton densus* L. ¶Leaves opposite; stipules o except in involucre, where they adhere to the leaves; spike very short, recurved. Clear streams and ponds, mostly in England. Flo. May–Aug. ✻.

Potamogeton natans L. **Floating Pondweed.** ¶Submerged leaves without blades; blade of floating leaves elliptical, jointed at base. Lakes and ponds, common. Flo. May–Aug. ✻.

Potamogeton polygonifolius Pourr. **Bog Pondweed.** *P. oblongus* Viv. ¶Blade of submerged leaves lanceolate, of floating leaves elliptical, not jointed at base. Bogs and acid pools, common, except in mid and E. England, where it is local or rare. Flo. June–Sept. ✻.

Potamogeton coloratus Hornem. **Fen Pondweed.** ¶Leaves mostly elliptical, stalked, thin, beautifully net veined; fr. very small, green; stalk slender. Calcareous fen pools, mainly E. England and Ireland, local. Flo. June–July. ✻.

Potamogeton lucens L. **Shining Pondweed.** ¶Leaves all submerged, large, oblong, short stalked; stipules large; fr. spike 2 in.; stalk thickened above. Ponds, streams, etc., mostly S. and E. England and the Midlands, locally common. Flo. June–Sept. ✻.

Potamogeton alpinus Balb. **Reddish Pondweed.** *P. rufescens* Schrad. ¶Leaves narrowly oblong, reddish, short stalked; fr. spike 1½ in., stalk not thickened. Lakes and ditches, widespread, but local. Flo. June–Sept. ✻.

Potamogeton nodosus Poir. **Loddon Pondweed.** ¶Leaves long stalked, elliptical, beautifully net veined; fr. stalk long, stout, not thickened above. In R. Thames, Avon, Stour and Loddon, local. Flo. Aug.–Sept. ✻.

Potamogeton gramineus L. **Various-leaved Pondweed.** *P. heterophyllus* Schreb. ¶Densely branched at base; submerged leaves lanceolate, sessile; floating leaves oblong, long stalked; fr. stalk thickened above. Chiefly in acid waters in E. Anglia, N. England, Scotland and Ireland. Flo. Aug.–Sept. ✻.

Potamogeton × zizii Koch ex Roth. = *P. gramineus × lucens*. Like *P. lucens* but with some oblong, stalked floating leaves; submerged leaves sessile. Local.

Potamogeton × nitens Weber = *P. gramineus × perfoliatus*. Little branched at base; submerged leaves cordate below; floating leaves long stalked or o.

Potamogeton epihydrus Raf. **American Pondweed.** ¶Submerged leaves very long, linear, ¼ in. wide; with broad air tissue; floating leaves broad, elliptical, stalked; peduncle slender. Hebrides, introduced in W. Yorkshire.

Potamogeton praelongus Wulf. **Long-stalked Pondweed.** ¶Leaves submerged, strap shaped, narrowed to apex, rounded at sessile base; fr. stalk long. Lakes, etc., mainly Midland counties northwards. Flo. May–Aug. ✳.

Potamogeton perfoliatus L. **Perfoliate Pondweed.** ¶Leaves clasping the stem, cordate-ovate, but sometimes narrower; stipule small, soon falling; fr. stalk stout. Ponds, streams, etc., common. Flo. June–Aug. ✳.

PLATE 90

Potamogeton crispus L. **Curled Pondweed.** ¶Leaves oblong, blunt, sessile, wavy, denticulate; fr. with a long beak. Ponds, streams, etc., common. Flo. May–Sept. ✳.

Potamogeton rutilus Wolfg. **Shetland Pondweed.** ¶Leaves very narrow, 1 mm. wide or less, tapering to a fine point; stipules strongly veined, acuminate. Lakes, Outer Hebrides, and Shetland. Flo. Aug.

Potamogeton pusillus L. **Small Pondweed.** *P. panormitanus* Biv. ¶Leaves very narrow, 1 mm. wide, blunt; lateral veins faint; stipules ⅔ tubular; beak of fr. nearly central. Ponds, streams, etc., mainly England. Flo. June–Sept. ✳.

Potamogeton berchtoldii Fieb. **Small Pondweed.** ¶Leaves long, narrow, 1–2 mm., acute; lateral veins meeting central at right angles near tip; stipules open. Ponds, streams, etc., common. Flo. June–Sept. ✳.

Potamogeton trichoides Cham. & Schlecht. **Hair-like Pondweed.** ¶Leaf width 1 mm. or less, tapering to long point; stipules open; usually ripening only 1 fr. per flo. Ponds, streams, etc., mostly S. and E. England and the Midlands, local. Flo. June–Aug. ✳.

Potamogeton obtusifolius Mert. & Koch. **Grassy Pondweed.** ¶Leaf width 3–4 mm., rarely 2 mm.; tip rounded apiculate; midrib with air cell, lateral veins rejoining at wide angle; stipules broad; peduncle short. Ponds, streams, etc., widespread, but local.

Potamogeton compressus L. **Grass-wrack Pondweed.** *P. zosteraefolius* Schumach. ¶Stem flattened; leaves very long, 2–4 mm. wide; tip rounded; main veins 3–5, with others smaller. Ponds, streams, etc., mostly Central and E. England. Flo. June–Sept. ✳.

Potamogeton acutifolius Link. **Sharp-leaved Pondweed.** ¶Stem flattened; leaves with air tissue, long, linear, pointed; veins many; fr. stalk short. In still waters, S. and E. England. Flo. June–July. ✳.

Potamogeton friesii Rupr. **Flat-stalked Pondweed.** ¶Stem flattened, with many short, leafy branches; leaves 2–3 mm. wide, 5-veined fr. whorls separated; stalk 1–2 in. Ponds, streams, etc., mostly England, local. Flo. June–Aug. ✳.

Potamogeton filiformis Pers. **Slender-leaved Pondweed.** ¶Leaves slender, of 2 tubes; base sheathing; spike widely interrupted; stalk very long; fr. beak central. Lakes, etc., Scotland, Anglesey and Ireland, mostly near coast. ✳.

Potamogeton pectinatus L. **Fennel-like Pondweed.** *P. flabellatus* Bab. ¶Upper leaves slender, of 2 tubes; sheath long, open; ligule longer; fr. large; beak near inner margin. Lowland waters, common in England, except S.W., rare in Wales and Scotland, and local in Ireland. Flo. June–Sept. ✳.

RUPPIACEAE

Ruppia spiralis L. ex Dumort. **Spiral Tassel Pondweed.** ¶Leaf width 1 mm., sheath inflated; peduncle very long, often spirally twisted; fr. ovoid. Ditches near the sea, mostly S. and E. England and N.E. Ireland, rare. Flo. July–Aug. �.

Ruppia maritima L. **Beaked Tassell Pondweed.** *R. rostellata* Koch. ¶Leaves narrower, filiform, sheaths small; peduncle short, equalling pedicels; fr. gibbous. Ditches near the sea, local. Flo. June–Aug.

ZANNICHELLIACEAE

Zannichellia palustris L. **Horned Pondweed.** ¶Variable; leaves slender; stipules semi-tubular; flo. subsessile in minute spathe; carpels muricate. In fresh or brackish waters, mostly England. Flo. May–Aug. ✲.

NAIADACEAE

Najas flexilis (pronounced Nar-yas) (Willd.) Rostk. & Schmidt. **Flexible Naiad.** ¶Leaf width less than 1 mm., subentire; sheaths ciliate; fr. 3 mm. In lakes, N. England, Scotland, W. Ireland. Flo. Aug.

*Najas graminea Del. ¶Similar, leaves tufted on branches. Alien. Formerly in Reddish canal, near Manchester, but now extinct.

Najas marina L. **Greater Naiad.** ¶Leaves with many, larger, spinous pointed teeth; sheaths entire, not ciliate; fr. 4 mm., ovoid. In Hickling Broad, Norfolk. Flo. July–Aug. ✲.

ZOSTERACEAE

Zostera marina L. **Common Grass-wrack.** ¶Leaves very long, 4–8 mm. wide, rounded at apex; stigma twice as long as style; seeds ribbed. In the sea below tide-level, widespread, but local. Flo. June–Sept. ✲.

Zostera angustifolia (Hornem.) Reichb. **Narrow-leaved Grass-wrack.** ¶Leaf width about 2 mm. only; margin of flo. sheath 2 mm.; stigma equalling style; seeds ribbed. Estuary mud, half tide to low tide. Widespread, but local. Flo. June–Sept.

Zostera noltii Hornem. **Dwarf Grass-wrack.** *Z. nana* auct. ¶Leaves 3–6 in. × 1 mm.; flo. few, male enclosed in bracts; sheath inflated; seeds smooth. Estuary mud, half tide to low tide. Widespread but local. Flo. June–Sept.

ERIOCAULACEAE

Eriocaulon aquaticum (Hill) Druce. **Pipe-wort.** *E. septangulare* With. ¶Roots and rhizomes white, septate; leaves septate; flo. stalk furrowed, twisted flo. in scaly head, lead coloured. Watery places, Skye and W. Ireland. Flo. July–Sept. ✲.

CYPERACEAE

PLATE 91

Eriophorum angustifolium Honck. **Common Cotton-grass.** ¶Leaves triquetrous, 3–6 mm. wide; upper sheath loose; peduncle smooth; glumes 1 nerved, brown, margin broad, hyaline. Common in acid bogs. Flo. May–June. �.

Eriophorum gracile Roth. **Slender Cotton-grass.** ¶Leaves triquetrous, 1–2 mm. wide, short, obtuse; peduncles hairy; glumes ovate, many nerved, not hyaline. In acid bogs, mostly S. and E. England, rare and local. Flo. June–July.

Eriophorum latifolium Hoppe. **Broad-leaved Cotton-grass.** ¶Leaves flat with short triquetrous point; sheath close fitting; peduncles rough; glumes blackish green. Bogs on basic or calcareous soil, mostly in N. Britain. Flo. May–June. ✽.

Eriophorum vaginatum L. **Hare's Tail Grass.** ¶Leaf width 1 mm., triquetrous; upper sheath much inflated, usually leafless; spike solitary. In moorland bogs, mostly in N., common. Flo. May. ✽.

Eleocharis parvula (Roem. & Schult.) Link ex Bluff, Nees & Schau. **Dwarf Spike-rush.** *Scirpus parvulus* Roem. & Schult., *Scirpus nanus* Spreng., non Poir. ¶Small; runners whitish, capillary, tipped with tubers; stem 1½ in. with 1 leafless sheath; spikelet 2–3 mm. On estuary mud, S. England, N. Wales and Ireland, very local. Flo. July–Aug.

Eleocharis acicularis (L.) Roem. & Schult. **Slender Spike-rush.** ¶Runners slender, brown; stem 4 angled, subulate; lowest glume ½ length of spikelet; nut ribbed. Wet heathy places, mostly England, local. Flo. July–Aug. ✽.

Eleocharis quinqueflora (F. X. Hartmann) Schwarz. *E. pauciflora* (Lightf.) Link. ¶Rhizome creeping; stem with scales and 1 leafless sheath; obliquely truncate glume more than ½ length of spikelet. Moors and fens, mostly in N. Flo. June–July. ✽.

Eleocharis palustris (L.) Roem. & Schult. **Common Spike-rush.** ¶Rhizome creeping; stem 1 ft; sheath almost transversely truncate; stigmas 2; spikelet ½ encircled by glume; variable. Common in marshes, etc. Flo. May–July. ✽.

Eleocharis austriaca Hayek. ¶Stems less purple, vascular bundles widely open; spikes many, short and conical; fr. with wide style vase, and often with 5 bristles instead of 4. On moorland streamsides and marshes. N. England, local. Flo. May–July.

Eleocharis uniglumis (Link) Schult. **One-glumed Spike-rush.** ¶Similar to above with stigmas 2; but lowest glume encircling spikelet; nut biconvex. In open marshes, mostly near the coast. Flo. June–July. ✽.

Eleocharis multicaulis (Sm.) Sm. **Many-stemmed Spike-rush.** ¶Stems 6 in., tufted; sheath obliquely truncate, acute; stigmas 3; nut trigonous; spikelet often viviparous. Wet acid heaths, mostly in S.W. Flo. July–Aug. ✽.

Scirpus cespitosus L. **Deer Grass.** *Trichophorum cespitosum* (L.) Hartm. ¶Upper sheath fitting tightly, opening 1 mm., with short blade; glumes brown with yellowish midrib. The type on Ingleborough and Ben Lawers. ✽.
Subsp. *germanicus* (Palla) Broddesson. ¶Upper sheath fitting loosely, opening larger; glumes brown with green midrib. Common on acid moors. Flo. May–June.

Scirpus setaceus L. **Bristle Scirpus.** *Isolepis setacea* (L.) R. Br. ¶Bract longer than inflo.; spikelets 1–3; glumes dark brown, margins white, keel green; nut trigonous, ribbed. Sandy soil, fairly common. Flo. June–July. ✽.

Scirpus cernuus Vahl. *S. filiformis* Savi, non Burm. *S. pygmaeus* (Vahl) A. Gray. ¶Bract not exceeding inflo.; longer, usually solitary spikelet; glumes green and brown; nut subglobose, nearly smooth. Sandy places by estuaries, mainly western. Flo. July.

Scirpus fluitans L. **Floating Mud-rush.** *Eleogiton fluitans* (L.) Link. ¶Stem floating, leafy; spike small, solitary, greenish. In ponds and dikes. Flo. June–Aug. ❀.

Scirpus lacustris L. **Common Bulrush** or **Club-rush.** *Schoenoplectus lacustris* (L.) Palla. ¶Stems 4–6 ft, sometimes with long basal leaves; bract stem-like; glumes smooth, shortly awned. In rivers and ponds. Flo. Aug.–Sept. ❀.

Scirpus tabernaemontani C. C. Gmel. **Glaucous Club-rush.** *Schoenoplectus tabernae-montani* (C. C. Gmel.) Palla. ¶Stems 3–4 ft, glaucous; bract stem-like; glumes clothed with dark brown papillae. Wet peaty places, often near the sea. Flo. June–July. ❀.

Scirpus triquetrus L. **Triangular Club-rush.** ¶Stems 3–4 ft, triquetrous; bract exceeding inflo.; glumes brown with shallow rounded lobes. In muddy estuaries, very local. Flo. Aug.–Sept.

Scirpus americanus Pers. **Jersey Club-rush.** ¶Stems triquetrous; leaves 2–3; bract long; spikelets dense, sessile; glumes with acute lobes. Ponds near the sea, Jersey. Flo. June–July.

Scirpus maritimus L. **Sea Club-rush.** ¶Stem 1–3 ft; leaves long and keeled; bracts several; spikelets large; glumes chocolate-brown, sharply 2 lobed, awned. Estuary mud. Flo. July. ❀.

Scirpus sylvaticus L. **Wood Club-rush.** ¶Stems 2–3 ft; leaves broad; bracts many; inflo. compound; spikelets many, green; glumes entire. Wet shady places, local. Flo. July. ❀.

Scirpus holoschoenus L. **Round-headed Club-rush.** *Holoschoenus vulgaris* Link. ¶Stem terete, 3–4 ft; upper sheaths with short blades; spikes many in stalked globular clusters. On sea sand, N. Devon, Somerset, Glamorganshire. Flo. Aug.

Blysmus compressus (L.) Panz. ex Link. **Sedge-like Club-rush.** *Scirpus caricis* Retz. ¶Leaves flat, keeled, rough; spikelets 10–12; lowest bract long, green; upper shorter than spikelets, many ribbed. In open marshes, local. Flo. June–July. ❀.

Blysmus rufus (Huds.) Link. **Red Blysmus.** *Scirpus rufus* (Huds.) Schrad. ¶Leaves involute, smooth; spikelets 4–8; bracts mostly equalling spikelets, 1–3 ribbed. In salt marshes on N. and W. coasts. Flo. June–July. ❀.

Cyperus fuscus L. **Brown Cyperus.** ¶Annual; stem 6 in.; inflo. subcapitate or small umbels; glumes reddish. On mud from ditches or dried pools. S. England, rare. Flo. Aug.–Sept. ❀.

Cyperus longus L. **Sweet Galingale.** ¶Rhizome aromatic; stem 3 ft; inflo. an irregular umbel; bracts very long. By ponds and ditches, mostly in S. England, very local. Flo. Aug.–Sept. ❀.

Schoenus nigricans L. **Black Bog-rush.** ¶Stem wiry, 1–2 ft; sheaths black; leaves $\frac{3}{4}$ length of stem; spikelets 5–10, blackish, sessile. Bogs on calcareous or basic soil. Flo. July. ❀.

Schoenus ferrugineus L. **Brown Bog-rush.** ¶Stem 6–12 in.; sheaths reddish brown; leaves $\frac{1}{4}$ length of stem; spikelets 1–3, reddish. By Loch Tummel, Perthshire, only. Flo. July.

Cladium mariscus (L.) Pohl. **Fen Sedge.** ¶Stem 3–6 ft; leaves long, sharply serrate; inflo. of many branches, each with small reddish spikelets. In fens and marshes, locally abundant. Flo. Aug. ✿.

Rhynchospora alba (L.) Vahl. **White Beak-sedge.** ¶Stems tufted; lower sheaths leafless; bracts about equalling inflo.; spikelets white. Bogs on acid moors. Flo. July–Aug. ✿.

Rhynchospora fusca (L.) Ait. f. **Brown Beak-sedge.** ¶Rhizome creeping; lower sheaths mostly with blades; bracts exceeding inflo.; spikelets brown. Damp peaty soil, local and rare. Flo. July–Aug. ✿.

Kobresia simpliciuscula (Wahlenb.) Mackenzie. *K. caricina* Willd. ¶Stem 4–8 in.; leaves slender; upper flo. (or spikelets) male, lower female, with 2 glumes. Moors, N. England, Perthshire, Argyll, local. Flo. June–July. The figure is labelled *K. calicina*. ✿.

PLATE 92

Carex
See *British Sedges*, by A. C. Jermy and T. G. Tutin (1968).

1. *Primocarex*. ¶Spike solitary, of one or both sexes.

Carex microglochin Wahlenb. ¶Stem 4 in.; leaves short; 4–8 yellow fr., with a bristle exserted at apex beside the stigma. Mountain bogs in Perthshire, very rare. Flo. July. ✿.

Carex pauciflora Lightf. **Few-flowered Sedge.** ¶Stem 4 in.; leaves short; spike male at top; fr. 3–4 only, yellow or reddish, without central bristle. Wet moors in the N. Flo. June. ✿.

Carex pulicaris L. **Flea Sedge.** ¶Stem and leaves 6–10 in.; spike male at top; fr. 5–6 mm., shortly stalked, brown and shiny. Frequent on wet moors. Flo. June. ✿.

Carex dioica L. **Dioecious Sedge.** ¶Stem 4–6 in.; leaves short; male and female spikes usually on separate plants; fr. 3·5 mm., sessile. On wet moors, local. Flo. May. ✿.

Carex rupestris All. **Rock Sedge.** ¶Leaves 2 mm. wide, equalling stem, point wavy; spike male at top; glumes ovate; fr. obovoid. Mountain rocks in Scotland, local. Flo. June–July. ✿.

2. *Arenariae*. ¶Creeping plants; spikes clustered, mostly male at top.

Carex maritima Gunn. **Curved Sedge.** *C. incurva* Lightf. ¶Creeping; terete stems and leaves curved; spikes clustered in dense head, male at top; fr. smooth. Coastal sand dunes, Scotland, N. England. Flo. June. ✿.

Carex arenaria L. **Sand Sedge.** ¶Creeping stems triquetrous, ½–1 ft; spikes separated a little, upper male; fr. ribbed and winged. Coastal sand dunes, common. Flo. June. ✿.

Carex disticha Huds. **Creeping Brown Sedge.** ¶Stems triquetrous, 1–2 ft; lowest and uppermost spikes female, central narrower male; fr. ribbed and serrate. Wet meadows and fens, local. Flo. June. ✿.

Carex divisa Huds. **Salt Meadow Sedge.** ¶Creeping; stems slender; bract often long and green; spikes oval, mostly contiguous, terminal male at top. Meadows near sea or estuaries. Flo. May–June. ✿.

Carex chordorrhiza L. f. ¶Stem stout, trigonous; leaves few, short; bract small; inflo. subcapitate, small. In bogs, W. Sutherland, very rare. Flo. June–July.

3. *Paniculatae.* ¶Spikes many, male at top, inflo. panicled or spike-like; stigmas 2.

Carex diandra Schrank. **Two-stamened Sedge.** *C. teretiuscula* Good. ¶Stem slender; leaves grey-green; ligule very short; glumes 3 mm.; fr. suborbicular, beaked, reddish. Damp meadows, local. Flo. May–June. ❀.

Carex appropinquata Schumach. **Lesser Tussock Sedge.** *C. paradoxa* Willd., non J. F. Gmel. ¶Tufted; stems 2 ft; leaves 1–2 mm. wide; inflo. branched; fr. ribbed below, abruptly narrowed above. Calcareous meadows and fens, local. Flo. June. ❀.

Carex paniculata L. **Greater Tussock Sedge.** ¶Tufted; stems 3–6 ft; leaves 3–7 mm. wide; inflo. branched; fr. gradually narrowed above. Wet shady places, common. Flo. June. ❀.

Carex otrubae Podp. **False Fox Sedge.** *C. vulpina* auct. ¶Stem triquetrous, not winged; ligule long, 10–15 mm.; 1 or 2 bracts very long; fr. greenish, ribbed. Damp, shady places, common. Flo. May–June. ❀.

Carex vulpina L. **Fox Sedge.** ¶Stem angles winged; ligule 2–5 mm.; bracts all short; fr. reddish brown. In damp, grassy places, mostly S. England, local. Flo. May–June. ❀.

4. *Spicatae.* ¶Spikes subsessile, male at top; stigmas 2.

Carex spicata Huds. **Spiked Sedge.** *C. contigua* Hoppe. ¶Leaf width 3–4 mm.; ligule 5 mm.; spikes male at top; glumes long, purplish; fr. tapering at base. On basic and gravelly soil. Flo. June. ❀.

Carex muricata L. **Prickly Sedge.** *C. pairaei* F. W. Schultz. ¶Leaf width 2 mm.; ligule short, 1–2 mm.; spikes male at top; glumes 3 mm.; brown fr. rounded at base. On dry basic soil, scarce. Flo. June. ❀.

Carex polyphylla Kar. & Kir. **Chalk Sedge.** *C. leersii* F. W. Schultz, non Willd. ¶Stems and leaves rough; ligule short; spikes male at top, upper close, lower separated; glumes brown; fr. tapering at base. Chalky pastures. Flo. May–June. Now regarded as a variety of *C. divulsa.*

Carex divulsa Stokes. **Grey Sedge.** ¶Slender; ligule short; spikes male at top, greyish, more distant, lowest often branched; fr. rounded at base. In woods and hedges, common. Flo. June–July. ❀.

5. *Elongatae.* ¶Spikes male at base; stigmas 2.

Carex echinata Murr. **Star Sedge.** *C. stellulata* Good. ¶Spikes about 4, slightly separate, male at base; glumes reddish brown; fr. spreading, star-like. Common in wet acid meadows. Flo. May–June. ❀.

Carex elongata L. **Elongated Sedge.** ¶Stem 2 ft; spikes several, oblong, overlapping, male at base; glumes 2 mm., brown, edges pale; fruit 4 mm. In marshes, local. Flo. June. ❀.

Carex ovalis Good. **Oval Sedge.** ¶1–1½ ft; spikes oval, clustered, male at base; glumes brown, edges pale; fr. 4–5 mm. Common on acid soils. Flo. June. ❀.

6. *Canescentes.* ¶Spikes male at base; stigmas 2; glumes short and pale.

Carex lachenalii Schkuhr. **Hare's-foot Sedge.** *C. lagopina* Wahlenb. ¶6 in.; spikes 3–4, contiguous, male at base; glumes short, reddish, edges pale; fr. yellow, beak short. Mountain bogs and wet rocks, Scotland. Flo. July.

Carex curta Good. **Pale Sedge.** *C. canescens* auct. ¶1 ft; spikes 4–6, oblong, male at base; glumes 2 mm., white, midrib green; fr. yellowish, beak short. In bogs on acid soils. Flo. July. ❀.

Carex remota L. **Distant-flowered Sedge.** ¶Bracts very long, leaf-like; spikes very distant, male at base; glumes white, midrib green; fr. green. Common in damp shady places. Flo. June. ❀.

PLATE 93

7. *Atratae.* ¶Terminal spike partly male; stigmas 3.

Carex norvegica Retz. **Alpine Sedge.** *C. alpina* Liljeb. ¶Bract leaf-like; spikes small, erect, black, terminal male at base; fr. small, obovoid. Wet alpine rocks, Central Scotland. Flo. June–July. ❀.

Carex atrata L. **Black Sedge.** ¶Leaves broad, 5 mm.; bract leaf-like; spikes oval, black, stalked, terminal male at base. Wet rocks on mountains, Scotland, N. England, Caernarvon. Flo. July. ❀.

Carex buxbaumii Wahlenb. **Dark Sedge.** *C. fusca* auct. ¶Leaves narrow, glaucous; bract leaf-like; spikes subsessile, terminal male at base; glumes narrow, blackish; fr. broad, glaucous green. W. Inverness-shire. Flo. July. ❀.

Carex atrofusca Schkuhr. *C. ustulata* Wahlenb. ¶Leaves short and broad; bracts brown, sheathing; spikes black, lower nodding, terminal male above or throughout. Mountain bogs, Perthshire, Hebrides. ❀.

8. *Acutae.* ¶Spikes dense flowered, terminal male; bracts leafy; stigmas 2; beak very short.

Carex recta Boott. **Caithness Sedge.** *C. kattegatensis* Fr. ex Krecz. ¶Stem 1½ ft; leaf ligule 2–3 mm.; lower spikes long stalked; female glumes long, 4–5 mm., midrib pale excurrent. Estuary sands, N. Scotland. Flo. July–Aug.

Carex elata All. **Tufted Sedge.** *C. hudsonii* A. Benn. ¶Stem 2–3 ft; leaf ligule 5–10 mm.; upper bracts small; spikes long, subsessile; fr. in straight rows. Riversides and fen ditches. Flo. June. ❀.

Carex acuta L. **Slender-spiked Sedge.** *C. gracilis* Curt. ¶Stem 2–3 ft; leaf ligule 2–3 mm.; lowest bract equalling inflo.; spikes long; glumes narrow, black, nerve often excurrent. By ponds, common. Flo. May–June. ❀.

Carex aquatilis Wahlenb. **Mountain Water Sedge.** ¶Stem 2–3 ft; leaf ligule 10 mm.; 2 or 3 bracts equalling inflo.; female spikes narrowed below; glumes dark. By mountain lakes and streams. Flo. July. ❀.

Carex bigelowii Torr. ex Schwein. **Stiff Sedge.** *C. rigida* Good. ¶Stem 6 in., stoutly triquetrous; leaves keeled and recurved; spikes shorter, ½ in.; glumes short and black. Stony places on mountains. Flo. June–July. ❀.

Carex nigra (L.) Reichard. **Common Sedge.** *C. goodenowii* Gay. ¶Stem 1 ft; lower bract leaf-like; spikes dense, cylindrical, obtuse; glumes black, narrower than green fr. Wet grassy places on acid soils. Flo. May–June. ❀.

9. *Limosae.* ¶Peduncles slender; fr. elliptic; beak very short; stigmas 3.

Carex flacca Schreb. **Glaucous Sedge.** *C. glauca* Scop., *C. diversicolor* auct. ¶1 ft stem and leaves glaucous; spikes cylindrical; stalks slender; glumes dark; fr. minutely papillose. Common on calcareous soil. Flo. May–June. ❀.

Carex limosa L. **Mud Sedge.** ¶1 ft stem and narrow leaves rough; spikes nodding, 10–20 flo.; male glumes lanceolate, female glumes ovate; fr. elliptic, ribbed. In peaty pools, local. Flo. June. ✿.

Carex rariflora (Wahlenb.) Sm. **Few-flowered Sedge.** ¶6–8 in. stem and leaves smooth; spikes nodding, 8–10 flo.; male glumes ovate, female glumes obovate. High mountain bogs in Scotland, local. Flo. June.

Carex paupercula Michx. **Broad-leaved Mud Sedge.** *C. magellanica* auct. ¶1 ft stem smooth; leaves broader, 3 mm.; spikes nodding, 8–10 flo.; female glumes lanceolate, narrower than pale, ovate fr. Bogs, Scotland, N. England, rare. Flo. June. ✿.

10. *Digitatae.* ¶Inflo. finger-like; flo. few; fr. pale, pubescent; beak short.

Carex digitata L. **Fingered Sedge.** ¶6–8 in.; leaf width 3–4 mm.; spikes lax, 6–8 flo.; glumes pale; fr. pubescent. On limestone and chalk, N. Somerset to N. England. Flo. April–May. ✿.

Carex ornithopoda Willd. **Bird's-foot Sedge.** ¶3–5 in.; leaves narrower; spikes small, lax, 4–5 flo.; glume shorter than pyriform fr. Limestone banks, Derbyshire to Cumberland, local. Flo. May. ✿.

Carex humilis Leyss. **Dwarf Sedge.** ¶Dwarf, 2 in.; leaves very narrow; bracts broad, enclosing 3–5 flo. female spike. Dry limestone turf and crevices. Herefordshire to Hampshire. Flo. April. ✿.

11. *Montanae.* ¶Spikes sessile subglobose or oblong; fr. pubescent; beak short.

Carex montana L. **Mountain Sedge.** ¶Shortly creeping; stem 8–12 in.; leaf width 2 mm.; glume dark, shorter than pubescent fr. Calcareous pastures, S. England and Wales. Flo. May. ✿.

Carex ericetorum Poll. **Heath Sedge.** ¶Stems tufted, 3–6 in.; leaves wider, 3–4 mm., short; glumes dark, edges pale; fr. obovate, pubescent. Calcareous soil, Suffolk to Westmorland. Flo. April–May. ✿.

Carex pilulifera L. **Pill Sedge.** ¶Stem 1 ft; leaves narrow, 2 mm.; glumes light brown; fr. globose, green; bract sometimes long. Damp heaths, common. Flo. May–June. ✿.

Carex caryophyllea Latourr. **Spring Sedge.** *C. praecox* auct. ¶Stem 6–8 in.; bracts sheathing; spikes oblong; glumes ovate, brown, midrib green; fr. elliptic, green. In short grass, common. Flo. April–May. ✿.

Carex filiformis L. **Downy-fruited Sedge.** *C. tomentosa* auct. ¶1 ft; leaves narrow; bracts shortly leaf-like; spikes oblong: fr. small, obovoid, very downy. In wet meadows, Gloucestershire to Sussex, local. Flo. May–June. ✿.

12. *Paniceae.* ¶Spikes stalked; fr. large, oval, glabrous, pale.

Carex pallescens L. **Pale Sedge.** ¶1 ft; bract leaf-like; female spikes dense, slender stalked; glumes white with green midrib; fr. bright green. Damp meadows and woods. Flo. June. ✿.

Carex panicea L. **Carnation Grass.** ¶1 ft; leaves very glaucous; bract sheath tight; spikes lax, few flo.; fr. curved. In damp pastures, common. Flo. May–June. ✿.

Carex vaginata Tausch. **Wide-sheathing Sedge.** ¶6–12 in.; leaves bright green; bract sheath very loose; spikes lax, few flo.; fr. curved. On high mountains in Scotland. Flo. July. ✿.

13. *Nutantes.* ¶Lower bract sheath long; spikes nodding; fr. narrow beaked.

Carex capillaris L. **Hair Sedge.** ¶Small, 2–4 in., very slender; spikes lax, few flo. nodding; glumes and fr. small, brown, shiny. Mountain slopes, Teesdale to N. Scotland, local. Flo. June–July. ❀.

PLATE 94

Carex strigosa Huds. **Loose-spiked Wood Sedge.** ¶Stem 2 ft; leaf width ¼ in.; female spikes lax, flo. slender, 2 in. long; fr. lanceolate, green. Damp shady places, local. Flo. May–June. ❀.

Carex pendula Huds. **Pendulous Sedge.** ¶Stem 3–6 ft; leaf width ½ in.; flo. spikes dense, very long, 4–6 in., drooping; fr. lanceolate, green. Damp woods and shady places. Flo. May–June. ❀.

Carex sylvatica Huds. **Wood Sedge.** ¶Stem 1½ ft; female spikes 1–1½ in., lax, nodding; stalks slender; glumes pale; fr. green with long beak. Woods on stiff soils, common. Flo. May–June. ❀.

14. *Distantes.* ¶Bracts long sheathing; spikes distant, oblong; beak long, bifid.

Carex depauperata Curt. ex With. **Starved Wood Sedge.** ¶Spikes with few flo., 3–4 only, lower distant, stalked; fr. very large, 8 mm., ribbed; beak long. N. Somerset and Surrey, very rare. Flo. May.

Carex binervis Sm. **Green-ribbed Sedge.** ¶Spikes distant, lowest 1 in., dense, long stalked; glumes dark; fr. with strong green submarginal ribs. Acid moors and meadows, common. Flo. June. ❀.

Carex distans L. **Distant Sedge.** ¶Spikes distant, ½ in.; stalks included in sheath; glumes greenish brown; fr. many, ribbed. Wet places, mostly near sea. Flo. May–June. ❀.

Carex hostiana DC. **Tawny Sedge.** *C. hornschuchiana* Hoppe, *C. fulva* auct. ¶Spikes distant, ¾ in., lower long stalked; glumes brown with white margin; fr. many, ribbed. On acid moors and meadows. Flo. June.

Carex punctata Gaudin. **Dotted Sedge.** ¶Spikes distant; stalks included in bract sheath; glumes pale reddish; fr. pale green with pellucid dots. Wet places by the sea, local. Flo. June–July.

Carex lasiocarpa Ehrh. **Downy-fruited Sedge.** *C. filiformis* auct. ¶Leaves narrow, glabrous; female spikes distant, subsessile, 1 in.; glumes brown; fr. very downy. Peat bogs and reed swamps, local. Flo. June. ❀.

Carex hirta L. **Hairy Sedge.** ¶Wider leaves and sheaths hairy; spikes distant; glumes long, greenish, awned; fr. green, very pubescent. Damp meadows and shady places, common. Flo. May–June. ❀.

15. *Extensae.* ¶Bracts deflexed; female spikes short, dense; fr. spreading.

Carex extensa Good. **Long-bracted Sedge.** ¶Leaves narrow, involute; bracts very long; spikes subsessile; glumes light brown; fr. ribbed. In salt marshes, locally common. Flo. June. ❀.

Carex serotina Mérat. **Late-flowering Sedge.** ¶Leaves 2–3 mm. wide, channelled; male spike sessile; glumes yellowish; fr. not curved, abruptly contracted to short beak. Mostly near sea. Flo. July–Aug.

Carex lepidocarpa Tausch. ¶Stems slender; male spike stalked; female spikes rarely contiguous; fr. deflexed, tapering to slender beak. Wet places on basic soils. Flo. May–June. ✳.

Carex demissa Hornem. **Low Sedge.** *C. tumidicarpa* Anderss. ¶Stems spreading; male spike short stalked; lowest female spike often distant and stalked; fr. swollen, green, lower deflexed. Common on acid soils. Flo. July. ✳.

Carex flava L. **Yellow Sedge.** ¶Stems stout; leaves 4–7 mm. wide; terminal spike sessile, often partly female; fr. large, 6–7 mm., deflexed, golden. In peat on limestone, N. Lancashire, W. Yorkshire. Flo. June. ✳.

16. *Vesicariae.* ¶Stems leafy; lower spikes on slender stalks; fr. ovoid; beak long.

Carex pseudocyperus L. **Cyperus Sedge.** ¶Stem 2–3 ft; leaves wide; ligule 12 mm.; female spikes nodding; fr. 5–6 mm., ribbed; beak long. By ponds and slow rivers, local. Flo. May–June. ✳.

Carex laevigata Sm. **Smooth Sedge.** *C. helodes* Link. ¶Stem 2 ft; leaf ligule 10 mm.; male spike 1; lower female spike nodding; glumes 3 mm.; fr. 5–6 mm., ovoid, inflated. Shady places on acid soil. Flo. June. ✳.

Carex rostrata Stokes. **Beaked Sedge, Bottle Sedge.** *C. ampullacea* Good. ¶Stem 1–2 ft; leaf ligule 2–3 mm.; male spikes 2–3; lower female spikes 2 in., suberect; glumes 5 mm.; fr. 5–6 mm., yellowish. Wet peaty soil. Flo. June. ✳.

Carex vesicaria L. **Bladder Sedge.** ¶Stem 1–2 ft; leaf ligule 5–8 mm.; female spikes 1 in. long; glumes 3 mm.; fr. 4–5 mm., ovoid, yellow. Wet places, local. Flo. June.

Carex stenolepis Less. **Thin-glumed Sedge.** *C. grahami* Boott. ¶1–1½ ft; leaf ligule 3–4 mm., acute; female spikes broadly oval; fr. 4–5 mm., inflated, ribbed. Mountain bogs in Argyll, Perthshire, Angus, rare. Flo. July. ✳.

Carex saxatilis L. **Russet Sedge.** *C. pulla* Good. ¶½–1 ft; leaves concave; ligule 1 mm., rounded; male spike usually 1; female spikes oval; fr. 3 mm., smooth. Bogs on high mountains, Scotland, local. Flo. July. ✳.

17. *Paludosae.* ¶Plants tall; leaves wide; spikes many, large, erect, dense.

Carex acutiformis Ehrh. **Lesser Pond Sedge.** *C. paludosa* Good. ¶Stem 2–3 ft; leaf width 7–10 mm.; ligule ½–1 in.; male glumes 5–6 mm., obtuse; female spikes 1–1½ in.; glumes 4–5 mm.; fr. 4 mm. Ponds and canals. Flo. May–June. ✳.

Carex riparia Curt. **Great Pond Sedge.** ¶Stem 3–4 ft; leaf width ½ in.; ligule ½ in.; male glumes long, 8 mm., pointed female spikes 2–3 in.; female glumes 7 mm.; fr. 8 mm. Ponds and dikes. Flo. May–June. ✳.

GRAMINEAE   **PLATE 95**

Much fuller accounts of the Grasses will be found in Dr C. E. Hubbard's *Grasses* (Penguin Series). The lines of that work have been followed here as far as possible. We are also indebted to Dr Hubbard for permission to use some of his 'points of difference' and for looking through the text below and making useful suggestions.

Digitaria ischaemum (Schreb.) Muhl. **Smooth Finger Grass.** *Panicum glabrum* Gaudin. ¶Annual; leaf ligule membranous; spikelets stalked, on 1 side of axis; lower glume suppressed; lower lemma barren. Arable land, S. and S.E. England. Flo. Aug.

Cynodon dactylon (L.) Pers. **Creeping Finger Grass.** ¶Perennial; leaf ligule a ring of hairs; spikelets sessile on 1 side of axis; glumes narrow, subsequal. Coastal sand, S.W. England. ❀ on plate 96.

Setaria viridis (L.) Beauv. **Bristle Grass.** *Panicum viride* L. ¶Annual; inflo. spike-like; spikelet stalks bearing long rough bristles; upper glume equalling spikelet, lower very short. Rare weed. Flo. Aug.–Oct.

Spartina maritima (Curt.) Fernald. **Cord Grass.** *S. stricta* (Ait) Roth. ¶Stems 1 ft; leaf width ¼ in.; spikelets ½ in., hairy; upper glume 3 nerved; anthers 4–6 mm. Salt marshes mostly in S. England. Flo. July–Sept.

Spartina × townsendii H. & J. Groves = *S. alterniflora × maritima*. **Rice Grass.** ¶Stems 2–3 ft; leaf width ½ in.; spikelets ¾ in. long, hairy; anthers 8–11 mm. Spreading on coastal mud flats, S. England to Scotland, planted. Flo. July–Nov. ❀.

Spartina alterniflora Lois. **American Cord Grass.** ¶Stems 2–3 ft; leaf width ¼ in.; spikelets ½ in. long, subglabrous; upper glumes 5–9 nerved; anthers 4–6 mm. Mud flats, Hampshire, now very rare. Flo. July–Nov.

Sieglingia decumbens (L.) Bernh. **Heath Grass.** *Triodia decumbens* (L.) Beauv. ¶Stems spreading; leaf ligule of short hairs; spikelets plump and shiny; flo. usually self-fertilizing. Damp peaty soils, common. Flo. July. ❀ on plate 96.

Molinia caerulea (L.) Moench. **Purple Moor Grass.** ¶Stems tufted, 1–3 ft; leaves long, dying in winter; ligule of short hairs; inflo. up to 1 ft long, purple. Moors and fens, common. Flo. July–Sept. ❀ on plate 97.

Phragmites australis (Cav.) Streud. **Common Reed.** *P. communis* Trin., *Arundo phragmites* L. ¶Stems stout, 6–9 ft; leaf width ½ in.; ligule of hairs; inflo. densely branched; spikelet ½ in. Marshes, pools and fens. Common. Flo. Aug.–Oct.

Leersia oryzoides (L.) Sw. ¶Stems 1–3 ft; leaf sheaths hairy, often enclosing inflo.; glumes 0; lemma and palea hairy. Brook sides, Surrey to Somerset and Dorset. Flo. Aug.–Oct.

Nardus stricta L. **Mat Grass.** ¶Stems and inrolled leaves wiry; spikes 1 sided, very slender; spikelets narrow, pointed. Heaths and moors, common. Flo. June–Aug. ❀ on plate 99.

Parapholis strigosa (Dumort.) C. E. Hubbard. **Sea Hard-grass.** *Lepturus filiformis* Trin. ¶Stem ½–1 ft; leaves 1–2 in.; spikes long, narrow; spikelets alternate embedded in the stem; anthers 2–4 mm. Salt marshes. Flo. June–Aug. ❀ on plate 99.

Parapholis incurva (L.) C. E. Hubbard. **Curved Hard-grass.** *Lepturus incurvatus* Trin. ¶Smaller, up to 6 in.; stems and spikes curved; leaves ½–1 in.; anthers very small, 0·5–1 mm. Salt marshes, Somerset and Dorset to Lincolnshire. Flo. June–July.

Phalaris arundinacea L. **Reed Canary Grass.** ¶Stem 3–5 ft; leaf width ½ in.; ligules ¼ in.; panicle with many rough branches; small sterile lemmas and fertile one hairy. Wet places. Flo. June–Aug. ❀.

Phalaris canariensis L. **Canary Grass.** ¶Stem 1–3 ft; inflo. spike-like, 1–2 in. long; glumes large, pale yellowish with green, winged keels. Introduced as bird seed. Flo. July–Sept.

Milium effusum L. **Wood Millet.** ¶Stem 3–4 ft; leaf width ½ in.; ligule long; inflo. long and wide spreading; spikelets isolated, oval, green. In woods. Flo. May–July. ❀.

Alopecurus alpinus Sm. **Alpine Foxtail.** ¶Stem 1 ft; spikes short and broad; glumes very hairy; lemma ovate, awn short or 0. Wet places on mountains, Scotland and N. England. Flo. June–Aug. ✻.

Alopecurus pratensis L. **Meadow Foxtail.** ¶Stem 3 ft; spikes soft, 2–3 in. long; spikelets 4–6 mm.; glumes acute, united below; lemma awn long. Common in meadows. Flo. April–July. ✻.

Alopecurus geniculatus L. **Marsh Foxtail.** ¶Stem prostrate below; leaf sheaths pale, inflated; spikelets 3 mm.; glumes blunt, nearly free. Wet margins of pools and ditches. Flo. June–Aug. ✻.

A. geniculatus × *pratensis* is fairly common. Spikelets 3·5–4·5 mm.; glumes subacute.

Alopecurus bulbosus Gouan. **Bulbous Foxtail.** ¶Stem ½–1 ft, bulbous at base; upper sheaths inflated; glumes sharply pointed; lemma awn long. Salt marshes in England. Flo. May–Aug. ✻.

Alopecurus aequalis Sobol. **Orange Foxtail.** *A. fulvus* Sm. ¶Prostrate at base; sheaths inflated; glumes blunt; lemma awn short; anthers orange. Margins of pools and ditches, local. Flo. June–Sept. ✻.

Alopecurus myosuroides Huds. **Slender Foxtail.** *A. agrestis* L. ¶Stems 2 ft; spikes 2–4 in., narrow; glumes pointed, half united; lemma awn long. Arable land, common. Flo. May–Aug. ✻.

Phleum alpinum L. **Alpine Cat's-tail.** *P. commutatum* Gaudin. ¶Stem 1 ft; leaf ligule short; spikes short and broad; glumes truncate; keel ciliate; awns 2–3 mm. High mountains, Scotland, N.W. England. Flo. July–Aug. ✻.

Phleum pratense L. **Cat's-tail, Timothy Grass.** ¶Stem 2–3 ft; leaves rough; ligule 4–6 mm.; spike 3–4 in.; glumes truncate; keel ciliate; awn 1–2 mm. Meadows, common. Flo. June–Aug. ✻.

Phleum bertolonii DC. **Lesser Cat's-tail.** *P. nodosum* auct. ¶Stem swollen at base; leaf ligules 2–4 mm.; spikes 1–2 in., dense; glumes truncate, ciliate; awn short. Grassy hills, common. Flo. June–Aug. ✻.

Phleum phleoides (L.) Karst. **Purple-stalked Cat's-tail.** ¶Leaves narrower, ligules 1–2 mm.; spikes 1–3 in.; glumes bluntly narrowed; keel hairs very short. Dry sand and chalk, E. England. Flo. June–Aug. ✻.

Phleum arenarium L. **Sand Cat's-tail.** ¶Stem 2–8 in.; leaves short, ligules long; spikes dense, narrowed below; glumes gradually narrowed above. Coast sands, locally common. Flo. May–July. ✻.

*Lagurus ovatus L. **Hare's-tail.** ¶Stems 1 ft, hairy; leaves short, softly hairy; spikes ovoid, hairy, bristly; glumes narrow, subulate, hairy. Channel Islands, naturalized in S. England. Flo. July.

Mibora minima (L.) Desv. **Early Sand Grass.** ¶Slender, tufted, 1–6 in.; leaves small; spike slender, 1 sided; spikelets 1 flo.; glumes blunt. Anglesey, Glamorgan and Channel Islands (Dorset). Flo. Feb.–May. ✻ on plate 96.

Agrostis stolonifera L. **Creeping Bent.** *A. alba* auct. ¶Stolons leafy; stem 1 ft; panicle contracted, branches short, palea ⅔ length of lemma. Common everywhere. Flo. July–Aug. ✻.
Var. *palustris* (Huds.) Farw. ¶Stolons leafless; stem 2 ft; panicle more open. Wet places.
A. stolonifera × *tenuis*. ¶Intermediate in form, is widespread.

Agrostis tenuis Sibth. **Common Bent.** *A. vulgaris* With. ¶Rhizome short; stem ½–2 ft; ligule short; panicle spreading, brown; lemma awnless; palea ½ length of lemma. Abundant everywhere. Flo. June–Aug. ❀.

Agrostis gigantea Roth. **Black Bent.** *A. nigra* With. ¶Rhizomatous; stem 2–3 ft; leaves large; ligule long; panicle open; lemma awnless; palea 1–1·3 mm. On waste and arable land. Flo. June–Aug.

Argrostis canina L.

Subsp. *canina* **Velvet Bent.** ¶Stolons creeping, bearing tufts of slender leaves; panicle branches bare below; lemma awned; palea minute. Moors and meadows, abundant. Flo. June–Aug. ❀.

Subsp. *montana* (Hartm.) Hartm. ¶With scaly rhizomes and dense tufts of leaves. ❀.

Agrostis setacea Curt. **Bristle-leaved Bent.** ¶Many shoots of very fine leaves; panicle narrow; lemma awned; palea very small. Heaths and moors, mostly in S.W., abundant. Flo. June–July. ❀.

Polypogon monspeliensis (L.) Desf. **Annual Beard-Grass.** ¶2 ft; leaves and ligules long; panicle spike-like; ripe spikelets falling; glumes rough, long awned. Coasts and saltings, S. and S.E. England. Flo. July. ❀.

PLATE 96

Apera spica-venti (L.) Beauv. **Loose Silky Bent, Wind Grass.** ¶1–3 ft; leaves and ligules long; panicle branches long, spreading; lemma awn long; anthers 2 mm. On light soils in S.E. England. Flo. June–Aug.

Apera interrupta (L.) Beauv. **Dense Silky Bent.** ¶Stems and leaves short; panicle branches short, erect, dense; anthers minute. Sandy soil, W. Norfolk and Suffolk, rare elsewhere. Flo. June–July.

Gastridium ventricosum (Gouan) Schinz & Thell. *G. lendigerum* (L.) Desv. ¶Stems 1 ft; leaves short; panicle spike-like, pale green; spikelets swollen at base, shiny. Calcareous land, S. England, scarce. Flo. June–Aug. ❀ on plate 95.

Calamagrostis epigejos (L.) Roth. **Wood Small-reed.** ¶3–6 ft; leaves wide, glabrous; ligule long; panicle dense; glumes narrow; hairs much exceeding lemma. Damp woods and fens. Flo. June–July. ❀.

Calamagrostis canescens (Weber) Roth. **Purple Small-reed.** *C. lanceolata* Roth. ¶Stem 3–4 ft; leaves hairy above; panicle loose; glumes rather narrow; hairs slightly exceeding lemma. Marshes and fens, rather rare. Flo. June–July. ❀.

Calamagrostis stricta (Timm) Koel. **Narrow Small-reed.** *C. neglecta* auct. ¶1–3 ft; leaves hairy above; ligule short; panicle narrow, dense; glumes 3–4 mm., broadly lanceolate; hairs shorter than lemma. Northern bogs, rare. Flo. July.

Calamagrostis scotica (Druce) Druce. **Scottish Small-reed.** ¶Stem 1–3 ft; leaves hairy above; panicle rather narrow, dense; glumes 4–6 mm., lanceolate; hairs shorter than lemma. Bogs, N. Caithness, very rare. Flo. July–Aug.

Ammophila arenaria (L.) Link. **Marram Grass.** *A. arundinacea* Host. ¶Rhizomes long; stem 3 ft; leaves inrolled, sharp pointed; ligule 1 in.; panicle large, spike-like; glumes ½ in. Coastal sands, abundant. Flo. July. ❀.

The hybrid *Ammophila arenaria × Calamagrostis epigejos* is found on the E. coast; leaves flatter; inflo. purplish; lemma hairs longer; anthers small.

Anthoxanthum odoratum L. **Scented Vernal Grass.** ¶Perennial; stem unbranched; spike 2–3 in.; glumes hairy, unequal; awns of sterile lemmas not conspicuous. Abundant everywhere. Flo. April–June. ✾ on plate 95.

*_Anthoxanthum puelii_ Lecoq & Lamotte. **Annual Vernal Grass.** *A. aristatum* auct. ¶Annual; stem branched; spike ½–1 in.; glumes glabrous; awns of sterile lemmas conspicuous. Sandy fields, rare. Flo. June–Aug.

Hierochloe odorata (L.) Beauv. **Holy Grass.** ¶Creeping; stem 1 ft; upper leaves short, pointed; panicle spreading; spikelets rounded; glumes broad. Wet places, N. Scotland, N. Ireland. Flo. March–May.

Holcus mollis L. **Creeping Soft Grass.** ¶Rhizomes creeping; stems hairy at nodes; glumes ovate, acute, hairy; upper lemma long awned. Grassland, cultivated ground, troublesome weed. Flo. June–Aug. ✾.

Holcus lanatus L. **Yorkshire Fog.** ¶Tufted; stems downy; glumes ovate, blunt, hairy, upper aristate; upper lemma short awned. Common. Flo. May–Aug. ✾.

Aira caryophyllea L. **Silvery Hair Grass.** ¶Stems 2–12 in., slender; leaf sheaths rough; panicle spreading; glumes silvery; lemmas awned. Dry soils, banks and wall tops, common. Flo. May–July. ✾.

Aira praecox L. **Early Hair Grass.** ¶Tufted, 2–6 in., slender; leaves very small; sheaths smooth; panicle spike-like; glumes shiny; lemmas awned. Sandy and acid soils, common. Flo. April–June. ✾.

Corynephorus canescens (L.) Beauv. **Grey Hair Grass.** *Aira canescens* L. ¶Tufted; leaves many, very slender, rough; panicle narrow; lemma awn with apex club-like. Sand dunes, Norfolk, Suffolk, Channel Islands. Flo. June–July. ✾.

Deschampsia setacea (Huds.) Hack. **Bog Hair Grass.** ¶Leaves very narrow, bristle-like; sheaths smooth; ligules long, pointed; lemma broad, unequally 4 pointed. Boggy heaths, local. Flo. July–Aug. ✾.

Deschampsia flexuosa (L.) Trin. **Wavy Hair Grass.** ¶Leaves narrow, bristle-like; sheaths slightly rough; ligules blunt; lemma ovate, apical teeth microscopic. On moors, abundant. Flo. June–July. ✾.
Var. *montana* Huds. ¶Has smaller panicles, with larger spikelets. Alpine.

Deschampsia cespitosa (L.) Beauv. **Tufted Hair Grass.** ¶Large tussocks; stem 2–4 ft; leaves flat, coarse, ribs rough; ligule long; lemma tip toothed. Wet fields and moors, common. Flo. June–Aug. ✾.

Deschampsia alpina (L.) Roem. & Schult. **Alpine Hair Grass.** ¶Stems ½–1 ft, tufted; leaves short, channelled; sheath smooth; ligule long; panicle smaller; flo. often proliferous; lemma toothed. High mountains. Flo. July–Aug.

Trisetum flavescens (L.) Beauv. **Yellow Oat Grass.** ¶Stem 1–2 ft; leaves flat, pointed; ligule short; panicle yellow; spikelets about 3 flo.; lemma 2 toothed, awned. Common in England. Flo. June–July. ✾.

Koeleria cristata (L.) Pers. **Crested Hair Grass.** *K. gracilis* Pers. ¶Tufted, 1 ft; leaves mostly inrolled; sheaths hairy; panicle dense, spike-like, pale. Calcareous soils, common. Flo. June–July. ✾ on plate 97.
Var. *albescens* (DC.). ¶Is a sand-dune form with whiter panicles. ✾ on plate 97.

Koeleria vallesiana (Honck.) Bertol. ¶Similar to *K. cristata*, but with the basal leaf sheaths persisting, split and fibrous, forming a dense thickened base to stems. On limestone, N. Somerset. Flo. June–July.

Avena ludoviciana Durieu. **Winter Wild Oat.** ¶Spikelet jointed and breaking only above the glumes; lemmas awned, hairy; apex 2 toothed, without bristles. Introduced weed. Flo. July–Aug.

Avena fatua L. **Common Wild Oat.** ¶Spikelet jointed and breaking between the lemmas; lemmas hairy, awned; apex 2 toothed, without bristles. Weed of cultivation. Flo. June–Aug. �.

Avena strigosa Schreb. **Bristle Oat.** ¶Spikelet not jointed; lemmas hairy and awned (except 3rd lemma) with 2 fine bristles from apical teeth. Cultivated in Wales and W. Scotland. Flo. July–Aug.

The chief oat of cultivation, *A. sativa* L., has lemma without hairs or apical bristles.

Arrhenatherum elatius (L.) J. & C. Presl. **Oat Grass.** *A. avenaceum* Beauv. ¶3–4 ft, often bulbous at base; spikelets 2 flo.; lower lemma long awned, 7 nerved. Waste ground and hedgerows, everywhere. Flo. June–Sept. ✻.

Helictotrichon pratense (L.) Pilg. **Meadow Oat Grass.** *Avena pratensis* L. ¶1–2 ft; leaf sheaths glabrous; spikelets large, 3–6 flo.; axis short haired; lemmas long awned. Commons on chalk downs. Flo. June–July. ✻.

Helictotrichon pubescens (Huds.) Pilg. **Downy Oat.** *Avena pubescens* Huds. ¶1–2 ft; leaves and lower sheaths hairy; spikelets 2–3 flo.; axis with long hairs; lemmas long awned. Damp calcareous soils. Flo. May–July. ✻.

Sesleria caerulea (L.) Ard.
Subsp. *calcarea* (Čelak.) Hegi. **Blue Moor Grass.** ¶½–1 ft; leaves flat, blunt, hooded; spike bluish with scales at base; spikelets 2–3 flo. On limestone, N. England, Scotland, W. Ireland. Flo. April–June. ✻.

PLATE 97

Melica uniflora Retz. **Wood Melick.** ¶Slender; leaf sheath with small pointed extension; panicle branched; 1 flo. fertile and sterile lemmas in each spikelet. Woods and shady banks, common. ✻.

Melica nutans L. **Mountain** or **Nodding Melick.** *M. montana* Huds. ¶Leaf sheaths without pointed extension; panicle usually unbranched; 2–3 flo. in spikelet; peduncle bent. Calcareous banks, Gloucestershire northward. Flo. May–July. ✻.

Glyceria maxima (Hartm.) Holmberg. **Reed Sweet Grass.** *G. aquatica* (L.) Wahlb., non J. & C. Presl. ¶Stems 3–6 ft; leaves 1–2 ft; panicle much branched; spikelets many, 4–10 flo.; lemmas oval, 3–4 mm. Ponds, fens and slow rivers. Flo. June–Aug. ✻.

Glyceria fluitans (L.) R. Br. **Floating Sweet Grass.** ¶Stem 1–3 ft; leaves ½–1 ft; panicle branches few, appressed; spikelets long, 8–16 flo.; lemmas long, 6–7 mm., bluntly pointed. Ponds and streams. Flo. May–Aug. ✻.

Glyceria plicata Fr. ¶Stem 1–2 ft; leaf sheaths rough; branches spreading; lemmas rounded, 3–5 mm., palea teeth included. Ponds, ditches and moorland pools. Flo. June–Aug. ✻.

Glyceria × pedicellata Townsend = *G. fluitans × plicata*. Intermediate between the parents, with minutely scabrid sheaths; sterile. Widespread.

Glyceria declinata Bréb. ¶1–1½ ft; leaves grey-green; branches few, appressed; lemmas 3 lobed, 4–5 mm.; palea teeth projecting. Marshes and moors. Flo. June–Sept. ☙.

Catabrosa aquatica (L.) Beauv. **Water Whorl-Grass.** ¶Stoloniferous, 1–1½ ft; leaves blunt; spikelets mostly 2 flo.; lemmas much exceeding glumes. Sides of ponds and streams, local. Flo. May–July. ☙.

Cynosurus cristatus L. **Crested Dog's-tail.** ¶1–2 ft; leaves pointed; inflo. spiked; sterile spikelets of empty glumes concealing fertile spikelets of 3–4 flo. Common. Flo. June–Aug. ☙.

*Cynosurus echinatus L. **Rough Dog's-tail.** ¶Leaves wide; inflo. dense, oval; lemmas with long rough awns; sterile glumes short awned. Introduced, mostly in S. England. Flo. June–July.

Dactylis glomerata L. **Cocksfoot.** ¶Stout plant, 2–3 ft; leaves valuable grazing; inflo. in dense clusters; keels of glumes and lemmas rough or hairy. Meadows, abundant. Flo. June–Sept. ☙.

Briza media L. **Common Quaking Grass.** ¶Perennial; leaf width about ⅛ in.; ligules short; lemmas as broad as long; anthers long. Dry calcareous pastures, common. Flo. June–Aug. ☙.

Briza minor L. **Lesser Quaking Grass.** ¶Annual; leaves soft, width about ¼ in.; ligules longer; lemmas small, broader than long; anthers small. Roadsides, arable land, S.W. England. Flo. June–Sept. ☙.

*Briza maxima L. ¶Spikelets very large, 7–20 flo. Is naturalized in Channel Islands.

Poa infirma Kunth. **Scilly Isles Meadow Grass.** ¶Annual, 1–6 in.; inflo. lax; spikelets small, 2–4 flo.; glumes small; lemmas short and hairy; anthers small. W. Cornwall, Scilly Isles and Channel Islands. Flo. March–May.

Poa annua L. **Annual Meadow Grass.** ¶6–12 in.; leaves broad and blunt; spikelets usually about 6 flo.; lemmas longer, overlapping; anthers medium. Abundant everywhere. Flo. all the year. ☙.

Poa bulbosa L. **Bulbous Meadow Grass.** ¶Shoots bulbous at base, ½–1 ft; leaves very narrow; inflo. dense; spikelets 3–6 flo.; short hairs on nerves of lemmas. Sandy coasts, S. and E. England. Flo. March–April. ☙.

Poa alpina L. **Alpine Meadow Grass.** ¶½–1 ft; leaves broad, blunt; spikelets large, 2–5 flo.; glumes and lemmas large, ovate, margins broad and white; anthers long, 2 mm. Stony places on mountains, often proliferous. Flo. July–Aug. ☙.

Poa flexuosa Sm. *Poa laxa* auct. ¶Similar to *P. alpina*, but leaves narrow, tapering; inflo. narrower; spikelets fewer, smaller, not proliferous; anthers 1 mm. High mountains in Scotland. Flo. July–Aug.

Poa nemoralis L. **Woodland Meadow Grass.** ¶1–2 ft; leaves narrow, pointed; ligules short; inflo. long, slender; spikelets small, few flo. Woods and shady places. Flo. June–July. ☙.

Poa balfourii Parnell. ¶Slender; leaves narrow, greyish; ligule 1–3 mm.; branches with 1–5 longer spikelets, 5–7 mm.; lower glume lanceolate. Mountains, N. Wales to N. Scotland. Flo. July–Aug.

Poa glauca Vahl. ¶Stiff stems and leaves glaucous, whitish; inflo. branches short, erect; glumes broader ovate. Highest Scottish mountains and Snowdon, rare. Flo. July–Aug.

Poa palustris L. **Marsh Meadow Grass.** ¶1–4 ft; leaves pointed; sheaths smooth; ligules long, blunt; inflo. large; lemma tips yellowish. An early introduction, by ponds, local. Flo. June–July.

Poa chaixii Vill. **Broad-leaved Meadow Grass.** ¶Large, tufted, 2–4 ft; leaves long and broad; ligules short; spikelets 5–6 mm.; lemma nerves glabrous. Naturalized in woods, local. Flo. May–July.

Poa trivialis L. **Rough Meadow Grass.** ¶Stoloniferous; leaves glossy below; sheaths keeled, rough, often purple; ligule long, pointed; lemma base long haired. Very common. Flo. June–July. ⚘.

Poa pratensis L. **Meadow Grass.** ¶Rhizomes slender; stems tufted; sheaths smooth; ligules short; spikelets up to ¼ in.; glumes abruptly pointed. Old pastures and road-sides, common. Flo. May–July. ⚘.

Poa subcaerulea Sm. **Spreading Meadow Grass.** *P. irrigata* Lindm. ¶Rhizomes long; stems scattered, solitary; lower inflo. branches in pairs; spikelets ¼ in.; glumes finely pointed. Wet meadows and sands. Flo. June–July. ⚘.

Poa angustifolia L. **Narrow-leaved Meadow Grass.** ¶Rhizomes slender; stems tufted; leaves stiff and narrow; ligules short; spikelets smaller, ⅛ in. Hill grassland and wall tops. Flo. May–June.

Poa compressa L. **Flat-stalked Meadow Grass.** ¶Rhizomes long; stems scattered, flattened, wiry; inflo. branches short; spikelets ⅛ in. Dry banks and old walls. Flo. June–Aug. ⚘.

PLATE 98

Puccinellia fasciculata (Torr.) Bicknell. **Tufted Salt-marsh Grass.** *Glyceria borrei* (Bab.) Bab. ¶Perennial; tufted; inflo. rather dense, branches short; spikelets up to ¼ in.; lemmas small, 2 mm.; anthers short. Salt marshes, S. England, Ireland. Flo. June–Sept. ⚘.

Puccinellia distans (L.) Parl. **Reflexed Salt-marsh Grass.** *Glyceria distans* (L.) Wallenb. ¶Perennial; leaves narrow; inflo. branches long, deflexed; spikelets ¼ in.; lemmas small. Salt marshes and seaside banks. Flo. June–July. ⚘.

Puccinellia maritima (Huds.) Parl. **Common Salt-marsh Grass.** *Glyceria maritima* (Huds.) Wahlb. ¶Stoloniferous; stems spreading; spikelets up to ½ in.; lemmas large, 4 mm.; anthers long. Salt marshes and brackish areas, common. Flo. June–July. ⚘.

Puccinellia pseudo-distans (Crép.) Jansen & Wachter. ¶Intermediate between *P. distans* and *P. fasciculata*. Branches spreading, not reflexed; lemma with middle nerve minutely projecting. Thames estuary, rare.

Puccinellia rupestris (With.) Fernald & Weatherby, *Glyceria procumbens* (Curt.) Dumort. ¶Stems spreading or prostrate; leaves flat; spikelets ¼ in.; lemmas large; anthers short. Salt marshes and shingle banks. Flo. May–Aug. ⚘.

Catapodium rigidum (L.) C. E. Hubbard. *Poa rigida* L. *Desmazeria rigida* (L.) Tutin. ¶Stems rigid, 6–10 in.; inflo. branches stiff, spreading on 1 side of axis; often purplish. On dry, mostly calcareous soils. Flo. May–July. ⚘.

Catapodium marinum (L.) C. E. Hubbard. *Festuca rottboellioides* Kunth. *Desmazeria marina*

(L.) Druce. ¶Stems short and stout; inflo. narrow, spike-like; branches short, appressed. Rocks and shingle by the sea, local. Flo. May–July. ❁.

Vulpia membranacea (L.) Dumort. **Dune Fescue.** *Festuca uniglumis* Ait. ¶Upper sheath inflated; spikelets large, ½ in., and awn ½ in.; lower glume minute or o, upper 3 nerved. Sand dunes, S. and E. coasts, E. Ireland. Flo. June. ❁.

Vulpia ambigua (Le Gall) More. **Bearded Fescue.** *Festuca ambigua* Le Gall. ¶Sheath nearly reaching straight inflo.; spikelets ¼ in.; awn ⅜ in.; lower glume very small, upper 1 nerved. Coast sand dunes, Devon to Norfolk and Breckland. Flo. May–June. ❁.

Vulpia myuros (L.) C. C. Gmel. **Rat's-tail Fescue.** *Festuca myuros* L. ¶Stem sheathed to top; inflo. long, curved; spikelets ⅜ in.; awn ½ in.; lower glume about ¼ length of upper. Cultivated and waste, sandy land. Flo. June–July. ❁.

Vulpia bromoides (L.) Gray. **Squirrel-tail Fescue.** *Festuca sciuroides* Roth. ¶Stems and sheaths slender; spikelets few, ½ in.; awn ½ in.; lower glume ½–¾ length of upper. Dry banks and sandy heaths, common. Flo. May–July. ❁.

Festuca altissima All. **Wood Fescue.** *F. silvatica* Vill., non Huds. ¶Tall, 2–4 ft; leaves wide and flat; ligules long; inflo. large; spikelets ¼ in.; lemma awnless. Woods and shady places, mainly N. and W. England. Flo. May–July. ❁.

Festuca tenuifolia Sibth. **Awnless Sheep's Fescue.** *F. capillata* auct. ¶Slender, tufted· leaves inrolled, hair-like; ligules short; sheaths open; spikelets up to ¼ in.; lemma awnless. On acid or peaty soils. Flo. May–June. ❁.

Festuca ovina L. **Sheep's Fescue.** ¶Without rhizomes; leaves narrow, inrolled, up to 8 in.; sheaths open; spikelets ¼–⅜ in.; lemma awn short, about 1 mm. Heaths and moors. Flo. May–July. ❁.

Festuca vivipara (L.) Sm. ¶Similar to *F. tenuifolia* but spikelets always producing young plants. N. Wales to Scotland.

Festuca longifolia Thuill. **Hard Fescue.** *F. duriuscula* auct. ¶Similar to *F. ovina* but stouter; leaves up to 1 ft; inflo. often pyramidal; lemmas a little longer; awn up to 4 mm. Sown and locally naturalized, S. England. Flo. June.

Festuca glauca Lam. **Grey Fescue.** *F. caesia* Sm. ¶Similar to *F. longifolia* but with leaves very bluish white. Native but rare on E. Anglian heaths, also introduced to gardens.

Festuca heterophylla Lam. ¶Tall, 2–4 ft, without rhizomes; basal leaves hair-like, 1–2 ft long, 3 angled; stem leaves short, flat, ⅛ in. wide. Woods, S. England, rare, introduced. Flo. June–July.

Festuca rubra L.
Subsp. *rubra*. **Creeping Fescue, Red Fescue.** ¶Rhizomes long; leaves narrow, basal, inrolled; sheaths tubular; spikelets ⅜–½ in.; lemma 5–6 mm., awned. Very common, glaucous in salt marshes. Flo. May–June. ❁.
Var. *arenaria* Fr. ¶Leaves very glaucous; spikelets large, hairy. Sand dunes.
Subsp. *commutata* Gaudin. ¶Like *F. rubra* with sheaths tubular, but without rhizomes. Introduced, established on dry soils, downs and roadsides.

Festuca juncifolia St-Amans. **Rush-leaved Fescue.** ¶Rhizomes long; stem 1–2 ft; leaves stiff, inrolled, sharply pointed; spikelets ½ in.; lemmas 7–10 mm., hairy, short awned. Sand dunes, S. and E. coasts. Flo. June–July. ❁.

Festuca pratensis Huds. **Meadow Fescue.** ¶Tufted, 1–3 ft; leaves flat; sheath auricles glabrous; shorter branch of each pair with 1–2 spikelets; lemma awnless. In meadows, abundant. Flo. June–Aug. ✳.

The hybrid *Festuca pratensis* × *Lolium perenne* = × *Festulolium loliaceum* is fairly widespread.

Festuca arundinacea Schreb. **Tall Fescue.** (Huds.) P. Fourn. ¶Tufted, 2–5 ft; leaves long, flat, coarse; sheath auricles hairy; shorter branch of each pair with 3–6 spikelets; lemmas 6–9 mm., often short awned. Grassy places. Flo. June–July. ✳.

Festuca gigantea (L.) Vill. **Giant Fescue.** *Bromus giganteus* L. ¶Tufted, 2–4 ft; leaves flat, 1–2 ft, up to ½ in. wide; sheath auricles glabrous, shorter branch with several spikelets; lemma awn ½ in. Woods, common. Flo. July. ✳.

PLATE 99

Lolium perenne L. **Rye Grass.** ¶Perennial; tufted, 1–2 ft; leaf width up to 6 mm.; glumes shorter than spikelets; lemmas awnless. In pastures, abundant. Flo. May–Aug. ✳.

*Lolium multiflorum Lam. **Italian Rye Grass.** *L. italicum* A. Braun. ¶Annual; 1–3 ft, soft; leaf width up to 10 mm.; glumes shorter than spikelets; lemma long awned. Cultivated and naturalized. Flo. June–Aug.

*Lolium temulentum L. **Darnel.** ¶Leaves wide; glumes equalling spikelets; lemmas board, oval, awned or awnless. On waste places, rare.

Bromus sterilis L. **Barren Brome.** *Anisantha sterilis* (L.) Nevski. ¶Annual; leaves hairy; inflo. branches long, mostly with single wedge-shaped spikelet; lemma long awned. Roadsides and waste places, common. Flo. May–July. ✳.

Bromus madritensis L. **Madrid Brome.** *Anisantha madritensis* (L.) Nevski. ¶Annual, 1–1½ ft; lower sheaths hairy; inflo. branches erect, shorter than wedge-shaped spikelets; lemma long awned. Limestone rocks, Bristol, etc. Flo. June. ✳.

Bromus ramosus Huds. **Woodland Brome.** *Zerna ramosa* (Huds.) Lindm. ¶Perennial, 2–4 ft; leaves wide; sheaths with reflexed hairs, auricled; inflo. branches in pairs; spikelets oblong, 1 in. Woods and hedgerows. Flo. July–Aug. ✳.

Bromus erectus Huds. **Upright Brome.** *Zerna erecta* (Huds.) Gray. ¶Perennial, 2–3 ft; leaves narrow; sheaths subglabrous; branches clustered, erect; spikelets oblong. Common on calcareous soils. Flo. June–July. ✳.

Bromus mollis L. **Soft Brome.** ¶Annual, 1–2 ft; leaves and sheaths softly hairy; spikelets ½–⅞ in., hairy; lemma 8–11 mm.; palea entire. Common. Flo. May–July. ✳.

Bromus thominii Hardouin. ¶Lemma 6·5–8 mm., glabrous; grain not projecting. Common.

Bromus ferronii Mabille. ¶Lemma 6·5–7·5 mm., densely hairy; spikelets crowded. On sea cliffs, S. coasts, local.

Bromus lepidus Holmberg. **Slender Brome.** ¶Similar to *B. mollis*; leaves and lower sheaths hairy, but inflo. dense; spikelets short stalked, usually glabrous, ⅜–⅝ in., lemma 5·5–6·5 mm.; the grain projecting at the top. Hayfields, frequent. Flo. May–June.

Bromus interruptus (Hack.) Druce. **Interrupted Brome.** ¶Leaves and sheaths hairy;

spikelets short, $\frac{3}{8}-\frac{1}{2}$ in., hairy, subsessile in clusters; palea split to base. Clover fields, very rare. Flo. June–July. ✖.

Bromus racemosus L. **Smooth Brome.** ¶1–3 ft; leaves and sheaths hairy; inflo. erect; spikelets $\frac{1}{2}-\frac{5}{8}$ in., glabrous, oblong; lemma 6·5–8 mm. In riverside meadows, England.

Bromus commutatus Schrad. **Meadow Brome.** *B. pratensis* Ehrh. ex Hoffm., non Lam. ¶1–3 ft; sheaths hairy; inflo. branches longer; spikelets $\frac{3}{4}$–1 in., usually glabrous; lemma 8–11 mm. Riverside meadows and arable land. Flo. June. ✖.

The alien *B. secalinus* L. in cornfields has glabrous leaf sheaths. This and other alien Bromes are described in Dr C. E. Hubbard's *Grasses*.

Brachypodium sylvaticum (Huds.) Beauv. **Wood False-brome.** ¶Stem 1–3 ft; leaves broad, soft and flat; spikelets hairy; awn as long as lemma. Hedge banks and shady places. Flo. July–Aug. ✖.

Brachypodium pinnatum (L.) Beauv. **Chalk False-brome.** ¶1–3 ft; leaves narrow, stiff and glabrous; spikelets glabrous; awn shorter than lemma. On chalk and limestone, locally common. Flo. June–Aug. ✖.

Agropyron donianum F. B. White. **Don's Twitch.** ¶Without rhizomes; leaves flat with slender ribs; spike rigid; lemma with short awn. High mountains, Perthshire and N. Scotland, rare. Flo. Aug.–Sept.

Agropyron caninum (L.) Beauv. **Bearded Twitch.** ¶Without rhizomes; leaves flat with slender ribs; spike slender, curved; lemma narrowed to long awn. Hedgerows and shady places. Flo. June–Aug. ✖.

Agropyron repens (L.) Beauv. **Creeping Twitch, Couch.** ¶Rhizomes long; leaves flat with slender ribs; lemma usually awnless; ripe spikelets falling entire. Weed of arable and waste land. Flo. June–Aug. ✖.
Var. *aristatum* Baumg. ¶Has lemmas long awned.

Agropyron pungens (Pers.) Roem. & Schult. **Sea Twitch.** ¶Rhizomes long; leaves with thick ribs, inrolled and pointed; sheath auricled; lemmas usually awnless. Salt marshes, seaside sand and gravel. Flo. June–Aug. ✖.
Var. *setigerum* Dumort. ¶Lemmas awned.

Agropyron junceiforme (Á. & D. Löve) Á. & D. Löve. **Sand Twitch.** *A. junceum* auct. ¶Rhizomes long; leaf ribs pubescent; sheath without auricles; spike brittle; glumes and lemmas blunt; awnless. Sand dunes. Flo. June–Aug. ✖.

The hybrid *A. junceiforme × pungens* is fairly common, also *A. junceiforme × repens*, chiefly in N. England.

Elymus arenarius L. **Lyme Grass.** ¶Rhizomes stout; stems 2–5 ft; leaves glaucous, sharply pointed; spikes $\frac{1}{2}$–1 ft; spikelets in pairs, 3–6 flo. Sand dunes on coast. Flo. June–Aug. ✖.

Hordelymus europaeus (L.) Harz. **Wood Barley.** *Hordeum europaeum* (L.) All. ¶Without rhizomes; 2–4 ft; sheaths mostly hairy; spikelets usually in threes and 1 flo.; glumes and lemmas awned. Woods on calcareous soil. Flo. June–July.

Hordeum murinum L. **Wild Barley.** ¶Annual, 1–2 ft; sheaths inflated; spikelets in threes, middle 1 fertile; glumes and lemmas long awned. Waste ground, common. Flo. May–Aug. ✖.

Hordeum marinum Huds. **Squirrel-tail Grass.** ¶Annual, 1 ft; sheath inflated; spike short with long spreading awns; glume of lateral spikelet widened at base. Edge of salt marshes. Flo. June–July. �.

Hordeum secalinum Schreb. **Meadow Barley.** ¶Perennial, 1–2 ft; sheath not inflated; spike with shorter awns; all glumes bristle-like. Meadows on heavy soils. Mostly S. England. Flo. June–July. ✿.

Gymnospermae

PINACEAE

PLATE 100

*Picea abies (L.) Karst. **Norwegian Spruce.** ¶Twigs pendulous; leaves $\frac{1}{2}$–$\frac{3}{4}$ in.; many on each leaf cushion. Much planted.

*Larix decidua Mill. **European Larch.** ¶Leaves deciduous, $\frac{1}{2}$–1 in., bright green, many on each shoot. Much planted.

Pinus sylvestris L. **Scots Pine.** ¶Bark reddish brown, in scales; old trees flat topped; leaves 2 on each short shoot; cones about 2 in. Native, abundant in Scotland, local in England. ✿.

*Pinus nigra Arnold. **Austrian Pine.** ¶Tree pyramidal; bark greyish; buds sticky; scales flat; cones about 3 in. Planted.

*Pinus pinaster Ait. **Clustered Pine.** ¶Bark reddish; leaves 2; buds not sticky; scales reflexed; cones large. Planted, naturalized near Poole, Dorset.

*Pinus radiata Don. *P. insignis* Dougl. ¶Has 3 leaves to each short shoot.

TAXACEAE

Taxus baccata L. **Yew.** ¶Small male and female cones usually on separate plants; ovule 1, surrounded by a red fleshy cup or aril. On limestone and chalk. Flo. March–April. ✿.

CUPRESSACEAE

Juniperus communis L. **Juniper.**
Subsp. *communis.* ¶Shrub suberect and prickly; leaves spreading, narrow, tapering to a point. Chiefly on chalk and limestone, rather local. Flo. May–June. ✿.
Subsp. *nana* Syme. *J. sibirica* Burgsd. ¶More procumbent; leaves wider and ascending, bluntly pointed. On mountains. ✿.

Abbreviations

OF AUTHOR'S NAMES FOR THE PLANT SPECIES

No dates are given for living authors

Aellen–P. Aellen
Airy Shaw–H. K. Airy Shaw
Ait.–W. Aiton, 1731–1793
Ait.f.–W. T. Aiton, 1766–1849
All.–C. Allioni, 1725–1804
Allman–G. J. Allman, 1812–1898
Anderss.–N. J. Andersson, 1821–1880
Andreas–C. H. Andreas
Andrz.–A. L. Andrzejowski, 1784–1868
Arcangeli–G. Arcangeli, 1840–1921
Ard.–P. Arduino, 1728–1805
Arn.–G. A. W. Arnott, 1799–1868
Arrondeau–E. T. Arrondeau, d. 1882
Aschers.–P. F. A. Ascherson, 1834–1913
Ashe–W. W. Ashe, 1872–1932
auct.–auctor, auctores; author(s)

Bab.–C. C. Babington, 1808–1895
Backh.–J. Backhouse, 1825–1890
C. Bailey–C. Bailey, 1838–1924
Bak.–E. G. Baker, 1864–1949
H. G. Bak.–H. G. Baker
J. G. Bak.–J. G. Baker, 1834–1920
Balb.–G. B. Balbis, 1765–1831
P. W. Ball–P. W. Ball
Bartal.–B. Bartalini, 1746–1822
Bast.–T. Bastard, 1784–1846
Baumg.–J. C. G. Baumgarten, 1765–1843
Beauv.–A. M. F. J. Palisot de Beauvois, 1752–1820
Bechst.–J. M. Bechstein, 1757–1822
Beck–G. Ritter Beck von Mannagetta und Larchenau, 1856–1931
W. Becker–W. Becker, 1874–1928
Beeby–W. H. Beeby, 1849–1910
Béguinot–A. Béguinot, 1875–1940
Bellardi–C. A. L. Bellardi, 1741–1826
A. Benn.–A. Bennett, 1843–1929
Benth.–G. Bentham, 1800–1884
Bernh.–J. J. Bernhardi, 1774–1850
Bertol.–A. Bertoloni, 1775–1869
Bess.–W. S. J. G. von Besser, 1784–1842
Betcke–E. F. Betcke, 1815–1865
Bicknell–C. Bicknell, 1842–1918
Bieb.–F. A. Marschall von Bieberstein, 1768–1826

Bigel.–J. Bigelow, 1787–1879
Biv.–A. de Bivona-Bernardi, 1774–1837
Blanche–E. Blanche, 1824–1908
Bluff–M. J. Bluff, 1805–1837
Boenn.–C. M. F. von Boenninghausen, 1785–1864
Boiss.–P.-E. Boissier, 1810–1885
Bonnier–G. E. M. Bonnier, 1853–1922
Boott–F. Boott, 1792–1863
Bor.–A. Boreau, 1803–1875
Borbás–V. von Borbás, 1844–1905
Borkh.–M. B. Borkhausen, 1760–1806
Börner–C. Börner
Borrer–W. Borrer, 1781–1862
R. Br.–R. Brown, 1773–1858
M. E. Bradshaw–M. E. Bradshaw
A. Braun–A. Braun, 1805–1877
Bréb.–L. A. de Brébisson, 1798–1872
Britton–N. L. Britton, 1859–1934
Brodesson–E. Brodesson, fl. 1906–1912
Bromf.–W. A. Bromfield, 1801–1851
Brot.–F. da Avellar Brotero, 1744–1828
Brummitt–R. K. Brummitt
Bub.–P. Bubani, 1806–1888
Buchen.–F. G. P. Buchenau, 1831–1906
Bunge–A. von Bunge, 1830–1890
Burgsd.–F. A. L. von Burgsdorf, 1747–1802
Burm.f.–N. L. Burman, 1734–1793
Burnat–E. Burnat, 1828–1920
Buser–R. Buser, 1857–1931
Butcher–R. W. Butcher

Caruel–T. Caruel, 1830–1898
Casp.–J. X. R. Caspary, 1818–1887
Cass.–A. H. D. de Cassini, 1781–1832
Cav.–A. J. Cavinilles, 1745–1804
Cavara–F. Cavara, 1857–1929
Čelak.–L. J. Čelakovsky, 1834–1902
Chaix–D. Chaix, 1730–1799
Cham.–A. L. von Chamisso, 1781–1838
Chatel.–J. J. Chatelain, 1736–1822
Chaub.–L. A. Chaubard, 1785–1854
Chazelles–M. de Chazelles, fl. 1790
Chevall.–F. F. Chevallier, 1796–1840
Chouard–P. Chouard
Clairv.–J. P. de Clairville, 1742–1830

Clapham–A. R. Clapham
Clarion–J. Clarion, 1780–1856
Clavaud–A. Clavaud, 1828–1890
Colem.–W. H. Coleman, 1816–1863
Compton–R. H. Compton
C. D. K. Cook–C. D. K. Cook
D. E. Coombe–D. E. Coombe
Corb.–L. Corbière, 1850–1941
Coult.–J. M. Coulter, 1851–1928
Court.–R. J. Courtois, 1806–1835
Coutinho–A. X. P. Coutinho, 1851–1939
Coville–F. V. Coville, 1867–1937
Crantz–H. J. N. von Crantz, 1722–1799
Crép.–F. Crépin, 1830–1903
Cronq.–A. Cronquist
Cunn.–A. Cunningham, 1791–1839
Curt.–W. Curtis, 1746–1799
Custer–J. L. Custer, 1755–1828

Dahl–O. C. Dahl, 1862–1940
Dahlst.–H. G. A. Dahlstedt, 1856–1934
Dandy–J. E. Dandy
Davey–F. H. Davey, 1868–1915
Davies–H. Davies, 1739–1821
DC.–A. P. de Candolle, 1778–1841
Decne–J. Decaisne, 1807–1882
Del.–A. R. Delile, 1778–1850
Delarb.–A. Delarbre, 1724–1814
Déségl.–P. A. Déséglise, 1823–1883
Desf.–R. L. Desfontaines, 1750–1833
Desv.–A. N. Desvaux, 1784–1856
Dickson–J. Dickson, 1738–1822
Dippel–L. Dippel, 1827–1914
Don–D. Don, 1799–1841
G. Don–G. Don, 1798–1856
Donn–J. Donn, 1758–1813
Dougl.–D. Douglas, 1798–1834
Drej.–S. T. N. Drejer, 1813–1842
Druce–G. C. Druce, 1850–1932
Duby–J. E. Duby, 1798–1885
Duchesne–A. N. Duchesne, 1747–1827
Dumort.–B. C. J. Dumortier, 1797–1878
Durieu–M. C. Durieu de Maisonneuve, 1796–1878
Duroi–J. P. Duroi, 1741–1785
Dyer–W. T. Thiselton Dyer, 1843–1928

Edmondst.–T. Edmondston, 1825–1846
Ehrh.–J. F. Ehrhart, 1742–1795
Ehrend.–F. Ehrendorfer
Ell.–S. Elliot, 1771–1830

Fenzl–E. Fenzl, 1808–1879
Fernald–M. L. Fernald, 1873–1950
Fieb.–F. X. Fieber, 1807–1872
Fiori–A. Fiori, 1865–1950

Fisch.–F. E. L. von Fischer, 1782–1854
Foggitt–W. Foggitt, 1835–1917
Forsk.–P. Forskål, 1732–1763
E. Forst.–E. Forster, 1765–1849
G. Forst.–J. G. A. Forster, 1754–1794
J. R. Forst.–J. R. Forster, 1729–1798
T. F. Forst.–T. F. Forster, 1761–1825
Fouc.–J. Foucaud, 1847–1904
P. Fourn.–P. Fournier, 1877–1964
Fourr.–P. J. Fourreau, 1844–1871
Fr.–E. M. Fries, 1794–1878
Franch.–A. R. Franchet, 1834–1900
Fritsch–K. Fritsch, 1864–1934

Gaertn.–J. Gaertner, 1732–1791
Garcke–F. A. Garcke, 1819–1904
Gaudich.–C. Gaudichaud-Beaupré, 1789–1854
Gaudin–J. F. A. T. G. P. Gaudin, 1766–1833
Gay–J. E. Gay, 1786–1864
Gilib.–J. E. Gilibert, 1741–1814
Gilmour–J. S. L. Gilmour
Girard–F. de Girard, fl. 1842
Gled.–J. G. Gleditsch, 1714–1786
C. C. Gmel.–C. C. Gmelin, 1762–1837
S. G. Gmel.–S. G. Gmelin, 1744–1774
Godfery–M. J. Godfery, d. 1945
Godr.–D. A. Godron, 1807–1880
Good.–S. Goodenough, 1743–1827
Gouan–A. Gouan, 1733–1821
Graebner–K. O. R. P. P. Graebner, 1871–1933
R. A. Graham–R. A. Graham, 1915–1958
Gray–S. F. Gray, 1766–1836
A. Gray–A. Gray, 1810–1888
Gregory–Mrs E. S. Gregory, 1840–1932
Gremli–A. Gremli, 1833–1899
Gren.–J. C. M. Grenier, 1808–1875
Grimm–J. F. K. Grimm, 1737–1821
Griseb.–A. H. R. Grisebach, 1814–1879
H. Groves–H. Groves, 1855–1912
J. Groves–J. Groves, 1858–1933
Gunn.–J. G. Gunnerus, 1718–1773
Guss.–G. Gussone, 1787–1866

Hack.–E. Hackel, 1850–1926
Hagerup–O. Hagerup, 1889–1961
Haller f.–A. von Haller, 1758–1823
Halliday–G. Halliday
F. J. Hanb.–F. J. Hanbury, 1851–1938
Hardouin–J. Hardouin, 1800–1858
Hartig–H. J. A. R. Hartig, 1839–1901
Hartm.–K. J. Hartman, 1790–1849
Harz–K. O. Harz, 1842–1906
Hassk.–J. C. Hasskarl, 1811–1894
Hausskn.–H. K. Haussknecht, 1838–1903
Hayek–A. E. von Hayek, 1871–1928
Hayne–F. G. Hayne, 1763–1832

Hedlund–T. T. Hedlund, 1861–1953
Heg.–J. J. Hegetschweiler, 1789–1839
Hegi–G. Hegi, 1876–1932
Henry–L. Henry, 1853–1913
Henslow–J. S. Henslow, 1796–1861
Hepper–F. N. Hepper
Herbert–W. Herbert, 1778–1847
F. Hermann–F. Hermann
Heynh.–G. Heynhold, fl. 1838–1850
Heywood–V. H. Heywood
Hiern–W. P. Hiern, 1839–1925
Hiit.–H. I. A. Hiitonen
Hill–J. Hill, 1716–1775
Hoffm.–G. F. Hoffmann, 1760–1826
Hoffmanns.–J. C. Hoffmannsegg, 1766–1849
Holmberg–O. R. Holmberg, 1874–1930
Honck.–G. A. Honckeny, 1724–1805
Hook.–W. J. Hooker, 1785–1865
Hook.f.–J. D. Hooker, 1817–1911
Hoppe–D. H. Hoppe, 1760–1846
Hork.–J. Horkel, 1769–1846
Hornem.–J. W. Hornemann, 1770–1841
Hose–J. Hose, d. 1800
Host–N. T. Host, 1761–1834
House–H. D. House, 1878–1949
Houtt.–Houttuyn, 1720–1798
Howard–H. W. Howard
Howell–T. J. Howell, 1842–1912
C. E. Hubbard–C. E. Hubbard
Huds.–W. Hudson, 1730–1793
Hull–J. Hull, 1761–1843
P. F. Hunt–P. F. Hunt
Hyland.–N. Hylander

Ilse–H. Ilse, 1835–1900
Ives–E. Ives, 1779–1861

Jacq.–N. J. von Jacquin, 1727–1817
Jacq.f.–J. F. von Jacquin, 1766–1839
Jalas–J. Jalas
Jansen–P. Jansen, 1882–1955
Johans.–K. K. Johansson, 1856–1928
Jord.–A. Jordan, 1814–1897
Juss.–A. J. de Jussieu, 1748–1836
Juz.–S. V. Juzepczuk, 1893–1959

Kar.–G. S. Karelin, 1801–1872
Karst.–G. K. W. H. Karsten, 1817–1908
Kenyon–W. Kenyon, fl. 1847
Ker-Gawl.–J. Gawler (né J. B. Ker), 1764–1842
Kerner–A. J. Kerner von Marilaun, 1831–1898
Kir.–I. P. Kirilow, 1821–1842
Kirschleger–F. R. Kirschleger, 1804–1869
Kit.–P. Kitaibel, 1757–1817

Kittel–M. B. Kittel, 1796–1875
Knuth–R. G. P. Knuth, 1874–1957
Koch–W. D. J. Koch, 1771–1849
K. Koch–K. (C.) H. E. Koch, 1809–1879
Koel.–G. L. Koeler, 1765–1807
Koerte–F. Koerte, 1782–1845
E. H. L. Krause–E. H. L. Krause, 1859–1942
Krecz.–V. I. Kreczetowicz, 1901–1942
Kunth–K. S. Kunth, 1788–1850
Kuntz.–K. (C.) E. O. Kuntze, 1843–1907
Kütz.–F. T. Kützing, 1807–1892

L.–C. von Linné (C. Linnaeus), 1707–1778
L.f.–C. von Linné, 1741–1783
Laest.–L. L. Laestadius, 1800–1861
Lag.–M. La Gasca y Segura, 1776–1839
Lagr.-Foss.–A. R. A. Lagrèze-Fossat, 1814–1874
Laichard.–J. N. von Laicharding, 1754–1797
Lam.–J. B. A. P. de M. de Lamarck, 1744–1829
Lamotte.–M. Lamotte, 1820–1883
Láng–A. F. Láng, 1795–1863
Lange–J. M. C. Lange, 1818–1898
Lapierre–J. M. Lapierre, 1754–1834
Latourr.–M. A. L. C. de Latourette, 1729–1793
Lebel–J. E. Lebel, 1801–1878
Lecoq–H. Lecoq, 1802–1871
Ledeb.–C. F. von Ledebour, 1785–1851
Leers–J. D. Leers, 1727–1774
Le Gall–N. J. M. Le Gall, 1787–1860
Lehm.–J. G. C. Lehmann, 1792–1860
Leight.–W. A. Leighton, 1805–1889
Lejeune–A. L. S. Lejeune, 1779–1858
Le Jolis–A. F. Le Jolis, 1823–1904
Less.–C. F. Lessing, 1809–1862
Léveillé–A. A. H. Léveillé, 1863–1918
Ley–A. Ley, 1842–1911
Leyss.–F. W. von Leysser, 1731–1815
L.-Garland–L. V. L. Garland, né Lester, 1860–1944
L'Hérit.–C. L. L'Héritier de Brutelle, 1746–1800
Liebl.–F. K. Lieblein, 1744–1810
Lightf.–J. Lightfoot, 1735–1788
Liljeb.–S. Liljeblad, 1761–1815
Lindl.–J. Lindley, 1799–1865
Lindm.–C. A. M. Lindman, 1856–1928
Link–J. H. F. Link, 1767–1851
E. F. Linton–E. F. Linton, 1848–1928
Lois.–J. L. A. Loiseleur-Deslongchamps, 1774–1849
Lönnr.–E. Lönnrot, 1802–1884
Loret–H. Loret, 1810–1888
Lousley–J. E. Lousley

A. Löve–A. Löve
D. Löve–D. Löve
Lyons–L. J. C. Lyons, 1792–1874

Mabille–P. Mabille, fl. 1864–1872
Mackenzie–K. K. Mackenzie, 1877–1934
Macreight–D. C. Macreight, 1799–1868
Manton–I. Manton
Marsh.–H. Marshall, 1722–1801
E. S. Marshall–E. S. Marshall, 1858–1919
Martyn–T. Martyn, 1735–1825
Mattuschka–H. G. von Mattuschka, 1734–1799
Mauri–E. Mauri, 1791–1836
Maxim.–K. J. Maximowicz, 1827–1891
Medic.–F. K. Medicus, 1736–1808
Meerb.–N. Meerburgh, 1734–1814
Meikle–R. D. Meikle
Meissn.–C. F. Meissner, 1800–1874
Melderis–A. Melderis
Melville–R. Melville
Merát–F. V. Merát, 1780–1851
Mert.–F. K. Mertens, 1764–1831
Mey.–C. A. Meyer, 1795–1855
E. Mey.–E. H. F. Meyer, 1791–1858
Michx.–A. Michaux, 1746–1802
Michx.f.–F. A. Michaux, 1770–1855
Mikan f.–J. C. Mikan, 1769–1844
Mill.–P. Miller, 1691–1771
Moench–C. Moench, 1744–1805
Moq.–C. H. B. A. Moquin-Tandon, 1804–1863
More–A. G. More, 1830–1895
Moss–C. E. Moss, 1872–1931
Muhl.–G. H. I. Muhlenberg, 1753–1815
Murb.–S. S. Murbeck, 1859–1946
Murr.–J. A. Murray, 1740–1791
A. Murr.–A. Murray, 1812–1878
J. Murr–J. J. Murr, 1864–1932

Naeg.–O. Naegeli, 1871–1938
Neck.–N. J. von Necker, 1729–1793
Nees–C. G. D. Nees von Esenbeck, 1776–1858
Neves–J. de Barros Neves
Nevski–S. A. Nevski, 1908–1938
Newbould–W. W. Newbould, 1819–1886
Neygenf.–F. W. Neygenfind, fl. 1821
Neid.–F. J. Niedenzu, 1857–1937
Nordb.–G. Nordborg
Nutt.–T. Nuttall, 1786–1859
Nyman–C. F. Nyman, 1820–1893

Oborny–A. Oborny, 1840–1925
Ockendon–D. J. Ockendon
Oeder–G. C. von Oeder, 1728–1791
Opiz–P. M. Opiz, 1787–1858

Ostenf.–C. H. Ostenfeld, 1873–1931

Pall.–P. S. Pallas, 1741–1811
Palla–E. Palla, 1864–1922
Panz.–G. W. F. Panzer, 1755–1829
Paol.–G. Paoletti, 1865–1941
Parl.–F. Parlatore, 1816–1877
Parnell–R. Parnell, 1810–1882
Pedersen–A. Pedersen
Pennell–F. W. Pennell, 1886–1952
Pers.–C. H. Persoon, 1762–1836
Peter–G. A. Peter, 1853–1937
Petermann–W. L. Petermann, 1806–1855
Petrak–F. Petrak
Pilg.–R. K. F. Pilger, 1876–1953
Piré–L. A. H. J. Piré, 1827–1887
Planch.–J. E. Planchon, 1823–1888
Podp.–J. Podpera, 1878–1954
Poggenb.–J. F. Poggenburg, 1840–1893
Pohl–R. W. Pohl
Poir.–J. L. M. Poiret, 1755–1834
Polatschek–A. Polatschek
Poll.–J. A. Pollich, 1740–1780
Porter–T. C. Porter, 1822–1901
Pourr.–P. A. Pourret de Figeac, 1754–1818
Prantl–K. A. E. Prantl, 1849–1893
C. Presl–C. (K.) B. Presl, 1794–1852
J. Presl–J. S. Presl, 1791–1849
Pritchard–N. M. Pritchard
M. C. F. Proctor–M. C. F. Proctor
Pugsl.–H. W. Pugsley, 1868–1947
Pursh–F. T. Pursh, 1774–1820

Rabenh.–G. L. Rabenhorst, 1806–1881
Raf.–C. S. Rafinesque-Schmaltz, 1783–1840
Rafn–C. G. Rafn, 1769–1808
Raunk.–C. Raunkiaer, 1860–1938
Räusch.–E. A. Räuschel, fl. 1772–1797
Rech.f.–K. H. Rechinger
Regel–E. A. von Regel, 1815–1892
Rehd.–A. Rehder, 1863–1949
Rehm.–A. Rehman, 1840–1917
Reichard–J. J. Reichard, 1743–1782
Reichb.–H. G. L. Reichenbach, 1793–1879
Reichb.f.–H. G. Reichenbach, 1823–1889
Req.–E. Requien, 1788–1851
Retz.–A. J. Retzius, 1742–1821
Reut.–G. F. Reuter, 1805–1872
Rich.–L. C. M. Richard, 1754–1821
Riddelsd.–H. J. Riddelsdell, 1866–1941
Ridley–H. N. Ridley, 1855–1956
Robson–E. Robson, 1763–1813
Rochel–A. Rochel, 1770–1847
Roem.–J. J. Roemer, 1763–1819
Roffey–J. Roffey, 1860–1927
Ronn.–K. Ronniger, 1871–1954

Rostk.–F. W. G. Rostkovius, 1770–1848
Rostrup–F. G. E. Rostrup, 1831–1907
Roth–A. W. Roth, 1757–1834
Rothm.–W. Rothmaler, 1908–1962
Rouy–G. C. C. Rouy, 1851–1924
Royle–J. F. Royle, 1779–1858
Rupr.–F. J. Ruprecht, 1814–1870
Ruthe–J. F. Ruthe, 1788–1859
Ryd.–P. A. Rydberg, 1860–1931

St Amans–J. F. B. St Amans, 1748–1831
St John–H. St John
Salisb.–R. A. Salisbury, né Markham, 1761–1829
Salmon–C. E. Salmon, 1872–1930
Samp.–G. A. da Silva Ferreira Sampaio, 1865–1937
Sauter–A. E. Sauter, 1800–1881
Savi–G. Savi, 1769–1844
Savigny–M. J. C. L. de Savigny, 1777–1851
Savouré–H. S. Savouré, 1861–1921
Schau.–J. C. Schauer, 1813–1848
Scheele–G. H. A. Scheele, 1808–1864
Scherb.–J. Scherbius, 1769–1813
Schiffn.–V. F. Schiffner, 1862–1944
Schinz–H. Schinz, 1858–1941
Schischk.–B. K. Schischkin, 1886–1963
Schkuhr–C. Schkuhr, 1741–1811
Schlecht.–D. F. L. von Schlechtendal, 1794–1866
Schleich.–J. C. Schleicher, 1768–1834
Schleid.–M. J. Schleider, 1804–1881
Schmidt–F. W. Schmidt, 1764–1796
F. Schmidt–F. Schmidt, 1832–1908
C. K. Schneid.–C. K. Schneider, 1876–1951
Schönh.–F. C. H. Schönheit, 1789–1870
Schönl.–S. Schönland, 1860–1940
Schott–H. W. Schott, 1794–1865
Schousb.–P. K. A. Schousboe, 1766–1832
Schrad.–H. A. Schrader, 1767–1836
Schrank–F. von Paula von Schrank, 1747–1835
Schreb.–J. C. D. von Schreber, 1739–1810
Schult.–J. A. Schultes, 1773–1831
C. H. Schultz–C. H. Schultz, 1805–1867
F. W. Schultz–F. W. Schultz, 1804–1876
K. F. Schultz–K. F. Schultz, 1765–1837
O. E. Schulz–O. E. Schulz, 1874–1936
R. Schulz–R. Schulz, 1873–1926
Schumach.–H. C. F. Schumacher, 1757–1830
Schur–P. J. F. Schur, 1799–1878
Schwarz–O. Schwarz
Schweigg.–A. F. Schweigger, 1783–1821
Schwein.–G. A. Schweinfurth, 1836–1925
Scop.–G. A. Scopoli, 1723–1788
Seb.–A. Sebastioni, 1782–1821

P. D. Sell–P. D. Sell
Senn.–Frère Sennen (E. M. Grenier-Blanc), 1861–1937
Sibth.–J. Sibthorp, 1758–1796
Sieb.–P. F. von Siebold, 1796–1866
Silva–A. R. Pinto da Silva
Simmons–H. G. Simmons, 1866–1943
Sims–J. Sims, 1749–1831
Sm.–J. E. Smith, 1759–1828
G. E. Sm.–G. E. Smith, 1804–1881
H. Sm.–H. Smith
Small–J. K. Small, 1869–1938
Sobol.–G. F. Sobolevski, 1741–1807
Sobrinho–L. G. Sobrinho
Soland.–D. C. Solander, 1736–1782
Soó–R. de Soó
Soy.-Will.–H. F. Soyer-Willemet, 1791–1867
Spach–E. Spach, 1801–1879
Spreng.–C. (K.) P. J. Sprengel, 1766–1833
Stapf–O. Stapf, 1857–1933
Stearn–W. T. Stearn
Stefánsson–S. Stefánsson, 1863–1921
Steph.–F. Stephani, 1842–1927
T. Stephenson–T. Stephenson, 1855–1948
T. A. Stephenson–T. A. Stephenson, 1898–1961
Sterneck–J. von Sterneck, fl. 1864–1901
Sterner–K. R. Sterner, 1891–1956
Sterns–E. E. Sterns, 1846–1926
Stev.–C. von Steven, 1781–1863
Stokes–J. Stokes, 1755–1831
Suksd.–W. N. Suksdorf, 1850–1932
Summerhayes–V. S. Summerhayes
Sutton–C. Sutton, 1756–1846
Sw.–O. Swartz, 1760–1818
Syme–J. T. I. B. Syme, né Boswell, 1822–1888

Tausch–I. F. Tausch, 1793–1848
Ten.–M. Tenore, 1780–1861
Thell.–A. Thellung, 1881–1928
C. Thomas–C. Thomas
Thuill.–J. L. Thuillier, 1757–1822
Timm–J. C. Timm, 1734–1805
Torr.–J. Torrey, 1796–1873
Tourlet–E. H. Tourlet, 1843–1907
Towns.–F. Townsend, 1822–1905
Tratt.–L. Trattinick, 1764–1849
Trin.–K. B. von Trinius, 1778–1844
Turcz.–N. Turczaninow, 1796–1864
D. Turner–D. Turner, 1775–1858
Turra–A. Turra, 1730–1796
Turrill–W. B. Turrill, 1890–1961
Tutin–T. G. Tutin

Ucria–B. Ucria, 1739–1796
Ulbr.–E. Ulbrich, 1879–1952

Vaarama–A. Vaarama
Vahl–M. H. Vahl, 1749–1804
Valentine–D. H. Valentine
Van Hall–H. C. Van Hall, 1801–1874
Vermeul.–P. Vermeulen
Vest–L. C. von Vest, 1776–1840
Vierh.–F. Vierhapper, 1876–1932
Vig.–A. L. G. Viguier, 1790–1867
Vill.–D. Villar(s), 1745–1814
Viv.–D. Viviani, 1772–1840

Wachter–W. H. Wachter, 1882–1946
Wahlb.–P. F. Wahlberg, 1800–1877
Wahlenb.–G. G. Wahlenberg, 1780–1851
Waldst.–F. A. Graf von Waldstein-
  Wartemberg, 1759–1823
Wall.–N. Wallich, 1786–1854
Wallr.–K. F. W. Wallroth, 1792–1857
Walp.–W. G. Walpers, 1816–1853
Walters–S. M. Walters
E. F. Warb.–E. F. Warburg, 1908–1966
H. C. Wats.–H. C. Watson, 1804–1881
W. C. R. Wats.–W. C. R. Watson, 1885–1954
Weatherby–C. A. Weatherby, 1875–1949
Webb–P. B. Webb, 1793–1854
D. A. Webb–D. A. Webb

Weber–F. Weber, 1781–1823
Weig.–C. E. von Weigel, 1748–1831
Weihe–K. E. A. Weihe, 1779–1834
C. West–C. West
Weston–R. Weston, 1773–1806
Wettst.–R. Ritter von Wettstein, 1863–1931
W. Wettst.–W. von Wettstein
L. C. Wheeler–L. C. Wheeler
F. B. White–F. B. W. White, 1842–1894
Wibel–A. W. E. C. Wibel, 1775–1814
Willd.–C. (K.) L. Willdenow, 1765–1812
Willk.–H. M. Willkomm, 1821–1895
Wilmott–A. J. Wilmott, 1888–1950
Wimm.–C. F. H. Wimmer, 1803–1868
Wirtg.–P. Wirtgen, 1806–1870
With.–W. Withering, 1741–1799
Wolf–J. Wolf, 1765–1824
Wolfg. J. F. Wolfgang, 1776–1859
Wulf.–F. X. von Wulfen, 1728–1805

D. P. Young–D. P. Young

Zahn–K. H. Zahn, 1865–1940
Ziz–J. B. Ziz, 1779–1829
Zucc.–J. G. Zuccarini, 1797–1848

Index of Botanical Names

Species only are indexed. Synonyms are shown in *italics*. ❀ indicates illustration

Index of Common English Names